20727

D0773532

# The Emergence of Spanish America

VICENTE ROCAFUERTE

# The Emergence of Spanish America

*Vicente Rocafuerte and Spanish Americanism*
*1808—1832*

BY JAIME E. RODRÍGUEZ O.

UNIVERSITY OF CALIFORNIA PRESS

*Berkeley • Los Angeles • London*

University of California Press
Berkeley and Los Angeles, California

University of California Press, Ltd.
London, England

Copyright ©1975 by The Regents of the University of California

ISBN: 0-520-02875-9
Library of Congress Catalog Card Number: 74-22972

Printed in the United States of America

*A*
*mi maestra*
*NETTIE LEE BENSON*

# ACKNOWLEDGMENTS

The debts I have incurred during the research and preparation of this work are numerous. Professor Nettie Lee Benson directed the initial research for my Ph.D. dissertation. Her continuing counsel and assistance have contributed greatly to this study. Thus, it is with great pleasure that I dedicate this book to her.

When I began research in Mexico during the summer of 1968, I had the good fortune to receive support and encouragement from several distinguished Mexican scholars. I am grateful to Daniel Cosío Villegas, Ernesto de la Torre Villar, and Ignacio Rubio Mañé who helped me obtain permission to investigate in the Archivo General de la Secretaría de Relaciones Exteriores when it was officially closed because of internal reorganization. Romeo Flores Caballero, Roberto Moreno, and John Womack, Jr., then researching in Mexico, kindly discussed various aspects of the study with me. Indeed, it was on Professor Womack's advice that the work eventually took its present form. I am indebted to Masae Sugawara and José Guzmán for their assistance at the Archivo General de la Nación in Mexico.

The directors and staff of the institutions in which I have worked were extremely helpful. I take this opportunity to thank them for their kindness and to applaud their important work of preserving our heritage. The Organization of American States, the Institute of Latin American Studies and the Graduate School of the University of Texas, Austin generously provided financial assistance during the early stages of my research.

I have also benefited from the advice and encouragement of various historians. Professors Germán Tjarks and J. León Helguera read an earlier version of this work and provided suggestions for its improvement. Michael P. Johnson, Colin M. MacLachlan, Keith I. Polakoff, and William F. Sater read the manu-

script and offered valuable criticism. I am particularly grateful to
Hugh M. Hamill, Jr., for his detailed commentary on the manuscript. James W. Wilkie gave me support and encouragement
during some difficult times. Noel L. Díaz prepared the maps.
Finally, I wish to thank my wife, Linda Alexander Rodríguez, who
took time from her own scholarly pursuits to read and criticize the
work in its several versions.

Irvine, California                          Jaime E. Rodríguez O.

# CONTENTS

## MAPS

# INTRODUCTION

The independence of Spanish America has long been regarded as a heroic period, a time when military leaders violently severed ties with Spain. Contemporary writers argued that new, liberal, bourgeois ideas, imported from England, France, and the United States, had overwhelmed the traditional, conservative, "feudal" institutions of the mother country. However, the subsequent history of conflict in Spanish America demonstrated that conservatism remained strong. Thus, many later observers concluded that the "alien" liberalism was not suited to Spanish America and that Spanish American liberals had been misguided in attempting to introduce bourgeois institutions in their countries. Indeed, many scholars, impressed by the essentially conservative nature of contemporary Spanish American society, have come to believe that nineteenth-century Spanish American liberalism was an aberration.[1]

It is the contention of this work that Spanish American liberalism was neither alien nor aberrant. Rather it was part of the complex and contradictory Spanish colonial inheritance. The struggle between liberals and conservatives began in Spain in the eighteenth century and was not settled by the wars of independence. All Spanish America achieved in that struggle was separation from Spain; virtually all the issues that had earlier divided Hispanic society remained unresolved. Thus, it is not simply a coincidence that the first half of the nineteenth century was a period of chaos and conflict both in Spain and in Spanish America.

This study concentrates on one aspect of the independence and early national period. It seeks to understand the activities of a group of Spanish Americans who were profoundly influenced by Spanish liberalism. Initially, they had favored the creation of a constitutional Hispanic commonwealth. But the subsequent failure of the Spanish Cortes (1810–1814 and 1820–1823) forced those Spanish Americans who favored Hispanic unity within a constitutional structure to seek independence and to adopt a new vision of

Spanish American community. Thereafter they worked together to achieve recognition and to foster the development of their countries. They hoped that this cooperation might result in alliances or perhaps a formal union. Although they called themselves *Americans* and constantly referred to the structure they wanted to forge as the *American system*, this study uses the term *Spanish Americanism* to refer to their efforts because Spanish Americanists did not include Canada, the United States, or Brazil in their definition of America.

Spanish Americanism was not a consciously developed ideology and, in that respect, not an *ism*. It grew out of the enlightened, modernizing tendencies initiated by the eighteenth-century Spanish reformers. And it crystallized during the early constitutional period. After independence the Spanish Americanists continued to support the goals and aspirations of Spanish liberalism. Nevertheless, they believed that the future lay with the New World.

Spanish Americanists differed from other Spanish Americans in three ways. First, they accepted and cherished the Spanish liberal tradition. Second, they were for a time champions of a Hispanic constitutional commonwealth. Third, when this failed they viewed Spanish America as an entity and collaborated in furthering the interests of the region. Together with other liberals they worked for constitutionalism and representative government. They believed in progress not only through economic development but also through social reform. In general, they favored the creation of a middle class society.

Although members of the Spanish American elite, the Spanish Americanists represented a growing bourgeoisie. They were part of the creole minority that formed the "effective nation" and guided the destinies of Spanish America in the early nineteenth century. The overwhelming majority of the people of Spanish America, the mestizos, blacks, mulattos, and Indians, played little or no role in the political life of their nations. Indeed, many had no concept of nationality until late in the century.

While only a segment of a small minority, the Spanish Americanists had great influence. They came from many countries and engaged in a variety of activities. Some, like the Ecuadorean, Vicente Rocafuerte, were the heirs of large landed fortunes. Others, like the Peruvian Manuel Lorenzo de Vidaurre, had been high ranking members of the imperial bureaucracy. A few, like the

Argentine, José Antonio Miralla, were merchants. Still others, like the Mexican, José Miguel Ramos Arizpe, were clergymen. All were well-educated, widely traveled, and had believed in and supported the Spanish reforms. What distinguished them as a group was their supranational views.

This work traces the rise and decline of Spanish Americanism by following the activities of one of its representative members, Vicente Rocafuerte. He is a particularly good vehicle for the study because he participated in multiple phases of the movement from its inception in the first constitutional Cortes (1810–1814) to its decline in the 1830s. Rocafuerte's activities provide a sense of unity and continuity to this work. His interest in education, economic development, and social reform, as well as in politics, was characteristic of Spanish Americanists. Thus, Rocafuerte's involvement in a variety of causes and projects provides an opportunity to discuss the wide-ranging concerns of Spanish Americanists.

The years that saw the dissolution of the Spanish Empire in America and the creation of new nations were exceedingly complex. Only by presenting the richness of the epoch is it possible to demonstrate the threads of continuity between Spanish liberalism, Spanish Americanism, and Spanish American liberalism. Thus the study begins with a chapter entitled "The Spanish Heritage." The title was chosen to emphasize the impact Spanish liberalism had on Spanish America. Chapter I briefly surveys the Bourbon reforms and presents a discussion of the Spanish attempt at a bourgeois revolution. Special attention is paid throughout the chapter to the interaction between Spain and Spanish America in the creation of a Hispanic commonwealth. The theme is further developed in chapter II, which considers the crucial second constitutional period. These two chapters demonstrate (1) why the Spanish Americanists believed they could achieve home rule within the Spanish commonwealth, (2) the stresses that led to the failure of Spanish constitutionalism, and (3) the ambiguous nature of Spanish American independence.

With the advent of independence the new nations faced various problems in which the Spanish Americanists played a prominent role. New governments had to be established and the last remnants of Spanish power destroyed. Chapters III and IV, which are primarily concerned with the nature of government in Mexico and the independence of Cuba, are illustrative of the way in which Spanish Americanists cooperated to obtain their ends.

No issue aroused more concern among Spanish Americanists than the consolidation of independence. Since the early 1820s, most Spanish American leaders believed that England's friendship was of paramount importance in achieving that goal. Although Spanish Americanists agreed that Britain had to play a key role in foreign relations, they warned that the new nations should not depend on any one power. They insisted on establishing relations with various European countries in order to balance competing interests. Since Vicente Rocafuerte was one of the most active of the Spanish Americanist diplomats, his role as Mexico's chargé d'affaires serves as an example of Spanish Americanist diplomacy in Europe. Accordingly, chapters V, VI, and VII deal with Mexico's relations with England, while chapters VIII and IX are concerned with Mexico's relations with the Continent.

Although the Spanish Americanists succeeded in obtaining European recognition and thus consolidating independence, their countries did not prosper as they had hoped. The 1820s had begun as a period of great expectation but by the end of the decade economic difficulties exacerbated social and regional divisions and many countries underwent profound political crises. Chapter XII discusses Rocafuerte's role in Mexico's internal conflict, one of the many internecine quarrels that were afflicting Spanish America.

Economic, social, and political problems forced the Spanish American nations to abandon or reduce their relations with one another. In general, the 1830s witnessed a growing sense of isolation in the area. This is true not only on the governmental level, but also on the social and cultural levels. One need only contrast the broad interest that Spanish American newspapers showed in international questions in the 1820s with the relatively insular nature of periodicals in the 1830s to see the magnitude of the change. Although they did not completely abandon international relations, most Spanish Americanists turned inwards to concentrate on national matters. In this respect, Rocafuerte's return to Ecuador in 1833 is symbolic of the demise of Spanish Americanism.

# I

## THE SPANISH HERITAGE

The Spanish ship *Monserrat* docked in Havana harbor on the afternoon of April 15, 1820. Within minutes the information it brought spread throughout the city. The Spanish Empire was once again a constitutional monarchy. A revolt had forced Ferdinand VII to accept the Constitution of 1812. Excitement mounted. Great crowds gathered to comment on the news.

The following day, Sunday, large numbers assembled waiting to learn what was going to happen. The Plaza de Armas, the city's principal square, was filled with throngs of people, many of them soldiers. Everyone expected Captain General Juan Manuel Cagigal to swear allegiance to the constitution. When the government made no announcement, the multitude began to stir. Rumors circulated. The captain general, it was alleged, refused to govern under the 1812 charter. Within a short time the crowd became a mob that invaded the government palace and forced Cagigal to the balcony where he swore to uphold the constitution.

On Monday, April 17, two days after the *Monserrat's* arrival, Captain General Cagigal held a formal ceremony in which he, as well as other government officials and the hierarchy of the clergy, took an oath of allegiance to the restored constitution. If he meant to make this a private affair, he was thwarted. Once again masses of people forced their way into the palace to witness the event. Calm was restored only when the bishop of Havana celebrated a *Te Deum* in the cathedral in honor of the Constitution of the Spanish Monarchy.[1]

1

Similar scenes were enacted in countless cities in Spain and Spanish America. Everywhere, the Constitution of Cádiz stood as the great symbol of Hispanic unity. This had not always been true. In the previous three hundred years—first under the Habsburgs and then under the Bourbons—the king had provided the bond of cohesion.

During the two-century-long rule of the Habsburgs, the monarch's authority was enhanced by the support of the Catholic Church. Habsburg kings entrusted much of their administration to clergymen. Traditionalists viewed this union of church and state as the essence of Spanishness and identified the great events of their history, the victory over the Moors, the discovery and conquest of America, and the Counter Reformation, with their religion. The Spanish empire reached the heights of power and glory in the fifteenth and sixteenth centuries. Thereafter, a decline began which reduced it to a second class power. By the end of the seventeenth century Spain was exhausted. When Charles II died without an heir in 1700, the struggle for the throne triggered a European war that lasted fifteen years. By its end, a new dynasty, the Bourbons, ruled Spain.

Philip V's victory in the War of the Spanish Succession allowed the new monarch to initiate a series of changes designed to centralize Spanish government, restore finances, and reorganize the armed forces.[2] French advisers and Spanish reformers such as José Patiño and José del Campillo revived the economy by applying mercantilist policies. The most important transformation, however, was the establishment of the intendancy system of administration. The intendant was a provincial administrator with military, financial, economic, and judicial authority. Directly responsible to the king, the new official reduced regionalism and strengthened the national government.[3] As Spain began to prosper, the forces of change gathered momentum.

During the reign of Charles III (1759–1788), education, administration, agriculture, industry, trade, and transportation were all attacked by zealous officials bent on creating a more efficient and more rational society. These men of the Enlightenment wanted a better, more equitable, and more effective government. They also believed in a secular community and sought to reduce the Church's immense role in the Spanish world by espousing the cause of regalism. The expulsion of the Jesuits in 1767 was a spectacular event in the struggle for secularization. More important, however, was the

Bourbon concept of government, which rejected the Habsburg reliance on the Church in favor of an administration of civil and military bureaucrats. Under the Bourbons four generations of reformers carried out a revolution in government.[4] Like twentieth-century liberals, the men of the eighteenth century believed that the state was the institution best equipped to promote the prosperity and well-being of the people. Therefore, they worked to create a strong and unified government. These changes were opposed by the traditionalists. On various occasions the defenders of Habsburg institutions reversed or delayed Bourbon innovations. The reformers, nonetheless, were often successful because their programs furthered the cause of monarchy.

The Bourbon program of regeneration was not limited to Spain. In 1743, José del Campillo turned his attention to the empire in a study entitled *A New System of Government for America*. He proposed that a general inspection be carried out to gather precise data. Then, on the basis of this information, improvements could be made. He also suggested that the cornerstone of American reform might be the introduction of intendancies and the establishment of "free trade."[5] Little was accomplished, however, until the advent of the Seven Years War. Shocked by Britain's capture of Havana in 1762 and dismayed by the trading boom that resulted, Spain moved to initiate changes upon the cessation of hostilities. Trade restrictions were gradually relaxed allowing relatively free trade within the empire. Furthermore, a series of *visitas* or inspections were carried out, beginning with Cuba in 1763 and 1764, continuing with one of Mexico from 1765 to 1771, and ending with that of Peru from 1776 to 1784. Subsequently, intendancies were established in Cuba in 1765, in the Rio de la Plata in 1782, in Peru in 1784, in Mexico in 1786, and later in New Granada.[6]

Although the innovations were generally beneficial, some areas suffered. The creation of the Viceroyalty of the Rio de la Plata and the relaxation of trade restrictions produced grave economic dislocations in Peru and Quito.[7] Once the Atlantic ports were opened to trade with Spain, the Pacific ports faced a cost disadvantage that could not be overcome until an isthmian canal shortened the distances to Europe. Nonetheless, these changes achieved the restructuring of the old order desired by the Bourbon officials.

The Habsburg empire had consisted of a group of federated

kingdoms each governed by a viceroy and each possessing a series of *fueros* or privileges. In America, the most important institutions were the Church, the *audiencia*, the *ayuntamiento*, and the *consulados* (merchant guilds) of Mexico City and Lima. Society was hierarchical and its laws and privileges were designed to maintain distinctions. The Bourbons, however, wanted to establish a centralized empire with uniform laws and administration. Therefore they implemented reforms to achieve that goal. The intendancy decreased the power of the viceroy. New bureaucracies reduced the role of the *audiencia* to that of a high court. The Cádiz, Mexico, and Lima trade monopolies ended with the establishment of new merchant guilds and the introduction of free trade. Similarly, the power and prestige of the Church diminished as many of its former functions were secularized and its ecclesiastical *fuero* curtailed. At the same time the influence of the military increased with the establishment of its own *fueros*. Other institutions, such as the mining guild, also received *fueros*. Although it was contradictory to abolish some *fueros* while establishing others, the crown believed it necessary to redress the balance of power in society. Nothing symbolized the new state of affairs as much as the decline of Church power and the corresponding rise of the military. Indeed, it became common for viceroys and presidents of *audiencias* to be chosen from among military administrators.[8]

To facilitate the desired change, the Bourbon state encouraged American reformers to come to the Peninsula while it sent Spaniards to the New World. Thus regional loyalties would not interfere with the proposed transformation. This policy spawned an empire-wide elite with similar training and a common belief in progress fostered by the state. These men envisioned themselves as enlightened individuals fighting local obscurantism, unjust regional practices, and provincial corruption. Their opponents, however, saw them as reckless innovators who were destroying the traditional system. But as long as the king supported them and as long as they were successful, the reformers felt scant cause to heed their critics.

2

Charles III's long and glorious reign ended in 1788. He was succeeded by Charles IV, a weak and ineffectual man, incapable of guiding the nation through the great upheaval unleashed by the French Revolution. At first the new king continued his father's policies by retaining the Count of Floridablanca as first secretary. Business, however, could not continue as usual. Events in France were moving too rapidly and becoming too radical for Floridablanca who attempted to seal the Spanish world from news of France. This proved impossible. Charles's cousin, Louis XVI, had sworn to uphold the French constitution. If he were to remain on the throne of France, he needed the understanding of his fellow monarchs. On February 28, 1792, the king of Spain removed Floridablanca and replaced him with the francophile Count of Aranda.

The change in ministry permitted news from France and revolutionary propaganda to pour into Spain. Most traditionalists were horrified, but many reformers, including Gaspar Melchor de Jovellanos, Francisco Cabarrús, and Mariano Luis de Urquijo, welcomed the change and hoped that Spain might also establish a constitutional monarchy. However, the Jacobin reign of terror and Louis XVI's execution shocked all Spain. Charles IV joined the other monarchs of Europe in war against the regicide French Republic only to see his country defeated. The humiliating peace treaty which ended the conflict bound Spain to France. Since England continued to wage war, Spain's alliance with the French Republic made her an enemy of England. As the mistress of the seas, Britain effectively cut off Spain from her overseas possessions and took control of Spanish American trade. Despite these events, most Spanish Americans remained staunchly loyal to the crown. Unfortunately for the monarchy, further complications strained that loyalty to the breaking point.

Manuel Godoy, a former guardsman and a favorite of the monarchs, had become first secretary. Rumors circulated that he was the queen's lover and exceedingly corrupt. These stories damaged the people's image of the royal family at a time when the grave international situation was creating discontent with the government. The long series of wars that began with the French Revolution, first against France, then against England, and later against Portugal, were an immense drain on the Spanish treasury. To finance the hostilities, desperate measures were necessary. One of these, the Royal Law of Consolidation—first enacted in Spain in 1798, and extended to the entire empire in 1804—was an amortization decree requiring the Church to turn over its lands and valuables to the government in return for a small interest. The king then auctioned these properties to finance the wars. Since the Church served as the empire's banker, execution of the order created economic chaos.[9] This and other unpopular decrees were attributed to Godoy's malign genius. Because he was influential for many years, he tainted the imperial bureaucracy with the mark of corruption, at least in the popular mind.[10]

Many who despaired at Spain's misfortunes and hoped to restore the nation to her former prosperity looked to Crown Prince Ferdinand as their champion because he opposed Godoy and resented his parents' dependence on the favorite. In March, 1808, his followers proclaimed him king. Although Charles IV abdicated, he did so under pressure. Later he requested Napoleon's aid in regaining his crown. Ferdinand VII also asked the French emperor to approve his accession to the throne of Spain. Thus Napoleon became the arbiter of Spain's dynastic politics.

The quarrel coincided with the intrusion of French troops into the Peninsula. In 1807, Napoleon had obtained permission to move his troops across Spain to occupy Portugal. Once his armies had entered the Peninsula, the Emperor of the French decided to remove the Spanish Bourbons. Using the dispute over the Spanish crown as an excuse, Bonaparte lured the royal family and Godoy into France where he forced them to abdicate in his favor. Then he granted Spain to his brother Joseph.

Nearly all Spanish authorities accepted Joseph Bonaparte as king of Spain. But if the imperial bureaucracy, the nobility, the clergy, and the army accepted the intruder, the people did not. On May 2, 1808, Madrid rose against the French and the example was followed throughout Spain.[11] The Spanish Revolution had begun.

3

The first impulse after May was centrifugal, that is, regional juntas (committees) were formed to govern individual provinces. In the absence of the king, sovereignty reverted to the people and each provincial junta acted as though it were an independent nation. Finally, the need for a unified defense led to the organization of a national governing committee, the Central Junta, which met in September. Although some provincial bodies did not recognize the authority of the Central Junta, most agreed that it should be the government of national defense to wage a war of liberation.

The Spanish reformers were deeply divided. To some Joseph represented an opportunity to continue the modernization of the Spanish world. He could be the social engineer for whom the *philosophes* had yearned. After all, such a man was remolding the world from Paris.[12] To others, however, the French were foreign invaders, whatever their ideology, and the defense of Spain came first. Yet these nationalist reformers were not willing to end their quest for a better future. Indeed, many were no longer content with enlightened despotism. Now they hoped to establish some sort of constitutional government. Furthermore, the king's absence and the revival of the concept of popular sovereignty seemed to offer an opportunity to create a representative government.

The nationalists did not have to borrow a foreign ideology in order to invoke the formation of a parliament. Since the beginning of the eighteenth century a new interest in history had slowly created a national myth. Enlightened Spaniards discovered that the early Visigoths had enjoyed a form of tribal democracy. Supposedly, these German ancestors forged the first Spanish constitution. Later, in the thirteenth century, Spain developed its own representative body, the Cortes. According to this interpretation of history, the late Middle Ages had witnessed the golden age of Spanish democracy only to see it destroyed by the Catholic Sovereigns and their despotic descendants, the Habsburgs.[13] Although earlier cortes had represented individual kingdoms such as Aragon and Castile, not the entire nation, reformers had a unified national body in mind when they suggested convoking a new cortes. Even Spain's most distinguished legal historian, Francisco Martínez Marina, author of the massive *Theory of the Cortes*, concluded that a national body was necessary to revitalize the nation.[14] Many Spaniards believed that the Central Junta should convoke a cortes in order to unify the country and establish legitimacy until the king returned.

The Central Junta, however, was not convinced that calling such a congress would be beneficial. Its principal task was to defend the nation from the French and to preserve the throne for Ferdinand VII, now recognized as the rightful king of Spain. The body faced grave problems. Some provinces of Spain did not recognize its authority and others were lukewarm in their support. No provincial junta was prepared to surrrender local power. The Central Junta also needed the support of the American kingdoms to win the struggle against the French. But others, including individual Spanish juntas, Princess Carlota Joaquina (Ferdinand's sister and wife of the Prince Regent of Portugal), and Bonaparte, also demanded American loyalty. Moreover, events in the New World further complicated the situation. Argentina had successfully repelled a British invasion even though the viceroy, the Marquis Sobremonte, fled before the enemy. As a result the area was left virtually independent. Mexico had seen the viceroy overthrown by conservatives in order to prevent the creation of a local provincial junta. Both Charcas and Quito attempted to form local juntas only to face the ruthless repression of the Peruvian viceroy. And other areas were seething with unrest. Many Americans believed that Spain would be overrun by Napoleon and they were unwilling to fall under French control. Thus the status of the Central Junta was very uncertain.

In order to establish a firm authority over the provinces of Spain and the kingdoms of America, the Central Junta dispatched Royal Commissioners to these areas. These delegates, often natives of the region, would serve as liaison agents between local government and the Central Junta. Unfortunately, they were not always successful. Therefore, the Spanish national government decided to strengthen the bonds of unity by inviting the provinces of Spain and the kingdoms of America to elect representatives to the Junta. Its decree of January 22, 1809, emphasized the equality of Spain and America and instructed local authorities to elect representatives to the Central Junta.[15] Some Spanish provinces elected delegates, but others could not because of French occupation. All the American representatives were elected, but distance delayed their arrival.[16]

Before membership in the Junta could be expanded, the French renewed their drive to conquer the Peninsula. As Spanish forces were driven south, various members of the Central Junta insisted on calling a cortes. Others, including Spain's new ally, Britain, wanted to establish a regency. However, the pro-cortes group convinced them that it was necessary to learn the people's wishes. Therefore, the Central Junta issued a "Consultation to the Nation" requesting provincial juntas, city councils, tribunals, bishops, universities, and erudite individuals to recommend the best method of organizing the government.[17] The replies indicated that most people desired a cortes. The Junta remained divided on the question. Some members favored convoking such a body to marshal support for the war and not to function as a legislature. For this reason, they preferred that, if a cortes met, it should meet not as one body but in the traditional three estates representing the clergy, the nobility, and the cities. New French victories, however, forced action.

The Central Junta decreed on January 1, 1810, that elections be held. In Spain each provincial junta and each city entitled to representation in earlier cortes was to elect a deputy. Also, a deputy was to be elected for every 50,000 inhabitants. In America a deputy was to be elected for each province, a vague and undefined term.[18] The Junta had no idea how large Spanish America was. By allowing each New World province individual representation, it inadvertently provided America with great power. Apparently the Central Junta also intended to summon the clergy and the nobility, but this was never done. The Junta could not compile a membership roll for these two groups and their supine attitude towards the invader made it unlikely that they could gain much support with the people.[19] Therefore, the Spanish Cortes met as one body and became a national assembly.

In spite of its best efforts the Central Junta could not halt the French advance. Forced to retreat into the southern corner of Spain, it was bitterly criticized for its failure. In an attempt to create a more effective government, the Junta dissolved itself and appointed a regency of five. One of them, the Mexican delegate to the Central Junta, Miguel Lardizabal y Uribe, was to represent America in the new government. The other members of the Junta, including the elected delegates who had not arrived, were relieved of their duties. As its last act, the Central Junta charged the Regency with convening the Cortes.

The new government, however, was slow in implementing this instruction. Some members believed that the nation's "constitutional" process merely required the establishment of a regency and not the convening of a national assembly.[20] Finally pressure from the Junta of Cádiz, where the government now resided, and from various deputies elected under the January 1 decree, forced the Regency's hand. It decreed that the Cortes should meet in September 1810. But because many of the occupied provinces of Spain could not hold elections, because those elected had difficulty in arriving, and because distance delayed the arrival of many American deputies, the Regency decreed that fifty-three substitutes be elected by persons then in Cádiz from the occupied provinces and from America.[21] As a result when the Cortes opened on September 24, 1810, all areas of the Spanish Monarchy were represented. Eventually some of the proprietary deputies arrived. They were seated, but the substitutes were also permitted to remain. Thus, parts of America and some of the occupied provinces in Spain received more than their share of representation.

Unlike earlier cortes, the congress which met in September 1810, was truly a modern national assembly. It met as one body and its members represented the entire Spanish commonwealth. Furthermore, the electoral process was among the most democratic of its time. Deputies were chosen in their native provinces and represented the will of all regions rather than merely the wishes of the capital city.[22] As a result the composition of the Cortes was varied: one-third were clergymen, about a sixth were nobles, and the remainder were persons of the third estate who, because of their professions, might be called middle class. Approximately a fourth of the delegates represented America.[23]

In its first session the Cortes declared that since it represented the people, the body was the repository of national sovereignty. Then the national assembly divided the government into three branches: the legislative, the executive, and the judiciary. Of the three, the legislature was the most important. The Regency would act as the executive until Ferdinand VII, the legitimate king and chief executive of the nation, returned.[24] "When the Regency objected to what it considered usurpation of its authority, its members were ordered arrested by the Cortes, tried, found guilty, and imprisoned or banished; a new Regency was then appointed."[25] The new parliament faced an enormous task. It assumed the job of creating a constitutional monarchy while prosecuting a defensive war in Spain and preserving the empire intact.

Regionalism was strong both in Spain and in America. Since the peninsular bureaucracy discredited itself by submitting to Napoleon, the provinces of Spain had no difficulty in taking control of the government. In contrast to Spain, local juntas that organized or attempted to organize in America faced an intransigent imperial bureaucracy, which either prevented juntas from forming or labeled them subversive and waged war against them. This forced many creoles into radical positions, some even advocated independence. However, the radicals were in a minority. Most Americans, like peninsular Spaniards, merely wanted home rule.

To reduce the danger of secession, the Cortes reaffirmed equal rights for inhabitants of the overseas provinces and granted a general amnesty to those who had rebelled.[26] In this way the national parliament hoped to gain the loyalty of recalcitrant juntas in Spain and America and to promote national unity. The Cortes also realized that the provinces of Spain and America resented the earlier Bourbon efforts toward centralization. Therefore, it recognized the diversity of the Spanish commonwealth by creating two new home rule institutions: the provincial deputation and the constitutional city council. The provincial deputation was an administrative body consisting of locally elected members and an executive appointed by the national government. Thus, Spanish provinces already governed by local juntas and rebellious American provinces could retain local administration while maintaining strong ties with the central government.[27] The new institution supplanted older territorial divisions such as viceroyalties, presidencies, captain-generalships, and the like, and divided the commonwealth into provinces that dealt directly with the central government. The second local body, the constitutional city council, replaced the hereditary elites who had hitherto controlled city government, with popularly elected officials.[28] After acting to unite the fortunes of local administration with the future of the Cortes, that body felt that it could turn to the restructuring of society.

The first Cortes remained in session from September 24, 1810, until September 20, 1813. During that time it attempted to transform the Spanish world. It abolished feudal institutions, ended the Inquisition, and established a firmer control of the Church. Freedom of the press, although already a fact, was formally introduced. These and other reforms were embodied in the Constitution of the Spanish Monarchy, promulgated in March 1812. The new charter created a unitary state with equal laws for all parts of the commonwealth. A unicameral legislature, the Cortes, would meet yearly in the capital. The king was substantially restricted and the Cortes entrusted with decisive power. Thus an absolutist nation became one of the most radical constitutional monarchies in Europe.[29] This extreme restructuring of society was opposed within the Cortes by a group of deputies known as *serviles.* They subjected the plans of the reformist majority, known as *liberals,* to strong criticism. Although the American deputies were, in many respects, a group apart, most sided with the liberals because reform benefited their areas.

The outstanding Spanish liberals such as José María Queipo de Llano (Count Toreno), Augustín Arguelles, Joaquín Lorenzo Villanueva, José de la Canga Argüelles, Francisco Martínez de la Rosa, Antonio Alcalá Galiano, Manuel José Quintana, and others are well known both because of their writings and because historians of Spain have studied their activities.[30] The Americans who also contributed much to reform are less well-known. José Mejía Llequerica from Quito was one of the finest orators and one of the most profound thinkers of the Cortes. "Called the American Mirabeau by his friends, he supplemented his political activities with work as editor of the liberal newspaper *La Abeja,* one of the most fighting reformist papers in Cádiz."[31] He was ably supported by his compatriot from Guayaquil, José Joaquín de Olmedo. The Peruvian delegation also had an outstanding representative in the deputy from Lima, Vicente Morales Duarez, an outspoken defender of American rights.[32] Argentina was well represented by Francisco López Lisguer, Manuel Rodrigo, and Luis Velasco.[33] However, it was the Mexican delegation, including the deputies from Central America, which acted most effectively to further reform and American interests.[34] José Miguel Ramos Arizpe was the chief architect of the provincial deputation.[35] His compatriots José Miguel Guridi y Alcocer and José María Coutó distinguished themselves as parliamentarians. Two Mexican clergymen who subsequently became conservative bishops, Antonio Joaquín Pérez and José Miguel Gordóa, often sided with the liberals. As a member of the constitutional commission, Pérez supported the liberals against the traditional faction in the committee.[36]

Once the constitution was promulgated, the special first session of the Cortes should have ended. But practical realities forced it to continue. The constitution stipulated that the Cortes should inaugurate its yearly meeting in March. However, since the constitution was adopted in March 1812, it was impossible to elect members to a new session that year. Therefore, the same deputies remained in office. The three-tiered electoral process, parish, city, and province, was slow and cumbersome. It was especially so because Spain was at war and because some parts of America were in rebellion. Realizing that more time was needed to hold elections and to permit the new representatives to travel to Cádiz, the Cortes issued a new decree postponing the opening of the next session of congress until October 1, 1813. Even this precaution did not allow all the deputies to arrive in time. For this reason some deputies from the previous session were permitted to remain as substitutes until the proprietary delegates arrived from their respective provinces.[37]

This first regular session, which met from October 1, 1813, until February 19, 1814, continued the process of reform begun in the previous special session. During this period the French were driven from Spain. Therefore, the Cortes moved to Madrid. As other Spanish provinces were liberated and conducted elections, more moderate and conservative deputies arrived.[38] This trend towards the right was checked by the arrival of new American deputies who tended to be increasingly radical because the imperial bureaucracy had thwarted New World attempts at local control. For example, Vicente Rocafuerte, the newly elected deputy from Guayaquil, was more liberal than his cousin, Olmedo, who had formerly represented the area.[39] Once again the Mexican delegation continued to lead the struggle for reform.[40]

When the second regular session convened in Madrid on March 1, 1814, nearly all of Spain was free. For the first time all the deputies of the Cortes were proprietary. Many of them were moderate or conservative. A majority of the Cortes now felt that reform had proceeded far enough.[41] Some conservative Spanish deputies believed that the liberals had gone too far. They did not view the king as a "mad dog" to be caged by legislative restrictions and they did not believe that any self-respecting monarch could accept the role assigned him by the constitution.[42] Nevertheless, the over-whelming majority of the members of the Cortes were committed to the principle of constitutional monarchy. They believed that the Cortes represented the people and were certain that no one could reject the authority of the national assembly. The revolution had been accomplished and could not be overturned. Therefore, they continued their legislative labor "in resolute, painstaking daily sessions and often in special night sessions."[43]

Unfortunately for the Cortes, the legal structure created by its members did not have time to win the full support of the Spanish people. On the contrary, everything that had been done in the previous six years—the war of national liberation and the acts of the Cortes—had been carried out in Ferdinand's name. Everywhere people longed for the return of their "well-beloved" king. The monarch was a great symbol, but an unknown personality. Now that the Napoleonic wars were ending, Ferdinand VII prepared to return. How would he react to the revolution carried out in his absence? A majority of the Cortes was certain that the king *had* to accept the new order. Therefore, the congress decreed that "only after having sworn allegiance to the Constitution in Madrid would he be recognized as Spain's legitimate sovereign."[44] A minority disagreed. Sixty-nine deputies, including ten Americans, sent the king a document known as the *Manifesto of the Persians*. In it they urged Ferdinand not to accept the Constitution of 1812. The Persians favored absolutism which, they argued, differed from arbitrary government because the power of the monarch was limited by the rights of the people. Using Martínez Marina's constitutional study, *The Theory of the Cortes*, the Persians argued that all the acts of the Cortes, including the constitution, were contrary to the traditions, laws, and history of Spain. They believed that the king should declare all the actions of the national assembly null and void. Then, in order to institute reforms, His Majesty should convoke a traditional cortes with three estates.[45] The Persians were willing to accept a national assembly because the country had undergone great changes during Ferdinand's captivity.[46]

The transformation had created a group of discontented men who were willing to support the king. Local governing bodies and local men had replaced the traditional institutions and the imperial bureaucracy. The dispossessed, naturally, hoped to return to power with Ferdinand. The regular army had also suffered. At first the Spanish army refused to fight the French on the grounds that resistance was illegal. Later when the army did fight, it was destroyed in the early battles. Irregular troops, the guerrillas, were much more successful against the invader. Quite rapidly young provincials, such as Francisco Espoz y Mina, Juan Díaz Porlier, Luis Lacy, and *El Empecinado*, became colonels and generals. The regular army meanwhile suffered a series of defeats and its generals were relegated to minor operations. The old professional army felt insulted and shunted aside while the upstart guerrilla leaders gained glory and rewards as national heroes.[47] Like the unemployed bureaucrats, the regular army officers waited for the king's arrival in the hope that he would restore them to their rightful place.

Ferdinand VII returned to a nation that had prosecuted six bitter years of war in his name. Although they did not know him, the people expected the king to be the finest of men and the best of rulers. Only a small minority feared that the monarch might be different. Ferdinand was careful not to commit himself until he learned more about the Cortes. He knew that Arthur Wellesley, the Duke of Wellington and supreme allied commander in the Peninsula, was openly hostile to the constitution. Moreover, the conservative Wellington had a favorable opinion of Ferdinand. The king also knew that the pro-constitutional Third and Fourth Spanish armies were in France under Wellington's command and were not likely to interfere with him should he choose to oppose the Cortes.[48] But the king did not know how much the people of Spain supported the parliament. As he traveled to Madrid he waited for an occasion to act. That opportunity came in Valencia on April 17, 1814. As usual the people received him with great enthusiasm. More importantly, however, General Francisco Javier Elío, a conservative regular army officer in command of the region, offered to support the king if Ferdinand wished to oppose the Cortes.[49] Ferdinand hesitated. But when he discovered that the Persians, the regular army, the bureaucracy, and many ultra-conservatives would support him, and that the guerrilla armies could not defend the constitution, he made his choice. Certain that the people would acquiesce, Ferdinand abolished the Cortes and all its acts on May 4, 1814.

The constitutional structure fell like a house of cards. The regular army pursued the liberals and the people did not rise up to defend them. Some, like the Count of Toreno and Rocafuerte, escaped to France, or Italy where they remained in exile. Countless others, including Argüelles, Quintana, and Ramos Arizpe, were imprisoned. The number of liberals imprisoned or exiled has been estimated to be between four and twelve thousand.[50] They and the *afrancesados*, who fled to France when the Napoleonic armies retreated from Spain, constituted "the country's most important men of letters, professionals, scientists, and the most capable and intelligent public officials."[51]

The Cortes collapsed for a variety of reasons. First, there had been little time to win the people's support for the new institutions. Since most of Spain had been occupied by the French until 1813, the constitutional government had little opportunity to exercise authority over the country. Neither the provincial deputation nor the constitutional city council had an opportunity to demonstrate its value at the local level. Second, the guerrilla armies that might have defended the Cortes were fighting Napoleon in France while the hostile regular army took Madrid. Third, the clergy, which had supported earlier reforms, turned against the Cortes when its interests were threatened. Finally, the people retained an innocent faith in Ferdinand VII. They did not know that he had betrayed them while in France nor that he was a despot. All they knew was that they had endured six years of immense sacrifices in his name. If he opposed the Cortes, he must have good reasons and they would not question those reasons.

4

Ferdinand's return meant not only repression in Spain and America, but also the recovery of the higher clergy, the nobility, the old bureaucracy, and the regular army. The very groups that had failed to defend Spain from the French attack prospered while the guerrilla generals, the heroes of the struggle, who had expected rewards and high positions in Ferdinand's government, were dismissed. Only a few received minor provincial posts. Most were expected to return quietly to their farms or shops after having been generals in charge of entire provinces.[52] It is hardly surprising that these men grew resentful. They understood that the government had to economize, but they did not want savings at their expense.

The Spanish government faced a dilemma. The army and the bureaucracy grew immensely during the war while revenues declined to nearly half their prewar level. American silver no longer arrived and Spanish industries suffered because they were unable to trade with the New World. Deprived of outlets, Cataluña's large textile industry nearly collapsed.[53] If Spain were to recover, it was imperative to regain control of America, restore trade, and revive the flow of silver. This seemed possible because once the Cortes collapsed, the old bureaucracy returned to power. Viceroys, governors, and other officials resumed their former posts. No longer restricted by the constitution or by local control, they were able to destroy insurgency with a ruthlessness previously impossible. In Mexico, Viceroy Félix María Calleja defeated the insurgent José María Morelos by the end of 1815.[54] The short-lived United Provinces of Cundinamarca was overwhelmed in 1816 and its president, José Fernández de Madrid, exiled.[55] Captain General Gabino Gaínza defeated the rebels in Chile in 1817.[56] Only Buenos Aires remained isolated and therefore beyond Spanish control. Although a majority of the imperial bureaucracy returned to absolutism gladly, some of its members had been infected by the liberal virus. For example, Colonel Toribio Montes, then president of Quito, permitted the constitutional city council to continue. As late as March, 1817, the crown was forced to reissue orders for its abolition.[57]

Despite the reassertion of Spanish authority in America, the insurgents did not give up. José de San Martín won a decisive victory in Chile in April 1818. Simón Bolívar renewed the struggle in Venezuela, and in 1819 the tide turned against Spain. Therefore, if Ferdinand wished to retain control of America, he would be forced to send more men. Yet the formation of another expedition to reconquer the New World could only mean increased discontent in Spain.

The struggle in America was but one source of dissatisfaction. The king associated with disreputable elements, forming a *camarilla*, which reputedly undermined the official ministers. Once again, a Spanish monarch discredited himself in the eyes of the people. The restored Inquisition added to the unrest by relentlessly tracking

down reputed liberals and masons. Ferdinand also permitted the
Jesuits to return to Spain and to resume their former positions.
However, it was the reestablishment of centralized administration
which affected Spaniards more than any other restoration. The
provinces, which had grown accustomed to home rule as a result of
six years of war, began to realize that the constitution had permitted
them more local control than any previous Spanish government.
Finally, the economy continued to decline. Thus as the years
passed, discontent increased. Many Spaniards, particularly those in
the cities, came to believe that since absolutism was bad, perhaps a
return to constitutionalism might be good.[58]

5

Opposition to Ferdinand's absolutism began as soon as the constitution was abolished. Political conspiracy in Spain and insurrection
in America were often carried out through secret societies, such as
the masonic lodges.[59] In order to understand the importance of
freemasonry in the political milieu of the period, it is necessary to
review certain related events. During the reigns of Charles III and
Charles IV, reformist attitudes had been disseminated through
three channels: the new periodic press, the reformed universities,
and the economic societies for useful knowledge.[60] The Napoleonic wars disrupted the universities and Ferdinand's return ended
the freedom of the press. As a result, the economic societies
became the chief vehicles of liberal communication. These societies
had once been primarily concerned with fostering the new knowledge and had established extensive contacts with like-minded
economic and philosophic societies in other nations of the Atlantic
world. This international network of communication became politically important during the Napoleonic wars. Spanish and Spanish
American revolutionaries and adventurers traveled across the
Western World under the aegis of such societies. However, conspiracy required a more clandestine organization. Since most
revolutionaries were members of the educated classes and since
learned societies had already served as a vehicle for communication, it was only natural that freemasonry, another creation of the
Enlightenment, should be made to serve political ends. Masonic

lodges had much to recommend them as conspiratorial oganiza-
tions. First, they were secret. Second, the elaborate ritual allowed
its members to scrutinize new applicants. Third, they instilled a
sense of comaraderie. Finally, they were international. Therefore,
the revolutionaries of the Hispanic world eagerly embraced freemasonry. When they could not join or organize official masonic
lodges, they created secret societies patterned after them. Ultimately, both the economic societies and the masonic lodges served
as political cells.

At first, Spanish Americans were the principal conspirators.
London became the great revolutionary center in 1810. Simón
Bolívar, José de San Martín, Bernardo O'Higgins, Vicente Rocafuerte, José Servando Teresa de Mier, and Francisco Miranda—the
greatest conspirator of them all—passed through the British capital. All joined secret societies at one time or another. After
Ferdinand's return most Spanish Americans moved their base of
conspiratorial activity to the United States. There the Venezuelans,
Pedro Gual and José Revenga, and the Mexican Miguel Santamaría, sought unsuccessfully to win the United States' support for
their cause. Because of its strategic location, Cuba also became an
important center for revolutionary activity. The Cuban capital
affords an example of how extensive conspiratorial ties were.
When the Colombian, José Fernández de Madrid, was exiled to
Havana in 1816, he immediately joined that city's economic society.
There he encountered the recently arrived Argentine, José Antonio
Miralla. In 1817, they met the ex-deputy and liberal exile, Vicente
Rocafuerte, who was stopping in Havana on his way to Guayaquil
after three years of wanderings in Europe. Later they were joined
by the Peruvian, Manuel Lorenzo de Vidaurre. Each was in contact
with secret societies in his homeland and each established new contacts through the Havana Economic Society. Because these and
other Spanish Americans traveled extensively, such contacts
expanded rapidly and were constantly being reinforced.[61]

It is not possible at this time to unravel all the threads of international intrigue. It is, however, clear that economic societies and
masonic lodges facilitated travel and put its members in contact
with like-minded individuals in other lands. Even persons of
limited means could aspire to fantastic adventures if they joined
the right groups. For example, the Cuban, Antonio José Valdez, a

self-educated man of humble background, joined the Havana Economic Society. By virtue of his ability he became a distinguished member of that association. Later he traveled to Buenos Aires, where he served the independent government. Eventually he was sent on a secret mission to Spain. In 1821, he was in Mexico serving in the capacity of secretary to the new national leader, Agustín Iturbide. Valdez remained in Mexico serving the government in various capacities until his death.[62] Others, like the Mexican, Tadeo Ortíz de Ayala, journeyed extensively on their own initiative. For a time Ortíz de Ayala traveled through South America allegedly representing revolutionary groups in Mexico. He also served the Buenos Aires government for a time. Finally, he returned to Mexico and later represented the insurgents in the United States.[63] Many other Spanish Americans pursued equally varied careers.

These international conspirators had other things in common besides their uncanny ability to travel and their membership in economic and masonic societies. They were well-educated members of the Enlightenment and were distinguished writers, some of them poets. However, in spite of their similar conspiratorial activities, they held varied political views. Some, including Simón Bolívar, Carlos María Bustamante, and José Servando Teresa de Mier, desired total independence. Others, like Vicente Rocafuerte, José Fernández de Madrid, José Antonio Miralla, and Miguel Ramos Arizpe, who would become Spanish Americanists, sought home rule within the Spanish commonwealth. Still others were not certain what road to follow. Nevertheless, as liberals they were united in a virulent opposition to Ferdinand VII's absolutism.[64]

Although Americans were the first to form conspiratorial groups, Spaniards soon followed. After Ferdinand's return Spanish liberals and the men of the new army formed secret societies to organize opposition to the absolute king. Because the war against the French had debilitated peninsular economic societies, Spanish conspirators relied on masonic lodges and other secret societies. The revolutionaries had a variety of motives. Many merely wanted jobs. Others wanted to restore constitutional rule. A few saw no difference between the American desire for home rule and the Spanish liberals' wish for constitutional government. Indeed, one of them,

Javier Mina, believed that the insurgent struggle in America was really an attempt to restore the constitution.

The Mina insurrection is a good example of the interrelation that existed between Spanish liberals and American rebels. Mina was a hero of the Spanish War of Independence who, like other guerrilla leaders, could find no employment at home after the war ended. He indignantly refused the command of a division in Mexico, where he was expected to defeat the Morelos revolt; in his view "the cause the Americans defend" was no different than the cause of Spain.[65] Instead, he and his uncle Francisco Espoz y Mina, another great guerrilla general, rebelled in September 1814 and demanded the restoration of the constitution. The insurrection failed and its leaders were forced to flee.[66] In exile, at the request of Father Mier, Javier Mina agreed to lead an invasion of Mexico. After obtaining the support of other Spanish Americans, like Pedro Gual, Miguel Santamaría, and José Revenga, the conspirators landed in northern Mexico in mid-1816. There they struggled for a year, but in the end, Mina was captured and executed and Father Mier imprisoned.[67] Mina had hoped to restore constitutional rule in Mexico and extend it from there to Spain and other parts of the commonwealth. Although the plan was fantastic, it was not entirely illogical. Mexico was the wealthiest part of the empire and, if captured, could serve as a base for a constitutional conquest of the Spanish Empire. However, it is unlikely that Morelos would have agreed to such a proposal. In any case, the Mexican insurgent had been defeated before Mina launched his expedition.

Another rebellion occurred in Spain even before Mina attempted an invasion of Mexico. Juan Díaz Porlier, a native of Buenos Aires and a hero of the Spanish guerrilla war against the French, rebelled in La Coruña in September 1815, demanding the return of the constitution. At first the movement appeared successful, but strong government action triumphed. Like Mina, Díaz Porlier was captured and executed. Thereafter, the two men entered the liberal pantheon. Poems and songs were dedicated to them in Spain and America.

The execution of the rebels did not deter other insurgents. In 1816, Vicente Richard plotted to assassinate the king in a brothel. In 1817, Lieutenant General Luis Lacy rebelled in Cataluña. Shortly thereafter, the Inquisition uncovered another conspiracy known as the Grand Masonic Plot of 1817. The following year, government officials thwarted an attempt to restore Charles IV to the throne as a constitutional monarch. When this plan failed, Colonel Joaquín Vidal led an insurrection in Valencia. All these attempts to restore the constitution failed and their leaders forfeited their lives.[68] However, regardless of the measures taken by Ferdinand's government, the opposition persisted.

Like the renewed rebellions in America, opposition in Spain increased despite the king's attempts to end it through violent repression. Although the countryside suffered as much as any other sector of the country, the rural population, the source of traditional strength, did not blame the monarch for its misfortunes. In the cities, however, many held absolutism directly responsible for the nation's ills. It was there that a new appreciation of the provincial deputation and the constitutional city council developed. Many urban provincials came to realize that the Cortes had established an acceptable equilibrium between the desire for provincial home rule and the need for an effective national government. Therefore, as the years passed, more and more people participated in the rebellions.

At first the insurrections in Spain had been chiefly military affairs. Quite rapidly, however, civilian liberals joined the movements. Although the conspirators disliked Ferdinand's rule, they did not agree on the form of government Spain should have. The constitution and the Cortes were a clear alternative to absolutism. But some liberals believed that the executive had to be strengthened if constitutional government were to succeed. Others felt that the legislature had to have a second chamber to prevent radicalism. Still others were committed to the 1812 charter and would condone no change. However, all agreed that constitutional government should be restored. But as late as 1819, none of the insurrections had found support among the masses. If the liberals were to return to power, they had to gain wider backing. The discontent caused by the growing struggle in America seemed to provide the basis for such support.

The war in northern South America had turned against Spain by 1819, and the army that had originally been intended to conquer Buenos Aires was now being sent to fight Bolívar in Venezuela. This expeditionary army had been encamped in Andalucía for months awaiting transportation to America. The delay and the soldiers' wretched living conditions only served to increase dissatisfaction. No one wanted to participate in the bitter fratricidal struggle in the New World. Liberals hoped to exploit the troops' reluctance to leave Spain. "Revolution meant no American campaign," they argued, and the rank and file agreed.[69] Cádiz masons also attempted to convince the commanding general, Enrique O'Donnell, Count La Bisbal, to join them. Unfortunately for liberal aspirations, La Bisbal betrayed the movement. Although the conspirators were forced to flee, a sudden outbreak of yellow fever among the troops prevented the government from taking strong measures. Therefore, some radicals attempted to renew the conspiracy.

Antonio Alcalá Galiano returned to Andalucia and approached several younger officers. Colonels Antonio Quiroga and Juan O'Donojú, who had been implicated in the Grand Masonic Plot, were receptive. However, it was Major Rafael Riego, commander of the Asturias Regiment, who acted. On January 1, 1820, he raised the banner of rebellion, demanding the restoration of the constitution. Other units followed, but rapid government action prevented the Cádiz liberals from supporting the military uprising. New government troops, dispatched to quell the rebellion, took control of the cities in the south. For nearly two months the rebels marched through southern Spain hoping to obtain support but found none. The expeditionary army had risen but accomplished little. It seemed certain that the crown would destroy this insurrection as it had others. The intense discontent in the army was not enough to make a successful revolution. Stronger forces were necessary.

Regionalism succeeded where armed insurrection had failed. On February 21, La Coruña rebelled. It immediately restored the provincial deputation and the constitutional city council. Other northern towns also restored their constitutional municipalities. By March 5, even large cities such as Saragossa and Barcelona had reestablished provincial deputations and constitutional city governments. The provincial cities of Spain simply restored the home rule granted them by the Constitution of 1812. Nevertheless, the liberal officers who began the revolt claimed success and the rest of the army hastened to join them. Even La Bisbal saw the error of his ways and returned to the liberal fold.[70]

Only Madrid remained in government hands by March 6, 1820.

Even there Henry Wellesley, the British minister, estimated that two thirds of the population sympathized with the rebels.[71] The liberals, who had organized clandestinely, capitalized on the economic crisis and the general disenchantment with the government to mobilize the masses. Crowds poured into the streets demanding the restoration of the constitution. To appease them, Ferdinand VII ordered the Cortes to convene. Pleased with the results, people of all sorts mingled in the streets embracing one another. Liberals sought to channel the euphoria to their own ends. Agitators convinced the multitude to march to the municipal palace and restore the constitutional city council. When the masses reached the cabildo, they discovered that several liberals, among them the noted Mexican playwright Manuel E. Gorostiza, were there to guide the people in "electing" officials. From the balcony of the municipal building Gorostiza shouted, "Citizens, do you want the Marquis de las Hormazas as constitutional *alcalde primero*?" Some replied yes. But others yelled that the Marquis was General Elío's uncle. They wanted nothing to do with a relative of the man who had destroyed the constitution in 1814. Gorostiza offered additional names until the crowd had "elected" all the members of the new constitutional city council. Thereafter the multitude celebrated in the streets. Hoping to regain the initiative, Ferdinand announced on March 8 that all political prisoners would be released. But the liberals were not satisfied with minor concessions. They induced the crowd to demand that the king swear allegiance to the constitution before the city council and also forced him to abolish the Inquisition.

The king appointed a junta of liberals to advise him until the Cortes met. Then he named a ministry of "jailbirds," liberals released from prison. But the national government controlled only Castile. Elsewhere, provincial deputations and constitutional city councils proclaimed their sovereignty much as local juntas had done in 1808. Six years of despotism had demonstrated the value of home rule and the institutions that guaranteed it. Nothing is more striking than the rapidity with which cities proceeded to organize and elect municipal governments.[72] Earlier during the first constitutional period, many local notables had been hesitant about holding elections. In some instances they had been apathetic. It was not so in 1820. Even in America, elections were held rapidly and enthusiastically as soon as news arrived that the constitution had been restored.[73]

In Spain and in America the return of constitutional government raised the hopes and aspirations of liberals. It appeared that once more they were being allowed to rule the Spanish world. For the small group who believed in the concept of a Spanish commonwealth, it was the last opportunity to maintain the unity of Spain and America. The men of the New World who loved the constitution, the future Spanish Americanists, were particularly concerned with maintaining that union.

# II

## THE SPANISH CONSTITUTION RESTORED

Countless liberals believed that the restoration of the Spanish Constitution would end the "civil war" in the New World because the charter of 1812 granted the autonomy desired by many creoles. Under it, Americans obtained representation at three levels: at the commonwealth level through the Cortes, at the regional level through the provincial deputation, and at the local level through the constitutional city council. Furthermore, the constitution guaranteed civil liberties, uniform laws, and the abolition of the special privileges of the old regime. For these same reasons conservatives looked with dismay upon the return of constitutional rule. The new order not only threatened their privileges but also seemed to favor the insurgents. The bureaucracy, in particular, viewed the new civil liberties as an obstacle to its efforts to end all rebellion in America. Nor were those insurgents committed to independence pleased. Representative government for the Spanish world provided an alternative way of achieving autonomy without the rigors of war. Moreover, the Spanish Constitution was more liberal than their own charters. Therefore, rebel leaders feared that the restored constitution might reduce their appeal to creoles and increase the difficulties of creating new nations.[1]

1

Strategically located along the route between Spain and America, Cuba soon became a center of activity for advocates of competing political views. The first publications lauded the reestablished constitution. The Colombian, Fernández de Madrid, published a poem entitled *To the Restoration of the Spanish Constitution*, which praised the virtues of that "sacred code."[2] Later he founded *El Argos*, a newspaper devoted to defending the constitution and to fostering useful knowledge. There he published another poem, *To the Memory of Porlier and Lacy*, which extolled the greatness of the

26

martyred constitutional heroes; one from America, the other from Spain, yet both devoted followers of representative government.[3] The constitution also had its detractors, primarily the bureaucrats. The official newspaper, *The Daily of the Constitutional Government of Havana*, became the chief vehicle for such critics. Antonio María Escobedo, a conservative, argued in one issue that the provincial deputation was a first step in the dismemberment of the Spanish commonwealth since it created a series of federal republics. Fernández de Madrid replied that Escobedo erred in not realizing the vast difference between the Cortes, a legislative body, and the provincial deputation, an administrative body. The Cortes was the great parliament that governed the entire commonwealth while the provincial deputation merely allowed local administration of national laws. Through this division of authority, he argued, the constitution had combined the best aspects of federalism with the best of monarchy.[4]

Pamphlets arguing a variety of views appeared daily. A majority favored the constitution.[5] Diego Tanco brought out *A Patriotic Notice* and Dr. Tomás Gutiérrez de Piñérez issued a proclamation to the Cuban people. Both publications emphasized that the need for change could best be accomplished under the constitution.[6] The Peruvian, Manuel Lorenzo de Vidaurre, recently appointed judge to the Audiencia of Puerto Príncipe, published a study entitled *American Votes for the Spanish Nation*. Vidaurre reviewed the existing grievances between creoles and peninsulars and concluded that they could be reconciled. He maintained that the real division was not between Americans and Spaniards but between those who supported representative government and those who favored absolutism. The Constitution of 1812, he argued, formed a true "concordat between American Spaniards and European Spaniards."[7]

Although several people voiced criticism of the constitution, the most important attack came from the distinguished Cuban physician, Tomás Romay. In an article entitled *Purga Urbem*, Romay, then secretary of the provincial deputation of Havana, questioned the linking of the constitution to the alleged need for change. He argued that Cuba had been peaceful during the preceding twenty years while the rest of Spanish America was rent by fratricidal wars. These revolutionary movements had not produced great statesmen such as George Washington or Benjamin Franklin and that failure caused anarchy and bloodshed. Romay believed that Spanish rule had been benevolent as well as beneficial and that the constitution should be used to preserve that rule rather than to modify it. He urged that Cuba purge herself of those vile malcontents who were bent not only on anarchy and destruction but also were turning Americans against Spaniards.[8]

Vicente Rocafuerte, then in Havana, felt compelled to reply to this veiled attack. Few Spanish Americans were better qualified to defend the constitution than he. The heir to a large fortune, he had been educated in Spain and France and had traveled extensively through Western, Northern, and Eastern Europe. Besides his native Spanish, he spoke French, Italian, and English fluently and had an excellent command of Latin. During his travels he was received by the best of European society. However, he was most comfortable with European intellectuals such as David Ricardo, Count Constantín Volney, the Abbey du Pradt, and Alexander von Humboldt. His wide-ranging interests brought him into contact with many important persons and his learning earned him a reputation among fellow Americans. Vidaurre included him among the savants of the New World. Bolívar could find no greater compliment to pay the poet Olmedo than to call him another Rocafuerte. The Ecuadorean also had political experience, having served as alcalde in Guayaquil and later as deputy to the Cortes of 1814. But it was his devotion to the interests of Spanish America and his willingness to abandon his personal concerns for American causes which made him a much sought after patriot.[9]

In his reply, Rocafuerte argued that Romay was making an artificial distinction between Americans and Spaniards. There was no difference. They were all Spaniards, some of whom had been born in America and others in Spain. The real division was between those who believed in constitutionalism and those who supported absolutism. Rocafuerte accused Romay of being an apologist for absolutism. Cuba remained tranquil not because of absolutist benevolence, but because her favorable geographic location had shielded her from the despotism that other parts of the Spanish commonwealth had suffered. Unlike the rest of America, Cuba had enjoyed free trade and the resulting prosperity. Since the constitution guaranteed not only free trade but tolerance and liberty as well, Rocafuerte suggested that it alone provided the guarantees that all enlightened men sought. Instead of insulting their brothers, he continued, men of goodwill should be "seeking the happy pacification of America [so that] animated by the spirit of the great Spanish family and electrified by the effects of the Sacred Constitution, we will form institutions which have as their foundation the understanding of our reciprocal interest, fortified by the powerful ties of a common tongue and a common religion." He concluded that justice, benevolence, generosity, and moderation were the ties that bind peoples as well as individuals together.[10]

Rocafuerte's forceful defense of the constitution provided Diego Tanco an opportunity for criticism. In a pamphlet entitled *More and Less*, he insulted the Ecuadorean for not having refuted Romay's criticisms of the constitution. Tanco. a former *afrancesado* prefect in Joseph Bonaparte's Spanish government, argued that although change was needed it did not have to come through constitutional processes. The former Bonapartist bureaucrat suggested that a strong man, an enlightened despot, was necessary to restore peace and harmony to the Spanish world by bringing an end to the bloody struggle between creoles and peninsulars.[11]

Fernández de Madrid defended his friend Rocafuerte. In his newspaper, *El Argos*, the Colombian deplored the insults and vulgar allusions that Tanco directed at Rocafuerte. Fernández de Madrid's brief reply indicated that Tanco's arguments were confused and contradictory and that the pamphlet in no way disappoved Rocafuerte's assertions.

Another of Rocafuerte's friends, the Argentine, José Antonio Miralla, replied to Tanco with a twenty-page pamphlet. Miralla pointed out that Rocafuerte had intended to diminish and to soften the impact of Romay's statements, which might have created ill will between Spaniards and Americans. Then he criticized Tanco for asserting that the American continent was divided by a bloody struggle between creole and peninsular. This had also been Romay's argument and Miralla replied with Rocafuerte's answer: the true division was between absolutists and constitutionalists, between serviles and liberals. Some Americans, such as Romay, were absolutists while some Spaniards favored the cause of American autonomy. Miralla chided Tanco for aping French culture. One could favor the best that nation had to offer without accepting discredited institutions. No enlightened despot could aid the Spanish world now. The one and only hope was the constitution. It alone could guarantee reconciliation, peace, and liberty.[12]

The debate over the constitution intensified when Havana's liberal bishop and reputed mason, Juan José Díaz de Espada, ordered that the constitution be read from the pulpits of the churches in his diocese. Later Bishop Díaz de Espada proposed that the Havana Economic Society establish a course in constitutionalism. Then he authorized Father Félix Varela, professor of philosophy at the Seminary College of San Carlos, to apply for the chair should it be created. Since Romay, Miralla, and Fernández de Madrid were all respected members of the economic society, debate on the proposed course was heated. But in the end the liberals won. The chair was established and supported by the society. Varela became its first professor and devoted himself to preparing an adequate text. The first class met at the end of 1820, with an enrollment of 193. However, Varela's book was not completed until early 1821, when he published *Observations on the Political Constitution of the Spanish Monarchy.* Shortly thereafter, Varela was elected Havana's deputy to the Cortes and departed for Spain. Nevertheless, the course of study was firmly established.[13]

Throughout the entire period, Miralla and Fernández de Madrid continued to defend the constitution from the pages of *El Argos.* Indeed they and the paper became the most ardent champions of a constitutional Spanish commonwealth.[14] Both men believed that the American insurgents could be reconciled with the constitutional government. Fernández de Madrid was the leader of a secret society in Havana which had established contacts with other secret societies throughout America for the purpose of promoting such a compromise. Thus when a secret society in Caracas asked for assistance in determining the intentions of the Cortes, the Cuban group was glad to provide it.

2

The separatist movement in northern South America succeeded in creating the republic of Gran Colombia in 1819. However, the struggle remained in doubt when news arrived that the Spanish Constitution had been restored. The change placed both the Spanish administration and the Gran Colombian revolutionaries in a precarious position. Hoping to resolve the issue, the leaders of the contending forces arranged for a truce. The Spanish were plagued with what seemed an impossible situation. They could no longer act with unity and authority because the Constitution of 1812 restricted their actions by restoring local autonomy. Although the viceroy retained military command, he no longer had political authority over the former viceroyalty of New Granada. Instead, he became the superior political chief of the provincial deputation of Bogotá. Other political chiefs in Quito and Caracas shared equal administrative power with him. Moreover, cities had the right to elect independent municipal governments. Finally, freedom of the press and other civil liberties guaranteed by the constitution were obstacles in defeating the insurgents. The separatists also faced a grave dilemma. The local autonomy and civil liberties provided by the restored constitution won many adherents and diminished the appeal of independence. Some, who advocated complete separation from Spain, wanted the constitution implemented because they expected the Spanish bureaucracy to oppose it. Then its admirers would be disabused and realize that only independence would provide the government they sought. A few leaders of the Gran Colombian government also hoped that the Cortes might be willing to negotiate a peace whose terms would grant virtual independence. Thus the new republic needed accurate information about the Cortes before it could act.[15] Yet it could not act officially without endangering its cause; a private inquiry seemed best.

The Caracas secret society contacted Fernández de Madrid in Havana requesting that a trusted patriot be sent to Spain to obtain reliable information regarding the attitude of the new Cortes on the question of American autonomy. The Havana secret society selected Vicente Rocafuerte for that delicate mission. There were several reasons for the choice. The Ecuadorean was an intimate friend of Gran Colombian President Simón Bolívar and Foreign Minister Pedro Gual, as well as being a friend and relative of influential bureaucrats in Spanish American government. He also knew many of the deputies to the Cortes and would have little difficulty in learning their attitude toward America. Moreover, he had the means to travel and to contact important persons in Europe. Finally, since the Havana society was committed to the union of the

Spanish world under the constitution, it expected that "as always, he would work for the important reconciliation of Spain with America."[16]

Another secret agent was also dispatched to Spain with a mission similar to Rocafuerte's. Francisco Lemus, a Cuban in the Gran Colombian army, traveled by way of Havana. He and Rocafuerte left in May 1820. Little is known about Lemus's activities in Europe. He returned to Cuba in February 1821, shortly before Rocafuerte. Later, in 1823, both men would collaborate, indirectly, in a conspiracy to free Cuba.[17]

When Rocafuerte arrived in Madrid early in August, he found the capital pulsating with a new excitement. His old Mexican friend, Manual Eduardo Gorostiza, took him to the café La Fontana de Oro where the young radicals—*exaltados*—who had made the revolution, such as Antonio Alcalá Galiano, Evaristo San Miguel, and Gorostiza himself, discussed politics. The first such club had been formed at the café Lorencini near the Puerta del Sol shortly after the constitution was restored. Soon other cafés, like the Gran Cruz de Malta and the San Sebastian, became gathering places for young politicians eager to change society. Francisco Martínez de la Rosa and other moderates organized the Society of Friends of Order, which met at La Fontana de Oro in the hope of creating a forum for less radical opinion. Their expectations were rapidly frustrated as the *exaltados* took over the café, making La Fontana de Oro the most famous of the radical clubs.[18]

Partisan newspapers further enlivened the political scene. The *Aurora de España* was the first to appear after the constitution was reestablished. It was followed by the radical *El Conservador* as well as by *El Sol, El Correo*, and the *Redactor General de España*. A few papers, like José Joaquín Mora's and Manuel Eduardo Gorostiza's *El Constitucional*, which appeared as literary and scientific journals during the absolutist period, changed their names and devoted themselves to politics. Newspapers, both in the capital and in the provinces, defended partisan views. In general, however, absolutist tracts had little appeal. The best Spanish men of letters were constitutionalists, many of them radical.[19]

Rocafuerte found the lively debate stimulating, but he also noted that potentially dangerous divisions had emerged. The elections of April 30 had returned an overwhelming liberal majority to the

Cortes. Most of them were "men of 1812" (*doceañistas*), as the liberals of the first constitutional period were called. Sobered by their imprisonment and exile, the men of 1812, considered government a grave responsibility and accordingly called themselves moderates. They were not only a majority in congress but they also controlled the ministries and through them patronage. Agustín Argüelles, the most famous *doceañista*, was minister of government and acting first minister while José de la Canga Argüelles held the ministry of the treasury. On the other hand, the "men of 1820," those who had actually carried out the revolution, received little. They were a minority in the Cortes because they had just come to public attention while the older men were already famous. A few *exaltados* received appointments to provincial posts. Most, however, remained outside of government, deprived of the rewards and patronage they believed were theirs by right of revolution. The men of 1820, younger and more reckless than the moderates, wanted rapid change and were proud to call themselves radicals (*exaltados*). The difference between the two groups of liberals was partly the difference between older and younger men, as well as between the "ins" and the "outs." The "division [also reflected the differences] between liberals and democrats, between men of property and position and urban radicals."[20] Not unnaturally, the moderates appealed to the wealthier classes while the radicals appealed to the urban proletariat.

Both groups of liberals were confident that constitutional government would succeed this time. Indeed, Ferdinand VII himself seemed to guarantee such an outcome by his wholehearted acceptance of the new system. When the Cortes began its sessions on July 9, the king explained that "wicked ministers" had hidden evils from him in the past. Now he promised to join the representatives of the nation in resolving the present ills, and offered to respect and support the constitution. Most deputies believed in Ferdinand's sincerity and cheered when he referred to himself as their constitutional monarch. In an emotional session the Cortes granted the king the title of Ferdinand the Great. Thereafter the patriotic cry became, "Long live the king and the constitution."[21]

The new liberal government faced a very difficult task. The nation was in a state of collapse. Roads and canals were in total disrepair, preventing effective commerce within the country. Industry and agriculture were in a pronounced depression. Inflation and unemployment were rampant. Few people wanted to pay taxes, yet the government desperately needed revenue to cover enormous deficits. Despite these grave difficulties, everyone expected the restored constitutional government to resolve the problems rapidly.

Although a majority of liberals believed that a policy of laissez-faire was best for the nation in the long run, they also realized that strong government intervention was necessary to remedy the country's immediate plight. Since the agricultural sector seemed to be hardest hit, the Cortes passed a law prohibiting the importation of grain. Deputies hoped that Spain's farmers would be able to expand production and sell more. For similar reasons, they granted the industrial provinces of the periphery protection from foreign competition. Since many liberals believed that all internal restraints on trade should be removed, they passed laws abolishing guilds as well as monopoly companies. They would have liked to end the state tobacco and salt monopolies but could find no other income to substitute for those lucrative sources. Similarly, many legislators believed that the tithe was the most oppressive of agricultural taxes, yet supported the fee because no other method of sustaining parish priests existed. Indeed, much to their grief, liberals were forced to impose new taxes to keep the administration solvent. Canga Argüelles proposed foreign loans as a means of preventing still higher taxes. However, he warned that such expedients were not a true solution; the nation itself would have to bear the cost of reconstruction. Some legislators suggested reducing the number of government employees. Others believed that the most important issue was the pacification of America. Only if trade with the New World were restored would the Spanish economy recover.[22]

In spite of the grave difficulties facing the nation, the American liberals shared their Spanish counterparts' belief that constitutional rule would save the commonwealth. Time did not permit elected American deputies to arrive in Madrid before the Cortes convened. Therefore, once again, substitutes were elected by Americans residing in Spain. Many had participated in the earlier Cortes. Some, like José Miguel Ramos Arizpe, were just out of jail. In contrast to the Spanish moderates, the American *doceañistas* had been made more radical by their imprisonment and exile. Now they were determined to obtain a greater degree of autonomy for their native lands than they had hoped for during the first constitutional period.

Rocafuerte contacted Ramos Arizpe and Francisco Fagoaga, another substitute deputy for Mexico, to ascertain the possibility of ending the conflict in Spanish America. They received the Ecuadorean warmly and introduced him to two other substitute deputies for Mexico, Juan de Dios Cañedo and José Mariano Michelena. The Mexicans assured Rocafuerte that reconciliation was not only possible but quite probable. Indeed, they were already considering new plans to present to the Cortes.

Eager to ascertain the government's attitude, Rocafuerte contacted Minister of Treasury Canga Argüelles whom he had known during the first constitutional period. Canga Argüelles told him that some sort of reconciliation between Spain and America was imperative and that the government would foster it. The Cortes had already decreed amnesty for the insurgents. If the separatists could be convinced to accept the constitution, there was no reason why some satisfactory compromise could not be reached. Other Spanish moderates, such as Deputy Joaquín Lorenzo Villanueva, also informed Rocafuerte that the Cortes would concern itself with finding the best means of reconciling American aspirations with the necessity for national unity. *Exaltados* were even more vocal in their assurances that America would receive just treatment in the Cortes.[23] Pleased with the reaction, Rocafuerte published an article in Gorostiza's newspaper, *El Constitucional*, encouraging the Spanish parliament to seek an understanding with the Spanish American separatists.[24]

Unfortunately, hopes for accord with America were dashed by dissention in Spain. The absolutists would not accept constitutional rule. They were unimportant so long as Ferdinand VII was willing to cooperate with the Cortes. But in the summer of 1820, the administration learned that the king was contemplating flight. Only with great difficulty was it able to restrain him. Thereafter, the Argüelles ministry had to maintain the fiction of the king's devotion to the constitution while it kept strict watch over the monarch.

The greatest threat to the government, however came from the left. Deprived of patronage and influence, the *exaltados* turned to the clubs and the press as a means of influencing the government.

Realizing that the radicals desired some rewards, the moderates had promoted Riego to the rank of general and allowed him to retain command of the revolutionary army known as the Army of Observation. Originally formed to defend the revolution, the ten-thousand-man Army of Observation provided the men of 1820 with opportunities for advancement and prestige. By August, however, the moderates felt that this army could no longer be justified. The absolutists seemed defeated, the king was under control and, most important of all, the Army of Observation was too expensive to maintain. Therefore, the army was disbanded and Riego transferred to a command in Galicia. The *exaltados* saw this as a move to deprive them of jobs and influence. Accordingly, when Riego came to Madrid, the speakers of La Fontana de Oro organized mass demonstrations on his behalf. The government controlled Madrid easily, but provincial disturbances were more widespread.

The moderates, frightened by the violence of the masses and disturbed by what seemed to them demagoguery on the part of the *exaltados*, enacted a series of measures designed to limit public expression. The role of the political clubs became a heated question. Thus, late in the summer of 1820, the liberals were bitterly divided between moderates and radicals. Although they agreed on a program of clerical reform, which included expelling the Society of Jesus, abolishing certain regular orders, and subjecting all churchmen to civil authority, the unity originally hoped for had ended.[25]

In November, foreign danger further complicated the political crisis. The Spanish revolution of 1820 brought new hope to liberals in Europe. Portugal and Naples soon followed Spain's example and adopted the Constitution of 1812 as their own. The Spanish charter became a symbol of liberalism on the Continent. Even in far-off Russia, a group of dissidents known as the Decembrists would adopt the Spanish constitution as their platform. Therefore, the conservative powers, Austria, Prussia, and Russia, prepared to take remedial action. Prince Metternich, the Austrian foreign minister, called a conference at Troppau to settle the affairs of Italy and to consider how revolutionary Spain might be contained. England refused to participate, but France remained ambivalent. The French Bourbons could not side with revolutionary "attacks" against the Spanish and Neapolitan Bourbons, nor could they support the conservatives without exasperating French liberals. As a result, France merely sent an observer. Since France was not an official party to the conference, the anti-constitutionalist Troppau Protocol, issued on November 29, 1820, became identified with the three conservative powers known as the Holy Alliance.

Historians have indicated that the Quadruple Alliance of England, Austria, Russia and Prussia, and not the Holy Alliance, directed Europe's actions. This distinction, however, was not meaningful to Hispanic liberals. They believed that England would not intervene; and they hoped that France would follow Britain's example. *El Constitucional* expressed these feelings when it said, "We have faith in France. Surely there are in that generous nation thousands of friends of liberty who know, through their own sad experience, [the ills of] foreign interference."[26] As long as France remained neutral, the Holy Alliance could not intervene in Spanish affairs. But the political divisions and the intense agitation of the clubs in Spain reminded many observers of the French Revolution on the eve of the Terror. Such comparisons could only increase France's anxiety.

By the end of January, 1821, France began to consider taking some measures to prevent the further radicalization of the Spanish revolution. The English government, also worried by the grave internal divisions in Spain, attempted to convince the contending factions that only harmony could save the constitutional process. Both France and England urged a revision of the constitution to moderate some of the more radical provisions. The *doceañistas* were inclined to accept such proposals but the *exaltados* declared that the constitution was sacred and refused to consider any changes.

The destructive division within the liberal ranks and the ominous Troppau Protocol convinced Rocafuerte that his first impressions had been wrong. He now believed that constitutionalism would be short-lived. Eventually the Cortes would be destroyed and absolutism restored. He concluded that America's only hope of establishing a liberal constitutional government was separation from Spain. Regretfully, he informed Fernández de Madrid of his conclusions so that the Havana secret society might notify their corresponding group in Caracas. Then he returned to Cuba.[27]

Convinced that a compromise was possible, the Gran Colombian government dispatched José Revenga and José Echeverría to

Madrid in January 1821 with instructions to seek recognition.[28] If this were not feasible, some sort of federation would be acceptable as long as Gran Colombia became independent. There was reason to believe that the Spanish liberal government might be willing to make concessions. The Gran Colombian government controlled much of the territory of the former viceroyalty of New Granada and Spain was faced with serious rebellions in many other parts of South America. Argentina had declared its independence in 1816, and Chile had been free since 1818. Moreover José de San Martín was attempting to liberate Peru.

Spain, however, viewed the situation from a different perspective. Large parts of New Granada, including the Andean regions of Pasto and Quito, were in loyalist control. Strong Spanish armies dominated Peru where San Martín had barely succeeded in establishing a foothold. Moreover, the Chileans were politicaly divided and, as long as loyalist forces controlled Peru, it was possible that the southern country could be restored to Spanish hands. Argentina was also rent by factionalism. That area's attempt to bring a Spanish prince to rule seemed to indicate that reconciliation with Spain was not out of the question. Finally, the great and wealthy viceroyalty of New Spain was peaceful and appeared to be thriving under constitutional rule. Therefore, while the Cortes might be willing to compromise, it would not acknowledge the independence of any American kingdom.

3

The American deputies insisted that the Cortes give priority to New World problems. The liberal government decided that the strict application of the constitution in the New World would regain the loyalty of American dissidents. However, as the Mexican deputies made clear, Spanish bureaucrats in America often violated the constitution. Therefore, it was imperative to send convinced constitutionalists to the New World to make certain that the constitution took strong roots there. Since New Spain was peaceful and since its representatives were among the most active and vocal of American deputies, the government decided to appoint a liberal to that area. It chose General Juan O'Donojú, a distinguished *doceañista* who had served as minister of war during the earlier constitutional period and was then the political chief of the provincial deputation of Seville. In accordance with the constitution, O'Donojú was appointed captain general of New Spain and political chief of the provincial deputation of Mexico on January 24. The council of state clearly indicated that the post of viceroy no longer existed. The new appointee could only hold political power over the province of Mexico. However, he would exercise military authority over the territory of the former viceroyalty of New Spain through his appointment as captain general.[29] O'Donojú received extensive instructions requiring him to enforce the constitution and the laws of congress. He was also to use his influence to promote the new system and to demonstrate that Mexican grievances could be resolved without violence.[30] However, the new political chief had no opportunity to carry out his instructions.

Fearing the radicalism of the Spanish Cortes, conservatives in Mexico decided to break relations with Spain. Spanish bureaucrats and merchants, Mexican oligarchs, the Church, and the army joined the conservative Mexican, Colonel Agustín Iturbide, who declared independence. His program, known as the Plan of Iguala, was designed to maintain their privileged positions in Mexico which the Cortes sought to diminish or to end. The Mexican conservatives hoped to attract Mexican liberals as well as former insurgents to their side with a plan that called for the creation of a constitutional monarchy. A Spanish prince would be invited to the throne and traditional interests would be preserved by writing a conservative charter that would maintain the status quo of the old order.[31]

When O'Donojú arrived in Mexico in July 1821, he was surprised to find most of the country in the hands of the conservative led insurgents. Only Mexico City and its environs remained under Spanish control. The situation in the capital, however, was complicated by divisions among the loyalists. Viceroy Juan Ruíz de Apodaca, a moderate, had been overthrown by General Francisco Novella because the viceroy had implemented the constitution while the Iturbide insurrection raged. Novella, an absolutist, commanded a sizable Spanish army in the capital when O'Donojú arrived. The new captain general faced a dilemma. Only Novella could help him regain control of New Spain but that absolutist officer would be unlikely to support his new superior when he learned that O'Donojú's principal mission was to see that the constitution was enforced in Mexico. It was in these circumstances that Iturbide offered to negotiate with O'Donojú. After much consideration, on August 24, the Spanish liberal signed the Treaty of Córdoba, which recognized Mexico's independence. As in the Plan of Iguala, a Spanish prince would be invited to the throne of a constitutional monarchy. Until the Spanish Cortes approved the treaty, a junta, which included O'Donojú, would govern Mexico.[32] Under the circumstances O'Donojú, could have done little else. As a Spaniard, he strove to retain whatever ties were possible with the mother country. As a liberal, he attempted to insure that constitutional rule was firmly implanted in Mexico. Unlike his new conservative allies, O'Donojú expected the new Mexican constitution to be liberal. Shortly thereafter, however, O'Donojú became ill and died.

4

Once again, problems in the Peninsula prevented the Spanish government from dealing with an American crisis. The liberals' economic reforms were often counterproductive. Prices, particularly of food, increased, while agriculture and industry failed to expand. Although the urban masses were increasingly restless, it was the countryside that erupted. Many churchmen, fearful of the anti-clerical attitude of the liberals, incited the rural masses against the government. Guerrillas went into operation but the army had no difficulty in controlling the absolutist insurgents. Fear of counterrevolution and a possible invasion by the Holy Alliance inflamed city mobs. Yet the liberals managed to keep order because both moderates and radicals understood that unity was essential to the success of constitutional government. The men of 1812 were willing to make concessions and the men of 1820 expected to win the next elections. Thus, both groups agreed on a political truce.

All harmony ended when the king dismissed the Argüelles ministry in March 1821. Both moderates and radicals were caught unprepared and refused to help the monarch appoint a new government. The council of state recommended a lackluster ministry of unknown *doceañistas*. Many observers interpreted Ferdinand's action as a move to discredit constitutional government. In retaliation, some extremists among the *exaltados* formed their own group, the *comuneros,* named after sixteenth-century rebels. The *comuneros* appealed to the masses from the clubs, inciting them to turn against the government. The new moderate ministry was able to control Madrid, but the *comuneros* dominated provincial cities. In Barcelona, they took over the municipality and deported alleged absolutists. Similar acts occurred in Galicia, Cádiz, Seville, Málaga, Algeciras, and Cartagena. In Alcoy, workers burned the textile mills. These actions reflected urban unrest, the result of unemployment and high prices. Spain was rapidly becoming an armed camp where the radical masses of the towns opposed a conservative countryside. Driven by the *comuneros,* the radicals turned against the moderates. Thus the *doceañista* government found itself less and less able to resolve conflict.[33]

Notwithstanding such internal difficulties, the American deputies insisted that more attention be paid to the problems of the New World. The distinguished moderate Count Toreno agreed and proposed that a commitee of four Spaniards and five Americans be appointed to study the matter. The Americans included four Mexicans—Lorenzo de Zavala, Lucas Alamán, Francisco Fagoaga, and Bernardino Amati—and the Venezuelan, Fermín Paul. The committee soon became deeply divided and was unable to provide any guidelines. Therefore, the American deputies formed their own committee to present proposals for pacification in the New World. Led by the Mexicans, José Mariano Michelena and José Miguel Ramos Arizpe, the Americans attempted to formulate a plan acceptable to the separatists in the New World. In June 1821, they proposed that America be divided into three kingdoms: (1) New Spain and Guatemala, (2) New Granada and the provinces of Tierra Firme, and (3) Peru, Chile, and Buenos Aires. Each of these kingdoms would have its own cortes and govern itself according to the Constitution of 1812. A Spanish prince or a person appointed by the king would preside in each kingdom. Spain and the American kingdoms would have special relationships in the areas of trade, diplomacy, and defense. Finally, the new kingdoms would pay portions of Spain's foreign debt. The provisions of the plan were similar to those of the Treaty of Córdoba. It went beyond the Mexican accord by creating a Spanish commonwealth not unlike the later British Commonwealth. The Gran Colombian envoy, who had been in Madrid seeking his country's recognition, reported to Pedro Gual that the project of regencies, as the proposal was called, was being discussed. He explained that the Mexican delegation was winning the support of other American deputies and he feared that, if the project were approved, "it would augment the difficulties which we have to overcome" to achieve independence.[34]

However, Spanish liberals were preoccupied with the internal crisis of the Peninsula, which had become so grave that France was considering intervention.[35] Only reluctantly did the Cortes agree to consider the problems of the New World during a special summer session. However, no acceptable solution was found. In September 1821, Pedro Gual, Gran Colombia's foreign minister, decided that Rocafuerte's analysis had been correct and insisted that "our ministers leave Spain so that they will not continue playing the role of fools."[36]

As time passed, more and more American deputies lost hope and returned to their countries. In an attempt to retain American participation in the Cortes, some Spanish liberals proposed a conciliatory measure in January 1822. As in previous attempts to deal with the American issue, a decision was postponed. Moreover, the Cortes rejected the Treaty of Córdoba and instructed the government to inform other nations that recognition of the independence of any part of Spanish America by another government would be considered an unfriendly act. Finally, the majority voted to postpone further action on the American question until the next session of the Cortes.

It was too late because by that time most American deputies had departed convinced that only independence could provide their areas the government they desired. Nevertheless, the kinship between American and Spanish constitutional liberals remained. Gual voiced those sentiments when he said: "we must have compassion for them because with our ten years of experience we know how much it costs to go from slavery to freedom."[37]

When the Cortes opened its session in March 1822, Spain was sinking into anarchy. In the north, the absolutists declared that the king was a prisoner of the liberals, that he could not exercise his sovereignty, and that they were establishing a regency to wage war against the constitutionalists. But they could not overthrow the government without foreign intervention, which they courted assiduously. Such activities increased urban unrest. The provincial cities were the most unruly, but even in Madrid crowds harassed the government and insulted the king. Finally, the Royal Corps, Ferdinand's devoted guards, rebelled on June 30, 1822. The king seized the opportunity to declare that he was resuming absolute power. During the week that followed, the Royal Corps fought with the militia for the possession of Madrid. The militia, led by the *exaltado*, Colonel Evaristo San Miguel, won. The *comuneros*, however, demanded radical changes, hinting that the king should be deposed. Ferdinand was forced to name a radical ministry led by San Miguel. Shocked by the excesses of July, most moderates withdrew from politics. Thereafter San Miguel and the *exaltados*, who had won control of the Cortes in the previous elections, governed a bitterly divided nation. Caught between the absolutists' guerrilla action and the *comuneros'* violent criticism and resort to mob influence, the radicals were forced to rely more and more upon military force to govern. Finally, after months of diplomatic threats, France invaded Spain in April 1823. The government retreated, first to Seville and then to Cádiz, hoping that the nation which had destroyed Napoleon's army would once again defeat a foreign invader. Unlike 1808, no united people rose to oppose the French. The liberals could not unify their warring factions and the people, tired of promises, allowed the well-behaved French army to pass. The absolutists had triumphed. Ferdinand abolished the Cortes and all its acts and took violent vengeance on any liberals unable to escape. He wanted to restore the Inquisition, but deferred to the protests of the French commander. In spite of the king's severity, absolutists were not satisfied.[38] There followed a dark period of reactionary rule, known as the "ominous decade," during which a French army of occupation was necessary to keep the king on his throne. Once again thousands of Spanish refugees in the countries to the north kept Spanish constitutionalism alive and waited for an opportunity to return to their homeland. They came back after Ferdinand's death to restore parliamentary government.[39]

5

Even before the French intervention in Spain, American rebels decided to win total independence. Once the Cortes rejected the

Treaty of Córdoba, Mexico was free to determine its own future. Quito, the last Spanish stronghold in what had formerly been the viceroyalty of New Granada, fell to Gran Colombian forces on May 24, 1822, Only Peru remained in loyalist hands. There, however, the loyalists were divided by constitutionalist-absolutist rivalries.

Viceroy Joaquín de la Pezuela, a member of the old army and an absolutist, had not permitted the constitution to be restored in Peru because, he argued, it would aid the separatists. However, his leading generals, José de la Serna, José Canterac, and Jerónimo Valdéz, were men of the new army. They had achieved distinction fighting Napoleon during Spain's war of independence and were now loath to fight their American brothers. They sincerely believed that the fratricidal struggle could be ended if the constitution were fully implemented. The liberal officers forced Pezuela to abdicate on January 29, 1821. La Serna was named captain general and superior political chief. He implemented as much of the constitution as possible. The Spanish constitutionalists reorganized the army and nearly drove San Martín's forces from the coast. However, in Upper Peru—present day Bolivia—the absolutist General Pedro Antonio Olañeta opposed La Serna. Pezuela had been a friend whom the absolutist respected. But most of all, Olañeta despised the very idea of representative government. For years he had nurtured a hatred against the liberals, but as long as they were popular he could do nothing.[40]

As the political situation in Spain deteriorated in 1822 and 1823 Olañeta was determined to restore Peru to the absolutism the king desired. However, Bolívar's invasion postponed the matter. The Spanish constitutionalist army dominated the highlands of Peru and by the end of 1823 their forces were advancing on Lima. General La Serna was making preparations to drive the separatists, who were embroiled in political rivalries, into the sea. Then he planned to advance north to Gran Colombia. But on December 25, General Olañeta suddenly abandoned his position and retreated with his army to Upper Peru. There he announced that Ferdinand had been restored to his absolutist throne and that he would defend His Majesty against the treacherous liberals. This saved Bolívar and his army from defeat. Now the Spanish constitutionalist army was caught between the separatists on the coast and Olañeta's absolutist army. For nearly a year, while Bolívar and his men recovered, the Spanish constitutionalist and absolutist armies waged a civil war in the highlands. Bolívar hoped to win the absolutist general to his side by granting Olañeta the title of "Liberator" and by authorizing General Antonio José de Sucre to negotiate a defensive alliance with him. Olañeta refused.[41]

Although the Spanish loyalist army was larger and better equipped than the separatists, General Sucre was able to inflict upon them a crushing defeat at Ayacucho on December 9, 1824. La Serna and other leading generals surrendered but Ayacucho merely witnessed the defeat of the Spanish constitutional army. Olañeta's absolutist army remained intact in Upper Peru and it was still formidable. Disregarding all separatist attempts to negotiate, Olañeta was determined to defend Ferdinand's absolutist claims in America. Indeed, Sucre believed that Spain would be able to send the absolutist general supplies through the southern port of Iquique and thus prolong the struggle indefinitely.

Political intrigue intervened to bring the conflict to an end. Realizing that Spain's cause was lost, conservative Bolivians opted for independence in order to establish a government that would protect their interests.[42] They had Olañeta assassinated in April 1825. The death of that absolutist officer marked the end of Spanish power on the American continent. His army joined the separatists. This was not unusual because the troops on both sides of the struggle were American and only the officers' sentiments made an army 'Spanish" or "American."[43] Although the New World had won its independence, the liberal-conservative struggle continued. The elites of Spanish America had agreed upon the need to separate from Spain, but for different reasons.

6

Independence merely meant separation from Spain; all the issues formerly dividing Hispanic society remained. Independence failed to dictate the form of government the new nations would have. Everyone agreed that a constitution had to be written, but such a charter could serve different ends. Some factions preferred a monarchy while others favored a republic. Even within these groups there were divisions. Liberal monarchists believed that a liberal constitution would best serve the needs of their countries, while conservative monarchists wanted a charter that would restrict representation and sustain privilege. The two monarchist factions agreed only upon the stabilizing effect of a hereditary chief executive, or king. On the other hand, republicans were united in rejecting a monarch, but on little else. Liberal republicans counted upon a liberal constitution while conservatives preferred a charter that would reflect their own views. The leaders of the new nations were further divided into federalists and centralists, and since both republics and monarchies could be either federal or central, the number of disagreements increased. The liberals who favored centralism argued that only a strong government could maintain the national unity needed to carry out reforms. Conservatives favored centralism because only a strong state could maintain the law and order necessary to sustain privileged classes. The liberals who favored federalism argued that only a decentralized administration could provide local autonomy and prevent the national government from becoming authoritarian. Similarly, conservative federalists maintained that decentralization would prevent zealous reformers from interfering in their lives while it preserved their privileges.

Given the variety of political choices and the new freedom of the press, it was natural that countless men would promote their particular points of view in print. Such propaganda had begun with the first Cortes in 1810, the parliament that had provided experience for many Americans. Long years of viewing the issues in empire- or commonwealth-wide terms had accustomed many publicists to continue thinking of Spanish America as one. This attitude was particularly true of the men who had hoped that the second constitutional period might bring about the reconciliation of Spain and America. Now that Spain was under the yoke of absolutism and their dream of a Hispanic commonwealth was over, these men turned to a new vision of Spanish Americanism. They not only proposed their views to the new nations but they also worked for the recognition and success of these nations. Ultimately they hoped that a confederation or a united states of Spanish America might be achieved. One of the most influential of these Spanish American publicists was the Ecuadorean, Vicente Rocafuerte, who wrote under the pseudonym "A True American."

# III

## POLITICS AND PROGRESS

Rocafuerte returned to Cuba from Spain on March 4, 1821, ten days after Iturbide had pronounced the Plan of Iguala. That event, naturally, interested him and confirmed his view that only separation from Spain could allow the New World to form the kind of government it wanted. His friends Fernández de Madrid and Miralla continued to hope that constitutionalism would triumph in Spain. But news of events in the Peninsula soon convinced them that Rocafuerte was right.[1] The situation in Mexico also intrigued the three South Americans. At first they believed that the new government might be a liberal constitutional monarchy. They were soon disabused of that notion. Secret societies in Mexico informed Fernández de Madrid's Havana group that the Mexican "liberator" was really a tyrant.

### 1

There were three major political divisions in Mexico: (1) the legitimate monarchists who wanted a Bourbon king and demanded adherence to the Plan of Iguala and the Treaty of Córdoba; (2) a second group of monarchists who, after Spain rejected the Treaty of Córdoba, were willing to accept a Mexican ruler, preferably Iturbide; and (3) the republicans, who opposed any sort of monarchy. While the legitimate monarchists were conservative traditionalists, the Iturbidists and the republicans had both liberals and conservatives in their ranks. Conservative monarchists who favored Iturbide believed that he could provide strong rule. Liberal monarchists supported Iturbide because he was the strongest candidate for the throne and because they expected to restrict his actions by writing a liberal constitution. Liberal and conservative republicans were united in their opposition to a hereditary executive, but

47

divided on the type of constitution they would accept. When the
Iturbidists gained ascendancy, the others joined forces in opposition.

The Mexican republicans feared that Iturbide might convince
the Spanish units that had capitulated to join him and with their aid
establish an absolutist government. His opponents were determined to thwart such an attempt. In Veracruz, a secret society,
whose membership included the noted republican Carlos María
Bustamente, asked the Havana group for help in ridding Mexico
of Spanish forces. Under the provisions of the Plan of Iguala,
Spanish troops in Mexico were to be evacuated to Cuba. Although
many units had already accepted those terms, some—notably
General Novella in Mexico City and General José Dávila, commander of the fortress of San Juan de Ulúa—refused. Therefore,
Mexican republicans requested that Rocafuerte procure ships in
the United States to evacuate the Spaniards and, because he was a
noted publicist, they also asked him to write a pro-republican treatise to counter the drift towards monarchy, which had begun with
the Plan of Iguala.[2]

The Mexican request presented Rocafuerte with a timely opportunity to further the cause of Spanish Americanism as well as his
own interests. Spain's experience with Ferdinand VII had convinced Rocafuerte that no king could be trusted and that only a
republic would serve the needs of the new nations. The Ecuadorean now favored a central or unitary republic because he believed
that it alone could provide the strong government needed to maintain independence and to modernize the new nations. He was
pleased to accept a commission that would allow him to express his
views while he requisitioned ships for Mexico. The trip would also
give him an opportunity to further a business venture. Rocafuerte
was negotiating with the Gran Colombian government for an
exclusive franchise to form a steamship line. He had been preparing to travel to the United States to investigate the possibilities of
having ships built there when the Mexican request arrived. Now he
could combine his own maritime interests with the need to charter
ships to evacuate the Spanish soldiers from Mexico. The trip would
also provide him with material for the tract on republicanism. He
departed for the United States in May, 1821.[3]

Although Rocafuerte had never before traveled to the North
American republic, he expected to be well received because he was a

member of that international community of men which developed during the Enlightenment. Although few in number, they had great influence. There were many differences among these men, but their similarities were important enough to foster cooperation. They were educated gentlemen whose interest and ability to participate in politics increased with the American, French, and Spanish revolutions. Since they were generally men of means, usually landowners and businessmen, they often used their wealth to participate in public life. What set them apart as a group, however, was their interest in learning. Although they came from many countries and spoke different languages, nearly all of them were conversant in French. By the beginning of the nineteenth century, the ideas of the *philosophes* were part of the necessary baggage of educated men. While familiar with the classics, they were more interested in "modern philosophy," science, technology, and political economy. These men were also concerned with education, social problems, economic development, and the machinery of modern industry. But their principal fascination was politics. This interest in politics frequently led to an intense concern with foreign affairs. Two organizations provided rapid contacts among these men: the societies for useful knowledge and masonic lodges. Thus, educated gentlemen could travel anywhere in the Western World with the assurance that they would be well received by like-minded individuals. Since such men were among the most powerful and influential in their countries, it was only natural that the representatives of the new nations should seek their support. It was such men whom Rocafuerte hoped to contact in the United States.

Flirtation with the republic of the north was dangerous. The United States was an expanding, English-speaking, Protestant power, which looked with profound suspicion and distaste on the newly independent Spanish-speaking, Catholic nations. Some North Americans, like John Quincy Adams, doubted that the new states could ever achieve representative government and could not overcome their distrust of what they considered to be the authoritarian and despotic heritage of Spanish Catholic culture. Others, like Andrew Jackson, were openly hostile to the "inferior mongrel" peoples to the south. The Floridas had already fallen to the United States and expansionists were certain that their country was destined to rule over the continent. Thus they could hardly accept the

Spanish Americans as equals. A few North Americans, like Henry Clay, believed in the future of the New World and hoped to create an "American System" to offset the power of the Old World. The Spanish Americanists were naturally drawn to men like him and agreed with those aspirations.[4]

Rocafuerte landed in Baltimore and journeyed to Philadelphia where he visited Manuel Torres, the Gran Colombian agent in the United States. Father Jose Servando Teresa de Mier was staying with Torres at the time. The three men agreed to cooperate to further the interests of an independent Spanish America. As Gran Colombia's agent in the United States, Torres had obtained credit and purchased large quantities of arms for his country. Moreover, many years of living in Philadelphia had permitted Torres to develop important contacts among the banking and business community. Among the influential supporters of Spanish American independence whom Rocafuerte met through Torres was the great shipping magnate and chief stockholder of the Bank of the United States, Stephen Girard. Although Girard had assisted Gran Colombia, he was unwilling to provide ships for Mexico because Rocafuerte did not represent the Mexican government and could, therefore, give no assurance that the ship masters would be paid.

Rocafuerte also met Thompson D. Shaw, an officer in the United States Navy who had visited Peru and was an enthusiastic supporter of South American independence. Shaw introduced Rocafuerte to Nicholas Biddle, the future president of the Bank of the United States. The banker was interested in Spanish America because his brother Thomas, then in the U.S. Navy in South American waters, was an ardent supporter of the new nations. Thus Nicholas Biddle received the Ecuadorean warmly. Rocafuerte and Biddle were nearly the same age and had similar interests. Both were businessmen and landowners concerned with modern scientific farming and, as educated men, both were interested in culture and politics. Biddle introduced the South American to the Wistar Association, a club devoted to wide-ranging intellectual discussions. As a member of the American Philosophical Society, the Pennsylvania Academy of Fine Arts, and the Historical Society, Biddle was able to present Rocafuerte to Philadelphia's educated classes, as well as to introduce him to businessmen. Naturally, Rocafuerte was delighted and took the opportunity to learn as much as

he could about North American culture. He was particularly fascinated by social institutions and, as one newspaper later recalled, he
"visited all the hospitals, prisons and public charities."[5] However
interesting these visits were, Rocafuerte did not lose sight of his
mission. When he failed to charter ships for Mexico in Philadelphia, he decided to visit New York.

He arrived in New York on July 31, 1821, and immediately contacted a long time resident of the city and correspondent of
Fernández de Madrid's Havana society, the Cuban merchant Macedonio Chavez. They discussed the United States opinion toward
the new nations and particularly the possibilities for Cuban independence.[6] Rocafuerte was convinced that the United States could
be a source of assistance as well as inspiration for Spanish America.
Chavez agreed to introduce the South American to the leaders of
the New York business community so that he could negotiate for
ships to evacuate the Spanish soldiers from Mexico.

Rocafuerte also made other useful contacts in New York. He met
Reverend Dr. James Milnor, the secretary of the American Bible
Society. The South American was interested in the Society's program of Lancasterian education, which was carried out through the
Free School Society. The Spanish Cortes had once considered this
system as a way of establishing widespread literacy in the commonwealth. Rocafuerte was an enthusiastic supporter of the method.
He also became acquainted with David Hosack, an eminent doctor
and a member of the New York Historical Society. These friendships grew out of the Ecuadorean's curiosity about cultural ideas
and new methods in education, agriculture, and industry. The contacts would also prove useful when he attempted to obtain support
for Spanish American independence.

After conferring with prominent persons and observing government in the United States, Rocafuerte felt prepared to write a
track on republicanism. While in New York, he arranged with the
bookseller, David Huntington, to have his work published in Philadelphia. Then he returned to that city. Although the Mexicans had
commissioned him to write in favor of republicanism in their country, Rocafuerte addressed his pamphlet to all Spanish Americans,
entitling it *Ideas Necessary to Any Independent American People Who
Want to be Free*. He argued that in an age in which human knowledge had advanced so rapidly, the science of government should

not fall behind. In his opinion, the United States had developed the best form of government. But, he did not believe that Spanish America should adopt a North American style of federalism, which could only work in a cohesive society that had the benefit of excellent communications. He maintained that centralism was better suited for multiracial Spanish America where the distances were vast and communications clumsy. However, he argued that the new governments should be popular and representative. He rejected the idea that the United States had been trained in constitutional rule by the English, while Spanish America had no such preparation and would therefore be unable to apply the new form of government. Instead of accepting such nonsense, he asked Spanish Americans to put aside the obscurantism and superstition of Madrid and Rome and to evaluate the forty-five years of United States republican experience in the clear light of reason. To help Spanish Americans profit from the North American example, he translated certain documents which he believed embodied their experience. They were: Thomas Paine's *Common Sense*, John Quincy Adams's speech of July 4, 1821, the Articles of Confederation, and the Constitution of 1787. The pamphlet was distributed throughout Spanish America, but it had the most impact in Mexico. In 1823, the government of the state of Puebla published a second edition and, later, a third appeared in Mexico City.[7]

Rocafuerte found it more difficult to fulfill the rest of the assignment. The problem of obtaining ships was complicated because payment could not be made in advance and shipowners were reluctant to risk their vessels merely at Rocafuerte's request. He faced a similar difficulty with his own projected steamship line. No one wanted to assist him until he had exclusive rights from the Gran Colombian government to establish a line along her northern coasts. Finally in September, he was able to secure ships to evacuate the Spanish forces. News of the signing of the Treaty of Córdoba facilitated the accord since it appeared that Mexico's government would guarantee payment. Rocafuerte entrusted the final arrangements to Manuel Torres. On September 24, 1821, he traveled to Baltimore where he was to take a steamship to Havana. He returned to Cuba with several boxes of the pro-republican pamphlets, which he distributed in the island and in Mexico. Later, he instructed Chavez to provide Father Mier with funds drawn on

Rocafuerte's account so that the priest could return to Mexico to oppose Iturbide.[8] Thus, republicans opponents of the Mexican "liberator" had established a web of conspiracy that stretched from Mexico to Cuba and to the United States.

2

In Havana, Rocafuerte met his old friend José Miguel Ramos Arizpe, who had just returned from the Spanish Cortes. The Mexican deputy confirmed Rocafuerte's belief that only independence could allow Spanish America to have representative government. Both agreed that republics should be established. However, they differed on the form these republics should take. Ramos Arizpe, the originator of the provincial deputation, still maintained that only a government which recognized regional interests could be effective. Rocafuerte, on the other hand, believed that without a strong central government the new nations would disintegrate into petty principalities. Although they continued to disagree on this point, before Ramos Arizpe departed to his native land, the two men pledged to further the cause of republicanism in Mexico. They believed that Iturbide would not allow the constituent congress to decide the nation's fate. Sooner or later, he would seize power. Therefore, they decided to cooperate with the republican conspirators in opposition to Iturbide.[9]

In December, Rocafuerte learned that Manuel Torres had completed arrangements for leasing the ships. He notified the republican secret society in Mexico that it should make preparations to bring the Spanish troops to a suitable port. However, the task was complicated by recent political developments in Mexico. The Spanish troops who had surrendered were permitted to retain their weapons and were promised evacuation to Havana. At first everyone assumed that the Spanish Cortes would approve the Treaty of Córdoba. But when the Spanish government rejected the treaty, many Mexicans feared that the armed loyalist troops might attempt to reconquer the nation. Some radicals even suggested killing the soldiers to end the danger of a reconquest. The republicans believed that Iturbide manipulated and prolonged the feeling of insecurity which pervaded Mexico so that he could have an excuse to impose his authority on the country. They accused him of preventing the Spanish troops from leaving Mexico. Uncertainty was heightened by the activities of General José Dávila, the Spanish commander of the fortress of San Juan de Ulúa. As the leader of the last Spanish stronghold in Mexico, Dávila attempted to incite the Spanish troops who had already capitulated to join him in an effort to reconquer Mexico for Spain. Dávila's actions were particularly menacing because O'Donojú had just died of yellow fever and no Spaniard seemed to exercise legitimate authority over Spanish forces in Mexico. Many reasoned that Dávila, the most active Spanish leader, might fill this void.[10] As a result, all republicans agreed on the need to evacuate rapidly the Spanish troops who had surrendered.

Iturbide's government was aware that the republicans were making efforts to withdraw the Spaniards from Mexico. In February it received reports that Rocafuerte would arrive in Veracruz with ships to take the Spaniards to Cuba.[11] Unwilling to allow such an open challenge to its authority, the government announced that the point of departure was being changed from the nation's principal port to Tampico, where General Dávila would be unable to foment rebellion. However, the worst fears of the republicans seemed to materialize when no order was given to move the troops to the new port of embarkation.

Mexicans were not the only ones unhappy with the state of affairs. Spaniards also criticized Iturbide because the government had failed to meet all the obligations of the capitulation. Many Spanish soldiers complained that they were abandoned by the Mexican government, left ill, penniless, and hungry.[12] By March discontent among the troops was so great that, fearing revolt, General Pascual de Liñán, the titular leader of the Spanish forces, obtained permission to move to Jalapa one of the two divisions waiting to be evacuated. But rumors spread among the troops that the Mexican government intended to disarm them so the populace could kill them. The resulting tension and fear forced some Spanish commanders to move their troops closer to Mexico City where they hoped to be protected from mobs by the Mexican Army of the Three Guarantees.

Mexicans interpreted these troop movements differently. Some believed that the Spaniards were actually attempting to reconquer the capital. The republicans later argued that the rumors were spread by Iturbide's men to increase tensions so that the "liberator" would have a pretext to usurp authority. When Spanish troops reached the town of Juchi on April 2, they were attacked by the townspeople. Mexican troops were rapidly dispatched and the so-called revolt was controlled with only three hundred troops. Nevertheless, Iturbide called a special session of Congress for the following day to request extraordinary authority to deal with the crisis. He then published a proclamation emphasizing, on the one hand, the danger the nation faced and, on the other, declaring that "good" Spaniards were brothers and should not be harmed. Many interpreted the proclamation as an attempt by the regent to divide Congress into anti- and pro-Spanish elements on the eve of the special session. Since it suspected Iturbide's motives, the legislature would not permit him to appear without the other members of the regency. Congressmen also questioned the ministers. Soon it became evident that no one except Iturbide had a clear notion of the recent events. Therefore, a distrustful Congress refused to grant Iturbide the extraordinary powers he requested.[13]

While this was taking place, the Spanish Saragossa regiment, commanded by Lieutenant Colonel Mariano Herrero, left its quarters at Nopalucán and marched towards Veracruz. On the second day it was attacked by local militia, forced to surrender its arms, and then, permitted to march to Tampico where it was to embark for Havana. Rocafuerte, who was then in Mexico, contacted Lieutenant Colonel Herrero and arranged to have three ships evacuate his troops for thirty thousand pesos, the sum that the Mexican government had provided for their transportation. Since this was done without Iturbide's consent, the regent ordered a cavalry regiment to stop the evacuation. But the republicans managed to subvert his orders by having Colonel Felipe de la Garza, a relative of Ramos Arizpe, placed in command of the cavalry regiment. Thus, although the Mexican cavalry arrived in Tampico while the Spanish troops were boarding the ships, De la Garza did nothing to prevent their departure.[14] With part of the Spanish troops evacuated, the republicans believed that Iturbide no longer had any pretext for declaring himself emperor. However, the "liberator" found other means to achieve his goal.

In May, Iturbide again painted a dark picture of Mexico's situation. He declared that the government was threatened by internal anarchy and by Spanish plans to reconquer the nation. Therefore, he demanded that Congress create an army of thirty-five thousand regular soldiers to supplement the existing army and militia. Iturbide also asked for extraordinary powers to be used in case of an emergency and threatened to resign if his requests were not granted. Although Congress was reluctant to authorize such power, it agreed to do so on May 18. However, by that time Iturbide's supporters decided to take matters into their own hands. That evening Sergeant Pío Marcha proclaimed Iturbide emperor of Mexico and the capital's garrison supported him.[15]

3

The nomination of a native emperor accelerated the intrigues of the opposition. Republicans had been very active in Mexico City since March when Miguel Santamaría, a native of Veracruz who had participated with Father Mier in Mina's expedition, arrived as Gran Colombia's minister to Mexico. His mission was to establish friendly relations and to obtain a loan of a half-million pesos. Shortly after his arrival, Santamaría began to criticize Mexico's drift towards monarchy. After renting Count Pérez Galvez's large house in the San Cosme district of the capital, he made it a center for republican intrigues. Even though he was officially recognized by the Mexican government as the representative of a foreign power, Santamaría was determined to convince his friends and countrymen to support a centralist republic similar to the one established in Gran Colombia. Conspiratorial meetings at the Gran Colombian minister's residence became very active after Iturbide had been proclaimed emperor. At the end of May, Santamaría welcomed as a house guest his old friend and fellow republican intriguer, Vicente Rocafuerte.[16]

Many leaders of the opposition were friends of Rocafuerte. Two, Ramos Arizpe and Michelena, were busy organizing forces in the provinces. A large number gathered in the capital and frequented the Gran Colombian legation, among them Carlos María Bustamante, Father Mier, and José María Fagoaga. Their political activities were shielded by the secrecy of masonic lodges and other similar organizations. By the middle of June, a widespread conspiracy against the emperor had been organized.[17] Although Rocafuerte sympathized with his friends' efforts to overthrow the empire and establish a republic, he was reluctant to participate in the opposition while in Mexico. His sister was married to General Gabino Gaínza, the former captain general of Guatemala, who was coming to Mexico City to serve the new emperor. Since Rocafuerte had not seen her in twelve years, the South American was unwilling to do anything that would jeopardize their reunion.[18] Thus, he turned to other less politically embarrassing activities to benefit Mexico.

Rocafuerte joined a group who sought to establish Lancasterian schools in Mexico. The editor of *El Sol*, the liberal Spaniard Manuel Codorniu, who had arrived in Mexico with O'Donojú, had been attempting to organize such a school since January 1822. Codorniu proposed that a subscription be organized to support the school. He had little difficulty in finding interested persons because the Cortes had previously enacted legislation favoring Lancasterian schools. Various Mexican deputies to the Spanish Cortes had sponsored the bills and now they supported Codorniu's proposal. Even though some of those who favored establishing the new school were also conspiring against the government, Iturbide approved of this system of education. With his consent, the municipality of Mexico City permitted the Lancasterian Society to use a building that had formerly housed the Inquisition for the first school. The school, called the School of the Sun, was inaugurated on August 22, 1822. Rocafuerte thought it fitting and proper that "the halls of the inquisition so inimical to . . . [education], were converted into a public school, into a nursery of free men, into a temple of reason."[19]

In spite of his desire to remain aloof from politics, events in Mexico forced Rocafuerte to change his mind. The republican conspirators believed that they could overthrow Iturbide's government provided no foreign power extended recognition to the monarchy. Santamaría assured them that he would not let Gran Colombia recognize Iturbide. It was unlikely that any European nation would extend recognition. But there was the danger that the United States might do so. In March 1822, Henry Clay, the staunchest champion of Spanish American independence in the United States, had requested that Joel R. Poinsett be permitted to visit Mexico. The following month, Secretary of State John Quincy Adams had informed the new nation that his government would be pleased to exchange envoys. Although the offer was made before news of Iturbide's coronation reached the United States, the republicans feared that the northern republic might recognize the new Mexican empire. They did not know that when Adams learned of the new political situation in Mexico, he changed Poinsett's mission from that of envoy to unofficial critic of the new government. Fearing the worst, Mexican republicans asked Rocafuerte to travel immediately to Washington as their representative to oppose United States recognition of Iturbide.[20]

The South American was hesitant because he was preparing for the long awaited reunion with his sister and her family. But Mexican friends convinced him that it was more important for him to represent them in the United States. The republicans entrusted Rocafuerte with several tasks: to oppose Iturbide's recognition in every way; to organize if possible, an invasion from the United States; publish a documentary attack against the emperor; and finally, to write in favor of centralism. The republicans also provided him with documents and information they feared Iturbide might suppress or destroy, so that Rocafuerte could include it in his writings. Privately, Santamaría asked him to use his business connections to obtain a loan for Gran Colombia in the United States since it was now impossible to get one in Mexico. Santamaría and the others also provided Rocafuerte with letters of introduction to important people. Finally, the Lancasterian Society requested that he obtain a translation of the reader used by the Free School Society in New York. Thus armed and instructed, Rocafuerte left Mexico City on August 6, 1822.[21]

Shortly thereafter the Mexican government asked Santamaría if Gran Colombia would recognize the new emperor. The South American envoy temporized by replying that he was awaiting instructions from his government. Realizing that Santamaría was opposed to the empire and aware that republican meetings were held in the Gran Colombian legation, the Iturbide government decided to act. On August 14, it informed Santamaría that he would no longer be acknowledged as a diplomatic representative until such time as he received authority to recognize Mexico's new government. Two weeks later, Iturbide discovered a conspiracy against him and ordered wholesale arrests, including fifteen congressmen. Since most of those arrested were known to frequent Santamaría's residence, he was declared persona non grata and asked to leave the country. The Gran Colombian envoy traveled to Veracruz in November. But, instead of departing, he joined secret opposition groups there.[22]

4

Prior to Santamaría's expulsion from Mexico City, Rocafuerte had made his way to Veracruz where he secretly booked passage for Havana. In Cuba he wrote an attack against Iturbide entitled *A Very Brief Sketch of the Mexican Revolution*, Fearing that his friends and relatives in Mexico might be harmed if his identity were known, Rocafuerte published the book under the pseudonym "A True American." Although it was published in Havana, it carried the imprint of a fictitious press in Philadelphia. The work is a history of the Mexican movement for independence from the Plan of Iguala to the time Iturbide proclaimed himself emperor. It includes many documents given to Rocafuerte by the republicans and argues that Iturbide was a depraved and sadistic tyrant who had conspired to obtain the throne by fraud. It was designed to demonstrate that what Mexicans deserved and wanted was a republic. *A Very Brief Sketch* ends with the Cuban poet José María Heredia's "Ode to the Inhabitants of Anahuac," which exhorts Mexicans to find a Brutus among them who will kill the tyrant and preserve the nation's freedom.[23]

After completing the tract against Iturbide, Rocafuerte left Cuba for the United States. Upon his arrival in Philadelphia in November, the South American learned that Manuel Torres was dead. Richard Meade was handling Gran Colombia's affairs until a new minister arrived. Rocafuerte visited Biddle who told him that it was a poor time to seek a loan for Gran Colombia. The new republic was considered a bad risk by the United States financial community because she had recently repudiated a British loan. Nevertheless, Rocafuerte contacted various bankers in Philadelphia, New York, and Boston. The terms they offered were too onerous to accept.

Late in December, he journeyed to Washington hoping to convince the United States government to guarantee the loan.

Poinsett, to whom he had a letter of introduction from Santamaría, was no longer in the country, but Rocafuerte contacted Henry Clay and confided to him Gran Colombia's need. Clay counseled him to take no action because it would be useless. He explained that even if the president and the cabinet were willing to guarantee such a loan, they could do nothing without congressional approval. That, Clay felt, would be very difficult, if not impossible to obtain. Rocafuerte refused to give up. He cultivated the friendship of various important people in the capital hoping that they could help him. He was well received by William H. Crawford and John C. Calhoun who, together with Clay and Adams, were the principal aspirants to the presidency in 1824. He sought the friendship of Josiah S. Johnston, a congressman from Louisiana and a confidant of the secretary of state, as well as the support of Philip Barbour of Virginia, a partisan of General Andrew Jackson. Since rumor had it that General Jackson would be appointed minister to Mexico, Rocafuerte hoped that he might be friendly to Spanish America and favorably disposed to a Gran Colombian loan. By February 1823, however, Rocafuerte informed Gran Colombian Vice President Francisco de Paula Santander and Foreign Minister Pedro Gual that it was impossible to obtain a loan and that it would be better to seek money elsewhere or to wait for a more propitious time.[24]

While seeking the Gran Colombian loan, Rocafuerte also worked against Iturbide. First he persuaded Meade, who was acting commercial agent for Mexico, to discharge his duties more slowly. Then he contacted William Duane, editor of the influential Philadelphia newspaper, *Aurora*, and through argument and flattery convinced him to oppose the imperial government of Mexico. Rocafuerte wrote a series of articles for the *Aurora*, entitled "Outlines of Mexican Court Characters," which gave a detailed account of the Mexican revolution and empire. Painting the latter in dark colors, he suggested that the United States have nothing to do with it.[25]

The imperial government sent José Manuel Zozaya as envoy extraordinary and minister plenipotentiary to the United States in an effort to counter the moves of the Mexican republicans. Wary of republican efforts to stop Zozaya, Iturbide provided the envoy with a military escort to Veracruz. On November 25, 1822, a month after Zozaya set out, Santamaría confided to Poinsett that everyone believed the imperial envoy had been captured by corsairs. The government, apparently fearing foul play, took the precaution of appointing Eugenio Cortés as an alternate. All the rumors proved false and Zozaya arrived in the United States at the end of November, shortly after Rocafuerte.[26]

Zozaya reached Washington before the republican representative. By December 7, the monarchist was writing his first report to the imperial government. A week later, he met with the secretary of state, who all but assured him that Mexico would be recognized by the United States. On December 13, two days before Rocafuerte arrived in Washington, President James Monroe received the Mexican minister with all the honors due the representative of a sovereign nation. Although, as he reported to his government on December 20, Zozaya learned that an international conspiracy was operating against the Mexican empire, the following week was one of triumph for the Mexican minister. He was officially received as minister plenipotentiary and invited to dine with the secretary of state and the president. Then other members of the government visited him at his residence. However, Zozaya was convinced that the United States would await Poinsett's report before naming a minister to Mexico.[27]

After two weeks of triumph, the imperial minister was reduced to virtual isolation. The monarchical nature of his government and his total ignorance of English and French prevented Zozaya from developing relationships in Washington society. After government officials paid the required courtesy calls, protocol obliged the new minister to await the visits of congressmen and other members of the diplomatic corps. But North Americans disliked him because he represented a monarchy and since no other country recognized Mexico, no diplomat would officially acknowledge his arrival. Thus no one called on him. Zozaya rapidly learned to dislike and distrust the United States, which he believed, not without reason, to be a natural enemy of Mexico.[28]

Vicente Rocafuerte was partly responsible for Zozaya's isolation. He reached Washington in mid-December and immediately took up the task of discrediting the imperial government. He was able to

arrange an interview with Secretary of State Adams, whom he
assured that the monarchy would be short-lived because it lacked
popular support. Since Adams remained aloof after the interview,
Rocafuerte sought to influence him by cultivating the friendship of
one of his confidants, Josiah S. Johnston, a congressman from
Louisiana.[29]

Rocafuerte was also quick to take advantage of the political situation in the United States. He conferred separately with three of the
presidential aspirants, Clay, Calhoun, and Crawford. To each he
suggested that the United States oppose Iturbide's government
and secretly aid in its overthrow. Fully aware of the expansionist
tendencies of the northern republic, Rocafuerte insisted that no
territory could be annexed without the consent of the people who
lived there. Since Texas had always demonstrated its desire to
remain with the rest of Mexico, the Ecuadorean stressed that
United States' volunteers who went there to help end the despotic
empire had to refrain from any attempt to take that territory for
their country. However, he hinted that United States assistance
might be rewarded with Cuba. Rocafuerte explained that Cubans
desired to free themselves from Spain and join the United States. If
the North American nation helped topple Iturbide, republicans in
Mexico would not oppose the annexation of Cuba. Although they
coveted Texas, Clay and Calhoun were enthusiastic about the proposal and Crawford was not against it. With such influential men
on his side, the South American felt that it was only a matter of
time before some sort of action would be taken against Iturbide.[30]

Rocafuerte also courted United States public opinion. Zozaya
constantly informed his government that the republican envoy was
publishing articles against the empire. He characterized Rocafuerte as a dog who barks but does not bite. Nevertheless, the
Mexican minister worried because the northern republicans disliked having a monarchy on their border. Rocafuerte assidously
courted the press as well as politicians and was not above using
blatant flattery to win them to his side. On one occasion he told
Clay that the Gran Colombian congress would be pleased to have
the portrait of such an illustrious American hanging in its chambers. Knowing that the South American government felt indebted
to Clay, he proceeded to have his portrait painted by the best artist
in Washington and made arrangements to send it to Bogotá. He

also made certain that Clay received the vote of thanks wich the Gran Colombian congress had decreed for him in 1821. Naturally, Clay was flattered and became his partisan.[31]

5

While Rocafuerte plotted in the United States, the republicans in Mexico were very busy. Santamaría, General Guadalupe Victoria, and various other conspirators who had fled Mexico City, invited General Antonio López de Santa Anna to join the republican cause. After some consideration, he declared himself for a republic on December 2, 1822. Four days later, Santamaría composed the Plan of Veracruz, which was issued by Generals Santa Anna and Victoria. Shortly thereafter, Generals Vicente Guerrero and Nicolás Bravo, declaring that Iturbide had usurped the throne, adhered to the Plan of Veracruz. Thus three leaders of Mexico's early insurgent movement against Spain joined Santa Anna in opposing the conservative emperor. At first the rebellion seemed to be succeeding, but by mid-January the tables had turned. Zozaya was overjoyed to learn of the rebels' reverses. He informed his government that its victories had virtually ended support in Washington for the conspirators' plans to invade northern Mexico. He was premature in his celebration, however, because events in Mexico once again turned against Iturbide.

Ramos Arizpe and Michelena had done their job well in arousing opposition to the emperor in the provinces. When Iturbide sent an army to besiege the rebels, republican intriguers began to subvert it. They convinced the government's forces to join the opposition. Then on February 1, 1823, they issued a new declaration, the Plan of Casa Mata. A section of the new plan permitted the provincial deputation of Veracruz to govern that province. As soon as the plan was announced, provincial deputations in other provinces seized control of local government, even though such action had not been specified in the Plan of Casa Mata. Within a short time the imperial government lost control of most of Mexico. Like Ferdinand VII in 1820, the Mexican monarch found himself overwhelmed by regionalism when armed insurrection was failing. Abandoned by his army and unable to muster support in the provinces, Iturbide abdicated on February 19, 1823. A provisional government formed to decide the organization of the new republic.[32]

Although many of the republican conspirators were centralists, the most effective revolutionaries, like Ramos Arizpe and Michelena, were federalists. They had catered to the strong desire for provincial home rule when they formulated the Plan of Casa Mata. Their position was strengthened within a short time when the provinces of Mexico organized themselves into states. Many of the states were formed before a national congress could meet. Thus, if the nation were to remain united, the new constituent congress would have to agree to some form of federalism.


6


Pleased that the republicans had triumphed in Mexico, Rocafuerte turned to other projects to help the new American nations. He renewed efforts to organize a steamship line for northern South America. Rocafuerte proposed to form a company that would operate four steamboats along the west coast from Lima to Panama. To attract capital, he needed to resolve the question of exclusive rights to steam navigation in the area, which had thwarted his earlier efforts. In an attempt to sway Gran Colombian and Peruvian officials, he wrote a series of letters arguing that steamships would provide rapid and effective communications thus ending the isolation of different provinces and strengthening Gran Colombia and Peru. He maintained that the steam-operated boats would also be beneficial because their need for fuel would create a new industry in Peru, which had accessible coal deposits. The steamship line would also require whale oil for illumination and thereby foster another industry. Whale fishing would improve the sailing abilities of people in the coast and thus, indirectly, lead to the development of a merchant marine.[33] Unfortunately his requests were not answered and he was forced to abandon the project. Nevertheless, he continued to lobby for better communications whenever the opportunity arose.

Although one project had failed, Rocafuerte was soon involved in other schemes to transfer modern advances to the nations of Spanish America. Since he recognized the important role energy played in development, Rocafuerte sent to Caracas a scale model of a machine used to extract gas from minerals. He suggested that the device might be used to provide the city with gaslighting. Similarly, he sent models of windmills, cotton gins, looms, steamships, and other equipment, as well as new types of cotton and tobacco, to Guayaquil so that he might develop them into useful products when he returned.

Rocafuerte also hoped to introduce institutional innovations, particularly in education, prison reform, and health care. He visited the famous Pennsylvania Hospital, one of the first modern charity hospitals. The new system of prisons designed to rehabilitate rather than merely to punish also aroused his curiosity. Hoping to introduce such methods in Spanish American prisons, he made scale models of the treadmills used in the Pennsylvania and New York penitentiaries. He sent one of these to the Mexico City Council, suggesting that it could provide the inmates of the city's jails with useful work as well as rehabilitation.[34]

Everywhere he went, Rocafuerte took notes on the new social institutions. He intended to use this material to write on social reforms when he finally returned to his native land. The Ecuadorean was a firm believer in the idea of progress. He felt that it was his patriotic duty to look with critical eyes at the new developments in the United States and select the best and most suitable to introduce to Spanish America. He believed that the new nations were exceedingly rich and that properly developed they would become a great force in the world.

As a member of the Enlightenment, Rocafuerte believed that reason was the best tool to transform society. Therefore, it was imperative that the peoples of Spanish America be educated. He took every opportunity to visit schools in Washington, Philadelphia, Boston, and New York. The Reverend Dr. James Milnor, rector of St. George's Episcopal Church in New York, convinced him that the dissemination of Bibles was an excellent method of furthering education while spreading religious toleration in Spanish America. This and the Lancasterian system of education seemed to Rocafuerte the most reasonable and economical ways of fostering learning in the new nations. Mindful of the task entrusted him by the School Society of Mexico, Rocafuerte attempted to have the reader of the Free School of New York translated into Spanish.

When he was unable to find a translator, he decided to organize the text himself. He took a copy of Father Felipe Scio's authorized modern Spanish version of the Catholic Bible and, after comparing it with the excerpts included in the Free School's reader, formed a similar collection in Spanish. He then wrote a short introduction and published the work as *Lessons for Schools of First Letters Taken From the Sacred Scriptures*. In the introduction Rocafuerte expressed his hope that the *Lessons* would allow the youth of Spanish America to develop new virtues. Love of justice, love of country, and love of liberty, he stated, were the principles that should be engraved in the soul of the new generation.[35]

As a result of these activities, Milnor arranged to have Rocafuerte give the main speech for the celebration of the American Bible Society's seventh anniversary in New York. After a formal parade through the city led by the Society's president, John Jay, and New York Governor De Witt Clinton, Rocafuerte addressed the group in the city hall. He said that God intended Spanish America not only to be free but also to be blessed with civil liberty and true Christianity. A true Christian was one who loved liberty, religious toleration, and education. It was the glory of the United States, said Rocafuerte, to have achieved such liberty and tolerance. This had been accomplished in part through the dissemination of the Bible and widespread education. He, therefore, asked their help in circulating the Bible in Spanish America where it would become a tool for achieving instruction as well as religious tolerance. If all Christian sects would act with harmony, he declared, morality, tolerance, and freedom would follow. His speech was well received.[36]

After some discussion the members of the American Bible Society agreed to assist the Spanish Americans. They decided to distribute Bibles in Spanish as soon as possible. In the meantime, Rocafuerte sent a large shipment of his *Lessons* to the Lancasterian School Society in Mexico. There, however, opposition to the readers was strong. "Some old priests opposed the introduction of these, stating that it was prohibited to read extracts from the Bible without notes."[37] Fortunately, the Society was of a different opinion and the texts were adopted for use in the School of the Sun.

Although interested in social change and technological innovation, Rocafuerte did not forget politics. He knew that Chile, Peru, and Mexico would soon draft their constitutions and he felt there was a need for clear thinking about constitutional issues. During his two-month stay in Washington, he paid close attention to the government of the United States. "The classic land of liberty," as he called it, fascinated him. He wrote to Pedro Gual that he believed he understood how its politics worked and demonstrated his knowledge in a detailed analysis of the forthcoming presidential election. Later he returned to Philadelphia and then traveled to New York. Everywhere he avidly discussed the nature of government with journalists, politicians, and men of affairs. These discussions provided material for his work on republicanism, the *Political Essay*, which appeared late in 1823.[38]

The *Political Essay* is a juxtaposition of analysis and documents. Relying on the best European and North American constitutional authorities, Rocafuerte sought to prove that constitutional republics were the best form of government for America. He feared the old monarchies, which wielded arbitrary power and which, allied with religion, oppressed the people. And he opposed the union of church and state because history had shown that it led only to despotism. In his opinion, religious toleration was the sine qua non of any free government. He realized that a constitutional monarchy might provide the guarantees desired by liberals. But he believed that republics were better. To prove his point, he compared the United States and England and concluded that a republic was superior to the best monarchy. Although the United States had developed an excellent system of government, he doubted that the rest of America was ready for federalism. Instead he advocated Gran Colombia's centralist constitution as a compromise for Spanish America. Rocafuerte argued that only strong national governments could provide the leadership needed for development. To illustrate his views, he included key documents: Paine's *Common Sense*, Thomas Jefferson's inaugural address of 1801, Simón Bolívar's speech upon taking the oath of allegiance to the Constitution of Gran Colombia, and George Washington's Farewell Address.[39]

The pamphlet is not the profound study of government Rocafuerte intended to write.[40] He admits in the preface that it was hurriedly written, but he explains that constituent congresses were preparing to meet, and the essay would disseminate pertinent information. Another and more plausible reason for the haste is that Rocafuerte had become involved in a movement to free Cuba and felt compelled to finish the study before he turned to active participation in the conspiracy.

# IV

## THE GREAT CUBAN CONSPIRACY

The island of Cuba welcomed the restoration of the Spanish Constitution. Slowly, however, a process of transition took place between what might be called a desire for liberty with Spain and liberty by means of independence.

Rocafuerte returned from Spain in March 1821, disillusioned with the prospects for the survival of constitutional government. Although his attitude influenced his friends in the island, they made no attempt to organize an opposition. Francisco Lemus also returned to Havana from Spain in 1821. He too was disenchanted, but he chose to act. With other officers, he began to organize secret societies modeled on freemasonry.[1] At first, the new groups were primarily concerned with concealment and ritual. Then in November, deputies from the Cortes began to return. These men had also given up hope of reconciliation with Spain. Their arrival radically altered public opinion in Cuba. Many who had hitherto pinned their hopes on the Cortes began to work for independence. The Lemus and Fernández de Madrid groups joined forces to seek foreign aid and to prepare for a military uprising in the island.[2]

1

As a strategically located island, Cuba had little hope of retaining her independence once she separated from Spain. Both England and the United States wanted to control the area and France was also interested in exerting influence. If Cuba could not remain alone, it seemed best to join one of the American nations. Situated on the crossroads of Atlantic trade, the island would be an asset to the country that annexed it. Many Cubans believed that they could obtain easy entry into any new nation and, therefore, it was important to choose carefully. Gran Colombia, Mexico, and the United States were the most attractive choices. However, Gran Colombia was too far away and Mexico was burdened with a conservative emperor. Thus the United States seemed the logical choice. Everyone agreed that if Cuba joined the northern Union, Havana would become the greatest port in the land. The conspirators commissioned the Argentine, Jose Antonio Miralla, to travel to the United States to ascertain that country's views on Cuba. He was instructed to negotiate the annexation of the island as a full-fledged state or, failing that, to seek help for Cuban independence.[3] Since he was an exporter, Miralla found his business connections useful. But his most important contact was Vicente Rocafuerte who was also on his way to the United States.

When Miralla arrived in November 1822, he discovered that a mysterious Bernabé Sánchez had already been in the United States for some months on a similar mission. José del Castillo, Poinsett's confidant in Havana, describes Sánchez as an unknown "mad man" from Cuba who had neither instructions nor authority. Nevertheless Sánchez had been able to contact the highest circles in the United States government. He appears to have arrived in Louisiana in the company of Colonel James Bradburn early in March 1822. John Sibly of New Orleans reported that Sánchez was going to Washington in some official capacity.[4] By September, the Cuban was in contact with President Monroe and his cabinet. He informed them that he was a secret agent of the "principal inhabitants" of Havana with instructions to seek Cuba's entry into the United States. As soon as that proposal was agreed upon, the patriots would rise, drive the Spaniards out, and proclaim independence. Then a free Cuba would immediately enter the Union as a state. Secretary of War John C. Calhoun was much in favor of the proposal. But Secretary of State John Quincy Adams did not believe that the time was ripe for such action. He did not know how much support Sánchez had in Cuba and did not like the idea of the island entering the Union as a state. Adams believed that such an act was unconstitutional and instead preferred that Cuba, like Louisiana, be accepted as a territory and afterwards become a state. The president met with the cabinet on September 26 and 30 to consider the matter. In the end,

Adams' view prevailed because there was no certainty that Sán-chez had any real support. He was informed that the United States maintained diplomatic relations with Spain and that she could not promote rebellion in a friendly nation's territory. But in a secret letter Sánchez was asked to provide more concrete proof of Cuban aspirations.[5] The matter rested there until Miralla arrived.

Miralla and Rocafuerte began their activities on behalf of Cuba in Philadelphia, which was a center for Spanish Americanist activity in the United States. Many of the country's most important politicians resided there rather than in the new federal city of Washington. Not only was Philadelphia large and attractive, but it also had a long history of hospitality to Spanish American revolutionaries. Now that Spanish constitutionalism was collapsing, the city became a haven for Spanish and Spanish American constitutional liberals. Among them were exiled Cuban patriots like Father Félix Varela, the journalist Gaspar Betancourt Cisneros, and the philosopher José Antonio Saco. The Peruvian, Manuel Lorenzo de Vidaurre, arrived in December 1822. Realizing that Spanish constitutionalism was dying, Vidaurre abandoned his magistracy in the Audencia of Puerto Príncipe, opted for independence, and joined the republicans. Like Rocafuerte, the Peruvian soon became an enthusiastic admirer of the United States.[6] The Spanish Americanists formed a tightly knit unit. They not only helped one another in their conspiracies, but they also formed their own cultural group. Betancourt Cisneros taught English to those unable to speak it, Saco lectured on philosophy, and Vidaurre on law. Father Varela established an emigré newspaper.[7] New York was another important center of Spanish Americanist activities. Cuban merchants such as Macedonio Chavez and the brothers José and Antonio Iznaga settled there. Others, like José Agustín Arango, Fructuoso del Castillo, and José Ramón Betancourt, were in New York agitating for independence.[8] Since Rocafuerte had many acquaintances in both cities and since Miralla knew all the Cubans, the two men became coordinators for the two groups.

When Rocafuerte traveled to Washington in December 1822, Miralla accompanied him. In his conversations about Iturbide with Clay, Calhoun, Crawford, Johnston, and Barbour, Rocafuerte also raised the Cuban issue. The three presidential candidates were in favor of annexing the island and this soon became an open secret in

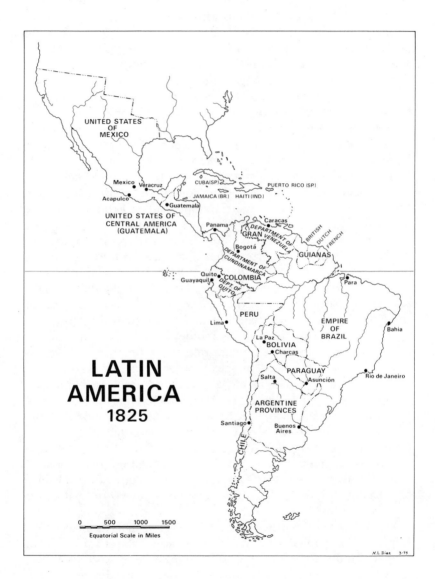

UNITED STATES
OF
MEXICO

Mexico● ●Veracruz
Acapulco●
●Guatemala

CUBA(SP.)
JAMAICA (BR.)   HAITI (IND.)
PUERTO RICO (SP.)

UNITED STATES OF
CENTRAL AMERICA
(GUATEMALA)

Panama●
Caracas●
DEPARTMENT OF
GRAN VENEZUELA
BRITISH
DUTCH
FRENCH
GUIANAS

Bogotá●
DEPARTMENT OF
CUNDINAMARCA

Quito●
Guayaquil●
COLOMBIA
DEPT OF
QUITO

Para●

PERU

Lima●

La Paz●
BOLIVIA
●Charcas

EMPIRE
OF
BRAZIL

Bahia●

PARAGUAY
Salta●
Asunción●

Rio de Janeiro●

ARGENTINE
PROVINCES
Santiago●
Buenos
Aires●

CHILE

**LATIN
AMERICA
1825**

0   500   1000   1500
Equatorial Scale in Miles

N. L. Diaz    3-75

the capital. The English and Mexican ministers reported the rumor to their governments. Secretary of State Adams was sufficiently concerned that he assured the British minister that the United States would not intervene in Cuban affairs.[9] Nevertheless, Rocafuerte and Miralla believed that public opinion might change the government's view.

In the press and in private conversations they argued that Cubans were unwilling to remain the colony of an absolutist government. Since the constitutional government of Spain appeared to be doomed, the only remaining choice was independence. However, they conceded that Cuba could not survive alone and that sooner or later the island would be forced to join Mexico, Gran Colombia, or the United States. They emphasized that Cuba, a wealthy island and a center of world trade, would be a great asset to the nation that annexed her. Therefore, they argued, if Cuba joined the United States, she should do so with the full dignity and power of a state. Since the island did not have a strong garrison, Rocafuerte and Miralla maintained that the Spanish government would be unable to defend itself. The people of Cuba favored liberty and, already, secret societies existed to direct the struggle for independence. The two men realized that England had a squadron in Cuban waters and that many people in the United States feared that England would take the island. But Miralla and Rocafuerte assured the public that the island would never be content with colonial status. They reiterated that the only choice was either total independence or statehood within the United States.[10]

Through Rocafuerte's introduction, Miralla was able to confer with Adams and present his proposals. Since they were similar to those offered earlier by Sánchez, the secretary of state was skeptical. Nevertheless, he informed President Monroe, who decided to investigate. The president asked his Latin American expert, Poinsett, to make inquiries in Cuba. By April 16, Poinsett had received an answer from the island. He reported that Miralla was indeed an agent from Havana, but that he had been unable to learn the strength of the movement. Poinsett also reported that Cubans were arming and that they would never accept colonial status under England. He suggested that the United States at least send an agent to Havana to evaluate the situation more carefully and volunteered his own services.[11]

President Monroe declined Poinsett's offer; instead, he consulted with Thomas Jefferson, as he had done in the past. Earlier, the elder statesman had advised that the United States do nothing in case England occupied Cuba. He made this recommendation because he believed that if Spain could not hold the island, England would not permit any other power to take it. Jefferson assumed that the Cubans would be willing to trade Spanish domination for British control and therefore saw no reason for the United States to challenge England. Knowing that Jefferson's opinion would be important, Rocafuerte advised Miralla to visit the former president. The Argentine did so, charmed the aging Jefferson, and changed his views on Cuba. On June 23, 1823, the elder statesman advised Monroe to try to obtain the island for the United States. The arguments that Jefferson advanced to support his new position were provided him by Miralla. If the United States could not obtain Cuba, Jefferson advised the president to prevent the island from falling into English hands. Monroe, however, decided to act cautiously. He contented himself with a warning to Spain not to cede Cuba to England.[12]

2

At this juncture new arrivals further complicated the activities of Spanish Americans. Four commissioners from the Central American province of El Salvador appeared in May 1823, hoping to obtain assistance from the United States. Like the Cuban rebels, they also wanted to enter the Union. José Manuel de Arce, the leader of the commission, sought out Rocafuerte as the person who could introduce his group to men in important government circles. The question of El Salvador was particularly difficult for Rocafuerte. The area was nominally part of independent Mexico. El Salvador had declared its independence in 1822, but Emperor Iturbide I dispatched an army under the command of General Vicente Filisola to crush the rebels. However, when the general realized that Iturbide's empire was in danger, Filisola appeased the Central Americans and was treated as a hero. Rocafuerte feared that the general might attempt to establish his own monarchy in Guatemala, as Central America was then called. Furthermore, as a friend and unofficial representative of Mexico, Rocafuerte could not help El Salvador secede. Since news of Iturbide's collapse had just reached the United States, Rocafuerte exhorted the Salvadorean commissioners to give the new republican government of Mexico a chance to treat them justly. Although the Central Americans did not seek immediate contacts with the United States government, Rocafuerte was unable to prevent them from presenting their case in the press.[13]

The *Philadelphia Gazette* published a long article on the question of El Salvador on June 18, 1823. The paper maintained that El Salvador had never been a part of Mexico. The Central American state had won its own freedom from Spain, and the Mexican Congress had recognized that independence. Nevertheless when Iturbide usurped power, his first act was to send an army to subjugate El Salvador. The Central Americans had successfully defended themselves against the unwarranted invasion. Thus, the article concluded, there was no reason why the United States should not receive the province into the Union.[14]

Although the Salvadoreans were publicly confident of obtaining their ends, news from Central America was disconcerting. Filisola appeared to be establishing his own empire in Guatemala and the commissioners feared that Central America would have to be liberated once again. With Rocafuerte's assistance, Arce traveled to New York and Boston seeking arms and credit. Early in September, Arce and the other commissioners went to Washington in an effort to obtain United States aid. In the capital they received news that the provinces of Central America had rejected a monarchy and, instead, had united to form an independent republic. Therefore, the commissioners decided to return to their own country to take part in forming a new government. However, the Central Americans, who wanted to retain contacts with the United States, persuaded Rocafuerte to represent them and empowered him to act in their behalf.[15]

The following month Rocafuerte informed Adams that the Central American commissioners had returned to their country. Guatemala had become a federal republic and General Arce had been elected president. Rocafuerte also notified the secretary of state that "the Mexican Congress had approved the separation of Guatemala and recognized the independence of the new republic."[16] Now that Central America's future was safe, Rocafuerte decided to continue with the project to free Cuba. He entrusted the affairs of Guatemala to Gran Colombian Minister José María Salazar.

3

While the Central Americans had been courting the government of the United States, Miralla, Rocafuerte, and the Cubans continued to work for the island's independence. Although President Monroe would not intervene to free Cuba or to unite it with his country, he appeared willing to follow Jefferson's advice and oppose a British takeover of the island. Therefore, the Spanish Americanists waged a propaganda campaign in the hope that United States public opinion might force Monroe to change his course. The conspirators also won the new representatives of Gran Colombia and Mexico to their side. Gran Colombia's Minister Salazar and Consul General Leandro Palacios both resided in Philadelphia.[17] After Iturbide's downfall, the Mexican legation was filled by José A. Torrens, who also settled in Philadelphia. The Spanish American diplomats agreed to assist the pro-Cuba group. As a result, a well-organized group of Spanish Americanists strained every resource to win Cuba's freedom.

Although the conspirators' efforts were unsuccessful, the Spanish representatives in the United States were frightened. On January 1, 1823, Joaquín Anduaga, the Spanish minister, informed Madrid that Vidaurre and the Cuban conspirators were agitating in New York. Two weeks later, he reported that the conspiracy was even more extensive. He accused Rocafuerte of convincing the Mexican representatives to obtain ships for an invasion of Cuba. Anduaga feared that despite his protests, President Monroe would be inclined to support an attack on the island.[18] Spanish fears began to subside when the dreaded invasion failed to materialize. As time passed the minister began to believe Secretary of State Adams's assurances that the United States would remain neutral in the Cuban affair. But since the conspirators' propaganda continued unabated, Spanish diplomats remained on the alert.

Hilario Rivas y Salmón, the Spanish consul in Philadelphia, repeatedly warned the captain general of Cuba, Francisco Vives, that Rocafuerte and his companions were publishing articles in the press which were promoting Cuban independence. Then on August 8, 1823, he informed Vives that the Spanish Americans had gone to New York where they "formed a [conspiratorial] *Club* headed by Rocafuerte and Miralla."[19] They were engaged in preparing a manifesto to Congress asking that it recognize Cuba's independence. Rivas feared that the United States might attempt to annex Cuba using the manifesto as an excuse.

This news from the United States arrived at a time when Vives was already worried about secret organizations in Cuba. The city of Puerto Principe, seat of the Audiencia of Santo Domingo, was alive with conspirators. If Vidaurre, a former magistrate of that *audiencia* and a leading conspirator, was now a member of Rocafuerte's secret society in the United States, it seemed likely that he retained contacts with the rebels in Cuba. Furthermore, Vives knew that a clandestine organization known as *Los Rayos y Soles de de Bolívar* was planning a revolt to free the island from Spanish rule. There was little that the captain general could do because the Spanish Constitution permitted freedom of the press and the conspirators used newspapers and pamphlets to promote their cause. Vives had repeatedly asked respectable persons to oppose such agitation, but they were unsuccessful in their opposition. Only the official newspaper printed articles favorable to the government. Moreover, magistrates at all levels seemed ready to assist agitators by following the letter of the law. In these critical circumstances Vives feared that his slender forces would be insufficient to forestall a revolt.

The uprising soon materialized. A manifesto addressed to the armies of the *Replublic of Cubaćan* was found on the outskirts of Havana on August 10. General José Francisco Lemus declared in the manifesto that Cuba was independent, that the slaves were free, and that all European Spaniards would be protected by the new government. The three guarantees were designed to prevent a division between Americans and Spaniards. But even if the liberal Spaniards had been willing to accept independence, conservatives were not. Since the Cuban rebellion coincided with the arrival of reports that French troops had restored Ferdinand VII to an absolutist throne, Captain General Vives felt safe in disregarding the constitution to take effective action against the rebels. He immediately stationed troops in strategic areas. Although most of

Camagüey province was in revolt, Havana and other principal cities remained in government hands. Wholesale arrests soon reduced the leadership of the insurgents to prison, hiding, or exile. By the end of September the uprising had been crushed. Lemus was in hiding, the poet José María Heredia in exile and, in Havana, Fernández de Madrid under surveillance.[20]

While the rebellion had been easily quelled, Vives, fearing an invasion, began to strengthen the island's defenses. Hoping to receive further support from Spain, Vives wrote to the conservative former deputy from Cuba to the Cortes, Tomás Gener. The captain general explained that Fernández de Madrid was the leading conspirator in Havana and that Miralla, Rocafuerte, and Vidaurre were in the United States seeking aid from that expanding republic. Since the Spanish government did not understand the perfidy of the Spanish Americanists, Vives asked Gener to use his influence to impress upon the overseas ministry the critical nature of the situation. The captain general emphasized that his forces were weak and that it was imperative that Cuba be reinforced.[21] But, realizing that reinforcements might not come, or come too late, Vives continued to prepare his defenses.

4.

The patriot disaster in Cuba ended all hope of United States aid in freeing the island. After being disappointed by the failure of Spanish constitutionalism, the Spanish Americanists had expectantly turned to the United States for help as well as for inspiration. They had embraced the Western Hemisphere Idea—the notion that there was kinship among the people of the New World because America was better than Europe. The Spanish Americanists admired the institutions of the United States. They especially valued the prosperity that seemed to be the fruit of that nation's open society. And they expected to find sympathy. After all, the United States was their elder sister republic. She more than any other nation would understand the hopes and aspirations of the new countries of Spanish America. In their desire for comfort and aid from the United States, the Spanish Americanists overlooked that country's interests, which were in conflict with their own aspirations. Even before the Cuban debacle, securing aid from the northern republic proved much more difficult than anyone had imagined. Rocafuerte and Vidaurre complained that the land was cold, both in weather and in its attitude towards the freedom of Spanish America. Thus, late in 1823, the Spanish Americanists realized that they would have to depend upon their own resources. If the invasion Vives feared were to take place, it would have to be a purely Spanish American enterprise.

During August 1823, prior to returning to Guatemala, General Arce had visited Rocafuerte and Salazar in Philadelphia. They talked about the future of Spanish America and about the need to end all Spanish power in the New World. They were convinced that Europe would be unlikely to recognize the new nations unless Spain were vanquished. The Spanish Americanists believed that no part of America was safe as long as the Spaniards retained a foothold on the continent. Mexico was threatened because the fortress of San Juan de Ulúa, which dominated Veracruz harbor, remained in Spanish hands. So far, attempts to take the fort had failed. Rocafuerte suggested that the best way to capture the fortress was to free Cuba. Since the island supplied San Juan de Ulúa, the fortress would have to surrender if Cuba were free. The Ecuadorean believed that a rebellion of Cuban patriots would triumph if it were supported by an invasion from Spanish America. The growth of republican sentiment in the island during the last two years had been too great to be stifled by Lemus's defeat.

The idea appealed to Arce. He informed Rocafuerte and Salazar that the army of four thousand men, which had been raised in El Salvador to oppose Iturbide, was intact and he was ready to lead it to Cuba. All he needed were a few artillery officers and funds. Arce suggested that Mexico contribute one-and-a-half-million pesos to the enterprise, since the republic had just obtained a twenty-two-million peso loan.

Salazar was also enthusiastic about the idea. Gran Colombia was already committed to the struggle to win Peru's independence but he thought that other forces could be obtained for the Cuban venture. Gran Colombia could not risk alarming England and France by openly endorsing an invasion of Cuba. But Salazar believed that it could be done secretly. General Mariano Manrique had just captured the cities of Maracaibo and Puerto Cabello on the

Venezuelan coast. He had an army of three thousand men and a naval squadron at his disposal. General Manrique was young and rash enough to undertake such an expedition without waiting for government orders. The Gran Colombian minister was certain that his government would not object. There were already too many soldiers in Venezuela and it would be useful to occupy them outside the country in order to avoid military revolts. If the expedition failed or if the European powers protested, Gran Colombia could reply that she had no knowledge of the affair and that General Manrique had acted on his own, without instructions. Salazar's proposal seemed acceptable to Arce and Rocafuerte. The three men agreed to cooperate in arranging a two-pronged invasion of Cuba to be carried out as soon as possible. They also contacted the Mexican chargé, José Torrens, who approved of the plan and advised his government to take part in the enterprise.[22]

The choice of General Manrique was shrewd. He was a romantic young officer seeking glory. Maracaibo had fallen to him and his naval commander José Padilla on June 18, 1823. Since that time he had been in conflict with the authorities and felt restricted by petty rules. He constantly complained to Vice-President Francisco de Paula Santander that the civil authorities did not supply the aid he needed. Already he had begun to think of Cuba as a new field of action. Cuban patriots contacted him secretly in August to tell him that the island was prepared to fight for independence, but lacked weapons. A secret agent calling himself "Avila y Compañía" asked the general for a thousand men and six thousand rifles and Manrique readily agreed to provide them.[23] From this involvement, it was only a short step to an agreement to lead an invasion of Cuba.

Rocafuerte contacted the Cubans in New York. After several meetings with the Cubans and the other Spanish Americans, all concerned agreed to an invasion of the island. General Arce would return to his country via Mexico where he would seek support and funds for the project. He believed that it would be possible to obtain sufficient funds to maintain an army of four or five thousand men. Salazar and Palacios accepted the task of convincing Gran Colombia to intervene in Cuba. Torrens offered to seek similar support from Mexico.[24] José Ramón Betancourt, who had already returned to Cuba to foment revolution, would be informed of the plan so that proper arrangements could be made in the island. Antonio Iznaga remained in New York to coordinate information arriving from Gran Colombia, Guatemala, Mexico, and Cuba. Miralla, José Agustín Arango, Fructuoso del Castillo, Gaspar Betancourt Cisneros, and José Iznaga agreed to travel to Gran Colombia to obtain the necessary support. Vidaurre, who was returning to his native Peru, also offered to assist the plan in any way possible.[25]

At first Rocafuerte intended to limit his role to providing letters of introduction. He still nurtured a faint hope of organizing a steamship line and there were several models and other equipment he wanted to purchase before returning to Mexico, where he planned to visit his sister and her family in Mexico. But Miralla and the Cubans were reluctant to leave Rocafuerte behind. Since he was an intimate friend of President Bolívar, they reasoned that he should be able to present their case more effectively. Rocafuerte was loath to abandon his interests, but finally agreed to accompany them. Then terrible news threatened to change his plans again. He learned that Gaínza and his sister had died in Mexico. Their numerous family was now alone. He prepared to return to Mexico immediately. His friends and conspirators mourned the loss but believed that a short delay would not inconvenience the family in Mexico. They begged him to go to Maracaibo, take stock of the situation, and convince General Manrique to support the invasion. Then Rocafuerte could return to Mexico. They argued that because of his tact, he alone was qualified to undertake the task. Reluctantly, he agreed.[26]

Vidaurre departed for Lima at the end of August. General Arce left for Mexico on October 18, 1823. Rocafuerte took a ship directly to Maracaibo, arriving there on November 21. Miralla and the Cuban commissioners left New York on October 23, bound for La Guayra. Since they expected Rocafuerte to convince Manrique to prepare for the expedition, they were traveling to Bogotá to obtain support from the Gran Colombian government. The Spanish Americans' departure could not be kept secret. The British minister in Washington reported the event, but assured his government that the United States had not provided them with any assistance. He seemed to believe that the United States refusal caused the conspirators to abandon their plans.

The Spanish consul, however, was not fooled. He slowly pieced together their activities and the reports he sent his government during the following year kept Vives under constant tension. Rivas notified the captain general of Cuba that Vidaurre had departed for Jamaica where he would seek passage for Panama and then Lima. The consul cautioned that Vidaurre had friends in the Peruvian government and might obtain aid for an invasion of Cuba. Rivas also reported the rumor that Rocafuerte would travel to Mexico on a similar mission. Later he announced the departure of Arce and Miralla, warning that if their project were carried out, Cuba could be attacked from all sides. In February 1824, he declared that the conspirators had obtained help from Gran Colombia and Mexico. Vives kept his forces in a state of readiness for months. Only in April did news warrant any relaxation. Rivas advised him that the invasion was unlikely to come in the near future because Gran Colombia was too involved in Peru. But he continued to admonish that neither Gran Colombia nor Mexico had given up their plans to invade the island.[27]

Rocafuerte arrived in Maracaibo on November 21, 1823, and conferred with Manrique. The general was enthusiastic, but told the Ecuadorean that he had to complete the siege of Puerto Cabello before he could undertake any other enterprise. Manrique was certain that the port would fall soon and he agreed to invade Cuba. The general was determined to win new laurels in the island rather than be swept into the Peruvian campaign. Gran Colombia's armies were mired on the coast of Peru. The Spanish forces were winning and Bolívar insisted that the troops from the Venezuelan front be sent to Lima immediately. If he allowed himself to be taken to Peru, Manrique knew that he would be overshadowed by many higher ranking generals. Therefore, he steadfastly refused to permit his troops to be transferred there. But ten days after Rocafuerte's arrival everything changed. General Manrique became ill and died.[28]

Rocafuerte attempted to find another Gran Colombian general willing to undertake the expedition. But no one was willing to disobey government orders. After Puerto Cabello fell, Manrique's three-thousand-man army was sent to Peru. Since Bolívar found himself in a desparate situation, Rocafuerte felt it useless to insist. He wrote Foreign Minister Pedro Gual to inform him that the Cuban commissioners were arriving and to recommend that Gran Colombia aid them. He also suggested that a warship be sent to take

Fernández de Madrid out of Cuba since his life was in danger.[29] After learning that Miralla and the Cubans had arrived in Gran Colombia, he departed for Mexico to join his sister's family.

The commissioners landed in La Guayra on November 14, 1823. There they met the Puerto Rican general, Antonio Valero, who had served Iturbide and was now seeking to enter the Gran Colombian army. When he learned of their mission, Valero immediately volunteered. But since he had no troops, the commissioners could not employ him. They proceeded to Bogotá and arrived there in January 1824. Gual and Santander received them, but could offer no support. Although Gran Colombia favored the independence of Cuba, she could not undertake another campaign until Peru was won. The vice-president and the foreign minister suggested that the conspirators wait. But the Cubans wanted a stronger commitment. Some of them continued on to Lima where they hoped Vidaurre might convince Bolívar, now dictator of Peru, as well as president of Gran Colombia, to help. Miralla remained in Bogotá working to win support. But all their efforts came to naught. General Arce also failed. Mexico could not provide him with funds and his own Guatemala lacked the resources to act alone.[30]

5

The Spanish Americanists failed in their attempt to free Cuba because they overestimated the strength of Spanish American cooperation and underestimated the growing power of nationalism. In the face of mounting internal problems, nationalists insisted that the scarce resources of the new countries be spent on internal questions rather than on costly foreign enterprises. The failure, however, did not end Spanish Americanist concern with Cuba nor did it terminate the activities of the conspirators. After several months of agitation in Bogotá, Miralla went to Mexico where he continued to work for independence. Death overtook him in 1826, just when General Antonio López de Santa Anna appeared ready to invade Cuba. Although the attack did not take place, the planning influenced the first Pan-American Congress, then meeting in Panama, which considered the possibility of a joint invasion. Michelena and Vidaurre, representing Mexico and Peru respectively, favored such a project. However, the United States, influenced by southerners as well as by expansionists, announced that: "This country prefers that Cuba and Puerto Rico should remain dependent on Spain. This government desires no political change in that condition."[31] The policy was designed to retain the possibility of annexing Cuba in the future. Moreover, North American planters, like their Cuban counterparts, feared that independence would bring with it black insurrections. Terror of Negro rebellions plagued all planter societies at that time. And that threat found a responsive chord in the Venezuelan born Bolívar. He apparently seized United States opposition as a pretext for not pressing the liberation of Cuba.

To free Cuba remained one of the most persistent goals of the Spanish Americanists. These men also cooperated in other ventures. Fernández de Madrid and his family were taken out of Cuba in 1825 as Rocafuerte had requested. He arrived in Bogotá in extremely ill health. After a period of recovery, he was entrusted with a mission to France and later became Gran Colombia's minister to England. There he and Rocafuerte worked for the well-being of Spanish America. General Arce remained a key figure in Guatemalan politics until he was expelled in 1830. He fled to Mexico and found temporary refuge in Rocafuerte's house. Later he returned to his country and to politics. Similarly, Vidaurre became prominent in Peruvian affairs and, like Arce, was exiled. He too returned and rejoined political life in Peru. These men were to remain close friends and to collaborate in Spanish American affairs. They wrote extensively and recalled their friendship by dedicating their works to one another.[32] They wanted a free and prosperous Spanish America and felt that they could turn to one another for help in achieving that goal.

# V

## THE POLITICS OF RECOGNITION

The new nations of Spanish America needed European recognition if they were to survive. The establishment of diplomatic relations would affirm their independence and facilitate commerce and foreign investment. The great powers, however, would not extend recognition unless they could be convinced that viable sovereign nations had come into being. The strength and stability of the new governments played a major role in determining their ability to gain European recognition. These factors were particularly important in the case of Great Britain, the country Spanish Americans believed most likely to favor their cause.

1

When Rocafuerte returned to Mexico in January 1824, the nation was preoccupied with drafting a constitution. The Ecuadorean, like Santamaría and several leading Mexican politicians, advocated centralism.[1] However, some of the provinces had already become states and their representatives insisted upon a federal constitution; one group of federalists demanded complete sovereignty for the states while others, like Father Mier, noted that only the nation could be sovereign. If each state were sovereign then each would be an independent country. Only if the states surrendered part of their power could the nation remain united. To demonstrate the validity of his arguments, Mier cited the example of the United States. Its first constitution, the Articles of Confederation, granted the states too much power; consequently, the national government failed. This situation was resolved with the Constitution of 1787, which forged a stronger union by dividing power more evenly between the federal and state governments. Thus Father Mier advocated the creation of a strong federal union in Mexico.

The constitutional debates intrigued Rocafuerte, who argued at length with his friends. Like Father Mier, Ramos Arizpe held that only federalism could maintain the unity of the former viceroyalty of New Spain. He declared that regionalism was too strong in Spanish America to be disregarded. Rocafuerte, however, considered federalism weak and associated the term with the disastrous regionalist struggles of the 1810s during the *Patria Boba* period in Nueva Granada. Then city had fought against city in a fratricidal struggle that devastated the country. But the Mexicans convinced him that there was a difference between the unbridled regionalism that had provoked the *Patria Boba* wars and federalism; the first had placed local interests above national goals while the latter allowed regional expression in state governments and national representation in a federal congress. Under federalism the national government could also be strong and effective if the constitution granted it sufficient power. The Ecuadorean decided to embrace federalism because it also seemed to encourage the development of civil responsibility by fostering state and local government. He now believed that the system would be better for the new nations than centralism. Although a new convert to federalism, Rocafuerte became one of the system's most ardent admirers.[2]

The Constituent Congress also was concerned with the manner in which power would be divided within the government. Like the Spanish Cortes, the Mexican Congress considered itself the most important branch of government. Most congressman believed that, following the precedent set by the Cortes of 1810, the executive should be required to carry out the policy established by Congress. Both Ferdinand VII and Iturbide had demonstrated that a strong ruler could become a despot. The Mexican Congress, like its Spanish predecessor, sought to forestall this by making the ministers responsible to the legislature. A majority in the Constituent Congress also wanted to further restrict the administrative branch by retaining the Supreme Executive Power, an ineffectual triumvirate then governing the nation. Others, like Ramos Arizpe and Michelena, believing that administration would suffer under a plural executive, favored a president. Since Michelena was one of the triumvirs, he was accused of seeking dictatorial powers. After a heated debate, the Constituent Congress voted to retain the plural executive. Nevertheless, the minority continued to press its case and finally convinced Congress to reexamine the question. Those who still supported the original decision were outraged at what they considered to be underhanded tactics and became even more adamant in their opposition. On January 20, the question was revived and, during the extensive debates, various compromise solutions were offered. All were rejected.[3]

The discussions coincided with a revolt in Mexico City led by General José María Lobato. The rebels demanded the dismissal of Spaniards from government jobs and their expulsion from the country. They also insisted that two of the triumvirs, José Mariano Michelena and Miguel Dominguez, resign. The reason for this demand is unclear. Both men were heroes of the early independence movement. Michelena had also fought in Spain against the French and represented Mexico in the Cortes. Although he had once favored a Spanish American constitutional commonwealth, Michelena was known to be an implacable enemy of Ferdinand VII and absolutism. Since he was acting president of the Supreme Executive Power when the rebellion began, it is possible that the incident was directed in part against the attempt to create a single executive and, therefore, against Michelena. The plural executive and the division of power within the government hampered action against the rebels. Lobato managed to win the support of the garrisons in the capital and the government seemed on the verge of capitulation when the Supreme Executive Power convinced Congress to declare Lobato an outlaw and grant it sufficient power to quell the rebellion. Although the government managed to suppress the Lobato revolt, Michelena was badly shaken. Whatever aspirations he may have had for the presidency ended. At the first opportunity he chose to retire from the executive office in favor of a mission to England.

The Lobato revolt convinced many congressmen that it was unwise to so weaken the executive branch that it was unable to act decisively in time of danger. This incident also convinced the Constituent Congress of the unwieldiness of the plural executive.

Instead, they substituted a presidential system. Logic dictated that the ministers should be responsible to the president, but most Mexican politicians continued to favor congressional superiority and insisted that the cabinet was responsible to the legislature. Thus they created an ambiguous situation that was not resolved until the Díaz era.[4]

2

Governmental stability was necessary, not only to maintain internal order, but also to initiate diplomatic relations with Europe. England and Mexico had originally established unofficial relations in 1822. The British government sent Dr. Patrick Mackie, who had previously lived in Mexico, to investigate Iturbide's government. The English physician arrived late in 1822 and sent favorable reports to Foreign Minister George Canning. Iturbide decided to take advantage of British interest in Mexico by appointing Arthur Wavell to represent him in England. The Mexican agent had just initiated talks with Canning when Iturbide's government collapsed in March 1823. In his reports to the foreign office, Mackie, who remained in Mexico while the new republican government was being formed, was sufficiently confident of the nation's future that England dispatched a commission composed of Lionel Hervey, Charles O'Gorman, and Henry G. Ward to study the feasibility of establishing diplomatic relations with the new nation. The republican government responded by appointing Francisco Borja Migoni, a Mexican merchant who had resided in London many years, as its agent in England.[5]

The main objective of the Hervey mission was to ascertain whether Mexico really wanted independence, and if so, whether she could survive. If these questions were answered affirmatively, the commissioners were instructed to suggest that the two countries exchange agents. The English commissioners reported to their government on January 18, 1824, that Mexico had publicly proclaimed herself independent and had formed a republican government. They also corroborated the popular notion that Mexico was immensely wealthy and suggested that England could profit by helping the new nation develop her great potential. Shortly thereafter, Hervey informed the Mexican government that Great Britain wished to exchange envoys.[6]

The Mexican government was pleased. Instead of sending a confidential agent to London, it could now dispatch an official representative. Mexicans realized the importance of selecting a man of importance and tact. Therefore, the Supreme Executive Power chose the distinguished botanist, Pablo de la Llave, as minister plenipotentiary and envoy extraordinary. Michelena recommended that Vicente Rocafuerte be appointed secretary to the legation. The other members of the executive agreed because of the Ecuadorean's previous diplomatic experience, his command of French and English—the languages necessary to carry out the negotiations—and his knowledge of the Continent and its statesmen.

La Llave's nomination was unopposed and Congress approved it on February 13. The appointee, however, declined, despite repeated attempts to convince him to accept the mission. The search for an alternate ended when Michelena agreed to go in La Llave's place.[7]

Other difficulties arose because Rocafuerte was unwilling to accept the appointment of secretary. He told friends that his arrangements to return to Guayaquil were complete and that he had to settle his personal affairs after several years of neglect. But Ramos Arizpe, Michelena, and Santamaría argued that Rocafuerte's help was desperately needed to obtain British recognition. If Mexico, the richest of the new nations, succeeded in establishing diplomatic relations with England, other American states would win recognition more easily. They also noted that, although the United States had recognized the new nations and President Monroe had spoken about the differences between the Old World and the New in a message to Congress, the independence of Spanish America could only be assured if England extended recognition. The United States had neither the power, the funds, nor the desire to assist the nations of Spanish America. Great Britain, on the other hand, had already shown that she could help with men, money, and influence. They appealed to him as a Spanish Americanist and a patriot to accept this mission, which would benefit the entire New World. He decided that without British recognition Spain and the Holy Alliance would surely attempt to conquer the New World. The interests of Spanish America were more important than concerns for family or personal gain. He made certain that his sister's children would be well cared for on their trip to Guayaquil and then accepted the post of secretary of the Mexican legation to England.[8]

The Supreme Executive Power, then chaired by Vicente Guerrero, nominated Rocafuerte on February 26. Although many Mexicans believed in Spanish Americanism and did not consider country of origin important, others felt differently. Nationalists in Congress refused to approve Rocafuerte's appointment on the the ground that he was not a citizen. The Ecuadorean, however, had important friends. General Guadalupe Victoria, who was to become the nation's first president, urged that his nomination be approved. Rocafuerte's supporters in Congress, among them Fray Servando Teresa de Mier, Manuel Crecencio Rejón, and Lorenzo de Zavala, proposed to resolve the question by awarding him Mexican citizenship. Opponents, however, argued that Rocafuerte was ineligible for citizenship because he was neither a resident of the country nor an owner of property in the nation. Despite heated discussion, Rocafuerte was awarded Mexican nationality in March and his appointment ratified.[9]

The mission carried both general and secret instructions. The envoy received the rank of commissioner, the same title held by the British agent in Mexico, which would be raised to minister when the English government recognized the United States of Mexico. Michelena's primary assignment was to obtain British recognition. Although he was not to involve himself in British politics in the pursuit of his task, the commissioner was to encourage England or any other power to mediate with Spain on Mexico's behalf. However, the envoy was also charged with impressing upon all governments that the nation's territorial integrity was not negotiable. Mexico would consider neither the United States' claim to Texas nor Russia's claim to California.

After England granted recognition, the minister was instructed to negotiate a treaty of commerce on the basis of strict reciprocity. Similar treaties were to be arranged with other countries that recognized Mexico. In the event that only England extended recognition and the Holy Alliance continued to threaten Mexico, the envoy was empowered to draw up an offensive and defensive treaty with Great Britain. He was also granted exclusive authority to contract loans and purchase ships and arms.[10]

Secret instructions directed the minister to work toward the independence of Cuba even if it required the expenditure of national funds.[11] He was to cooperate with other Spanish American ministers in this effort; under no circumstances was he to permit the United States to annex Cuba. Since the government of Mexico also wanted to attract artisans and craftsmen, especially those with technical knowledge of the paper and textile industries, as well as sailors who could establish whale fisheries in the Pacific, the minister was instructed to encourage their immigration. Impoverished Catholic Irish farmers were to be attracted by promises of free land. Both the general and the secret instructions had been drafted while La Llave was being considered for the post. When Michelena was named in his stead, the new envoy received two additional assignments. Michelena was told to keep ex-emperor Iturbide under surveillance and to acquire ships to blockade San Juan de Ulúa.[12]

3

Many Mexicans believed that with orderly government and foreign investment their country could be transformed into the wealthiest and most powerful nation in the world. Since they felt that Mexico's fabled wealth would induce European governments to recognize their independence, they wanted their country to negotiate from a position of strength. True, Spain and the Holy Alliance posed a grave threat. But it was temporary. Once Mexico organized her administration and armed forces, she could defeat the Spaniards and, if necessary, carry the struggle to the Peninsula. Consequently, the Mexican government refused to grant special privileges to any nation, even Great Britain. The new republic would assume her place as an equal among the great powers of the earth.

Europeans also believed that Mexico had a great future. During the eighteenth century Mexican silver had supported the Spanish Empire and various writers propagated the mistaken belief that Mexico was immensely rich. Among the most influential of these authors was Baron Alexander von Humboldt, whose *Political Essay on the Kingdom of New Spain* had been translated into English in 1811. The evidence he presented made investors and businessmen eager to enter into such a profitable market. Consequently, they exerted pressure on their governments to establish relations with the new nation.

Michelena and Rocafuerte and seven assitants left Mexico early in April. After some delays, they arrived in England on June 24, 1824.[13] A complex political situation confronted them in Europe. The Holy Alliance, the bulwark of legitimacy, opposed the recognition of the new American states. The danger of direct armed intervention by the Alliance ended when England threatened to use force to prevent the conservative powers from launching an invasion to reconquer Spanish America. Later, France also announced opposition to such actions. However, neither France nor England objected to Spanish efforts to regain control of the New World. Russia continued to encourage Spain to retake her former colonies. Although Austria and Prussia seemed to support Russian policy, the Spanish Americans hoped to win their friendship. Papal recognition was also very important to the Catholic countries of the New World. The Holy See, however, was under the influence of Austria and Spain and it appeared unlikely that the Vatican would recognize the new nations until Ferdinand VII allowed it. The smaller European states were unknown quantities. Since they were commercial nations, the Spanish Americans hoped to persuade them to recognize the New World in exchange for trade opportunities.

Although France opposed efforts by the Holy Alliance to dictate European foreign policy, she remained ambivalent in her attitude toward the new states. French conservatives had involved their country in a military intervention in Spain forcing their government into the arms of Ferdinand VII and the Holy Alliance. Some French statesmen deplored such a relationship because they realized that Spain's former colonies were free and eventually would have to be recognized. French merchants were particularly anxious to initiate diplomatic relations with America lest England reap all the benefits of trade with the new nations. French ministers hoped to solve their dilemma by creating monarchies in Spanish America. The British government also favored this solution, but the two European powers could not agree on the princes who were to rule the New World. Earlier in the decade, many Spanish American leaders had supported such an enterprise. By 1824, however, monarchies had lost appeal for Americans. Nevertheless, French officials refused to abandon the idea. England and France also suggested that Spain might be convinced to recognize the new nations if the Spanish Americans offered some sort of monetary compensation. But the New World was neither willing nor able to ransom its way into diplomatic society.

Great Britain hoped that the conflict between Spain and America could be settled amicably. His Majesty's government offered to help mediate between the mother country and the new states. But England also declared that she would not oppose a purely Spanish attempt to reconquer the rebellious provinces of America. Such declarations were predicated on the belief that Spain was incapable of reestablishing control over Spanish America. Nevertheless, England's official position inspired various Spanish attempts to invade her former colonies. As a result, Spanish American governments believed it necessary to establish diplomatic relations with Europe. Only then could they be certain of obtaining the loans and arms needed to protect and maintain their independence.

The Spanish Americans hoped to use enticements of trade as the bait in winning recognition. But they were handicapped in their dealings with Great Britain because the English were already trading with their countries and would continue to do so even if recognition were not forthcoming. Fortunately for the New World, the British Foreign Minister and Prime Minister George Canning favored recognition. His support, however, was of limited immediate value because the foreign minister wanted to be certain that the new states would survive before England recognized them. He also had to convince his monarch to abandon legitimist principles and accept the independence of Spanish America. Moreover, Canning's position was not strong because he had just become prime minister and was still attempting to establish himself firmly in the government. Until he succeeded, he would not enjoy the freedom of action necessary to recognize the new states.[14] As a result, the new nations felt compelled to take all possible steps to hasten British recognition.

4

Francisco Borja Migoni, Mexico's agent in England, was away in Brussels when the Mexican legation arrived in London. Unable to contact him, Michelena and Rocafuerte were disturbed by what seemed to them irresponsibility on Borja Migoni's part. After some inquiries, they located the agent's secretary, who agreed to forward a letter from Michelena.[15] Although he had been unable to secure details of recent developments in relations between Mexico and England, Michelena informed Canning that he had arrived as Mexico's confidential envoy. The English foreign minister immediately acknowledged the Mexican's note and gave him an appointment for an unofficial meeting on Sunday, June 27.[16]

Before conferring with Canning, Michelena and Rocafuerte tried to learn as much as possible about the state of their country's affairs in England. They visited the commercial house that had been negotiating a loan for Mexico, Barclay, Herring, Richardson and Company. Much to their surprise, Barclay informed them that his firm could not obtain the proposed loan because Borja Migoni had already contracted another loan for Mexico with B. A. Goldschmidt and Company and had agreed to a clause prohibiting the Mexican government from negotiating further loans for a period of one year. This left the Mexican legation without funds until Borja Migoni returned. The envoys were also dismayed to learn that Iturbide had left for France and was planning to return to his native land. Michelena was certain the ex-emperor had no backing in Mexico but realized that Iturbide's activities would be embarrassing for his country and might delay recognition.[17]

Rocafuerte accompanied Michelena to the interview with Canning on June 27. The foreign minister showed great interest in Mexico, asking a variety of questions about the new nation. He seemed well disposed to the new federal republic, but was reluctant to commit himself. As he explained to the Americans, Hervey had exceeded his authority by suggesting that Mexico exchange official envoys with England. Moreover, the British government was in the midst of a political crisis and no decision could be taken at that time.[18]

Michelena and Rocafuerte were pleased with their first conversations with the foreign office. Canning's friendly attitude seemed to imply that British recognition would soon be extended, so Michelena decided to dispatch confidential agents to France and the Low Countries. Tomás Murphy, a liberal Spanish merchant who had lived in Mexico many years and who had been elected to represent his adopted land in the Cortes, was sent to France to evaluate the situation in southern Europe. Manuel Eduardo Gorostiza, who fled Spain in 1823 and was in London when Michelena arrived, agreed to report on northern Europe from Holland. Brimming with confidence, the Mexicans planned to win European recognition with the lucrative trade the new republic offered. Michelena also believed that the English government might be induced to recognize Mexico immediately if it realized that other nations might obtain access to the Mexican market by establishing diplomatic ties with the country. Therefore, he arranged a conference with Canning so that the British minister would be aware of Mexico's efforts on the Continent.[19]

A few days later, Borja Migoni, displeased because the Mexican government had not appointed him minister to England and ready to oppose the man who had deprived him of that post, returned to London. Rocafuerte visited the Mexican merchant to inform him of Michelena's arrival, and to ask him to report on his activities on Mexico's behalf. The request angered Borja Migoni. When he visited Michelena he demonstrated his hostility to the minister and his contempt for the new government, which he called "revolutionary."[20] Furthermore, the economic agent was reluctant to turn over his papers to the new minister because he feared that the irregularities involved in negotiating the Goldschmidt loan might be discovered. (The loans to Mexico are discussed in chapter VI.) Finally, after some disagreement, he relinquished the documents. Thereafter both men complained to Mexico. It was clear that a great animosity had developed and that they could not work together. Unaware of the developments in London, the Mexican government appointed Borja Migoni its financial agent with sole responsibility to disburse funds from the Goldschmidt loan. Although he was instructed to provide whatever Michelena needed, the credentials authorized Borja Migoni to use his own discretion in financial matters. Thus Michelena was forced to request, rather than order, his diplomatic subordinate, Borja Migoni, to provide needed funds.[21]

The division of authority would have created difficulties had the men been on good terms; since they had become enemies, it was disastrous. Michelena, who believed that one of his principal tasks was to acquire arms and ships, made repeated demands for funds. But Borja Migoni refused to provide any money without the express authorization of the Mexican minister of the treasury. Borja Migoni considered himself secure because as a merchant he represented Mexico's powerful mining interests in the English bond market. Throughout the conflict, he retained the support of Foreign Minister Lucas Alamán, one of Mexico's most important mining entrepreneurs. In spite of Michelena's complaints, the Mexican government failed to remedy the situation. Instead, it created greater difficulties by naming Borja Migoni consul general, thereby granting him more extensive financial power.[22] The question became an international issue when the British government objected to Borja Migoni's appointment on the ground that he was an important member of the merchant community in London. Such an appointment, it argued, could lead to conflicts of interest or, at least, to charges of partisanship. Mexico ignored the objection and Borja Migoni acted as Mexico's consul general until his death in 1832, in spite of the fact that he was never recognized by the English government. The apparent intransigent position of the American nation is partially explained by the fact that Borja Migoni falsely informed his government that England had received him as consul general.[23]

Once Borja Migoni had consolidated his position, he attempted to undermine Michelena's influence and prestige in Europe. He not only embarrassed the minister by refusing to pay for the military equipment Michelena had ordered, but also delighted in attacking the Mexican government. When all London believed Iturbide might be able to return to power, Borja Migoni publicly defended the former emperor and attacked the republic, thus encouraging widespread speculation that the Mexican government would collapse. This led to a drastic decline in the price of the nation's bonds. On his frequent trips to the Continent Borja Migoni aggravated the already difficult situation by paying homage to Spain's ambassador to Paris and by appearing publicly with several Spanish nobles. Murphy reported on various occasions that Borja Migoni was a client of the Spanish Duke of San Carlos. The consul general also ingratiated himself with other Spaniards, including the Count of Puebla, the Duchess of Hijar, and the Marquess of Astorga, by giving them lavish gifts. At a party given by the Duke of San Carlos, Borja Migoni told the French minister of foreign affairs that Mexico's only hope of success was to establish a monarchy, preferably with a Spanish prince. Gorostiza reported that Borja Migoni made similar statements in Belgium. Murphy and Gorostiza both noted that the consul was fond of ridiculing Michelena and predicting that he would soon replace the minister.[24]

The diplomatic situation deteriorated on July 17, when it was reported that former emperor Iturbide was on his way to Mexico. The British government postponed various appointments with Michelena because Canning wanted to await the outcome of Iturbide's return. The Mexican minister noted that many Englishmen expected the emperor's arrival to precipitate a civil war, which would allow Spain to regain possession of Mexico. Therefore, he urged the republic to suppress pro-Iturbide rebellions since any hesitation would probably result in Britain's postponing recognition.[25]

To regain the initiative, Michelena and Rocafuerte urged the other Spanish American envoys to join Mexico in presenting a united front vis-à-vis England. However, none of the other Spanish American ministers felt strong enough to challenge Canning. Only the Brazilians, General Felisberto Caldeira Brant and Cavalier Manoel Rodríguez Gameiro Pessoa, seemed in a strong position. To fortify the bargaining power of the new nations, Michelena proposed that they form an American union. After several conferences the Latin American envoys decided on a strategy to win recognition from Great Britain. Mexico, Gran Colombia, Argentina, and Brazil agreed to establish an offensive and defensive alliance that would refuse to recognize or to admit to their ports the ships of any nation that did not in turn recognize the members of the alliance. The envoys planned to inform Canning jointly that they would withdraw from London immediately if England did not extend recognition. The allies also proposed to combine their fleets to capture San Juan de Ulúa; thereafter, the allied navy would patrol American waters enforcing their restrictions. Michelena and Rocafuerte believed that the program would force England to recognize the new states rapidly and to negotiate treaties with them on favorable terms. Brant and Gameiro accepted the plan, but would not act without their government's approval. Since Brazil seemed to be the strongest of the new nations, the others did not feel capable of acting without her. So action was delayed for several months.

The manner in which the proposed alliance was formed is

characteristic of Spanish Americanism. Previously, Gran Colombian Foreign Minister Pedro Gual had proposed that bilateral offensive and defensive treaties form the basis of a Spanish American union; Gran Colombia and Mexico had already signed such a treaty. Thus, there was a basis for joint action. When confronted with a crisis, the Mexican envoys first considered expanding that alliance to form a Spanish American union. However, Brazil was in a stronger diplomatic position than any Spanish American nation. Therefore, Michelena and Rocafuerte reluctantly invited the South American monarchy to join the proposed alliance.[26]

Mexican efforts on the Continent were also at an impasse. Gorostiza reported from Brussels that the people of the Low Countries had little knowledge of, or interest in, America. He hoped, however, that coastal cities like Amsterdam and Rotterdam might be induced to develop commercial interests in Mexico. News from France was even worse. Murphy wrote that most Frenchman believed that Mexico was unstable and that chaos would persist for some time. Although he was trying to dispel such notions, Murphy had little success.[27]

By the end of August, Michelena concluded that Mexico had to take steps not only to be recognized but even to survive. Spain was preparing an invasion. Spanish commissioners who had been thwarted when they attempted to purchase ships in England were negotiating with Austria. Furthermore, the Holy Alliance had not softened its position and planned to cripple the new nations by interfering with American trade. The Mexicans tried to counter the threat by offering England a treaty of commerce, but Canning remained reluctant. England was torn between friendship for America and consideration for Spain. Since she would continue to trade with Mexico in any event, Michelena feared that the inclination to appease Spain was a sign that British conservatives were growing stronger. Therefore, he warned his government against any act that might perpetuate the idea that Spain had a just claim to govern Mexico. It was necessary to convince the British of the nation's stability. Otherwise England might turn against America. Then French conservatives would be able to force their country into intervening in the New World just as they had forced the invasion of Spain. In Michelena's opinion, the only viable solution was to make a show of force. Iturbide must be destroyed and the fortress of San Juan de Ulúa taken immediately. The envoy suggested that Mexico and the other Spanish American nations should take the war to Spain and if necessary foment revolution in the Peninsula. American fleets should also sweep the Spanish navy from the sea and attack Spanish cities. Only in this fashion would Europe realize that the new Spanish American countries could not be kept waiting forever.[28]

The Spanish Americans were theoretically capable of uniting their fleets, bottling up the last remnants of Spanish power in America—the fortress of San Juan de Ulúa, the interior of Peru, and the island of Chiloé off the coast of Chile—and then taking the war to Spain. Presumably, Ferdinand VII's government would have fallen as a result of civil war in Spain, if France and the Holy Alliance did not send additional troops to protect Spanish absolutism. In the end, Spain would have been forced to recognize the new nations.

Nationalist tendencies in Spanish America, however, made pooling resources difficult. Michelena also ignored the fact that resources would have to be temporarily diverted from the land war in Peru to concentrate on a direct attack on Spain. Since many of the leaders of Spanish America were soldiers, it is unlikely that they would have accepted a plan that placed primary emphasis on naval operations. Furthermore, the famous meeting between Simón Bolívar and José de San Martín indicates that cooperation among the great generals was unlikely. For these reasons, the hopes of the Spanish Americanists were utopian. Nationalism and personal ambitions were too entrenched and the distances separating the new nations too great for such an enterprise to succeed.

The fears that prompted Michelena's plan were unfounded. Even if England reversed her policy and favored the complete return of Spanish power to America, it was unlikely that she would permit either France or the Holy Alliance to intervene. Britain wanted Spanish American trade and any interference by European powers would obstruct that commerce. Furthermore, it was unlikely that French ultra-conservatives would attempt to intervene in the New World if it meant fighting England. Nevertheless, the Spanish Americans were oppressed by the fear that, if England stepped aside, France and the Holy Alliance would intervene to restore

Spanish power in America. In that case, the Spanish American nations would not possess the strength to defend themselves. Nor is it likely that the United States could or would have assisted them.

Throughout this period the European public, as well as the diplomats, were eagerly awaiting the outcome of Iturbide's return to Mexico. The republic's credibility suffered a grievous blow when his departure became known. The problems of Spanish American diplomats were compounded when news of recent patriot setbacks in Peru were published. Newspapers in France and England counseled their governments to exercise the utmost caution in dealing with the new American states. Only in the manufacturing districts of Birmingham and Manchester were important interests in favor of recognition. Spain launched a propaganda campaign to take advantage of Iturbide's return to Mexico and Spanish spies circulated in Europe. In Belgium Spanish agents planned to watch Gorostiza, but local police warned him in time to take precautions. The attitude of the Belgian police gave Gorostiza some hope, although most newspapers were filled with alarmist reports about Mexico.[29]

In spite of these difficulties, two bright spots appeared on the diplomatic horizon. Gorostiza was heartened when he traveled to Amsterdam and met several important merchants who were interested in establishing trade with Mexico. Since they were afraid to proceed without approval from their government, Gorostiza went to The Hague in an effort to convince the Dutch government to establish some sort of relations with his country.[30] Michelena also received good news from his government; a French commissioner had arrived in Mexico and reported favorably to Count Joseph de Villele, president of the council of ministers. Foreign Minister Alamán believed that France might be willing to recognize Mexico. Therefore, Michelena instructed Murphy, who was then in the Pyrenees gathering information on Spain, to return to Paris and contact the French government.[31]

Before action could be taken, news arrived which changed the entire diplomatic situation for Mexico. On the morning of September 27, Michelena learned that Iturbide had been captured and executed shortly after landing on Mexican soil. All observers in Europe interpreted the swiftness with which he was dispatched as a sign of governmental strength. Accordingly, Michelena demanded that England recognize his country immediately. The English government, although impressed by Mexico's stability, was only willing to mediate between the American nation and Spain as she had earlier mediated between Brazil and Portugal.[32]

News of Iturbide's execution heartened all partisans of independence. The Argentine envoy to the United States, Carlos de Alvear, sent congratulations to Michelena and assured him that the new nations would soon be recognized as a result of Mexico's stern action. In the Low Countries, Gorostiza was also pleased. He met with Minister of Foreign Affairs Count Rheede who complimented Mexico on its stability and expressed a strong desire to initiate relations with the new nation. But, he explained, Holland was unable to act alone; she could not ignore the fact that the Holy Alliance would look unfavorably upon the Low Countries if the small nation acted precipitously. Holland, he claimed, would be happy to recognize Mexico as soon as England did so. Until then, his country could only show its friendship. However, he agreed to appoint unofficial consuls in Mexico. Feeling that relations would now develop rapidly, Gorostiza requested further instruction from Michelena.[33]

Murphy was less successful in France. Minister Villele was unwilling to take any step towards recognition without further reports from his commissioner to Mexico, Lieutenant Samouel. Murphy interpreted the delay as proof that the Holy Alliance still influenced French diplomacy. He believed that Villele wanted to establish relations with Mexico, but would not initiate a change.

French involvement in Spanish affairs had an important effect on her relations with America. Most French ministers would have preferred to withdraw French troops from the neighboring country, but conservatives—particularly the *Ultras*—favored Ferdinand VII and absolutism. Furthermore, the *Ultras* believed that the Spanish American nations had to be crushed in order to maintain the principle of legitimacy. Since Spain seethed with unrest, Ferdinand could send armies to America only if French troops remained to control internal disturbances in his country. As a result, French conservatives refused to consider the withdrawal of French troops from Spain.

Spanish Americanists, of course, wanted internal disorders in Spain so that Ferdinand could not attack America. They hoped that

Spanish liberals might even overthrow absolutism. When Spanish emigrés reported to Rocafuerte that the king of Spain was sending a large force to Havana even though the country was on the verge of civil war, the Mexican diplomat promised to support a revolutionary expedition. Michelena authorized the use of some secret funds and Rocafuerte convinced other Spanish American envoys to lend similar assistance. However, they were unable to obtain sufficient resources to mount an emigré invasion of Spain.[34]

In the weeks that followed the Mexicans pressured England and France to act. They argued that Ferdinand VII would never recognize the independence of the New World and that eventually Spanish America might have to carry the war to Spain in order to guarantee its safety. This bloodshed could be avoided if England and France extended recognition. Spain would then be forced to accept the independence of America. When these arguments failed to convince the two European powers, the Americans tried to get each of them to act by insinuating that the other was taking the lead and that if they wanted to retain American friendship, they should act decisively. Neither tactic was successful.[35]

Because neither England nor France seemed willing to take the necessary steps either to recognize Mexico or to induce Spain to acknowledge her independence, the Mexican diplomats decided to force the issue. Michelena and Rocafuerte circulated rumours that they were organizing an expedition of Spanish liberals to overthrow Ferdinand. Since Michelena, Rocafuerte, Gorostiza, and Murphy had all been active in recent Spanish politics and had openly reestablished ties with liberal Spanish exiles, the stories gained credence. The rumor soon spread to the Continent where the Spanish chargé d'affaires in Paris took the threat quite seriously. He informed Villele that Michelena was spending over a million pesos to foment revolution in Spain and requested that France deny entry to Spaniards not acceptable to the Spanish legation.[36]

Michelena also tried to reactivate the plan for a Latin American union. Since the Brazilian envoys had not received instructions from their government, he decided to act without them. The ministers of Gran Colombia, Chile, and Argentina agreed that England was merely procrastinating and that they would have to act in unison to force her to recognize their republics. But when Michelena proposed firm action, they, too, refused to act without explicit instructions from their governments. The envoy from Argentina, Bernardino Rivadavia, believed that in order to protect their extensive trade in his country, English merchants would insist on its recognition. Therefore, he demanded an interview with Canning and informed the British minister that unless recognition were granted, Argentina would be forced to take strong measures. In spite of the threat, the foreign minister remained evasive.

Although British trade with Spanish America had increased tremendously and was now three times greater than England's trade with the United States, the new republics were stymied in their efforts to force England to recognize them. In part, this was because Canning believed they could not afford to boycott British commerce since the United States was incapable of providing the trade, credit, weapons, and men that England supplied. British policy was also influenced by the strong legitimist attitudes of some members of parliament and the king. George IV was king of both England and of Hanover. Although a constitutional monarch in Britain, he was an absolute ruler in Germany. He surrounded himself with conservatives and his palace in London became a gathering place for the diplomats of the Holy Alliance. Canning thus faced great resistance when he sought to recognize Spanish America. Although the Duke of Wellington supported the minister's opposition to European intervention in America, he disapproved of Canning's desire to recognize the new nations. To establish relations with Spanish America, the foreign minister would ultimately have to override both the king and the influence of British conservatives. In this struggle the growing trade with the New World was very important but not decisive.[37]

Thus, late in 1824 Holland seemed the only bright spot for Mexico in an otherwise dismal diplomatic panorama. After his initial interview with Count Rheede on September 29, Gorostiza received new credentials and instructions from Michelena. The Mexican envoy then entered into conversations with the Dutch minister of foreign affairs, the minister of national industries, and the director of the New Commerce Society, a quasi-governmental corporation. The Netherlands attempted to maintain her policy of increasing trade with Mexico without antagonizing her large neighbors, France and Prussia, or the Holy Alliance. After intense negotiations, Holland agreed to recognize ships flying the Mexican flag both on the high seas and in Dutch ports. Late in November Gorostiza convinced the foreign minister to expand the talks. As a result, the Netherlands instructed A. R. Falk, the Dutch ambassador to England, to initiate conversations with Michelena.[38]

Gorostiza's success in Holland convinced Michelena that the time was ripe to approach Prussia. He believed that talks with a member of the Holy Alliance might divide the conservative powers and increase the possibility of early recognition. Gorostiza, however, doubting that the eastern power had any commercial interest in America, was reluctant and argued that Lubeck and Danzig, two cities of the Hanseatic League, handled Prussia's trade with the New World. Even that commerce was limited to Cuba where Spain regulated the exchange. The confidential agent also hesitated because he feared the Prussian police. Michelena sought to allay Gorostiza's fears by telling him that the minister from Argentina had recently been well received in Berlin.[39]

After making some inquiries, the Mexican envoy became more optimistic about the enterprise. He learned that the king of Prussia had chartered a Company of the Indies in 1821 for the sole purpose of trading with the new states. It had already engaged in commerce with Argentina, Gran Colombia, and Mexico. The Mexican expedition proved so successful that the king had just dispatched a commercial agent to Veracruz. On the advice of Count Rheede, Gorostiza visited Count Schladen, the Prussian minister to Holland, to obtain a passport. The count was cordial but apprehensive until the Mexican assured him he no intention of becoming involved with internal politics. Count Schladen then agreed to provide Gorostiza with a passport within a few days. The days, however, turned into weeks. As the new year approached, Gorostiza again sought the aid of the Dutch foreign minister. Count Rheede counseled patience. He told the Mexican that the Prussian minister did not have the authority to issue the passport. Rheede was certain that Schladen had asked Berlin to grant permission and, no doubt, the Prussian government would forward it soon. Until then, Gorostiza would have to be patient.[40]

Developments on the Continent were temporarily stalled, but the situation in England began to change rapidly. After a series of postponements, Canning granted Michelena an audience on November 30. He appeared to be concerned about the proposed

Spanish American alliance. The British minister asked Michelena about the power of the Gran Colombian and Mexican navies and whether they intended to invade Cuba. Michelena replied that the strength of both navies was increasing and that all independent states hoped to liberate Cuba. The Mexican reiterated the American position: the new states would not wait forever for Spain to recognize them. If it did not happen soon, they would attack the Peninsula. After requesting copies of the offensive and defensive treaties between Mexico and Gran Colombia, Canning assured Michelena that England would make her final decision regarding mediation as soon as the new Spanish ambassador arrived in London.[41]

Michelena thought he detected a softening in England's attitude and decided to apply some pressure by having Rocafuerte present a strong protest to Under-Secretary Planta. On December 4, Rocafuerte wrote that Spain continued to intrigue against Mexico and that she would stop at nothing to try to reconquer America. He argued that Spain did not have the power to succeed and that the American nations had grown tired of her plots. England could maintain peace, as well as protect her commercial interests, by recognizing the new states. He implied that if England did not recognize the new countries, she might endanger her commercial ties with them. To demonstrate his impatience with Britain, the Mexican did not include the treaty between Gran Colombia and Mexico in his correspondence.[42] The letter had the desired effect. Two days later Planta informed Michelena that England recognized the belligerency of the American nations and would remain neutral in their struggle with Spain. She would recognize their flag on the high seas, as well as receive their ships in her ports. Satisfied with the reply, the Mexican minister instructed Rocafuerte to provide the foreign office with the Gran Colombian treaty.[43] In making these assurances, England was only confirming previous declarations; however, this was the first time that the British government had committed itself in writing.

The Spanish Americans were pleased. They believed that recognition might follow in a few months. The event was nearer than anyone realized. Canning had exhausted his patience waiting for the Spanish government to take a reasonable attitude toward the new states. English merchants had been insisting for several months that it was in the nation's interest to recognize the new countries. But the king, several ministers, and many members of parliament were opposed to recognition. They sought to minimize the importance of trade with the New World while emphasizing diplomatic relations with Europe. Realizing that he must overcome such opposition, Canning attempted to demonstrate the danger inherent in such policy. On December 3, he asked the French government when it would evacuate its troops from Spain. Villele refused to commit his country to any timetable. Armed with this rebuff, Canning argued that not to recognize the new nations was tantamount to ensuring French ascendancy over the Spanish World. After much discussion most of the ministers capitulated. The king, however, remained adamant. Canning did not wait for the monarch's acceptance. He invited Michelena and Rocafuerte to a conference on the evening of December 30 and gave them the satisfaction of being the first to learn that England would recognize the new states. Shortly thereafter, the prime minister made similar announcements to the representatives of Gran Colombia and Argentina. The other American countries would have to consolidate their strength before being recognized.

It was, nevertheless, a major triumph and the Spanish Americans were extremely grateful to Canning. They had used various tactics, from trade enticements to threats of force, in their attempts to win recognition. Everything failed because European governments were dominated by conservatives who opposed American independence. Although most commercial interests in Europe favored recognition, they allowed the diplomats to overrule them because they were already benefiting from Spanish American trade and because they lacked the power to overcome the aristocrats who dominated European governments. Canning was one of the few statesmen who supported mercantile interests and who was determined to recognize the new nations. After mediating the dispute between Portugal and Brazil, he continued to press Spain to negotiate a settlement with her former colonies. But when Ferdinand refused all entreaties and when Canning realized that the Spanish Americans were determined to take desperate measures, he, too, acted boldly. He precipitated a government crisis in England by recognizing the American nations without waiting for the king's approval.

England's recognition ended all possibility of an attack by the Holy Alliance, but it did not ease diplomatic tension between Spanish America and Europe. Indeed, several years were to pass before France would take a similar step. However, British recognition made it easier for the new states to float loans and purchase the arms necessary to end the Spanish menace in America. Eighteen twenty-five promised to be a good year for the American republics.[44] Although Canning asked the Americans to keep their recognition a secret until he could announce it to the European powers, the information leaked out. The *Times* carried the story on January 4, 1825. "The Holy Alliance may protest," it declared, "but it will never be able to obstruct their path to prosperity, eminence, and honor."[45]

# VI

## THE POLITICS OF CREDIT

Although England's recognition was of paramount importance, the negotiation of foreign loans was also vital. The new governments were virtually bankrupt and needed money to function. Indeed, loans were negotiated even before the new countries were recognized.

1

Emperor Iturbide had commissioned Francisco Borja Migoni to contract a loan in England. After his fall in 1823, the Constituent Congress authorized a foreign loan of eight million pesos and the Supreme Executive Power sent Borja Migoni new credentials.[1] Shortly thereafter, Bartolomé Vigors Richards, the representative of the London commercial house of Barclay, Herring, Richardson and Company arrived in Mexico. The government took the opportunity to institute direct negotiations with Richards. On December 5, 1823, José Ignacio Esteva, the new minister of treasury, signed a contract for a loan of twenty million pesos. Mexico would issue bonds for that amount and Barclay would buy them at 70 percent of face value. The nation was liable for the entire sum and would pay 6 percent annual interest. However, before it could go into effect, the London office of Barclay would have to ratify and return the contract to Mexico by June 1824; otherwise the accord would be null and void.[2]

Meanwhile, in London Borja Migoni was also negotiating a loan for Mexico. Because he had complete authority to approve any agreement, the Mexican agent used his position for personal gain.

As a monarchist and former partisan of Iturbide, he was quite willing to exploit the new republican government. Instead of contacting the leading capitalists, such as Rothschild, Baring Brothers, or Barclay, who were eager to make the loan, he entered into a secret arrangement with B. A. Goldschmidt and Company. The firm agreed to act as agent for a group of London merchants headed by Borja Migoni. These men planned to purchase Mexico's bonds at a price considerably lower than face value. Once the merchants acquired the bonds, they would resell them at a large profit. To do this, they needed time to raise the capital. Accordingly, Borja Migoni stalled by informing Mexico that none of the great firms was willing to deal with an infant nation. He reassured the government, however, that the smaller but important banking house of Goldschmidt was interested. The negotiation, he said, had been delayed by news of the French invasion of Spain and the resulting fear that the Holy Alliance would take steps to reconquer Mexico. Borja Migoni promised to continue working to obtain the loan on favorable terms.[3]

While various members of the group gathered their funds, a new complication arose. Dr. Patrick Mackie, England's agent to Mexico, returned to London on November 15, 1823. Knowing that the Mexican government was eager to secure a loan, he contacted Borja Migoni and pledged to use his influence with the British government. Mackie, of course, expected to benefit from helping to secure the loan. Borja Migoni found himself in a quandary. His group was not yet prepared to make the loan and he could not deal with Mackie without endangering the enterprise. Again the Mexican decided to stall. Borja Migoni allowed Mackie to introduce him to several associates who agreed to finance the loan for Mexico. Fortunately for the merchant, Mackie's group did not have direct access to funds. During the following weeks they conducted a series of manipulations that afforded Borja Migoni the opportunity to break free from them by denouncing the group as adventurers. He charged that Mackie had abused his diplomatic post to take advantage of Mexico.[4]

After disentangling himself from Mackie, Borja Migoni returned to Goldschmidt to continue the secret arrangements. But Mackie and his friends could not be dismissed so easily. Feeling betrayed, they demanded a compensation of several hundred thousand pounds. Borja Migoni initially refused the demands although he eventually settled their claim with bonds worth thirty-nine thousand pounds, which he hid under administrative expenses in the Goldschmidt contract. Subsequently, Borja Migoni explained that he had authorized the gift in order to insure the goodwill of these influential men.[5] Mackie and his associates, however, were hardly capable of deciding the future of Mexico. The payoff was actually designed to protect the exorbitant profits that Borja Migoni and his friends intended to realize from the loan to Mexico.

Freed of Mackie and anxious to prevent any further threat to his enterprise, Borja Migoni entered into a verbal contract with Goldschmidt on January 12, 1824. Although the negotiations were secret, rumors that Mexico was going to float a loan had been circulating for some time. By January 20 the London *Times* was speculating that the details of the loan would be available soon because potential subscribers were eager for information. When no announcement was forthcoming either from Goldschmidt or from Borja Migoni, the *Times* started an investigation. It reported on January 27 that the bonds would soon be sold and that some buyers had received preferential scrip—they were Mackie and his associates. However, the newspaper could not provide the identities of these subscribers or the reason for their preferential treatment. In spite of general interest in the loan, and contrary to general practice, the bonds were sold in private to the few men who had been invited to participate. This maneuver forestalled the possibility of high bidding, which a public sale could have engendered. Borja Migoni's tactic was successful; when the bonds were later resold on the bourse, the original buyers realized a large profit.[6]

On February 9, Borja Migoni wrote the minister of treasury to announce the successful completion of the loan. He did not, of course, include information on the circumstances surrounding its negotiation and sale. Under the terms of the contract signed on February 7, 1824, Goldschmidt undertook to provide Mexico with £1,600,000 within fifteen months. The Mexican government agreed to issue bonds for £3,200,000 to mature in thirty years at 5 percent interest. The bonds were sold at a guaranteed price of 58 percent of face value. Mexico would receive 50 percent and the commercial house the remaining 8 percent as its commission for the sale of the bonds. Goldschmidt would also receive a 1½ percent commission on any funds that passed through its hands. In order to guarantee payment of the loan, the Mexican government agreed to mortgage one-third of its customs receipts beginning in April 1, 1825. The sum of £400,000 would be retained by Goldschmidt to pay interest and to establish an amortization fund. The commission on the interest, the cost of printing the bonds, and other administrative costs, which came to £62,768.6, would be deducted from Mexico's share. Finally, clause twelve of the contract prohibited Mexico from making another foreign loan for one year and required that one quarter of any subsequent loan be used to amortize the Goldschmidt transaction.

Borja Migoni assured the minister of the treasury that the loan had been negotiated with the best terms possible under the circumstances. He declared that the specter of the Holy Alliance had frightened investors who would otherwise have been interested in Mexican bonds. The agent acknowledged that Gran Colombia had received better terms, but maintained that the South American nation had obtained its loan when the market was more favorable to Spanish America. Indeed, Borja Migoni boasted that the loan he had negotiated carried the lowest interest rate that any nation had received in the London market. He believed that a 50 percent discount was justified because other countries had been forced to accept even less favorable terms. Finally, to demonstrate his selfless dedication, Borja Migoni indicated that he would refuse the commission customarily granted the person who negotiated a government loan.[7]

Borja Migoni's assertions were false. He sold Mexican bonds to his coterie of speculators at 58 percent. They, in turn, later resold the same issue at 84 percent, thus making a 45 percent profit. The speculators had known from the beginning that their profits would be great because there was an intense demand for Spanish American bonds in the London money market. Indeed, at the time of the original sale, the securities of Peru, Chile, Argentina, and Gran Colombia were selling in the London bourse at 80, 82, 85, and 88 percent respectively.

Borja Migoni lied when he declared that the influence of the Holy Alliance had depressed the bond market. Although there had been a decline in the value of Spanish American securities in April 1823, when French troops entered Spain, prices returned to normal as soon as it became evident that England would not permit European intervention in American affairs. Furthermore, since Borja Migoni kept the first sale of the Mexican issue at an artificially low price, he was forced to borrow sixteen million pesos—twice the amount authorized by Congress—in order to produce the requisite sum of eight million pesos.

The Mexican merchant, who had lived in London many years and had secretly become a British citizen, was supremely confident of his ability to deceive his former countrymen. His audacity is underscored by the fact that, during the same period, Gran Colombia obtained a loan at 86 percent from Goldschmidt. The South American country had not negotiated, as Borja Migoni maintained, at a time when the market was more favorable. Rather the difference in the terms of the two loans can be explained only if one assumes that the Gran Colombian agent had his country's interest in mind while Borja Migoni did not. Indeed, as table 1 demonstrates, the Mexican contracted the most onerous loan negotiated by any Latin American nation during the years preceding the great economic dislocation of 1826.[8]

2

The Goldschmidt contract produced other difficulties as well. Mexico had initiated negotiations with Barclay on the understanding that the money would be used to purchase ships and arms. But as soon as Borja Migoni made a verbal agreement with Goldschmidt, that commercial house took steps to prevent the Barclay loan. Three weeks before the signing of the official agreement, and acting without authority, Goldschmidt informed Barclay that Mexico could not negotiate a new loan until February 7, 1825. The admonition arrived after Barclay had advanced funds to Mexico and begun to purchase the war matériel urgently requested by the Mexican minister of war. Barclay suspended all acquisitions until some clarification was received. When no news was forthcoming by the end of March, David Barclay and Charles Herring demanded that Borja Migoni modify the restrictive clause of the Goldschmidt contract or reimburse their firm for sums advanced to

Mexico and employed to purchase equipment. The Mexican agent refused to discuss the matter, claiming that he could not act without instructions from his government.[9]

Table 1

British Loans to Latin America

| Country | Amount in £ | Sale Price (%) | Price in Bourse (%) | Year |
|---|---|---|---|---|
| Chile | 1,000,000 | 68 | 70 | 1822 |
| Gran Colombia | 2,000,000 | 82 | 84 | 1822 |
| Peru | 450,000 | 86 | 88 | 1822 |
| Brazil | 1,686,000 | 73 | 75 | 1824 |
| Argentina | 1,000,000 | 83 | 85 | 1824 |
| Gran Colombia | 4,750,000 | 86½ | 88½ | 1824 |
| Mexico (Goldschmidt) | 3,200,000 | 58 | 84 | 1824 |
| Peru | 750,000 | 80 | 82 | 1824 |
| Brazil | 4,000,000 | 83 | 85 | 1825 |
| Guatemala | 167,000 | 70 | 73 | 1825 |
| Mexico (Barclay) | 3,200,000 | 86¾ | 89¾ | 1825 |
| Peru | 616,000 | 76 | 78 | 1825 |

**Source:** Andreas Andreades, *History of the Bank of England* (New York, 1966), 249-250; Corporation of Foreign Bondholders, *Sixty-fourth Annual Report* (London, 1937), passim.

In an effort to resolve the impasse, Barclay dispatched two agents, William Marshall and Robert Manning, to Mexico with instructions to obtain an extension for the ratification of the contract negotiated by Richards. This, the firm hoped, would provide the time necessary to modify the Goldschmidt clause. In April, while the British agents were still en route to Mexico, Barclay received a new order from the minister of war to purchase arms.

Although the company informed the Mexican government that as long as the Goldschmidt clause remained in effect, all previous agreements were null and void, Barclay began to make arrangements to purchase two forty-four gun frigates for the American nation. When the Barclay Company learned that Mexico was sending a minister plenipotentiary to Great Britain, it hastened to express its "infinite satisfaction" and the hope that the envoy would be authorized to resolve the firm's dilemma.[10]

### 3

One of the purposes of the Michelena mission was to procure large quantities of arms and ships to seize the fortress of San Juan de Ulúa. Immediately after the plenipotentiary left Mexico, the minister of war began sending Michelena specifications for vessels. Since time was a crucial factor, the minister authorized the envoy to purchase the best available ships; even converted merchantmen would be acceptable. If difficulties arose in arming them in England, Michelena could send the ships to Philadelphia where the Mexican minister to the United States would finish outfitting them.[11]

Immediately upon his arrival in London, Michelena dispatched agents to search for weapons: Gorostiza and Murphy were to scour the Low Countries and France, while Michelena and Rocafuerte concentrated their efforts in England. The Mexican minister assumed that he could purchase the armament with the six million pesos on hand from the Goldschmidt loan. Despite Michelena's threats and exhortations, Borja Migoni, first as financial agent and later as consul general, refused to appropriate any money without specific instructions from the minister of treasury. The Mexican diplomat became so incensed that on August 1, 1824, he asked the Supreme Executive Power to resolve the matter immediately.[12]

In the interim, the search for arms and ships continued. Murphy reported that Parisian contacts assured him that England was the best source of armaments because British prices were momentarily low. He suggested that Barclay might agree to guarantee the cost of the weapons until Mexico resolved the loan question.[13] Gorostiza made his first arms inquiries in Antwerp where he learned that a Dutch ship had sailed for Mexico with fifty boxes of rifles. The Dutch commercial house of Ruess and Kirckhoff had established itself in the new nation, offering armaments to the government as its first product for sale. Gorostiza also stated that while there were no warships, numerous merchantmen were available which could be refitted for war. He indicated that these ships could be manned by recruiting sailors from various countries in Dutch ports. He particularly recommended Scandinavians because they were good sailors, considered dependable, and not likely to desert in time of war. Best of all, they would work for lower wages than English sailors. Finally, the Mexican agent informed Michelena that while Belgian arms were excellent, they were costly; instead, he recommended the less expensive British equipment.[14]

In London Michelena and Rocafuerte made repeated efforts to obtain resources to procure arms. Initially, the Barclay Company was willing to cooperate because it had already invested large sums and expected Mexico to correct the misunderstanding by quickly granting them a new contract. The firm agreed to provide and forward to Mexico two corvettes, a brig, and some small arms. Michelena also wanted to purchase three frigates, two with forty-four guns and one with thirty-two. But Barclay was unwilling to advance additional funds.[15]

In September Michelena once again attempted to convince Barclay to guarantee the acquisition of additional ships, implying that a grateful Mexican government would be likely to offer the company favorable concessions in the future. However, Barclay reminded the minister that the firm had already advanced Mexico more than three-quarters of a million pesos and that without a contract to protect its outlay, the commercial house could not continue to grant funds.[16]

In spite of the rebuff, Michelena, spurred by the fear of a Spanish invasion of Mexico, persisted in his efforts to acquire vessels on credit. The minister found himself in a humiliating position. Everyone knew he could not touch the six million pesos available to cover Mexican expenses because Borja Migoni, his diplomatic inferior, would not permit it. In August and September, Michelena located acceptable ships but lost the opportunity to buy them because he could not make the down payment. On both occasions, Borja Migoni absented himself from England in order not to accede to the minister's wishes.[17]

Then late in September, Michelena learned that a merchantman, the *Arvens Prindsen*, was for sale at a low price. Determined not to lose this opportunity, the Mexican minister convinced Barclay to lend him £3,800 at 10 percent interest to meet the down payment. The commercial house also agreed to cover the cost of converting the vessel for war. Since the Mexican government had no legal status in England at that time, Barclay purchased the ship in the name of Tomás Murphy, Jr., then attached to the legation in London. The shipyard of Carling, Young, and Company was chosen to convert the merchantman, but their naval engineers maintained that the vessel, now renamed the *Libertad*, could not support the heavy guns Mexico desired. Impartial experts were consulted, but they disagreed among themselves. Michelena became impatient and considered sending the ship to Philadelphia for repairs. However, after learning in December that the Mexican government had authorized a new contract with Barclay, he decided to have the work completed in England.[18]

4

The decision of the Mexican government to renegotiate the contract with Barclay did not mean that it was disenchanted with Borja Migoni. The government upheld the consul's right to disburse funds from the Goldschmidt loan. While Michelena was authorized to arrange a second loan, the terms of the agreement had to comply with the limitations established by the Goldschmidt contract. One-fourth of the amount derived from the new transaction was to amortize the earlier loan. Moreover, the Barclay contract could not go into effect until February 7, 1825. While Michelena would have authority to disburse the funds derived from the second loan, he still was not permitted to use the Goldschmidt funds.[19]

Michelena and Rocafuerte immediately negotiated a new contract with Barclay. Mexico agreed to issue thirty-year bonds for £3,200,000 at 6 percent interest; Barclay would receive 6 percent commission for the sale, and Mexico would guarantee the loan by mortgaging one-third of her maritime customs receipts. Michelena further stipulated that the bonds could not be sold below 85 percent of face value. During these negotiations Barclay indicated that the firm wanted to become Mexico's sole financial agent in London. Rocafuerte opposed the request because it would give the house excessive power and influence. Michelena agreed, but when the firm insisted, he referred the matter to his government. Although Michelena advised against granting such authority, Mexico approved Barclay's request as a reward for assistance rendered the nation and because the firm's agents in Mexico lobbied strongly for it.[20]

Table 2

Goldschmidt and Barclay Loans Compared
in Mexican Pesos

|  | **Goldschmidt** | **Barclay** |
|---|---|---|
| AMOUNT | 16,000,000 | 16,000,000 |
| Interest (%) | 5 | 6 |
| Commission (%) | 8 | 6 |
| Sale value (%) | 58 | 86¾ |
| Net amount after commission | 8,000,000 | 13,048,000 |
| Administrative costs | 313,843 | 33,902 |
| Amount received by Mexico after all costs were deducted | 5,686,157 | 11,333,298 |

Note: The pound sterling was worth five Mexican silver pesos at this time.

On Monday, February 7, 1825, Barclay sold Mexico's bonds. The company announced that the Mexican minister had established a minimum sale price, but did not divulge the amount. Within a short time the entire issue was purchased by B. A. Goldschmidt, who made the highest bid of 86.75 percent. The sale yielded £2,999,900. The Barclay Company received £166,560 of this sum as commission and £336,000 for a mortgage fund. The cost of printing the bonds and other administrative costs amounted to

£6,780 10s. Three days later Goldschmidt resold the bonds on the bourse at 89.75 percent of the face value. The *Times* declared that there had been enough subscribers to float a £40,000,000 loan, indicating "how rapidly [the credit of] this fine country is rising in public estimation."[21] Indeed, as table 1 demonstrates, the bonds from Mexico's second loan sold at the highest price of any Latin American securities on the London bourse. This is in stark contrast to the loan negotiated by Borja Migoni, which was sold to a few cronies at an artificially low price and later resold at the much higher prices normal on the bourse. Table 2 compares the Gold-schmidt and Barclay loans.

5

As soon as arrangements for the Barclay loan were completed, Michelena again turned his attention to securing armaments for Mexico. Barclay filled most of the orders while the Mexicans inspected the quality of the equipment. Michelena also negotiated the purchase of one eighty-four gun ship of the line and four forty-four gun frigates from Sweden.[22] His preoccupation with the Spanish threat also led the Mexican minister to investigate rumors that a strange ship was being built in a yard on the banks of the Thames. He learned that the proprietor of the Battersea Iron Works, Thomas Johnson, a disciple of the famous Robert Fulton, was perfecting an undersea craft. Johnson persuaded Michelena that his submarine would be able to isolate the fortress of San Juan de Ulúa. The vessel would carry thirty-two guns and some new devices called torpedos which, Johnson assured the Mexican, would travel underwater to destroy the enemy. Thrilled by the possibilities, Michelena ordered the inventor to construct such a ship for Mexico, advanced Johnson £10,000, and instructed him to name the ship the *Guerrero*. The minister hoped to take this marvelous vessel to Mexico as soon as the armament purchases were completed; various difficulties, however, delayed construction and he was forced to depart without it. He instructed Rocafuerte to forward the vessel as soon as possible.[23]

Michelena decided to return home because he was convinced

that his enemies were undermining his role as Mexico's envoy to England and supporting the candidacy of Borja Migoni. The diplomat hoped to convince the government that the merchant was not to be trusted. On February 6, 1825, the day before the Barclay loan was made public, Michelena informed Murphy that he would return home in a month. When Murphy realized that the minister could not be dissuaded, the agent advised him to have Rocafuerte appointed chargé d'affaires.[24] Gorostiza concurred. As a result of Michelena's recommendation, the Mexican government granted the post to Rocafuerte and empowered him to negotiate with all European nations.[25]

Michelena's plans to return with the Swedish ships collapsed because Russia would not permit Mexico to take possession of the vessels. Michelena departed in July 1825, leaving Rocafuerte to resolve the problem. The chargé also had to placate the Admiralty because the Mexican minister had recruited officers and men from the British navy to serve in the newly formed Mexican navy.[26] Michelena took the new Mexican squadron to Philadelphia where further repairs were made and more armament acquired. Then the flotilla sailed to Mexico where it encountered and dispersed a smaller Spanish fleet. Thereafter, the Mexican ships besieged the fortress of San Juan de Ulúa, which soon surrendered.

Following Michelena's departure, Rocafuerte attempted to expedite the acquisition of the Swedish ships. Stockholm's minister in London assured him that the vessels were being readied but would not arrive for a few months. Fearing that the Russian and Spanish ministers in Sweden were conspiring to stop the delivery of the warships, Rocafuerte proposed that if Sweden surrendered the vessels immediately, Mexico would complete repairs at her own expense in the United States. But Russia was determined to prevent delivery and resorted to a show of force when the Swedish government insisted on honoring its contract with Mexico. On October 31, news arrived that two Russian warships were stationed in the Baltic with orders to seize the vessels in the name of the king of Spain if they attempted to sail from Swedish ports. Not wishing to challenge Russia, the Swedish government canceled the contract and returned the £62,000 advance through a bank in Hamburg. Mexico was reimbursed for the costs incurred in the negotiations. Rocafuerte then recommended that new ships be purchased in the

United States. North American vessels were not only as good as British ships, he declared, but were also less expensive.[27]

6

Rocafuerte had ample cause to worry about finances. Unlike his predecessor, he did not have the power to administer the funds deposited with Barclay and he feared the growing instability of the English money market. Liberal policies were allowing credit to expand rapidly and British investors, enthusiastic about the future of Spanish America, seemed willing to finance any enterprise, from silver mining in Mexico to pearl hunting in Venezuela.[28] Since continental money markets were also gripped by speculative fever, Rocafuerte feared that the entire monetary structure of Europe might collapse. Barclay added to the chargé's fears by convincing Minister of Treasury Esteva to communicate directly with the firm or with its agents in Mexico, Manning and Marshall, thus keeping the diplomatic envoy in England uninformed. Angered by this action and disturbed because his warnings went unheeded, Rocafuerte criticized the minister of treasury in an unsigned article in the Spanish emigré newspaper, *Ocios de los españoles emigrados.* Consequently, relations between Esteva and Rocafuerte became acrimonious. Thereafter, the minister of treasury believed Borja Migoni's reassuring reports and failed to heed Rocafuerte's warnings.[29] As will be seen, these enmities, in conjunction with political divisions in the government, weakened Mexico's foreign policy. (Mexico's internal politics are treated in more detail in chapter VII.)

Powerless, Rocafuerte watched as Barclay and Company speculated with Mexico's money. The chargé believed that the only way to protect his country's capital was to remove it from Barclay's hands. Thus, on August 2, 1825, when he received instructions from Esteva directing the Barclay Company to pay interest on the funds deposited with them, Rocafuerte instead suggested to the firm that the money either be deposited in the Bank of England or invested in Bills of Exchequer. The chargé d'affaires hoped to protect his government's funds by placing them in safe institutions guaranteed by the British government and simultaneously to earn the interest desired by the minister of finance. Barclay refused to consider Rocafuerte's recommendations, since they would have reduced the firm's working capital and diminished its activity in the market. The chargé warned his government repeatedly that he was unable to restrain Barclay and insisted that Mexico's funds be deposited in the Bank of England. Despite his warnings, Esteva failed to act.[30]

The financial situation worsened in the succeeding months. Goldschmidt was the first major commercial house to fail. Rocafuerte informed his government on February 15, 1826, that the firm was in serious difficulties and had suspended payments. He noted that despite the critical circumstances the directors of Goldschmidt had acted with "great delicacy" and had not demanded the £50,000 from the Barclay loan destined to amortize part of Mexico's 1824 loan.[31]

The Goldschmidt disaster did not substantially affect the funds belonging to Mexico, since only £4,000 still in the firm's hands were lost. However, some of the bondholders of the 1824 loan had not collected their dividends for January, and with Goldschmidt bankrupt, they would not be paid. Rocafuerte arranged with Barclay to indemnify them with funds from the 1825 loan, thereby retaining the public's confidence in Mexico and momentarily halting the decline of the bonds from the Goldschmidt loan at 60 percent.

The situation also benefited Mexico. Rocafuerte used the £50,000 from Barclay, which had originally been earmarked to amortize the 1824 loan to buy the depressed Goldschmidt bonds. Since repayment at maturity or through Goldschmidt would have been at face value, Mexico not only retrieved part of the first bond issue but she also saved 35 to 40 percent. The large purchase also triggered a rally, driving the value of Mexican bonds to 70 percent. Considering the depressed state of the market, the rise was spectacular, renewing confidence in Mexico.[32]

Gran Colombia and Peru were not so fortunate. Both lost large sums when Goldschmidt failed. Creditors demanded payment for millions of pounds outstanding in Peruvian or Gran Colombian drafts on Goldschmidt accounts. The two nations also had to deal with nervous bondholders. If Gran Colombia or Peru did not meet their dividend payments, confidence would decline. Since Spanish

Americanists had fostered the belief that the new states were closely allied, the failure of one would reflect on the credit of the others. Action by Gran Colombia was particularly crucial because she and Mexico were then considered the most important Spanish American nations.[33]

In desperation, Gran Colombia's minister, Manuel José Hurtado, implored Rocafuerte to help the South American country meet its April dividends. Hurtado assured him that Gran Colombia would remit funds to cover her obligations, but they could not possibly arrive in time. The Mexican diplomat agreed with Hurtado that the "American system" (Spanish Americanism) required that the American nations help each other maintain their credit. Barclay concurred and advanced the funds. On April 6, 1826, Rocafuerte and Hurtado signed an agreement that advanced Gran Colombia an interest-free loan of £63,000, payable in eighteen months.[34]

While the loan permitted Gran Colombia to meet her April dividends, other means had to be found to make the remaining quarterly payments. Initially, Bogotá hoped that Peru would repay part of her wartime debt to Gran Colombia. However, Peru had also suffered losses and could not service her own bonds, let alone repay a sister nation. Hoping to resolve the crisis, Peru and Chile also requested assistance from Mexico. Rocafuerte turned them down because he did not believe those countries capable of repaying such loans punctually and because he had already overstepped his authority in making the loan to Gran Colombia. Chile managed to cover her dividends, but Peru did not.[35]

When the public learned that Peru would not meet her obligations, the price of Spanish American securities declined; even Mexico's bonds fell to 60 percent. Realizing the gravity of the situation, Rocafuerte, Hurtado, and the minister from Argentina, Manuel de Sarratea, suggested that Peru float a loan with the Paris branch of the House of Rothschild. The minister of Peru, the Ecuadorean, José Joaquín de Olmedo, refused, believing that this was a stopgap measure that would only give his government a temporary respite from its financial difficulties while substantially increasing its indebtedness. He regretted that by not acting he was undermining his cousin Rocafuerte's efforts to protect American credit, but he believed the attempt to be foredoomed. When it became known that Peru would not service her debts, English public opinion turned violently against the Spanish American states. Canning was savagely criticized for recognizing the new countries and for signing commercial treaties with Gran Colombia and Argentina. The public outcry threatened the pending commercial treaty with Mexico.[36]

The Spanish American nations were the victims of a European economic dislocation. Unemployment was increasing and, along with it, discontent. The British government had already used the army to quell riots in industrial centers.[37] The economic crisis frightened investors who hastened to dispose of their Spanish American interests. Consequently, as capital evaporated, many foreign, and particularly British, enterprised in America failed. As it became increasingly difficult for the new nations to try to service their foreign debts, the price of their securities declined drastically. In June, Hurtado, in a final desperate effort to secure money, demanded that Peru negotiate a special loan to repay one-and-a-half-million pesos owed to Gran Colombia. Since the best terms offered for Peru's bonds were 30 percent, Olmedo naturally refused. As a consequence, Gran Colombia's bonds fell to 34 percent, to the anger and anguish of Hurtado.[38] The financial crisis not only deprived the Spanish American nations of much needed capital and injured their international credit, but it also began to rupture their sense of solidarity.

Mexico's situation was better than most of the other republics. The government dispatched a half-million pesos to cover its debt. The arrival of these funds temporarily restored English confidence. As the *Times* expressed it, "Mexican bonds were rather in more demand."[39] However many bondholders knew that the market was shaky and that the Barclay Company itself might fail. Thus, in spite of Mexico's positive action, the decline of her securities resumed.

English creditors had ample reason for fear because, in spite of Rocafuerte's repeated warnings, the Mexican government was doing nothing to protect its funds. Quite the contrary, Minister of Treasury Esteva attempted to quiet the chargé's fears by estolling the "moral security" afforded by Barclay.[40] Sadly, this assurance proved unwarranted. Barclay, Herring, Richardson and Company failed in August. The bankruptcy left Mexico penniless. Earlier she had attempted to save Gran Colombia; there was no one to help Mexico. Public reaction was predictable. The *Times* reported on August 10 that rumors concerning the declining credit of Mexico and Gran Colombia had produced panic in the bond market.[41]

Even before the bankruptcy, Rocafuerte had contacted the influential Alexander Baring requesting that he become Mexico's financial agent in England. The failure of Barclay only strengthened Rocafuerte's resolve to transfer his government's agency to Baring Brothers. He argued that Mexico could meet her obligations but required time. In return for paying the September dividends, Baring Brothers could become Mexico's sole agent. Since the country was wealthy, with a bright economic future, Baring would benefit from the association. Furthermore, Rocafuerte assured the firm that Mexico was determined to protect her credit and as proof supplied copies of ministry of treasury directives instructing custom's officials to retain one-half of all receipts to pay the foreign debt. When Baring agreed to consider the matter, Rocafuerte convinced Barclay to relinquish its contract as Mexico's financial agent. Then, on September 13, Baring Brothers agreed to handle Mexico's financial affairs in Europe. The firm would pay the dividends as well as the salaries and expenses of the country's diplomats. The advances would earn 5 percent interest and were to be repaid as soon as possible. Baring also dispatched an agent to Mexico to ratify the provisional agreement and to negotiate a formal contract.[42]

Rumors of the pending agreement stabilized the market for Mexican securities. Rocafuerte announced on the fifteenth that Baring Brothers would pay Mexico's dividends for September. The press reacted favorably; it believed that Baring would not have agreed to represent Mexico without making certain that future dividends would be paid. Mexican bonds responded to the good news, climbing in value to 66 percent at a time when "the English market was [otherwise] totally deserted."[43] The following month, Minister Plenipotentiary Sebastián Camacho arrived with funds to cover the January dividends and to repay part of Baring's advances. As a result, Mexican securities advanced still higher, to 69 percent, while the bonds of other Spanish American nations remained below 30 percent.[44]

7

Such confidence seemed entirely justified late in 1826. The United States of Mexico was the largest nation in the Western Hemisphere, her resources were immense, her future unlimited. After a false start under an empire, the country had established a federal republic, which was prospering under the leadership of her first president, Guadalupe Victoria. The Mexican government, more than any other, appeared determined to maintain the nation's credit. Her chargé d'affaires in London had been the most resourceful of Spanish American diplomats in protecting that credit. Unfortunately, developments in Mexico were soon to destroy these expectations.

Guadalupe Victoria was a weak leader who had attempted to create harmony by forming a cabinet composed of men with widely differing views. The minister of interior and foreign affairs, Lucas Alamán, was a conservative; the minister of war and marine, Manuel Gómez Pedraza, a moderate; the minister of justice and ecclesiastic affairs, Miguel Ramos Arizpe, a liberal; and the minister of treasury, José Ignacio Esteva, a radical. These labels, of course, did not represent either pronounced ideologies or parties, but they did indicate potential divisiveness. Because of Victoria's indecision and the unresolved conflict between congressional sovereignty and executive authority, the most active ministers struggled for power and leadership. In late 1825 the liberals ousted Alamán. By the end of the following year the radicals, led by Esteva, seemed to be winning control of the executive branch.[45]

The growing power of the radicals frightened the conservatives and led Vice-President Nicolás Bravo to revolt against the government in 1827. Although the administration quelled this and other insurrections, the civil wars consumed revenues that could have liquidated Mexico's foreign debt. During these years the country also suffered from a contraction of European investment, as well as a decline in agricultural production because of droughts and the epidemic of 1827. Consequently, decreasing revenues could not cover the increasing demands made on the treasury. In such circumstances the Mexican government was soon unable to meet its foreign obligations.[46]

The North American nation managed to maintain dividend payments through April 1827. The October dividends, however, could not be met. The other American nations had not paid for nearly a year; now Mexico, the largest, wealthiest, and most stable of Spanish American states, seemed destined to repeat the pattern. Although Gran Colombia's new minister, José Fernández de Madrid, reported to his government that Mexico's failure to meet its October payment had harmed all the new nations, public reaction against Mexico was mild at first.[47] When Rocafuerte announced that money was en route, many bondholders hoped that payment was merely being delayed once more. When they finally realized that Mexico was not going to meet her obligations, the creditors reacted with fury, accusing the federal republic of fraud, deception, and treachery.[48] The *Morning Herald* charged, in a particularly vicious attack, that Mexico and her chargé d'affaires were lying and had prostituted their honor. Rocafuerte sued for libel, but lost because the court found that one could reasonably deduce that the Mexican government had not told the truth, since it had failed to implement official assurances.[49]

As a consequence of the public outcry, Parliament named a commission to investigate the Spanish American debt. Sir Robert Wilson, a friend of the new nations and a member of the commission, informed Rocafuerte that if the dividends could be paid, the entire question would lapse. If, one the other hand, payment were not forthcoming, relations between Great Britain and the new countries would deteriorate. The Spanish Americans were in a particularly vulnerable position because George Canning, their great friend and protector, had just died and been succeeded by the Duke of Wellington, the old enemy of Hispanic liberalism.[50]

Rocafuerte informed the government of the gravity of the situation and exhorted the president to act. Newspapers in Mexico also became concerned. *El Amigo del Pueblo* warned that action had to be taken because "a nation's credit, like virginity, can only be lost once."[51] Unable to raise funds at home, the Mexican government turned to Gran Colombia, hoping she could repay her £63,000 debt. The South American nation, plagued by even more severe financial problems than her northern neighbor, instructed Fernández de Madrid to tender Mexico the frigates *Cundinamarca* and *Colombia*—constructed in the United States and sister ships of the famous *Constitution*—as payment. Since the value of these ships exceeded the amount owed, Rocafuerte advised his government to accept the offer. Although the ministry of foreign affairs supported the chargé, the minister of treasury refused, claiming that Mexico needed money, not ships, to satisfy her obligations, and instructed Consul General Borja Migoni to press claims against Gran Colombia. Rocafuerte resented this act because he believed the matter should be resolved through diplomatic rather than consular channels. An acrimonious correspondence developed, which degenerated into a personal dispute. Consequently, the Gran Colombian debt to Mexico remained unresolved for many years.[52]

When it became apparent that Mexico could not pay her dividends in 1828, President Victoria authorized the recapitalization of the nation's foreign debt. However, Baring Brothers argued that it was futile to exchange new bonds for old, unless the government could give assurance that it would service the debt; the promised allocation of customs revenues, all too often diverted to other uses in cases of emergency, would not suffice to restore credit. Mexico had already broken too many promises; it would be wiser to make no new ones. Until substantial changes could be implemented in the tax structure, Alexander Baring suggested that things be allowed to remain as they were.[53]

Like the other nations of Spanish America, Mexico had begun with great hopes and aspirations. She shared with her sister republics the belief that Spanish America possessed great natural wealth that could be easily developed by foreign capital. Unfortunately, this was not true. The struggles for independence had substantially damaged their economies, while burdening the new nations with a vast foreign debt. Even when the armed struggle ended in 1825, they had been forced to maintain expensive armies and navies lest Spain attack them. This danger was largely illusory, since Spain's only act of war was a feeble and almost farcical invasion of Mexico. Yet the cost of defense was real and very large, in some cases devouring nearly eighty percent of the national budget. The European crisis further harmed the Spanish American nations; the economic dislocation only served to aggravate internal political tensions.

The external and internal crises strengthened nationalism,

which grew stronger in opposition to Spanish Americanism. Much of the friction among the new states resulted from their inability to repay loans to one another. Hounded by European creditors whom they could not pay, the Spanish American nations resented the failure of sister republics to repay their debts.

# VII

## THE ENGLISH TREATY

Once recognition was assured, the Spanish Americanists sought to strengthen their countries' position by negotiating treaties of friendship, commerce, and navigation with England. Talks between Mexico and Great Britain began in January 1825. Michelena and Rocafuerte hoped to use the negotiations as a vehicle for helping other Spanish American nations. They believed that their country was an important market for English manufacturers and a significant source of raw materials. Therefore, they attempted to tie treaty discussion with suggestions that England recognize other Spanish American nations, particularly Guatemala. They also hoped to obtain England's approval for Mexican liberation of Cuba and the possible annexation of the island.[1]

The English government took a different position. Canning preferred to have Spain retain control of the island so that Great Britain could continue to trade freely there. Cuban independence or union with another American nation might lead to a restriction of British trade. Furthermore, England viewed the negotiation of a treaty merely as a way of regulating existing commercial relations. Indeed, the British government wanted to establish restrictions on Mexican shipping. Canning also wished to use the treaty negotiations as a way of preventing Michelena, whom he considered too involved in Spanish politics, from officially assuming the post of minister to England.[2] Instead, the Englishman preferred that Mexico appoint a chargé d'affaires who could be raised to the rank of minister after the treaty was ratified. In this way England would retain the diplomatic advantage, since the post of chargé had both temporary and inferior status.

1

As a consequence of these differences and to facilitate talks, Michelena and Canning agreed that the treaty would be negotiated in Mexico, using the 1823 accord between Mexico and Gran Colombia as a working draft. Although Michelena believed that negotiations would begin automatically, Canning instructed England's plenipotentiaries in Mexico, James Mornier and Henry G. Ward, to enter into conversations only if that federal republic remained orderly and peaceful. Moreover, he insisted that the accord must include absolute assurance that British subjects would be permitted to exercise their religion. This matter was so important that he repeated the instruction in another letter, also suggesting that they seek an additional article permitting religious services in private homes or in places designated for that purpose. Aware that such demands would meet with public opposition, he suggested that if it were not possible to include such a clause openly, it should be done secretly. Canning also expected to encounter some difficulty with tariffs and fees as well as with the definition of the nationality of a ship. England wanted strict reciprocity and she would recognize as Mexican only those ships purchased by Mexico in England and owned and manned by Mexicans. Those who hoped to build a strong Mexican merchant marine wanted a much looser definition of a Mexican ship, as well as preferential tariffs and fees for Mexican bottoms. Canning understood the aspiration, but regarded it as illusory. Although it was England's principle not to grant any concessions, he authorized the negotiation of an additional article loosening the definition of a Mexican ship for a five-year period.[3]

Michelena and Rocafuerte visited Canning on May 21, 1825, to discuss the pending treaty. The Mexican envoy wished to ascertain the status of the negotiations before returning to Mexico. When he realized that England's narrow definition of a ship's nationality would be detrimental to Mexico, Michelena requested a revision.[4] The British Board of Trade considered the matter, ruling that for the purpose of paying duties in English ports, vessels built in England, purchased by Mexicans, and flying Mexican colors would be recognized as Mexican. Ships constructed in any of the Spanish American States, including Mexico, would be considered Spanish, regardless of their flag, until Spain recognized the independence of those nations. Vessels constructed elsewhere, purchased by Mexicans and flying Mexico's standard, would be classified as having no nationality.[5] Michelena was so astonished by the absurdity of these distinctions that he considered severing relations. He sent a sharp protest declaring that Mexico would never compromise her sovereignty by accepting such an offensive definition of her shipping. If England desired to maintain friendly relations with his country, she would have to alter her position radically. Shortly thereafter he returned to Mexico, leaving Rocafuerte in charge.[6]

Unaware of the difficulties in England, the negotiators had reached an agreement in Mexico. At the republic's insistence, the accord included a declaration of British recognition. The question of the carrying trade was settled in England's favor; British and Mexican ships were to pay no fees at each other's ports. Mexico, however, received a concession on the nationality of her vessels. For a period of ten years, a Mexican ship would be defined as one built, owned, and captained either by native-born or naturalized Mexicans, and manned by a crew three-fourths of whom were in government service. Although the treaty guaranteed British citizens freedom to exercise their religion, the constitutionality of the measure was in doubt. Moreover, since Minister of Foreign Affairs Alamán opposed this provision, congressional approval was unlikely. At England's insistence, Mexico granted Spain, as well as other Spanish American nations, special trading privileges for a decade. Thereafter Britain would receive most-favored-nation status. The agreement was concluded on April 6, 1825, and provided for ratification by England within four months.[7] James Mornier returned to London with the treaty, while Henry G. Ward remained in Mexico as Great Britain's chargé d'affaires.

The English government found the accord unacceptable. The Foreign Office was principally concerned with the loose definition of a Mexican ship. Because Canning was ill, Under Secretary of Foreign Affairs Planta and President of the Board of Trade William Huskisson met with Rocafuerte on July 27, 1825. Huskisson argued that in its present form the treaty would allow virtually any vessel to fly the Mexican flag. This would be particularly harmful to England in time of war because enemy shipping could easily acquire neutral status by flying Mexican colors. He insisted, therefore, that the treaty be modified. Rocafuerte refused. Although he was empowered to negotiate additional articles, Alamán had instructed him not to yield on the matter of a vessel's nationality.[8] The Mexican chargé recognized the validity of England's position but he preferred to return the treaty to Mexico to have the question settled there. Furthermore, he believed that Mexico would gain prestige by requiring Great Britain to send her emissaries back to America. Convinced that the English government desired the treaty, he requested that Mornier return to Mexico with new instructions. Canning agreed.[9]

The British government was further disturbed when news arrived that the unfinished treaty had been published in Mexico. Rocafuerte sought to placate Canning by explaining that Mexico's free and representative institutions made it difficult to keep diplomacy a secret. He assured the English minister that the Mexican government had not authorized publication of the tentative accord. Although the explanation did not satisfy Canning, the English government decided to ignore the matter because Mornier and Ward were well disposed toward Mexico and had sent excellent reports about the country.[10] As a result, Rocafuerte gained confidence that relations between the two nations would continue to improve; he suggested to his government that the amended treaty be returned by some outstanding citizen, like General Manuel Mier y Terán, who could assume the role of minister plenipotentiary as soon as the ratifications were exchanged.[11]

In Mexico, Ward was impatiently awaiting instructions from England. When no word arrived by December 1825, he asked the new minister of foreign relations, Sebastián Camacho, to grant his country more time to ratify the treaty. Shortly thereafter, Mornier arrived and the two men requested that Mexico name plenipotentiaries to renegotiate several articles. President Guadalupe Victoria appointed Camacho and Minister of Treasury Esteva. The talks concerned three issues—religious toleration, trade reciprocity, and the definition of a Mexican ship. Government advisors had already warned Victoria that since the constitution recognized Catholicism as the religion of the nation, he could not allow the English to practice other faiths freely. Furthermore, constitutional amendments could not be enacted because the 1824 charter stipulated that no changes could be considered for a six-year period. After explaining the constitutional limitation to the British envoys, President Victoria assured them that the Mexican government would reform the constitution to allow religions freedom as soon as it became possible to do so. He implied that the recent dismissal of Lucas Alamán, a leading opponent of religious toleration, was proof of his administration's desire to reach an understanding with England. Satisfied that Victoria was sincere, Mornier and Ward recommended to their government that it postpone the question to a more propitious time.

The remaining issues proved more difficult to resolve. Since immediate reciprocity would benefit only England, Mexico demanded a period of preferential treatment in order to develop her economy. The Victoria administration was also adamant on the question of a vessel's nationality. Mexico possessed only a few ships and sailors; she was forced to purchase vessels abroad and to hire foreigners to man them. If she acceded to the British requirement that three-quarters of the crew be Mexican nationals, the country would be unable to develop a merchant marine. Although the English plenipotentiaries sympathized with Mexico's plight, they could not change Great Britain's policy. Regretfully, they terminated negotiations.[12]

2

President Victoria, however, refused to allow the matter to lapse. He informed Ward and Mornier that he would appoint Sebastián Camacho plenipotentiary to England so that the treaty could be completed there. Although Congress immediately ratified the appointment, the mission was delayed because Camacho became ill. The president nominated Manuel Gómez Pedraza to replace him but Congress refused confirmation. As a consequence of political divisiveness, no compromise nominee could be found by mid-March when Mornier decided to return to England. Since he and Ward remained convinced that the Mexican government sincerely desired amicable relations with Great Britain, they recommended that their government await Camacho's recovery.[13]

After a delay of several months, Camacho arrived in England on

October 13, 1826, only to discover that Canning was in France.[14]
Talks finally began on November 29, with Camacho and Rocafuerte representing Mexico, and Mornier, Huskisson, and Canning
representing England. The British foreign minister was disturbed
because the article on religious toleration had been deleted.
Camacho managed to convince him that the Mexican government
favored religious freedom, but needed time to overcome old
prejudices; he reminded the Englishman that an analogous situation existed in his own country where complete civil liberties had
yet to be granted to Catholics.

The question of shipping posed greater difficulties. Mexico
demanded preferential treatment in the form of reduced duties
for Mexican bottoms and a broader definition of a Mexican ship.
After several meetings and much discussion, Huskisson suggested
that the treaty establish complete reciprocity, but that it include an
additional article whereby each party reserved the right to favor its
own shipping for ten years. England would unofficially agree not
to avail herself of that privilege. This would allow Mexico to
provide her ships with preferential treatment for a decade without
compromising England's traditional policy. When Britain offered
that concession, Camacho suggested that his country would be
willing to accept the English definition of a Mexican vessel,
provided that for the purposes of the treaty "Mexicans" include
naturalized citizens and people who had resided in Mexico more
than five years, as well as those born in the country. Canning
agreed to the compromises and the treaty was signed on December 26, 1826. Then, at Camacho's request, England provided a
ship so that Rocafuerte could return immediately to Mexico to have
the treaty ratified. The following day, the chargé departed on the
*H.M.S. Caliope.*[15]

Rocafuerte arrived in Veracruz on February 16, 1827, reaching
Mexico City six days later. He was pleased to deliver the treaty to
his government because the lengthy negotiations produced a
Mexican victory. England had begun the talks unwilling to grant
any concessions. However, as the discussions became protracted
and Mexico refused to abandon her goals, the British government
conceded the disputed items one by one. The treaty did not
guarantee Englishmen the right to practice their faith; it unofficially granted Mexico preferential treatment; and it accepted a very

broad definition of what constituted a Mexican ship. In the end, all that England obtained was a face-saving device and assurance that the treaty did not establish precedents other nations could exploit. Mexico's diplomatic victory is even more impressive when one considers that a decade earlier the United States had gone to war over many of these same issues and failed to obtain them.

3

Mexican political factionalism threatened to negate the nation's diplomatic victory. Since 1825, the more democratic political faction, the *yorkinos*, had attempted to drive the aristocratic *escoceses* from office. They succeeded in 1826 when they won the confidence of President Victoria and forced Alamán to abandon the ministry of internal and foreign affairs. The victory, however, only engendered division within the group. By the end of 1826 the *yorkinos* were engaged in an internecine struggle between the moderate wing, which controlled the government, and the radicals, who were outside the government or in minor positions. Because Mexican politicians considered the president to be chief of state rather than head of government, radical attacks in the press and in Congress were always directed against government ministers, never against Guadalupe Victoria. Only José Ignacio Esteva, the minister of treasury, was friendly with the radicals. Miguel Ramos Arizpe, Manuel Gómez Pedraza, and Juan José Espinosa de los Monteros, the new minister of internal and foreign affairs, were considered moderates and, thus, the enemy.[16]

Events in January 1827 gave the radicals an opportunity to reach for power. A Spanish priest, Joaquín Arenas, was discovered conspiring to restore Spanish power. The plot itself was never important, but it provided the radicals with a vehicle to destroy the *escoceses* and the moderate *yorkinos*. Newspapers were filled with commentaries on the conspiracy and many people demanded the immediate expulsion of all Spaniards from Mexico. Public sentiment was so inflamed that the radicals were able to act with impunity. General Ignacio Mora, the commander of the Federal District of Mexico City, imprisoned Pedro Negrete and José Echávarri, two retired Spanish generals who had fought for Mexican independence. Flushed with victory, the radicals demanded changes in the government; by the end of March it appeared that they were about to depose the moderate ministers. However, a strong public reaction to the treatment of Negrete and Echávarri steeled the nerve of the moderate *yorkinos*. Determined not to be destroyed individually, they gathered their forces. Early in April, Manuel Crescencio Rejón and seven deputies from Yucatan, once considered pro-radical, joined the moderate congressional faction, providing Ramos Arizpe, Gómez Pedraza, and Espinosa de los Monteros a majority on nearly every issue. Although the radicals failed to topple the government, they succeeded in creating a climate of hysteria that led to the expulsion of the Spaniards from Mexico.[17]

The radicals were also able to retain some positions of influence and did not abandon their attempts to gain control of the government. Early in 1827 José María Tornel, one of the most outspoken radical deputies, became confidential secretary to the president. Tornel hoped to use this post to secure appointment as minister to England. He and his allies decided that Tornel could become Mexico's representative in London by discrediting Rocafuerte. A senate investigation of the financial records of the mission to England, which had begun in January 1826, seemed to provide information that could be used against the chargé. While the inquiry had resulted in the approval of most of the legation's expenditures, one, involving Michelena's purchase of a mysterious brig that could navigate beneath the water, remained unsettled. The vessel, the *Guerrero*, had never arrived. Since the ministry of war and marine appeared unable to discover anything more about the submarine, Senator José María Alpuche, a radical, formed a senate committee to investigate the matter. When the committee learned that Rocafuerte was returning to Mexico with the English treaty, the senators agreed to await his arrival before continuing the investigation. The radicals hoped to prove that Rocafuerte was incompetent and thus force him from office.[18]

Upon his arrival, the chargé d'affaires explained that the submarine had never been completed. He noted that he had frequently visited the inventor, Captain Thomas Johnson, to see how the work progressed. At first Johnson was confident that the *Guerrero* would soon be finished. Late in 1825, however, the inventor asked for another six thousand pounds to complete the project, claiming that inflation had markedly increased the cost of materials and labor. Since Rocafuerte had no authority to grant the request, he asked Johnson either to return the original ten thousand pounds to Mexico or complete the vessel at the original price. The inventor, however, could do neither, having invested all his capital in the submarine.

Rocafuerte sought the counsel of lawyers, who informed him that Mexico had no legal recourse and suggested that he settle the question amicably. The chargé notified his government, asking for new instructions. In September 1826 Johnson sought a loan of a thousand pounds from Rocafuerte to repay debts he had incurred in building the submarine, promising to deliver the vessel if the sum were advanced. Since Sebastián Camacho was on his way to England, Rocafuerte decided to let the new minister decide. A few days later Johnson's creditors jailed him. The submarine remained unfinished. The senate accepted Rocafuerte's explanation and instructed the government to obtain the vessel as soon as possible. When Rocafuerte returned to England later that year, he learned that Johnson had sold the *Guerrero* for three hundred pounds, thereby depriving Mexico of her first submarine.[19]

Undaunted by the failure of senate radicals to discredit Rocafuerte, the radicals in the chamber of deputies decided to pursue two other matters involving the Mexican legation in London: certain discrepancies in the purchase of uniforms and the loan to Gran Colombia. Michelena had been ordered to buy one thousand army and one thousand navy uniforms. The *Correo de la federación mexicana*, the organ of the radical *yorkinos*, claimed that Michelena paid thirty pesos apiece for old uniforms that could have been purchased in Mexico for half the price. The most serious charge, however, was that the uniforms for the navy never arrived.[20]

When questioned by the chamber of deputies on February 22, 1827, Michelena replied that the navy uniforms had not been ready when he returned from England. Two days later Rocafuerte testified that the Barclay Company, which had handled the purchase, had shipped them aboard the *Sweetluce* on October 31, 1825. To support his assertions the chargé submitted a bill of lading and insurance forms.[21]

While the chamber verified this information, it investigated the charge that Michelena had paid high prices for old uniforms. To defend himself, the former minister to England asked José Morán, the officer who had inspected the equipment on its arrival in Mexico, to testify. Morán declared that the uniforms were new. He explained that when he had "said that the leather straps and knap-sacks were old, . . . [he] meant to make clear that the rest of the equipment was knew."[22] With this information and with copies of orders instructing Michelena to expedite the purchase of equip-ment, the chamber found it difficult to prove malfeasance. The only question remaining was the whereabouts of the uniforms.

In July 1827, Minister of War Gómez Pedraza learned that the uniforms had arrived a year and a half earlier and were stored in Mariano Raro's warehouse. They had not been released because the inspector found that although the total number of pieces was correct, some were mismatched. The quartermaster had been calmly waiting for someone to make note of the error and exchange the mismatched pieces.[23] Once again the radicals were unable to use the issue to further their ends.

They did not, however, abandon their attacks on Rocafuerte. On March 1, 1827, Deputy Tornel demanded to know whether the government had authorized the loan to Gran Colombia. If the chargé d'affaires had acted without instructions, the deputy de-clared, he should be tried for criminal negligence. Tornel argued that Rocafuerte cared more for the interests of Gran Colombia, the country of his birth, than for his adopted land, Mexico. Although the chargé was a naturalized citizen, Tornel still considered him an alien. Rocafuerte's friends, José María Coutó, Anastasio Zerecero, Manuel Crescencio Rejón, and Casimiro Liceaga, defended him. However, knowing that the nationalist radical *yorkinos* would not be swayed by Spanish Americanist arguments, they justified his ac-tions on practical grounds. Coutó explained that Rocafuerte had loaned Gran Colombia money in order to safeguard Mexico's funds from the impending bankruptcy of Barclay. He was unable to support his assertions, however, because the administration refused to discuss the matter. Ultimately, the radicals prevailed when they forced the chamber to pass a motion demanding that Rocafuerte be tried on criminal charges for having made an unauthorized loan to Gran Colombia.[24]

When the senate received the chamber's motion, it began its own investigation. Asked to testify, the minister of foreign affairs informed the senate that he could not provide Congress with any information because the loan was a matter of "high level diplomacy." Given the great importance and delicate circumstances of the question, the government could not answer now but would make the facts available at the "proper time." When asked if Rocafuerte should be permitted to return to his post in England, Foreign Minister Espinosa de los Monteros replied that the government was satisfied with his conduct. Since the minister's reply did not constitute a complete exoneration, Senator Alpuche insisted that Rocafuerte face trial. Then the chargé's old friend, Senator Juan de Dios Cañedo, shifted the line of argument. He maintained that Rocafuerte was merely a subordinate and, therefore, not responsible; the administration was liable for the conduct of its officers. The senate should not allow the government to hide behind the facade of "high level diplomacy," but should demand the truth. The executive branch refused to alter its position. Reluctantly, the senate accepted the administration's view. The senate investigating committee declared that although Rocafuerte had not been exonerated, it would reserve judgment until the government provided the relevant facts.[25]

Rocafuerte was embittered by the senate's action. He believed that the administration had unjustly prevented him from defending himself and had forced him to shoulder the blame for Esteva's failure to safeguard the nation's funds. Accordingly, he wrote a long letter to the newspapers explaining that he was innocent and asking the public to withhold judgment until he could present all the facts. Far from being guilty of criminal neglect, he maintained that he deserved the nation's gratitude for his actions.[26]

The radicals failed to oust Rocafuerte not only because the chamber and the senate could not agree to impeach him, but also because British Chargé d'Affaires George H. Ward opposed the appointment of a radical to a diplomatic post in England. When he learned that Tornel might be named to replace Rocafuerte, Ward protested, informing President Victoria that he would regard the appointment "as an insult to His Majesty's Government." Consequently, Victoria decided to send Rocafuerte back to England with the ratified treaty.[27]

4

The English treaty also faced opposition in Congress. Initially, Rocafuerte had hoped that it would be ratified quickly. President Victoria, pleased with the document, expected little opposition in Congress. However, the British chargé was less confident; the senate still had not approved a treaty with United States which remained in committee after four months, despite United States Minister Joel Poinsett's repeated attempts to have it expedited. As one of the founders of the York Rite Lodge in Mexico, Poinsett was reputed to exercise great influence among the radical *yorkinos* and Ward feared that the North American would convince them to oppose the English treaty. Although they were not a majority, they had sufficient strength to delay the ratification process indefinitely.

Ward's pessimism proved unfounded. Although some radicals in the chamber criticized the British treaty, most were willing to approve it in the belief that Tornel, the president's secretary, would be named minister to England. After two weeks of debate, the chamber sanctioned the treaty unanimously. This was a great victory because only a two-thirds majority of the combined membership of both houses of Congress was needed to ratify the treaty.[28]

In the senate, the treaty faced strong opposition from the committee on foreign affairs. Many committee members believed that the document favored Great Britain. But the minister of foreign affairs explained that the clauses favorable to England merely allowed her to preserve her reputation. The treaty, he argued, really favored Mexico. The committee eventually accepted the explanation and sent the accord to the floor. Although there was additional debate, the treaty won majority approval on April 2, 1827. The following day President Victoria signed the document, authorizing Rocafuerte to exchange ratifications in London.[29]

The English treaty won approval in part because the radicals hoped to profit by it. More importantly, it was accepted because most Mexicans believed that trade with England would produce great benefits for their country. Great Britain had amply demonstrated her wealth, power, and willingness to assist in Mexico's development. Any attempt to obstruct the treaty, particularly by partisans of the United States, was doomed to failure. The nation to the north had little to offer Mexico; she was still a second-class agrarian country. In the view of many Mexicans, their own republic was destined to become the colossus of North America. Few denied the ambitions and growing power of the United States, but in 1827 Mexico was larger and many believed the wealthier of the two nations. Thus, despite Poinsett's important ties with the radicals, the North American treaty languished in committee while the English treaty was quickly ratified.

Rocafuerte and Ward returned to England together. Although it was too late to stop him from returning to London, the radical *yorkinos* tried to smear Rocafuerte's reputation. On May 19 the *Correo de la federación mexicana* claimed that the chargé d'affaires had taken one of the accomplices in the Arenas conspiracy with him to England.[30] Since the public was still vehemently anti-Spanish, this was tantamount to branding Rocafuerte a traitor. His friends proved his innocence, but the suspicion engendered by the radical *yorkino* charges was never fully dispelled and continued to haunt Rocafuerte for many years.[31]

The Mexican chargé returned to England by way of Havana and New York, arriving on July 16, 1827. Although Sebastián Camacho had been instructed to return to Mexico as soon as Rocafuerte reached London, he remained to witness the exchange of ratifications. Camacho and Rocafuerte visited Canning, who was extremely ill but gratified that the negotiations had been completed. A few days later, the ratified treaties were exchanged in a formal ceremony; Camacho then prepared to return to Mexico. Before Camacho could depart, Canning died, on the morning of August 8, 1827. The Mexicans, indeed all Spanish Americans, felt an immense loss. Their great friend and protector was gone.[32]

Rocafuerte expressed the opinion of most Spanish Americanists when he wrote, "death unexpectedly snatched from the political scene that great luminary of modern civilization who had the sympathy, respect, and admiration of all the liberals of the world."[33] European conservatives, however, rejoiced, giving thanks to a merciful Providence for delivering the world from "that malevolent meteor." Four years later Metternich wrote, "The Ministry of Canning has marked an era in the history of England and Europe."[34] The Spanish Americanists agreed; they believed that without him England would not have recognized their countries until much later. In spite of their determined efforts, no other important European nation had yet done as much.

# VIII

## NORTHERN EUROPE

Spanish Americanists prized English recognition, but they were also eager to establish relations with other European countries because they feared that without such ties, Great Britain might try to dominate them. As soon as England granted recognition, the diplomats of Spanish America hastened to press the European states to establish diplomatic relations. Their legations in London became the headquarters for Spanish American diplomacy in Europe. Although all the Spanish Americanists sought to establish relations with Continental nations, this chapter concentrates on Mexico's activities as an example of such efforts by Spanish Americanists.[1]

1

Even before England granted recognition, Mexican diplomats had attempted, through a combination of trade enticements and threats of embargo, to force the Continent to establish relations with their country. As early as August 1823, Michelena had instructed Murphy and Gorostiza to inform France and Holland that unless they established relations with Mexico, their products might be barred from Mexican ports. While these declarations provoked concern in Paris and The Hague, they lacked force until England recognized Mexico in December 1824.

News of Britain's new policy did not immediately reach the Continent because Canning wanted to inform the European nations personally of his government's action. Thus Gorostiza, who was in Holland awaiting permission to travel to Berlin, remained unaware of the change in Mexico's diplomatic situation. The

Mexican agent hoped that German commercial interests might assist his country in obtaining recognition. When Gorostiza had not received a passport by January 1, 1825, he wrote Rocafuerte that he was considering travelling to the Prussian capital without documents. However, the Mexican legation in London admonished him not to enter Prussia without official permission, lest he run afoul of the police and the agents of the Holy Alliance.

The warning was unnecessary because within a few days the world learned of England's recognition of Mexico. This news altered the diplomatic situation; the Prussian ambassador gladly granted Gorostiza a passport.[2] On January 22, the Mexican reached Elberfelt on the Rhine where, to his surprise, he found that a large company had been formed to trade with Mexico. Two days later he met with the directors of the Rhine West India Company who assured him that Prussian merchants were eager to expand their trade with Spanish America. Indeed, they offered to use their influence to persuade the Prussian government to establish relations with Mexico. Before Gorostiza departed for Berlin, the merchants furnished him with letters of introduction to important government officials and other influential persons.[3]

In Berlin, the Mexican agent met with Minister of Trade and Commerce Count von Bulow, an advocate of expanded commerce between the two countries. Prussia was eager to enlarge and protect her trade with Mexico but she refused to recognize the American nation. Gorostiza informed Von Bulow that the Mexican government had permitted Prussian merchants to enter the country as a token of goodwill. For trade to continue, however, Prussia would have to exchange consuls with Mexico. Since such an act implied de facto recognition, Von Bulow arranged for Gorostiza to confer with the Prussian minister of foreign affairs, Count Bernstorff. Although the foreign minister received Gorostiza cordially, he explained that Prussia's position as a continental power did not allow her to deviate from the policy of the Holy Alliance. Gorostiza had several meetings with Von Bulow and Bernstorff but failed to convince them to change their policies. Indeed, these meetings and the strict surveillance of his activities both by Prussian police and agents of the Holy Alliance convinced Gorostiza that Prussia was not free to act independently. In his opinion, St. Petersburg and Vienna had the last word on Prussia's Spanish American policy. He wrote Michelena that while certain important commercial interests were eager to trade with Mexico, they had little influence in court. Trade alone, he concluded, was not sufficient inducement to obtain Prussia's recognition. Believing that further efforts were useless, the Mexican departed for the Republic of Hamburg.[4]

That city state handled a large percentage of Northern Europe's trade and its government was eager to strengthen its ties with Mexico. Hamburg also had important commercial dealings with Spain and the republic feared Ferdinand VII's wrath if she should negotiate openly with Spanish America. However, Gorostiza was confidènt that the wealth of the New World would overcome such concern. He initiated talks with Foreign Minister Karl Sieveking on March 1. Worried by Mexico's threat to bar the Hanseatic republic from her markets, Sieveking agreed in principle to recognize Mexico's flag and exchange commercial agents. Gorostiza wanted a more formal commitment and insisted that talks continue in London. As a result, Sieveking authorized Hamburg's consul general in England, James Colquhoum, to enter into conversations with Michelena and, if circumstances warranted it, to negotiate a commercial agreement. In the interim, Sieveking, who feared that England would monopolize Spanish American trade if immediate action were not taken, convinced the reluctant senate of Hamburg to ratify the agreements he had reached with Gorostiza.[5] Two months later, Hamburg established de facto relations with Mexico by exchanging consuls. Gorostiza considered the event a great triumph. He concluded that the Holy Alliance no longer intimidated small nations; otherwise, Hamburg would not have taken the lead in recognizing Mexico. He believed other European nations would soon extend de facto recognition.[6]

Negotiations in London were also fruitful. James Colquhoum, who had business interests in the Antilles, agreed with Sieveking on the need to establish relations with Spanish America. He began talks with Michelena and Rocafuerte on June 9, 1825. After some discussion, they reached a tentative agreement on a draft treaty of commerce and navigation similar to the one negotiated between Mexico and England. Since Michelena was returning to Mexico, the negotiators agreed to allow Gorostiza to resolve the details with the government of Hamburg. At the same time, Rocafuerte and Colquhoum would continue talks in London.[7]

The following month Colquhoum informed Rocafuerte that until the treaty was ratified, Hamburg would grant Mexican ships the same privileges as her own vessels. He asked, however, for reasons of international politics, that the news be kept secret. Hamburg hoped to expand commercial relations with Mexico while postponing a confrontation with the Holy Alliance. On July 12, Colquhoum notified Rocafuerte that Bremen, another Hanseatic republic, wished to negotiate a treaty on the same basis as Hamburg. Once again, he requested that the agreement remain secret until ratified. Rocafuerte willingly acceded to their requests, but indicated that once the Hanseatic consuls assumed their posts, the public had to be informed.[8]

Rocafuerte's declaration disturbed Hamburg, which unrealistically hoped that her trade with America would remain secret. The senate of Hamburg insisted that since the republic had exchanged "commercial agents" rather than consuls, she had not granted Mexico de facto recognition. Bremen, on the other hand, seemed willing to acknowledge and expand relations with Mexico. But Hamburg convinced her sister republic to postpone all action. During the following year, the Hanseatic states enjoyed increasing trade with America without openly challenging the Holy Alliance. Finally the Mexican diplomats grew impatient and threatened economic reprisals if the Hanseatic republics did not "honor their word." On November 7, 1826, Gorostiza informed the senate of Hamburg that the time had come to exchange "recognized" consular agents. From London, Colquhoum advised the republics to fulfill their earlier commitments if they wanted to preserve commercial ties with Mexico. In spite of threats and urgings, matters remained undecided.

By 1827 the diplomatic climate had begun to change. England and Mexico had negotiated a treaty of commerce. This prompted the large continental nations, which were recovering from the economic crisis of 1825–1826, to consider recognizing the American countries. The changed attitude of the larger nations forced the smaller states to act before the great powers divided Spanish American commerce among themselves. Thus, on January 31, 1827, Sieveking proposed a series of radical measures to the Hamburg senate; he asked the body to approve the treaty with Mexico, exchange consuls with Gran Colombia, and initiate relations with Guatemala, Chile, Peru, and Argentina. Sieveking argued that the Holy Alliance had ceased to exist except as a formality and that the measures would not compromise Hamburg's position in Europe. The senate, however, was not persuaded.

Sieveking's action convinced the Mexican, Gran Colombian, Peruvian, and Chilean ministers to England that the Hanseatic republics could be coerced into recognizing them if they publicized the growing contacts between the great powers and their countries. The tactic succeeded in disturbing many Hanseatic merchants. As a result, in March and April Sieveking arranged a series of conferences with the American diplomats in Brussels, Paris, and London. These discussions coincided with rumors that France, Prussia, and The Netherlands were on the verge of recognizing the new nations. Gripped by a sense of urgency, Hamburg and Bremen proceeded to complete negotiations with Gran Colombia and Mexico. Sebastián Camacho, Mexico's plenipotentiary, and Foreign Minister Sieveking agreed to a slightly modified version of the draft prepared by Rocafuerte and Colquhoum, granting the Hanseatic republics most-favored-nation status. Although the treaty was officially signed on June 16, 1827, internal political divisions in Mexico delayed ratification beyond the stipulated deadline. Since the Hanseatic republics believed Mexico was merely retaliating for their earlier refusal to honor the agreements, they were willing to negotiate a second treaty in 1831, which the Mexican Congress ratified.[9]

2

After initiating relations between Mexico and the Hanseatic states in March 1825, Gorostiza had returned to Brussels to continue negotiations with the Low Countries. The following month, he had a series of conferences with various Dutch officials, including Foreign Minister Count Rheede, which ultimately resulted in a formal exchange of consuls.[10] On May 5, the Dutch ambassador to England, A. R. Falk, informed Michelena that his government was appointing Charles Higgins consul general to Mexico. The proposed exchange of consuls extended de facto recognition. Since Mexico desired de jure recognition, the Mexican minister did not

immediately nominate a consul to Holland. At Count Rheede's
insistence, however, Michelena eventually appointed Gorostiza
consul general to The Netherlands. Determined to consolidate
Mexico's diplomatic position in Holland, Michelena instructed
Gorostiza to insist upon a treaty of friendship and commerce and
formal recognition. Reluctantly, the Dutch government began
informal talks.[11]

Holland, however, was not anxious to establish diplomatic relations with Mexico and treaty negotiations languished. Mindful of
the importance of growing trade with Mexico, the Dutch government attempted to maintain cordial relations with Mexican diplomats; Gorostiza was unofficially invited to court functions while, in
London, Rocafuerte was entertained by Ambassador Falk. Since
the Mexican diplomats were concerned with a number of complex
issues such as the English treaty negotiations, the efforts to
establish relations with other European states, and the protection
of Mexico's funds in London, they permitted the Dutch to procras-
tinate. Thus, the Netherlands enjoyed Spanish American trade but
avoided antagonizing her two large neighbors, France and Prussia.
However, in August 1826, the Mexicans renewed their pressure on
the Dutch. Rocafuerte instructed Gorostiza to inform Count
Rheede that he had been appointed chargé d'affaires to The
Netherlands. By this act, Rocafuerte hoped to force the Dutch
government into extending formal recognition. At first the government of Holland temporized, but finally Count Rheede declared
that his country could not exchange diplomats until the great
powers recognized Mexico. Rheede assured Gorostiza that the
Holy Alliance appeared to be softening its attitude towards the new
nations and that Holland would recognize Mexico at the first
opportunity.

Despite continued Mexican pressure, the Dutch government
refused to oppose the legitimists. Since the Netherlands had
protected her commerce by exchanging consuls, the Spanish
Americans were unable to apply economic sanctions to win her
recognition. The representatives of Spanish America, however, did
not relent. When the repeated warnings of possible reprisals finally
convinced Prussia and France to begin serious negotiations, the
Mexicans were quick to use their new advantages to pressure
Holland.

After protracted negotiations, Camacho and Gorostiza reached an accord with the Dutch. On June 15, 1827, Rheede signed the treaty of friendship and commerce and Camacho returned with it to Mexico for congressional approval. Again political divisions in the American nation prevented the immediate ratification of the long sought agreement. Although trade between the two countries continued to flourish, the treaty was not ratified and exchanged until May 7, 1828, when the king and queen of the Low Countries officially received Gorostiza as Mexico's chargé d'affaires.[12]

3

Earlier, in August 1825, when relations with Holland appeared so promising, Rocafuerte decided to contact the Russian government. Believing that Mexico's talks with England, Holland, Prussia, and the Hanseatic republics would disturb the Tsar, the Mexican diplomat hoped to pacify the autocrat by demonstrating that Mexico wished to live peacefully with all nations. Accordingly, Rocafuerte wrote Count Romanzoruf, the Tsar's confidant whom he had met in 1813 and with whom he had occasionally corresponded, in the hope of finding a way of overcoming Russia's antipathy to the Spanish American countries.[13]

Events in Prussia provided an opportunity to expand contacts with Russia. Late in August 1825, Gorostiza asked permission to return to Elberfeld to confer with Carl Becher, the director of the Rhine West India Company. The Mexican agent also requested authorization to meet in Cologne with representatives from the city of Stettin who desired to name commercial agents to Mexico. Rocafuerte, unperturbed by Prussia's earlier rebuff, approved Gorostiza's requests and suggested that he continue to Berlin and perhaps to St. Petersburg, if it appeared that the Russians would receive him. In order to encourage Gorostiza, Rocafuerte explained that he had visited St. Petersburg a decade earlier and that travel in the eastern monarchy was no more difficult than a journey through Prussia.[14]

When Gorostiza met with the representatives of the Rhine West India Company, he learned that they were concerned about the passage of a new Mexican law that required all states trading with

Mexico to appoint consuls, thus extending de facto recognition. The Mexican refused to allay their fears and indicated that his government was determined to apply economic sanctions to any nation that failed to recognize her. Furthermore, he declared that if Prussia did not establish formal relations with Mexico, she might be excluded from that profitable market. The Prussian businessmen were quite concerned but could promise no action on the part of their government.

Gorostiza continued to Cologne where he arranged for an exchange of consuls between Mexico and Stettin. Then, convinced that the legitimists who controlled Prussia and Russia would never allow their governments to recognize the Spanish American nations, Gorostiza returned to Brussels without going to Berlin or St. Petersburg. This was a regrettable decision because the two conservative governments were reconsidering their foreign policy. Had Gorostiza persevered, Mexico might have obtained recognition.

Prussian merchants, who were particularly concerned by the possibility of being excluded from American markets, demanded government action. Indeed, the Rhine West India Company insisted that Prussia recognize Mexico. In a memorandum sent to the minister of foreign affairs shortly after their meeting with Gorostiza, the directors of the company declared that Prussia's trade with Mexico was of the utmost importance. In the previous year, Mexico had purchased 250,000 bolts of linen and other cloth at the price of two-and-a-half-million Prussian tallers. Other interested parties also expressed concern. The governor of Westphalia warned that the Hanseatic states would eventually dominate trade between Germany and Mexico unless Prussia acted. News of the forthcoming Panama Congress added to the fears of many Prussians, because they believed that the Spanish Americanists might convince their governments to take economic sanctions against those countries that had not recognized them. In that event, warned Count Schuckman, Prussia would suffer great economic dislocation, widespread unemployment, and political unrest.[15]

Count Bernstorff, who was also under pressure from Prussian legitimists, decided to pursue a middle course by establishing commercial rather than diplomatic relations. Accordingly, Bernstorff instructed Baron von Maltzahn, Prussia's ambassador in

England, to contact Rocafuerte informally and attempt to gain trade concessions without abandoning the principle of legitimacy. Von Matlzahn invited Rocafuerte to dinner in March 1826. The Mexican chargé was astounded by the Prussian's cordiality and his much-repeated desire to establish formal relations between the two nations. Ambassador von Maltzahn added, however, that his government, which had commitments to Spain and the Holy Alliance, could not act immediately. He questioned Rocafuerte about the rumor that the Panama Congress would declare an embargo against nations that did not recognize the New World states. Rocafuerte replied that although the Congress lacked authority to impose its decisions on individual members, Mexico already had laws providing such sanctions. The Prussian ambassador then implied that relations between their two countries might develop more rapidly if Mexico refrained from applying the restrictions to Prussian merchants.

Puzzled by the vague overture, Rocafuerte later conferred with Canning to determine if England was aware of any shifts in Prussia's policy. Canning knew nothing, but instructed Viscount Strangford, England's ambassador to Russia, to inform the Tsar's government that Prussia was negotiating with Mexico. If this were a new policy of the Holy Alliance, Russia would not be surprised by the news. If it were not, Canning reasoned, knowledge of a division in the Alliance might induce the Tsar to modify his stance toward Spanish American recognition.

Strangford conferred with Russian Foreign Minister Count Nesselrode in April 1826. The Russian was surprised to learn that Prussia was taking an independent course, and he informed the Englishman that the Tsar had not changed his policy toward the new states. However, Strangford reported that the French ambassador in St. Petersburg believed that Russia was considering some sort of compromise that might allow Spain to reach an agreement with the American nations.[16]

This information convinced Rocafuerte that Russia was considering a change of policy toward the new republics. He believed that his letters to Count Romanzoruf and the realization that Prussia was abandoning the Holy Alliance had persuaded the Tsar to seek a rapprochement with Spanish America. Although he wished to dispatch an agent to St. Petersburg, the Mexican government instructed him to act with caution. Therefore, he conferred with Albert Gallatin, the United States' minister in London, on the propriety of sending an agent to Russia. Since the United States was the only American nation that had relations with the Tsar, Rocafuerte hoped that her minister might help break the deadlock. Although Gallatin believed that Russia might eventually recognize Mexico, he doubted that she would act without Spain's approval. He felt that the eastern monarchy had few commercial interests in Spanish America and that neither trade enticements nor fear of restrictions would have any effect on the Tsar's foreign policy.[17] Rocafuerte, who knew and respected the North American minister, was discouraged by Gallatin's observations and ended Mexico's early attempts to establish relations with Russia. If St. Petersburg had a change of heart, it was never made evident. Count Romanzoruf failed to answer Rocafuerte's letters and no feelers were put forth by the Tsar's government.

Although Russia was highly critical of Prussia's dealings with Mexico, the German nation continued talks with the American country. The demands of Prussian merchants had become insistent and Russia was occupied by the struggle with the Turkish empire. Thus, spurred on by extremely optimistic reports from her unofficial agents in America, Prussia grew eager to secure her commerce with the new nations. Berlin feared that England, Holland, and the Hanseatic republics might exclude her from Mexican markets if she did not act. Aware of this, Rocafuerte and Gorostiza increased pressure. They and other Spanish American envoys circulated rumors that France was about to recognize them, thus forcing the Prussian government to act decisively. When Sebastián Camacho arrived in London, the Prussian minister to England initiated talks. After several months of negotiations, they completed a preliminary agreement on trade and navigation. This time it was the Germans' turn to implore; they considered themselves fortunate in obtaining most-favored-nation status. Prussia extended formal recognition on June 18, 1827, when the agreement was signed.[18] Then Camacho returned to Mexico to receive his government's approval. There the Prussian treaty, like the Dutch treaty, met with opposition in Congress.

A growing sense of nationalism and the tensions that led to the expulsion of the Spaniards created a feeling of xenophobia in

Mexico. Many complained that the new foreign enterprises were simply continuing the exploitation begun by the Spaniards. Some Mexican nationalists were particularly concerned by the tendency of foreign companies in Mexico to hire their compatriots rather than Mexicans.[19] As a result, Congress was highly critical of the advantages granted to Prussia and was loath to approve the treaty while public opinion remained volatile. Later, political instability further delayed the ratification.

In London, the new Prussian minister to England, Count von Bulow, made repeated inquiries about the treaty. He was concerned that it might be rejected and the status of Prussian commercial agents in Mexico might be jeopardized. Rocafuerte attempted to allay his fears by explaining that Congress would approve the agreement after a detailed examination and that the delay was due, in part, to the recent illness of the minister of foreign relations. When Congress failed to ratify the treaty after a year, Prussia grew apprehensive that her growing trade with Mexico might be obstructed and agreed to make further concessions. Rocafuerte repeatedly admonished the government to ratify the new treaty as soon as possible, lest Mexico lose her momentary advantage. Little could be accomplished, however, until political turmoil subsided. Finally, a new government managed to win congressional approval in 1830. Fortunately for Mexico, other events in Europe had occupied Prussia. She accepted the treaty that was finally ratified and exchanged on February 8, 1831.[20] The lure of trade and political discord in Europe had saved Mexico from her internal divisions.

## 4

Mexican negotiations with other German states had also begun in 1825. Encouraged by the growing trade with Prussia, Rocafuerte approached Count Mandestohl, Württemburg's minister to England, whom he had met through their association with the British and Foreign School Society. The Mexican diplomat argued that trade with his country would be extremely beneficial to Württemberg. However, unless the German kingdom established relations with Mexico, her commerce would suffer economic sanctions.

Mandestohl, impressed by Mexico's activities in Europe, recommended that his government establish relations with the American republic. Count von Beroldingen, Württemberg's foreign minister, agreed, but was afraid to act against the established policies of Austria and Prussia. On February 22, 1826, the king resolved the nation's dilemma by appointing Egan Hundeiker commercial agent to Mexico. His credential, however, did not state whether the agent had been sent to deal with an independent nation or with a possession of Spain. Württemberg, like many of the smaller states, hoped to trade with Mexico without openly opposing the legitimist policy of the Holy Alliance. In a separate letter to Mexico's foreign minister, Von Beroldingen intimated that Württemberg was negotiating directly with Mexico and that his government would receive an agent from America.[21]

Rocafuerte recommended that Mexico accept the agent because, under international law, official communication and exchange of agents was equivalent to de facto recognition. President Victoria rejected Rocafuerte's argument, believing that international law tended to be whatever the great powers chose to accept; he was certain that the Holy Alliance would not agree to an interpretation favorable to Mexico. However, Minister of Foreign Affairs Camacho convinced him that Rocafuerte was correct. Camacho then instructed the Mexican chargé to seek formal relations and to begin negotiating a treaty of commerce.[22]

Because of delays in communications, several months passed before further action could be taken in London. On October 21, 1826, Rocafuerte conferred with Count Mandestohl to press the negotiations. Mandestohl informed his government of Mexico's desire, but Württemberg hesitated. Although Prussia and Bavaria were negotiating with Mexico, Austria and France still refused to recognize the American nations and the king of Württemberg feared reprisals from his two powerful neighbors if his government acted hastily. Rocafuerte authorized Gorostiza to continue conversations in Germany, but again Württemberg temporized. Despite continuing pressure by Rocafuerte and Gorostiza, the situation remained unresolved until France finally recognized Mexico. On January 18, 1832, Württemberg and Mexico exchanged ratified treaties.[23]

5

When Rocafuerte first made overtures to Württemberg in November 1825, he also approached Baron Von Cetto, the Bavarian minister to England. Bavaria was one of the most important of the German states and Rocafuerte believed that her recognition of Mexico might even influence the Holy Alliance. Unfortunately, Bavaria was a landlocked nation, unlikely to be won by offers of trade. In fact, a commercial treaty might be impossible to negotiate because Bavarian goods had to pass through Austria, France, or other German states to reach Atlantic or Mediterranean ports. Trade with Bavaria, therefore, would involve agreements with one or more of those countries.

In spite of these problems, Rocafuerte decided that a Mexican overture might succeed because King Ludwig of Bavaria was reputed to be a progressive monarch. Upon learning that his neighbor, the king of Württemberg, had initiated relations with Mexico, Ludwig appointed Herman Nolte commercial agent to Mexico and authorized Baron von Cetto to enter into talks with Rocafuerte. The two men had several meetings in June, 1826. Rocafuerte wanted to develop relations with Bavaria but since Camacho was coming to London, the chargé delayed talks until his arrival.[24]

Camacho did not share Rocafuerte's enthusiasm about relations with Bavaria. In his opinion, the difficulties were greater than any benefits that might accrue. Thus when Rocafuerte returned to Mexico with the English treaty, Camacho allowed the talks between Bavaria and Mexico to languish. Baron von Cetto accepted the setback as temporary and awaited more propitious times.[25]

The Bavarian's patience was rewarded in July 1827 when Rocafuerte returned to England. After Camacho departed for Mexico, Von Cetto and the chargé resumed private conversations that led Rocafuerte to contact the Bavarian foreign minister. The talks on the Continent were extremely cordial and considered the possibility of a treaty of commerce between Mexico and Bavaria. King Ludwig's government instructed Von Cetto to press negotiations with Rocafuerte. Bavaria's economy had prospered under the king's enlightened policies; it was wealthier than any other landlocked nation. Moreover Bavarian products had been popular in Mexico even before independence. Thus, Ludwig was eager to guarantee his country's access to the Mexican market.

Rocafuerte temporized while he attempted to overcome his government's reluctance to deal with Bavaria. The chargé argued that relations with Bavaria would be extremely useful because of the friendship between the courts of Munich and Vienna. Rocafuerte believed that Ludwig's influence in Austria would be helpful in initiating talks between Mexico and the empire. Hoping to gain President Victoria's approval to continue talks with Bavaria, Rocafuerte obtained a copy of the recently negotiated treaty between the United States and Switzerland, another landlocked nation. He forwarded the information to Mexico, suggesting that an agreement with Bavaria might be patterned on that treaty.[26] The Mexican government, however, remained unimpressed. Although Mexico's internal politics and the intransigence of the Holy Alliance were partially responsible for Mexican disinterest in the treaty, the principal obstacle remained Bavaria's inability to trade directly with the American nation. Therefore, despite Rocafuerte's insistence, Mexico remained unwilling to sign an agreement with King Ludwig.

The Mexican chargé in London refused to abandon talks abruptly. He was careful to assure Baron von Cetto that his government desired friendly relations with Bavaria and promised to resolve existing obstacles as soon as possible.[27] Since Ludwig was eager to continue talks, Rocafuerte's friendly attitude reassured Bavaria. However, as in the case of Württemberg, the situation did not change until France recognized Mexico. Then Gorostiza resumed negotiations with Bavaria, ultimately signing a treaty of friendship and commerce on May 14, 1832.[28]

Switzerland, like Bavaria, was a landlocked nation that reacted favorably to overtures by Rocafuerte and Gorostiza. By the end of 1826, talks had advanced to the point of naming commercial agents. Conversations languished after Sebastián Camacho arrived in London because the plenipotentiary believed that relations with Switzerland would be no more profitable than with Bavaria. Gorostiza was able to resume negotiations upon Rocafuerte's return from Mexico in 1827. In August 1827, Switzerland appointed a consul to Mexico. But no further progress was possible as long as France withheld recognition. Negotiations between

Mexico and Switzerland resumed after France recognized the North American nation. The Swiss treaty was completed on December 31, 1832.[29]

6

Sweden was the only important Northern European nation that had not signed a treaty with Mexico by the end of 1832. The international situation as well as internal politics in both countries combined to frustrate relations that began auspiciously in 1824, when Michelena sought Swedish ships and sailors for the Mexican navy. Rocafuerte, who traveled through Sweden in 1813, negotiated the sale of warships to Mexico. Unfortunately, the Tsar opposed the sale and when Russian warships entered the Baltic to prevent delivery of the vessels, the Swedish government thought it prudent to wait for a more opportune time to negotiate with Mexico.

Undaunted, Rocafuerte maintained official contact with the Swedish ambassador to England, Count von Brojesterna. When Prussia took the lead in initiating relations with Mexico in 1827, Sweden also decided to act. Von Brojesterna suggested that the two governments negotiate a treaty of commerce and navigation. Before talks could develop officially, Europe became embroiled in a war with Turkey. The tense international situation led to a postponement of negotiations.[30]

By October 1828, Turkish nationalists had halted Russia's drive on Istanbul and pinned large Tsarist contingents along Russia's southern front. Rocafuerte believed that the talks with Sweden should be renewed while Russia was too preoccupied to interfere. He contacted Count von Brojesterna, who agreed to a treaty similar to the one Mexico had negotiated with England. The Swedish minister was pleased with the result and assured the Mexican chargé that his government would ratify it rapidly.

Rocafuerte forwarded the treaty to Mexico with a strong recommendation that it be ratified immediately. He argued that Sweden produced the best and least expensive ships and naval equipment, and that her seamen, many of whom were already serving in the Mexican navy, were the finest in the world. The port of Gothenburg could serve as a northern entrepôt for Mexican goods in Europe and Sweden could provide many raw materials needed in Mexico. Rocafuerte maintained that the American republic had to build railroads to foster development and suggested that Swedish iron could be imported for the purpose since it was cheap and readily available. Finally, Rocafuerte explained that relations with Sweden would ultimately lead Russia to change her policy towards Spanish America. If all of Northern Europe extended recognition, the Tsar might feel compelled to force a change in Spain or recognize Mexico regardless of Ferdinand's actions.[31] A series of political upheavals in Mexico prevented timely ratification. When Gorostiza sought to renew conversations with Sweden in 1830, the international situation had changed. Russia was no longer occupied by war and Sweden did not believe it prudent to ratify a treaty with Mexico.[32] Negotiations were not renewed until Spain finally recognized Mexico's independence in 1836.

7

Although England had recognized Mexico, Gran Colombia, and Argentina in December 1824, the nations of continental Europe did not immediately follow suit. The Spanish Americanists attempted to entice them with commerce. Then they threatened the Europeans with economic sanctions if they did not recognize them. The policy was effective both because of the myth of Spanish American wealth and the reality of a burgeoning trade with the New World. Holland and the Hanseatic republics initiated trade contacts by exchanging consuls, but the small nations refused to recognize the Spanish American countries until France and Prussia acted. The Spanish Americanists also attempted to entice Prussia and Russia. To their surprise, Prussia was much more interested in their commerce than they had imagined. Threats, enticements, and rumors that other nations would recognize Spanish America worked to the benefit of the new nations. Afraid that other countries might monopolize the vast Spanish American market, the governments of Northern Europe extended de facto recognition and some of them even negotiated treaties with some Spanish American states in 1827. Thereafter, internal political divisions in

Mexico delayed the ratification of some of those treaties. However, to the dismay of the Spanish Americanists, France remained staunchly legitimist even after Prussia—the supposed bastion of conservatism—extended recognition in 1827.

# IX

## FRANCE AND ROME

England's recognition of Spanish America in December 1824 caught France by surprise. The French government was divided: the president of the council of ministers, Villele, favored establishing de facto relations to protect French trade with America, but the new minister of foreign affairs, Baron Ange Damas, refused to allow commercial considerations to dictate government policy. Other conservatives supported him and some assured Spain's ambassador to France, the Count of Puebla, that France would continue to support Ferdinand VII's claims to America. However, the French government decided to postpone comment on Britain's action until the Russian ambassador, who was then consulting with the Tsar, returned from St. Petersburg.

### 1

Murphy, the Mexican agent in France, believed that Paris might follow London's lead by recognizing Mexico. At the very least he expected Villele to appoint consuls. But by March 1825, Murphy began to doubt his earlier evalution and decided to consult with Michelena and Rocafuerte in London. Before departing, he met with Minister Villele who interpreted the rapid growth rate in trade between Mexico and France as a good sign. The minister warned, however, that it would take time to change France's special relationship with Spain. In the interim, relations with Spanish America would have to remain informal. Murphy was not encouraged by Villele's expressions of goodwill toward the New World, because the minister's sentiments were not reflected in French policy.[1]

The Mexican's fears seemed to be verified by rumors that France was supporting a Spanish attempt to reconquer her former colonies. In Mexico Minister of Foreign Affairs Alamán learned that a force of two thousand Spanish soldiers had departed from La Coruña bound for Havana. Since Alamán assumed that their final destination was Mexico, he urged Michelena to arrange for the immediate departure of the fleet he had purchased for the federal republic.[2] Michelena and Rocafuerte expressed their concern to Canning who, though sympathetic, declared that as long as Spanish forces continued to hold the fortress of San Juan de Ulúa, Ferdinand VII would attempt to reconquer Mexico. The American diplomats confidently replied that the fortress would capitulate as soon as Mexico could deploy her new fleet.[3]

Despite his public optimism, Michelena was shaken by a report that French warships were convoying Spanish troops in American waters. Although he believed Mexico could defeat Spain, he knew that the new republic was not prepared to fight France. He immediately asked Canning to investigate the rumor. The British ambassador in Paris determined that the French navy had convoyed Spanish troop ships from Puerto Rico to Havana at the instructions of the governor of Martinique. This unauthorized act, which not only jeopardized France's neutrality but also her relations with Great Britain, so upset Baron Damas that he forbade all activities that might result in a confrontation between his country and England.[4]

Although France hoped that Ferdinand VII would be reconciled to the new American governments, Spain continued to prepare her forces for the reconquest of America. The news in July 1825, that France had recognized her former colony, Haiti, in return for a large indemnity, prompted speculation that Spain might recognize the Spanish American states if they made similar payments. None of the American nations, however, would agree to such a humiliating demand.[5] Nevertheless, France continued to seek a compromise between Spain and America.

The French government believed that the issue of recognition could be resolved if the newly independent nations would accept princes of the Spanish royal house as monarchs. Confidential agents reported to Rocafuerte that the Holy Alliance had agreed to recognize Mexico provided Crown Prince Francisco de Paula became king. Since Murphy was in England, Rocafuerte asked the Gran Colombian agent to France, the noted scientist José Lanz, to investigate the rumor. Lanz learned that France supported a monarchy in Mexico because the government believed that many Mexicans, including the hierarchy of the clergy and the military, were not committed to independence.[6] This corroborated secret reports Rocafuerte had received from Madrid that important Mexican clergymen were assuring Ferdinand VII that he had strong support in the New World. Rocafuerte was certain that Villele realized that the majority of the clergy and the army supported the newly established republics, but he also understood that French conservatives would grasp at any pretense to sustain their legitimist principles. Therefore, he instructed Lanz to emphasize the fact that under no circumstances would Mexico accept a king. Spanish American opposition and Ferdinand VII's refusal to allow Spanish princes to rule America doomed the French plan.[7]

Although French conservatives were committed to upholding legitimacy, French merchants clamored for a change in policy. Trade with the new states, particularly Mexico, had expanded enormously. Indeed various French chambers of commerce urged their government to recognize Spanish America so that their products could better compete with English goods. The French government sought to reconcile the conflicting interests of legitimists and traders by encouraging commerce with Spanish America while withholding diplomatic recognition. By August 1825, France freely granted passports to Spanish Americans who desired to travel or reside within her borders. Aware that such a policy could delay recognition indefinitely, Rocafuerte instructed Murphy to demand the appointment of consuls by threatening to discriminate against French goods, perhaps even to bar them from Mexican ports. Villele wanted to please Mexico but the strength of the French conservatives, led by the Duque Anguoléme and the Prince de Polignac, restricted the minister's ability to act. He compromised by naming commercial agents, rather than consuls, to oversee trade with the American nation. Since the Mexican government was dissatisfied with the compromise, Villele demonstrated his goodwill by agreeing to Rocafuerte's demand that the agents be named publicly. Within a few weeks, the king announced the new appointments.[8]

In December, the French government appointed Admiral Guy Duperré its diplomatic agent to the Antilles; he was also to concern himself with Mexican and Gran Colombian trade. In addition, France wanted to send Alexander Martin as unofficial consul to Mexico, but the Mexican government refused to receive unofficial agents; France, of course, would not formally appoint a representative lest it imply recognition. The issue was finally resolved when Foreign Minister Camacho agreed to receive Martin as confidential agent, the same capacity Murphy enjoyed in France.[9]

French commerce with Mexico continued to increase rapidly. Murphy estimated that the volume of trade for 1825 amounted to 6,600,000 pesos, a sum which exceeded France's trade with her own colonies. In April 1826, the Chamber of Commerce of Bordeaux insisted that France reach an understanding with Mexico because it feared that trade, which in the first quarter of 1826 had already surpassed the volume of commerce for the entire previous year, might be curtailed if Mexico chose to retaliate for the failure to recognize her government.[10]

Aware that the obstruction of trade with Spanish America would cause serious dislocations in the French economy, the Spanish Americanists decided to apply pressure on the government of France. Although England and virtually all the nations of northern Europe recognized the colors of the American nations in their ports, France clung to the policy she had followed with new nations since the United States rebelled against England; Spanish American ships were permitted to enter French harbors if they did not fly their national standards. Since the Spanish Americanists considered the requirement humiliating, they decided to present a united front to France. Early in 1826, the envoys of Mexico, Gran Colombia, Peru, and Argentina delivered an ultimatum to Villele. They declared that if his government did not change its policy, French ships would be forced to lower their flags before entering American ports. And they emphasized that in that event, French goods would enjoy no protection whatsoever. As a consequence, worried French merchants soon pressured Villele into giving assurances that the flags of Spanish America would be respected.[11]

The first test of the new policy came in September 1826 when the Gran Colombian vessel, the *Ayacucho*, arrived in Le Havre. The authorities forced her to lower her colors before entering the

harbor. José Fernández de Madrid, the new Gran Colombian agent
to France, immediately issued a strong protest. Rocafuerte also
demanded an explanation. Even French merchants were outraged.
An embarrassed government attempted to save face by announcing
on September 13 that the king had decided to permit Mexican ships
to enter French harbors flying their own flags inasmuch as France
and Mexico had exchanged commercial agents. On September 28
Baron Damas announced that henceforth Gran Colombian vessels
would enjoy the same privilege.[12]

The Spanish Americanists interpreted the event as a diplomatic
victory. Their optimism was bolstered by France's decision to
withdraw troops from Spain, a move the Americans believed to be
indicative of a new policy, one less circumscribed by Ferdinand or
the Holy Alliance. Thus they were dismayed when these promising
developments were jeopardized by a Gran Colombian proposal of
truce with Spain.

The large contingents of troops that Spain had sent to Cuba and
Puerto Rico, disturbed Bolívar, who feared that the buildup was in
preparation for an invasion of Gran Colombia.[13] At first, he
considered forming a joint naval and military force with Mexico
and Guatemala to challenge Spain's growing power in the Carib-
bean. But since each of the two northern nations also believed that
she was the target of a Spanish invasion, they refused to divert their
armed forces to protect Gran Colombia. Their uncooperative
attitude and the unenthusiastic response of the Pan American
Congress in Panama persuaded the Gran Colombian government
to act independently, by asking the United States minister to Spain
to propose a truce "of three or four months in which to decide
whether she [Spain] prefers to continue the war or to make
peace."[14] Ferdinand VII rejected the offer and immediately notified Villele, who used the information to throw the activities of the
American diplomats off balance.

Since Camacho was en route to London, Rocafuerte thought it
prudent to await his arrival before taking any action. When the
Mexican plenipotentiary learned the news, he was angered by Gran
Colombia's failure to consult his government. In his opinion, the
action constituted a violation of the letter as well as the spirit of the
1823 treaty between the two American nations. He instructed
Murphy to present his view to French Minister Villele and Gran

Colombian envoy Fernández de Madrid. The South American, who had only recently learned of the truce initiative, was shocked to learn that Mexico knew nothing about his government's aims. Although he regretted the damage done by Gran Colombia to American solidarity, he could do nothing to remedy the situation. Indeed, Fernández de Madrid found himself in a particularly embarrassing situation because his friend Rocafuerte returned to Mexico while an indignant Camacho remained in England.[15]

Sebastián Camacho had come to Great Britain with the intention of completing treaty negotiations with various European nations. Once the issues of the English treaty were resolved in December 1826, he turned his attention to improving Mexico's relation with the continent, concentrating initially on northern Europe and France. In January 1827 Baron Damas invited him to visit Paris, but Camacho refused to leave London unless the French government received him as Mexico's plenipotentiary. Finally, in April, the king of France agreed.

Camacho arrived in Paris with the expectation that France would recognize Mexico and begin negotiations on a treaty of friendship and commerce. The French government, however, had no such intention. After a number of meetings with various French ministers, Camacho reached a preliminary agreement on trade: the Declaration of May 9, 1827. This document established commerce on a reciprocal basis and included provisions for the protection of citizens of the two nations. Both sides interpreted the arrangement to be to their own advantage: Camacho, who believed that France had extended de facto recognition by receiving him as a fully accredited minister from Mexico, considered the Declaration an unofficial treaty of commerce; the French, however, felt that they had preserved their policy of nonrecognition by naming "commercial agents," rather than consuls, to Mexico.[16] Although merchants and some liberal officials favored recognition, the king of France was totally opposed and, unlike their English counterparts, French ministers dared not act contrary to the king's will. Consequently, the rapid growth of trade between France and Spanish America did not lead to recognition.

Political divisions in France also retarded Spanish American recognition. The Villele ministry fell at the end of 1827. The following year Spanish American affairs languished because of

*France and Rome*

France's involvement in the Russo-Turkish War. Trade continued to expand, but talks were suspended. Viscount Jean Batiste Martignan headed a caretaker government until 1829. Then, tired of quasi-liberal ministers, the king of France chose the standard-bearer of conservatism, Prince Polignac, as president of the council of ministers.

The appointment of a conservative government augured ill for Spanish American hopes of recognition. Rocafuerte, who had been relieved of his duties and was preparing to return to Mexico, decided to visit France at the end of 1829 as an unofficial observer. He had known Polignac when the prince was ambassador to England and hoped, therefore, to learn what direction the new government intended to take. Rocafuerte also visited his friend the Marquis de La Fayette, a leader of the liberal faction in the chamber of deputies, and asked him to use his influence in obtaining recognition for Mexico. The marquis invited Rocafuerte to his estate at La Grange where, together with other important French liberals, they plotted to force the Polignac government to recognize Mexico and Gran Colombia. Rocafuerte agreed to remain in France for two months trying to win the support of French merchants for a proposal which La Fayette would introduce in the chamber. Although the plan was implemented, they could not exert sufficient pressure to force Charles X to change his policies. Polignac's legitimist government rejected all Spanish American overtures and talks came to an end. Negotiations were renewed only after the Revolution of 1830 deposed the Bourbon king; Mexico and France finally negotiated a treaty of friendship in March 1831.[17]

Although Spanish Americanists devoted substantial time and effort to winning French recognition, Paris continued to favor legitimacy until 1830. The Americans desired French recognition because many of them felt a special kinship to that nation, either because they had once lived there, like Rocafuerte, or because, like Fernández de Madrid, they identified with her culture. However, the Spanish Americanists underestimated the strength of legitimist sentiment in the French government. Even Prussia, the supposed bulwark of conservatism, entered into negotiations before France. Despite the enormous increase in trade with America, the king and the ultra-conservatives refused to abandon their principles. Various French governments attempted to reconcile these conflicting interests by reaching commercial understandings with Spanish America while refusing diplomatic recognition. In 1829 Charles X appointed Polignac to lead a conservative ministry. His oppressive administration provoked the Revolution of 1830 and the change of regime finally permitted France to join the other nations in extending recognition to Spanish America.

2

The diplomacy of two other states, Spain and the Holy See, was of great importance to Spanish America. Spain's recognition of American independence would eliminate a major obstacle to widespread diplomatic recognition of the new nations. That event, however, seemed unlikely as long as Ferdinand VII reigned. Thus Spanish Americans were resigned to lengthy negotiations with Spain. Papal recognition was of more immediate concern; the Catholic nations of Spanish America could not remain estranged from the head of the Church. There were, however, various disputed issues, the most important was the *patronato reál*.

The *patronato*, a series of privileges granted by various popes to Spanish monarchs, gave the Spanish government comprehensive control of the Church in America. During the first two centuries of Spanish rule the Church had been a branch of government. Through the *patronato* the Spanish state controlled the administrative functions of the clergy while granting them privileges, or *fueros*. But in the eighteenth century Spanish reformers sought to deprive the Church of its special status. This movement, known as "regalism" by its adherents and "jansenism" by its opponents, appeared to triumph during the reign of Charles III. Although the ultramontane Jesuits were expelled, the Church still retained vast influence when independence came.[18]

The *patronato* had been an issue in the Spanish world since 1808; it was discussed in the Cortes (1810–1814 and 1820–1823) where liberals maintained that the right of *patronato* was one of the sovereign powers of the Spanish state. When Spanish America seceded, American liberals claimed the right of *patronato* for their countries and sought papal confirmation of this prerogative.

As long as the Holy See did not dispute the right of the king of Spain to exercise the *patronato* in America, Mexican liberals believed that their sovereignty was not total. Conservatives, however, maintained that the *patronato* was not a right but a privilege granted by the papacy to the Spanish crown. Thus the *patronato* ended when Mexico gained her independence. Nevertheless, conservatives insisted that the Church retained the privileges it had gained as the partner of the Spanish state. The liberals objected not only because the Church would be exempt from state control but also because it would continue to exercise its great influence over the masses from a privileged position. Instead, they preferred a national church regulated by the state and staffed by secular clergy. They deemed the regular orders with their ties to Rome a threat to the nation. The liberals had the support of many secular priests who were themselves liberal and who would gain by the displacement of the regular clergy.[19]

Attempts to establish relations with the Vatican began as soon as the American nations became independent. In May 1824 Mexico appointed Canon Francisco Pablo Vázquez envoy to the Holy See. The government desired to negotiate with the papacy, provided two conditions were met: Mexico would enjoy the right to exercise the *patronato* and the diocese of Chiapas would be included in the archbishopric of Mexico so that religious and national boundaries would coincide.

Many Mexican liberals questioned Vázquez' appointment, fearing that the hierarchical nature of the Catholic Church would prevent the priest from negotiating in the best interests of Mexico. They suggested a layman be sent instead. The Supreme Executive Power, nevertheless, believed that Vázquez was well suited for the job and his appointment was ratified. Shortly after his departure, the triumvirate instructed acting Minister of Foreign Relations Juan Guzmán to contact the Holy See and express Mexico's desire to establish relations with the papacy.[20] Unfortunately, His Holiness was not in sympathy with the new states.

On September 24, 1824, Pope Leo XII issued an encyclical to the bishops of America deploring the state of the Church in those areas, which he characterized as festering with rebellion and contaminated by evil, incendiary, and heretical ideas. The pope, on the other hand, praised the Holy Alliance, declaring that the Holy

Religion could not remain intact in America unless the "present divisions" ended. His Holiness concluded by praising Ferdinand VII and urging bishops to convince Catholics of his special virtues.[21] The encyclical was printed in the *Gazeta de Madrid* and widely disseminated in Europe. At the same time the Spanish government forced the Vatican to expel Ignacio Tejada, Gran Colombia's envoy to the Holy See, who had been received as a private individual. The encyclical and Tejada's expulsion convinced many observers in Europe and America that the pope supported Spain's claims to the New World. Michelena reported from London that most European governments interpreted the encyclical as an exhortation to the conservative clergy to overthrow the existing governments in Spanish America.[22]

On October 27, 1824, before news of the encyclical reached Mexico, newly elected President Guadalupe Victoria sent the pope a letter expressing his desire to establish relations with the papacy.[23] Michelena received Victoria's letter in March 1825. At first he considered not forwarding the communication because he believed that the Vatican opposed Spanish American independence. When he did send the president's letter to Leo XII, he included a personal message to Cardinal Secretary of State Giulio della Somaglia explaining that President Victoria had written His Holiness before learning of the encyclical. Michelena informed the Vatican that while Mexico recognized Pope Leo XII as the spiritual head of the Catholic Church, she did not consider her independence a religious question. Accordingly, the Mexican government regarded the encyclical as the regrettably mistaken view taken by the temporal ruler of the Papal States and not an issue relevant to relations with the Holy See. The government of Mexico, he concluded, respected the pope as the leader of the Holy Faith but it would not tolerate anyone questioning the incontrovertible fact of independence entrusted to the nation by High Providence.[24]

As soon as the encyclical reached Mexico, the government sent new instructions to Vázquez. Alamán ordered him not to travel to Rome until Rocafuerte learned the Vatican's attitude toward Mexico. The foreign minister hoped that Michelena's letter would impress upon His Holiness the folly of serving the interests of the Holy Alliance. Alamán assured Rocafuerte that the encyclical had not undermined the authority of the government because "both the clergy and the people understand the limits of the ecclesiastical authority of the popes."[25]

While the Mexican envoy to the Vatican remained in London waiting for instructions, his assistant José Joaquín de Moral, a Mexican priest who had resided in Europe for many years, entered into talks with the papal nuncio in Paris. Early in August, Moral notified Rocafuerte that the nuncio had assured him Rome desired to establish contacts with Vázquez. Rocafuerte, however, did not believe the time propitious for talks. Furthermore, Miguel Ramos Arizpe, the new minister of ecclesiastic affairs, had instructed the chargé not to allow Vázquez to travel to Rome unless the Vatican received the priest as an official envoy of Mexico. Under no circumstances should the envoy compromise the nation's honor by going as a private citizen. Accordingly, Rocafuerte instructed Vázquez not to proceed to Rome or to contact the nuncio in Paris unless specifically ordered to do so by the Mexican government.[26]

The already difficult negotiations with the Vatican were further complicated by the conflicting personalities of the Mexican diplomats. Vázquez, a conservative priest who distrusted the liberal tendencies of his government, believed that by establishing relations with the Holy See, he could protect the Mexican Church from radicalism. Consequently, he was willing to accept onerous terms. On the other hand, Rocafuerte, who had visited Rome, was an avowed regalist and anti-clerical who regarded the Vatican as "a center of corruption, deceit, intrigue, and wretchedness," referring to it thereafter as that "miserable satellite of the Holy Alliance."[27] Fearful of the growing activity of the Jesuits in European politics, he advised the governments of Spanish America to sever relations with the pope and establish national churches.[28]

Relations between Rocafuerte and Vázquez deteriorated when the envoy obtained permission to live in Brussels. Rocafuerte opposed Vázquez' move fearing that, once there, the priest would be subject to pressures from Rome to place his faith above his duty to his country. The chargé's suspicions were confirmed when Gorostiza reported that the Mexican Jesuit, José Peña, a religious fanatic, was trying to convince Vázquez to travel to Rome as a private individual. Since many Europeans still believed that the clergy in America remained loyal to Ferdinand VII, any rash act by Vázquez would damage Mexico's prestige. As a result of Peña's and

Moral's insistence that he confer with the nuncio in Paris, Vázquez returned to London to discuss the matter with Rocafuerte. The chargé and Murphy, who was also in England, agreed that such a conference would harm Mexico. Vázquez, however, insisted upon the necessity of initiating talks. After much difficulty, Rocafuerte convinced the envoy to return to Brussels without seeing the papal representative, assuring Vázquez that he would request new instructions immediately. When he wrote the minister of foreign relations, however, Rocafuerte did not recommend conversations with the Vatican. Instead, the chargé suggested that Vázquez be given strict instructions to prevent him from acting in an irresponsible manner.[29]

Rocafuerte had reason to doubt the priest's loyalty to Mexico. Earlier, in July 1825, Ramos Arizpe had instructed Vázquez to protest the papal encyclical of September 1824. The envoy violated both the letter and the spirit of his instructions. In January 1826 Vázquez wrote to Leo XII that he had been authorized to make some observations about, and not a protest against, the encyclical. The Mexican began by explaining to His Holiness that Spanish intrigue had placed a false interpretation on the encyclical, leading some to believe that the pope was anti-American. Then, Vázquez declared that Mexico was Catholic and would remain so. He further indicated that Mexico's present government had not acted against the Church as the Spanish Cortes had done earlier when it permitted freedom of the press and allowed heretical and anti-religious books to enter Mexico. Iturbide, he stated, had restored censorship and the present government was continuing this policy by encouraging bishops to compile an index to restrict impious freedoms. He concluded that although the Spanish Cortes had revoked many of the rights and privileges of the clergy, the Mexican government was seeking to restore Church prerogatives. None of Vázquez' declarations to the Vatican was true. Guadalupe Victoria's government had no intention of surrendering to conservative views on the Church. The envoy knew this, yet he deliberately distorted Mexico's position. Concerning the right of *patronato*, which he had been instructed to sustain, Vázquez wrote that Mexico should be commended by the Pope because she had not exercised the *patronato* since becoming independent. He contrasted Mexico's actions to those of the constitutional government of Spain and other Spanish American nations who had arrogated that power to themselves.[30] He concluded by expressing his desire to enter into talks with the Vatican.

Rome was unwilling to make major concessions, but hoped to retain Church influence in Mexico. Michelena's earlier letter had impressed upon the Holy See the grave differences developing between the Vatican and Spanish America. As a consequence, the pope sought to conciliate the Mexican government by writing the "renowned leader" (*inclito duci*), Guadalupe Victoria, congratulating him upon the peace and harmony existing in Mexico, and expressing the pontiff's gratification that Mexico desired to remain Catholic.[31] Cardinal Secretary of State Della Somaglia also sent Count de Luchesi to persuade Vázquez to come to Rome as a private person. When this failed, Jesuit spies were dispatched to undermine Vázquez' resolve, overcome his scruples against acting without authority, and induce him to travel to Italy.[32]

Rocafuerte also believed that the moment had arrived for Mexico to initiate formal talks with His Holiness, since Rome had again received Gran Colombia's envoy, Tejada. The Mexican chargé, however, was equally certain that Vázquez was too awed by ecclesiastical authority to be an effective representative of Mexico. Moreover, he feared that the Roman curia would use the priest as an unwitting pawn in their attempt to destroy democracy.[33] Indeed, Rocafuerte reported that the pope was participating in the strong wave of reaction sweeping Europe. The pontiff had assisted the emperor of Austria in repressing liberals by excommunicating Masons and Carbonarists. The Jesuits and the *ultras*, a reactionary group, were attempting to destroy freedom in France. And, he declared, European liberals believed that the Jesuits were the most effective agents of the Holy Alliance. Under the circumstances, Rocafuerte recommended that the suggestible Vázquez not be allowed to travel to Rome. The Mexican government agreed and instructed the envoy to remain in Brussels until he received further instructions.[34]

The Vatican, however, was unwilling to accept the impasse. The cardinal secretary of state sent a long conciliatory letter to Vázquez expressing the Holy Father's desire that the Mexican envoy come to Rome for talks. The Mexican priest was ecstatic.[35] However, Rocafuerte continued to insist that Vázquez could proceed only if Pope Leo XII received him as Mexico's official envoy and, since the cardinal's letter explicitly avoided any mention of the priest's diplomatic status, the chargé d'affaires refused to approve the trip. In a private letter to the minister of foreign affairs, Rocafuerte pointed out that the cardinal secretary of state had not recognized Mexico or her president. Indeed, all the Vatican's actions were carefully calculated to avoid even a hint of recognition. Leo XII, for example, had addressed President Victoria as "renowned leader," Cardinal Della Somaglia referred to him as "commanding general"; neither of the letters mentioned the United States of Mexico, but only some vague "Mexican nation." Rocafuerte was also dissatisfied with Vázquez' uncritical attitude toward Rome. The envoy did not understand that the papacy was capable of using treachery to gain its ends. When Gorostiza discovered that a Jesuit spy was living in Vázquez' house in Brussels, the priest refused to believe it. The chargé argued that although Vázquez was a learned man, he was too conservative. What would he do, wondered Rocafuerte, if the envoy were to go to Rome where he would be surrounded by priests who were masters of deception and who had grown old amid the intrigues and corruption of an absolutist court? What priest, he asked, would not be seduced by the possibility of becoming a bishop? The greatest danger, in Rocafuerte's view, was that "the enemies of our system have their last hopes for victory in Rome."[36]

The chargé worried unnecessarily, because events in Mexico were to make Vázquez unwelcome in the Vatican. Since the pope's letter to Guadalupe Victoria was extremely well received in Mexico, Minister of Ecclesiastic Affairs Ramos Arizpe asked Congress to reevaluate the state of relations between Mexico and Rome. After considering the question, Congress declared on February 18, 1826, that nothing had changed; Mexico wished to establish relations with the papacy, but she would not abandon her sovereign right of *patronato*. When the pontiff learned that Mexico's legislature reserved the right to decide matters of Church administration and discipline, he withdrew Vázquez' invitation.[37]

Incensed at Congress and convinced that its actions had prevented him from being received in Rome, Vázquez published a pamphlet criticizing his government. Unwilling to rebuke the envoy publicly, Rocafuerte commissioned his Spanish emigré friends, José Canga Argüelles, Pablo Mendíbil, and Joaquín L. Villanueva, to defend Mexico in the press.[38] The polemic coincided with the arrival, in October 1826, of Mexico's plenipotentiary, Sebastián Camacho. He immediately demanded an explanation from Vázquez. After several conversations with the envoy, Camacho decided that Vázquez was not the man to represent Mexico in Rome. The plenipotentiary was further angered when he learned that the papal nuncio in Paris was publicly characterizing the action of the Mexican Congress as heretical. In a lengthy report to his government, Camacho suggested that a new, more carefully chosen envoy should be dispatched to Rome. In Mexico, the government reacted less strongly. Ramos Arizpe agreed that the actions of the Vatican were high-handed, but counseled patience.[39]

If Mexico desired to establish relations with Rome, patience and understanding were indeed required because the Vatican found itself in difficult straits. The pope had a dual role: he was the spiritual head of the Catholic Church as well as the sovereign of the Papal States. As a spiritual leader he wanted to deal with Spanish American Catholics but, as a temporal prince, he could not recognize the new states until the principal Catholic nations, Spain, France, and Austria, did so. Yet the longer the Vatican delayed in negotiating with Spanish America, the greater the danger of a schism became. Chile and Guatemala were already threatening to break away from Rome because the pope had failed to appoint new bishops to replace those who had either died or fled. Since only bishops could ordain priests, the Spanish Americans needed new prelates immediately. However, the pope, still accepting the prerogatives of the king of Spain under the *patronato*, would not approve Spanish American episcopal nominations unless Ferdinand VII endorsed them first. The American governments, interpreting this requirement as an infringement of their sovereignty, began to consider seriously the establishment of national churches.

Mexico, like the other Spanish American nations, had hoped that the Holy See would recognize her independence and immediately appoint new bishops. The Vatican's apparent intransigence, however, forced Victoria's government to reconsider its policy. As George Ward, the English chargé d'affaires in Mexico, reported in March 1827, the Mexican government was attempting to demonstrate to "the clergy of all ranks, the inconvenience and manifold disadvantages of a dependence upon a trans-Atlantic power [Rome]."[40]

Concerned with the growing estrangement of Mexico, the Vatican requested France's assistance in arranging a meeting between Camacho and the papal nuncio in Paris. On April 18, 1827, Baron Damas met with the two men. The nuncio asked the Mexican plenipotentiary to allow Vázquez to travel to Rome as an agent for the Mexican Church. Camacho refused, insisting that the Mexican envoy could travel to the Holy See only if he were accorded the status of an official representative of Mexico. Furthermore, he reminded the ecclesiastical diplomat that the United States of Mexico insisted upon her right of *patronato* and that, until the pope recognized that right, little could be discussed. The nuncio's attempt to explain Leo XII's delicate political position failed to arouse Camacho's sympathy. On the contrary, the Mexican accused the Church of mixing religion with politics. America, he reminded the papal delegate, had been conquered and destroyed by the Spaniards with the approval of Urban VI, who even rewarded their barbarity. Then, as today, the Mexican declared, the Court of Rome danced to the tune of imperial power. Furthermore, Camacho would not send Vázquez to Rome only to have him expelled at Spain's whim, as had happened earlier to the Gran Colombian envoy, Tejada.

Disturbed by the tone of the discussion, the nuncio implored the Mexican to have patience and to inform his government that the papacy was trying to resolve the differences between them. Camacho agreed, but warned that the situation of the Church in Mexico was grave. New bishops were needed immediately and they could be nominated only if the Vatican recognized the republic. If the Holy Father did not heed the call of the faithful, it was quite possible that they would listen to those who wanted to sever relations with Rome. In view of the gravity of the situation, Baron Damas suggested that Vázquez be authorized to enter into talks with the nuncio. Camacho, however, was unwilling to permit the Mexican priest to negotiate with his clerical superiors. He evaded the issue by promising to seek instructions on the matter.[41]

No further developments occurred in the months that Camacho remained in Europe. After his departure, Rocafuerte received a letter from Ignacio Tejada on August 17, 1827, informing him that

Vázquez had inquired about going to Rome. Although Tejada wanted another American in the Holy City to oppose Spanish influence, he believed that no priest, especially Vázquez, should be sent. Friends in Paris had given Tejada reports of the Mexican's attitude and the Gran Colombian felt that Vázquez' presence would be dangerous for both Mexico and Gran Colombia. Tejada also included his reply to Vázquez, leaving it up to the chargé to decide whether or not to forward the letter to the priest. Since Rocafuerte did not want Vázquez in Rome, he did not send Tejada's communication to him. Instead, the chargé informed his government of the Gran Colombian's attitude and suggested that Vázquez be relieved.[41]

In September Rocafuerte rushed to Belgium when he learned that Vázquez was leaving Brussels. The priest informed him that the cold climate had ruined his health and that he needed to move to Paris or perhaps to southern France to recuperate. The chargé d'affaires, however, suspected that the envoy was traveling to Paris principally to talk to the papal nuncio. Instead, he recommended that Vázquez return to Mexico where he could regain his health. When the envoy refused to abandon his mission, Rocafuerte reluctantly granted him permission to travel to southern France. But fearful that the priest would yield to the temptation to visit Rome, Rocafuerte decided to use Vázquez' illness to have him relieved. The chargé informed his government that Vázquez was in extremely bad health and that doctors warned he would die if he did not change climates. Rocafuerte's report, in conjunction with Tejada's letter and Camacho's recommendations, convinced Mexico to recall Vázquez; in October 1827, the government appointed José María Bocanegra as his replacement.[43]

When Vázquez learned that he had been relieved, he insisted on waiting for his successor. However, the growing political divisions in Mexico prevented Bocanegra's departure. While Vásquez waited, he protested that Rocafuerte had exaggerated his illness and had wantonly falsified his opinions. The priest was certain that he was a victim of political intrigue. He also suspected that Rocafuerte was harassing him by withholding the funds necessary for his sustenance. As a result, a heated correspondence ensued between the two men. Vásquez did not realize that Mexico was in financial straits and that in 1828 her diplomats in Europe were able to survive only because of Rocafuerte's personal efforts to obtain funds for them. Vázquez' mission was particularly expensive because he had a large entourage, including several young art students. His situation was further complicated because the minister of treasury failed to include Vázquez among those to be paid by Baring Brothers. Although the problem had arisen in 1827, while Camacho was in London, the plenipotentiary did not resolve it and the treasury did not instruct Baring Brothers to pay Vázquez until 1830. Despite the growing antipathy between the two men, Rocafuerte managed to provide some funds for the priest. Nevertheless, Vázquez blamed Rocafuerte for all his difficulties.[44]

When no one came to relieve him, the envoy decided to act without authority. Vázquez departed for Rome in 1828. After being delayed in northern Italy, he arrived in the Vatican in April 1829. Gran Colombian Envoy Tejada reported that, although Vázquez had been admitted as a priest to see his Vicar General, he had not been permitted to talk to Cardinal Secretary of State Della Somaglia. Tejada deplored Vázquez' actions as prejudicial to Mexico, warning Rocafuerte that the priest's loyalties were clearly divided. The chargé d'affaires reported Vázquez actions, requesting that his government send a replacement immediately. Rocafuerte also suggested that Mexico sever all ties with the Vatican because, though a new pope had been elected, the corrupt Court of Rome would never change.[45]

The Mexican government, divided politically, took no action. In 1830 the reactionary government of Anastasio Bustamante reappointed Vázquez to his mission. Certain that the political climate in Mexico had changed, Vázquez readily compromised his nation's interests. The most pressing problem of the Mexican Church was solved in February 1831, when the pope named new bishops, among them Vázquez. This was accomplished by maneuvers that preserved Ferdinand VII's right of *patronato* while granting Mexico a semblance of autonomy. The Vatican accepted Mexico's episcopal nominations after secretly obtaining Spain's approval. Moreover, the new bishops only received appointments *in partibus*.

After being consecrated in Rome, Vázquez returned home, leaving Tejada in charge of Mexican affairs. Conservatives were pleased. They believed that by obtaining the appointment of new bishops he had saved the Catholic Church in Mexico. Liberals,

however, were incensed. Vázquez had betrayed their principles.
His actions had the effect of forfeiting their demands for a
Mexican *patronato*. As a result, some liberals began to consider the
possibility of amending the constitution to separate the Church
from the state. Despite the appointment of new bishops, Rome
refused to recognize Mexico. The pope only established diplomatic
relations with Mexico after Spain did so in 1836, following the
death of Ferdinand VII.[46]

# X

## THE SPANISH LIBERALS, ROCAFUERTE, AND AMERICA

When Michelena and Rocafuerte arrived in England in 1824, they discovered that London had become a haven for liberals who had fled Spain following the French invasion of 1823. The refugees chose Great Britain because it was one of the few European nations free from the influence of the Holy Alliance. The Mexican diplomats, who already knew many of the exiles, rapidly developed friendships with others. Although some Spanish liberals did not approve of the independence of America, others accepted it and willingly furnished information about their country to the Spanish Americanists. Accordingly, the relationship was beneficial to Michelena and Rocafuerte. The British government, however, was displeased because the Mexican diplomats had too many close ties with Spaniards opposed to Ferdinand VII.[1]

1

Rocafuerte, convinced that the constitutional liberals of Spain and America had a common cause, was determined to continue these associations. While many of the exiles were men of outstanding ability, they found themselves in a strange land with little means of support. True to the spirit of Spanish Americanism, Rocafuerte sought to assist them and also benefit America by subsidizing Spanish intellectuals who agreed to write works useful to the new nations. On July 30, 1824, Rocafuerte contacted his old friend, the former Spanish minister of treasury, José Canga Argüelles, and suggested that there were few men as well qualified as he was to discuss political economy and public expenditures. The Spaniard was well acquainted with contemporary economic theory and had experience in applying these theories to concrete political situations.[2] Rocafuerte asked Canga Argüelles to write a work that would guide the governments of Spanish America in allocating their expenditures. The former minister, flattered by the request, agreed to revise his manuscript entitled "Science of the Treasury," which he had composed while imprisoned by Ferdinand VII.

Canga Argüelles completed the study in two months, dedicating it to Guadalupe Victoria, the newly elected president of Mexico. Entitled *Elements of the Science of the Treasury*, the book appeared early in 1825 and was immediately successful. It was so well received in Mexico that various editors wanted to publish a second printing. Canga Argüelles, however, asked the Mexican government to prohibit another printing until he could revise his work. The following year, he published a new edition in London.[3] Thereafter, Rocafuerte continued to sponsor Canga Argüelles, who was working on a massive five-volume economic dictionary of Spain.[4]

Canga Argüelles' success confirmed Rocafuerte's belief that Spanish intellectuals could advance the cause of Spanish Americanism if they could find an outlet for their publications. While most Spanish emigrés preferred to write literature, Rocafuerte convinced some of them to compose technical studies by arranging to have their literary works published by Rudolf Ackerman. Rocafuerte agreed to subsidize a series of manuals in religion, morals, grammar, geography, arithmetic, and technology, while the publisher undertook to print the Spaniards' literary works. Ackerman accepted the arrangement because the Mexican chargé d'affaires agreed to secure preferential treatment for his publications in Spanish America. In the years that followed, a series of technical manuals called catechisms were published and widely distributed in the New World. Since these books became the basic and, in many cases, the only texts used in the schools of Spanish America, the Spanish liberals exercised a profound influence on several generations of Americans. The literary works of the Spaniards—poems, plays, novels, and literary criticism—were also widely distributed to an avid public in Spanish America.[5] Thus the exiles insured the continuity of the Spanish liberal tradition in the New World.

Rocafuerte also sponsored important works issued by other publishers. He convinced José Joaquín de Mora to translate

Francisco S. Clavigero's *History of Ancient Mexico*, which had originally appeared in Italian, by paying for the publication of Mora's
history of the Arabs.[6] Later, he commissioned the famous former
*exaltado* and outstanding military leader, Evaristo San Miguel, to
write a manual for the instruction of young officers in America.
Although San Miguel envisioned a six-volume treatise, he was only
able to finish the first two.[7] Nonetheless, San Miguel's work became
the basic text in the military schools of Spanish America.

2

Rocafuerte's commitment to improving education in Spanish
America drew him to groups and individuals with similar interests.
Two associations, the British and Foreign Bible Society and the
British and Foreign School Society, were active in promoting moral
and intellectual learning. The Bible Society distributed scriptures
and religious works to all sectors of society, while the School
Society, or Lancasterian movement, stressed social improvement
through literacy. Since the two associations had similar aims,
individuals often belonged to both groups. Rocafuerte hoped that
the two societies would help improve learning as well as morality in
Spanish America by supporting the distribution of religious texts.
He had already won renown by translating the New York School
Society's primer, which was modeled on the British School Society's
reader, for use in Spanish America. Accordingly, Rocafuerte was
well received by the members of the Lancasterian movement. In
Rocafuerte's view, however, the primer was only the first step in
providing adequate instructional materials for America. He encouraged the Bible Society to publish Father Felipe Scío's authorized Spanish edition of the Bible for distribution in the New
World. He also suggested that some treatises used by both societies
be translated for the newly independent nations. To demonstrate
the feasibility of the suggestion, Rocafuerte convinced one of his
Spanish friends, the liberal priest Joaquín L. Villanueva, to translate William Paley's *Natural Theology*. In return, he subsidized the
publication of the Spaniard's memoirs. Impressed by the translation, the members of the two Societies formed the Society for

Spanish Translations, which contacted Spanish exiles and commissioned various translations.[8]

Rocafuerte used his personal friendship with the presidents of Gran Colombia and Mexico, as well as with the ministers of several Spanish American nations, to pave the way for the representatives of the School and Bible Societies in the New World. He provided letters of recommendation for individuals, sponsored schools and charitable institutions, and used his diplomatic status to safeguard the Bibles and treatises that the groups distributed in America. With his support, the Society for Spanish Translations published and distributed 11,500 volumes of educational and religious works by 1828. As society representatives developed contacts in the New World, they formed central distribution points in Mexico City, Guatemala City, Cartagena, Guayaquil, Lima, Valparaiso, Buenos Aires, and La Güaira.[9]

Participation in the British and Foreign School Society brought Rocafuerte into daily contact with many of its influential members, among them various Tory leaders: the Duke of Bedford, Lord Clarendon, Lord John Russell, the Marquis of Landsdowne, and Lord Holland. Charles Barclay, director of various commercial houses, was also a member, as were Ambassador M. de Falk of the Netherlands and Count Mandelstohl, ambassador of Württemberg.[10] His acquaintance with these men not only facilitated his diplomatic efforts, it also gave him an opportunity to win support for projects to assist Spanish American development. When the School Society invited him to prepare a report on the state of education in Latin America for its annual meeting in May 1826, Rocafuerte used the reunion to impress upon the members the necessity of furthering modern attitudes and education in America.[11] While depicting the progress of Lancasterian schools in Mexico, Guatemala, Gran Colombia, Peru, Chile, and Argentina in glowing terms, he exhorted the Society to continue its work for the well-being of humanity and particularly for the new nations of America.

Although the mutual system of education was growing in each Spanish American country, Rocafuerte believed that a unified effort would produce greater results. He convinced the British and Foreign School Society to propose a plan for the expansion of

Spanish American education to the second Pan-American conference to be held in Tacubaya, Mexico, in 1827. Then he collaborated with James Thompson, who had been designated to represent the Society, in preparing a formal manifesto to the Congress
of Tacubaya.[12]

Thompson left for Mexico in February 1827, carrying with him
several boxes of Bibles as well as printed copies of the Society's
manifesto. He arrived in Veracruz on April 29, where customs'
inspectors refused to allow the scriptures to enter Mexico because
they did not contain the Book of Macabees. Fortunately for
Thompson, Rocafuerte had returned to Mexico with the English
treaty and arranged for the entry of the Testaments. He also
provided Thompson with letters of recommendation to important
politicians and educators in the capital as well as to other Spanish
American officials who were in Mexico to attend the Tacubaya
Conference. Unfortunately, the Pan-American Conference did not
take place and the proposal of the British and Foreign School
Society could not be considered. Nevertheless, Thompson remained in Mexico to work for the Society and Rocafuerte's
introductions facilitated his task.[13] In London, the Society voted to
elect Rocafuerte an honorary member.[14]

Rocafuerte's activities in the School Society also allowed him to
meet prominent social reformers. Lord Henry Holland, a member
of the School Society, often invited Rocafuerte to gatherings at
Holland House, a noted London salon.[15] There the Mexican
chargé met important social workers, among them Mrs. Elizabeth
Fry, who had formed an association to improve conditions for
women prisoners at Newgate. Mrs. Fry believed that religious
instruction could rehabilitate the inmates. She and other ladies of
the group visited the jail to read the Holy Scriptures and to exhort
the prisoners to a better life. Rocafuerte approved of the program
of Christian rehabilitation. Since he had long standing interest in
prison reform, he expressed a desire to learn more about the
movement. Mrs. Fry introduced him to her brother-in-law, Sir
Thomas Buxtom, a businessman, Member of Parliament, and the
leader of the drive to improve conditions in Britain's jails. When
Buxtom offered to arrange an inspection of several nearby prisons,
Rocafuerte accepted gladly. Sir Thomas also invited the Mexican

chargé to attend his group's meetings and study their literature.[16] Later the American visited prisons on the Continent and studied new rehabilitation methods. Since criminality was a grave problem in the new nations, Rocafuerte hoped to publish a study advocating penal reform. Some of his preliminary reflections appeared in the Spanish exile newspaper *Ocios de los españoles emigrados*; he argued that prisoners should not be punished, but rehabilitated, and that jails should be considered but another aspect of education.[17]

3

The *Ocios* supported Rocafuerte's views because the chargé subsidized the journal by purchasing two hundred copies of each issue. Moreover, its directors, Canga Argüelles, Villanueva, and later Pablo Mendíbil, were indebted to Rocafuerte for arranging the publication of their literary works. Since the paper's political editor, Canga Argüelles, sympathized with the American's political attitudes, the *Ocios* published political opinions that betrayed Rocafuerte's influence. The paper opposed the Vatican, stood for federalism rather than centralism, praised religious toleration, and was concerned with social welfare.[18] As a result, Spanish Americans who favored other positions were often critical. The periodical flourished while Rocafuerte remained in London, but it began to decline at the end of 1826 when he returned to Mexico and suspended publication in October 1827. The *Ocios'* demise was related to the economic difficulties of the Mexican government. Rocafuerte was forced to curtail financial support by the end of 1827 because he was no longer receiving funds to meet legation expenses and faced the prospect of having to divert his personal income to support Mexico's agents in Europe.[19]

During the height of the *Ocios'* activity, Canga Argüelles collaborated with Rocafuerte on an important discussion on the nature of government in Spanish America. Late in 1824 the Chilean Congress began to dismantle the conservative constitution fashioned by Juan Egaña in 1823. During the debates, liberal and federal ideas gained popularity and there was the possibility that Chile would draft a federal charter. Since Mexico was the principal Spanish

American model of federalism, many Chilean conservatives, among them Egaña, wrote scathing criticisms of Mexico's constitution.[20] Consequently, the debate took on international overtones.

As Mexico's representative in England, Rocafuerte felt compelled to participate in the debate. He refuted Egaña's claims in a work analyzing the constitutions of Guatemala, Mexico, and the United States, in which he argued that those nations were peaceful and prosperous because they had adopted federalism. The study also contained a detailed criticism of Egaña's views. Rocafuerte completed a draft of the work, but hesitated to publish the book under his own name lest he antagonize Egaña's son, Mariano, then Chile's minister to England. Accordingly, Rocafuerte convinced Canga Argüelles to edit and publish the study.[21] Although the Spaniard reorganized the material, the book, which appeared as *Letters by an American on the Advantages of Republican Governments*, bore the unmistakable characteristics of Rocafuerte's style.[22]

Certain that the Mexican chargé had written the work, Mariano Egaña severed relations with him. Although Rocafuerte explained that his disagreement with Juan Egaña was ideological and not personal, Mariano considered the Mexican diplomat an enemy. He wrote his father that Rocafuerte was probably the paid agent of Chilean radicals like Francisco Antonio Pinto and Joaquín Campiño Salamanca who Mariano believed were intent on destroying his father. The Chilean minister was so ill-disposed toward Rocafuerte that he suspected the Mexican of being a puppet of Ferdinand VII because the chargé was involved with the Spanish exiles.[23] Thus, the publication of the *Letters* proved detrimental to New World cooperation. Although Spanish Americanists like Rocafuerte felt it was their responsibility to offer advice and criticism to any Spanish American government, nationalists were offended by these instrusions in their countries' internal politics.

4

The international debate on the nature of Spanish American governments drove Rocafuerte into a dispute with his friend Bolívar. The disagreement began as the result of an insurrection in Venezuela. General José Antonio Paéz, one of the area's most popular leaders, rebelled against the government in Bogotá. Seizing on the Paéz revolt as an opportunity to advance the cause of federalism, Rocafuerte wrote Bolívar a long letter on September 27, 1826, suggesting that Gran Colombia abandon centralism.[24]

Rocafuerte argued that Mexico and Guatemala were peaceful and prosperous because they had adopted the federal system. He knew that the Liberator believed only a strong central government could succeed in South America. But he reminded his friend that he, too, had once opposed federalism on theoretical grounds. Experience, however, had demonstrated that it was the best system of government because it permitted political and religious liberty. Rocafuerte knew that Bolívar had suffered hardships during the early days of confederation in Gran Colombia, but believed that the situation had changed. He declared, "What was then the reason for the failure [of the government] is today the means of its salvation."[25] Rocafuerte also warned Bolívar against forming a confederation of the three large sections of the country—Venezuela, Cundinamarca, and Quito—because each was large enough to develop as a separate unit and ultimately secede. Instead, Rocafuerte suggested the formation of twelve smaller states which would individually be too weak to threaten national unity.

The Constitution of Bolivia, which arrived in London the following month, convinced Rocafuerte that his advice would go unheeded. The document, written by Bolívar himself, was quite conservative, providing for a lifetime president and senate. Indeed, the Mexican chargé confided to Albert Gallatin, the United States minister to England, that Bolivia's new constitution would lend aid to the reactionaries who still hoped to destroy the existing republican institutions. He also feared Bolívar's ambition, which he believed responsible for the dissolution of Peru's congress and the introduction of a dictatorial system in that country. Thus, Rocafuerte was certain that Bolívar would make sure Gran Colombia's proposed constitutional convention would concentrate even greater power in the hands of the executive, rather than reforming the government by adopting the federal system.[26] Unwilling to allow liberalism to decline in South America, Rocafuerte availed himself of every opportunity to convince Gran Colombian officials that the South American republic needed more, not less, freedom.[27]

Since Bolívar exercised great influence and authority in Gran Colombia, Rocafuerte initiated a campaign to bring him back into the liberal fold. In June 1827, Rocafuerte wrote the Liberator a friendly letter reminding him of the quotation: "Caesar is great, but Rome is free."[28] Bolívar, however, was not swayed by the chargé's arguments or insinuations. On February 7, 1828, the Liberator wrote their mutual friend, Gran Colombia's minister to England, Fernández de Madrid, "Federation doesn't work, as proof of this Buenos Aires, Chile, Guatemala, and Mexico are lost."[29] The following year he expressed even stronger opinions, saying that it would be easier to become a Moslem than to adopt federalism, which he considered regularized anarchy.

Although Bolívar had been careful not to antagonize his friend, Rocafuerte became more and more critical, eventually concluding that the Liberator's ambition would destroy the new nations. Accordingly, when Spanish preparations for an invasion of Mexico coincided with redoubled efforts by Gran Colombia's agents to negotiate with the mother country, Rocafuerte interpreted the events as proof that Bolívar was willing to reach an agreement with Spain at Mexico's expense. It was well known, he asserted, that Ferdinand VII would accept the loss of South America, if he could regain Mexico. Rocafuerte concluded that Bolívar was trading Mexico's freedom for Spanish recognition of a monarchy in Gran Colombia with himself as king. The Mexican chargé feared the legitimist governments of Europe would be willing to reward the Liberator's betrayal of America by recognizing his dynasty, as earlier they had recognized another "traitor," Bernadotte of Sweden. Indeed, Rocafuerte's fears and suspicions prompted him to recommend that his government forestall such action by invoking the 1823 treaty of defense between Mexico and Gran Colombia, thereby forcing Bolívar to oppose the Spanish king.[30] The Mexican government, however, was not blinded by personal animosity. It wisely disregarded Rocafuerte's recommendations.

In 1829, the Liberator made a final effort to salvage their friendship by sending Rocafuerte a personally inscribed copy of his newly published memoirs. The Mexican chargé refused to change his opinions. Although he replied that no personal differences existed between them, the tone of his letter betrayed his feelings. Bolívar felt deeply insulted. Later, when he realized that he had judged the Liberator too harshly, Rocafuerte regretted his actions. Unfortunately, Bolívar died in 1830 before they could be reconciled.[31]

Although the Liberator had exaggerated when he said the federated states of Spanish America were disintegrating, there was some basis for his statement. Bitter political disputes had become common in Spanish America, not only in the federal republics, but also in the centralist nations. Unable to cope with growing internal crises, many observers advocated increasing the power of the national government, thus hoping to avoid provincial disturbances. Rocafuerte, in contrast, argued that it was necessary to control regionalism through an improved federal system, one which would foster local responsibility while it forged a stronger union. Hoping for enlightened constitutional reform, Rocafuerte wrote a comparative analysis of the constitutions of Spain and Spanish America, concluding that federalism was better than centralism.[32] Although the work was widely read, it merely reinforced the opinions of those already committed to federalism. Others continued to argue for a greater concentration of power in the national government.

5

The political divisions of Spanish America had an adverse effect on European public opinion. Many observers believed that this strife might precipitate civil wars and perhaps destroy the new nations. Temporarily discouraged by his inability to influence the affairs of other American nations, Rocafuerte concentrated his efforts on salvaging Mexico's reputation. Seeking to remind Europeans of earlier days of glory, he commissioned Pablo Mendíbil to prepare a one-volume abridgment of Carlos María Bustamante's four-volume history of Mexico's struggle for independence.[33] Rocafuerte also paid journalists in England and France to write favorable stories about Mexico. These public relations efforts failed because political strife continued in the federal republic.

Mexico's political divisions appeared to reach their apogee when the radical *yorkinos* forced the passage of a law expelling Spaniards from the nation in December 1827. Their victory seemed to have destroyed the conservative *escoceses* as a political force in Mexico as well as to have ended the basis for moderate *yorkino* control of the government. Indeed, observers feared that Mexico would become a popular democracy; in the view of many this was synonymous with anarchy. Moderate critics, like Rocafuerte, believed that radical *yorkino* leaders such as General Vicente Guerrero and Congressmen José María Alpuche and José María Tornel were responsible for political unrest in Mexico. The chargé hoped that trouble might be avoided in the 1828 presidential election if Vice President Nicolás Bravo abandoned his *escoces* friends and assumed the leadership of moderates in both groups. In this way, the radical *yorkinos* as well as the conservative *escoceses* would be defeated by the center, which could then consolidate the nation's institutions. Those prospects were destroyed when Bravo led a conservative revolt opposing the expulsion law. Since a federal army under the command of General Guerrero defeated the rebels, it appeared that the radical *yorkinos*, the extreme left, were certain to capture the presidency in the next election.[34]

The Mexican moderates, however, under the leadership of Ramos Arizpe and Michelena campaigned for Manuel Gómez Pedraza and gained sufficient support in the state legislatures to stage an election upset. Unfortunately for Mexico, the radicals refused to accept their electoral defeat. In December 1828, they organized violent mass demonstrations in the capital. Hoping to avoid civil war, President-elect Gómez Pedraza resigned before his inauguration and withdrew to Europe. Congress then elected Guerrero president and the conservative General Anastasio Bustamante, vice-president.[35]

Rocafuerte first learned about the political changes through reports from New York. Refusing to believe that such a calamity could have occurred, he requested verification from the minister of foreign affairs.[36] Within a few days he obtained most of the details from the defeated Gómez Pedraza who arrived in London as an exile. The former president-elect viewed the events with equanimity, believing that they should be interpreted in the best light possible to protect Mexico's reputation.[37]

On June 18, 1829, Rocafuerte finally received official notification of the change in government. He immediately contacted Lord Aberdeen, Britain's foreign minister, to inform him that order had been restored, that the republic was calm, and that Guerrero was the new president. He also provided Aberdeen a copy of Guerrero's inaugural address, in which the new president promised to assure internal order and to restore the nation's foreign credit. In an effort to influence English public opinion, Rocafuerte published the president's speech in the *Times*. He also wrote a series of articles stressing Guerrero's role in the independence movement and suggesting that, like Peter the Great, he would reform and modernize Mexico by the force of his indomitable will. The chargé d'affaires made similar assurances to the ministers of other European nations. Since Gómez Pedraza, who remained in London, did not criticize the new government, Rocafuerte's efforts reassured many Europeans.[38]

In his communications with the Guerrero administration, the chargé reiterated the importance of maintaining internal order and restoring the nation's foreign credit. Until the dividends could be paid, he declared, it was foolish to negotiate new loans or to expect entrepreneurs to invest in Mexico. As an economy measure, Rocafuerte suggested reducing the size of the legation in London. He recommended that the diplomatic mission be abolished and that a well organized consulate general be established. If the consul general were also provided with emergency credentials as minister extraordinary, he would be able to care for the nation's interests without having to bear the heavy expenses required of diplomats who had to attend affairs of state, court functions, and the like.[39]

6

Rocafuerte, who had continued to serve Mexico through various changes in government, was ill, disillusioned, and ready to end his diplomatic career. He had always considered his apointment temporary and had accepted it only to assist in obtaining diplomatic recognition for Mexico and the rest of Spanish America. He had asked to be replaced on various occasions in 1825, 1826, and 1827. The government of Mexico considered his requests but internal political divisions prevented the appointment of a new minister to England.[40] Rocafuerte understood the government's difficulties but, by May 1828, he was determined to resign his post. The political tactics of the radical *yorkinos* disgusted him and, after Bravo rebelled, Rocafuerte feared the government of Mexico would fall to the radicals. Furthermore, his chronic lung ailment afflicted him with particular severity in the winter of 1827–1828 and he felt that at forty-five he should return to his family and private affairs. Accordingly he asked his friend, Minister of Foreign Affairs Cañedo, to have him replaced. He requested a year and a half's leave to travel to Guayaquil. Afterwards, he would place himself once again at the disposal of the Mexican government.[41]

President Victoria agreed to relieve Rocafuerte as soon as a substitute could be appointed. This, however, proved difficult. José Ignacio Esteva, a friend of the president, suggested Borja Migoni be appointed minister to England. Protests against the nominee began immediately. *El Amigo del Pueblo*, then edited by Rocafuerte's enemy Tornel, was appalled at the recommendation. While the paper agreed that Rocafuerte should be replaced, it maintained that Borja Migoni was not suitable for the post. "Only with irony," it argued, "could such a man call himself a patriot."[42] When the British minister to Mexico learned that Borja Migoni might replace Rocafuerte, he protested that the merchant's activities in the London stock exchange would make it impossible for England to accept the appointment. British Foreign Minister Lord Dudley reiterated Pakenham's objections.[43]

As a consequence of the British protest, the Mexican government instructed Rocafuerte to determine Borja Migoni's official status in England. Believing that the chargé was exceeding his authority, Borja Migoni refused to provide Rocafuerte information. When the chargé d'affaires consulted British Under Secretary of Foreign Affairs Joseph Blackmore, he discovered that England had never recognized Borja Migoni's 1825 appointment as consul general and that, as a result, Mexico had no official commercial representative in England.[44]

Under normal circumstances such a revelation would have destroyed Borja Migoni's diplomatic career. Rocafuerte's report, however, did not reach Mexico until after Guerrero's election. Since the chargé was closely identified with the defeated moderates, the new government feared that Rocafuerte might abandon his post. In an act of desperation, it named Borja Migoni interim chargé d'affaires. The merchant, however, refused to accept the post until he learned the details of the legation's financial status. Rocafuerte informed him that the government had been unable to forward funds for some time and that the chargé d'affaires had to provide the five hundred pounds a month needed to sustain Mexico's agents in Europe. Borja Migoni, who desired the prestige of being Mexico's chief diplomat in Europe but did not want to shoulder the financial burden, refused to commit himself. Rocafuerte angrily demanded a reply in writing. Borja Migoni wrote directly to the minister of foreign affairs, rejecting the appointment. The merchant noted that Rocafuerte's rude behavior had made the prospect of a merely interim appointment, which required large personal economic sacrifices, unacceptable.[45]

Borja Migoni's refusal forced Rocafuerte to remain at his post. In a bitter note, he urged the new government to replace him. The Guerrero administration nominated Gorostiza and Congress approved the appointment with surprising ease. The new chargé d'affaires arrived in London on September 19, 1829. Before relinquishing his office, Rocafuerte obtained a small loan to cover the salaries of Mexico's diplomats in Europe until the government could provide the funds.[46] Then Rocafuerte traveled to France in an unsuccessful attempt to obtain Mexican recognition. When he returned to London ill and discouraged, he was asked by Guerrero's government to return to Mexico before going to Guayaquil. Rocafuerte suspected that the radicals who were now in power wanted to try him on the charges levied against him in 1827. In Mexico observers believed that Rocafuerte would not return. Even old friends like Alamán were uncertain about the course he would take.[47]

Rocafuerte decided to return to Mexico, face his enemies, and clear his name. Then he planned to retire from public life and devote himself to business and to social reform. He also sought a more settled existence; before returning to Mexico, he requested the necessary papal dispensation to marry his twenty-two-year-old orphaned niece, Josefa Gaínza.[48] Although Rocafuerte was adamantly opposed to papal interference in the political affairs of

America, he never questioned the pontiff's jurisdiction on religious matters. The man who had vigorously opposed diplomatic relations between the nations of Spanish America and the Vatican saw nothing incongruous in requesting the pope's permission to marry.

# XI

## ROCAFUERTE AND MEXICAN REFORMS

1

Rocafuerte left England dissatisfied with Guerrero's administration, depressed but ready to oppose José María Alpuche, José María Tornel and the other members of the cabinet.[1] By the time he reached Veracruz on March 12, 1830, Mexico had a new government. Vice-President General Anastasio Bustamante had ousted Guerrero. Although Rocafuerte was not acquainted with the new chief executive, he did know three of his ministers. His friend Lucas Alamán was minister of state for internal and foreign affairs; Rafael Mangino, a colleague from the Spanish Cortes, was minister of the treasury; and José Antonio Facio, who had been attached to the legation in England, was minister of war.[2]

Rocafuerte had great confidence in Alamán, whom he considered capable and enlightened. The former chargé d'affaires knew that Alamán was considered conservative but believed the label to be a fabrication of the radical *yorkinos*. In fact, when Alamán had been minister of foreign affairs, during the early years of the Victoria administration, Rocafuerte had expressed his liberal and, often, anti-clerical sentiments openly, yet Alamán never reproved him. Thus Rocafuerte immediately wrote the new foreign minister congratulating him on his appointment and expressing his high hopes for the new regime.[3]

Alamán and Mangino were pleased by Rocafuerte's arrival and hoped he would support them, lending his talents to the government. At the very least, they wanted to prevent his formidable pen from being used against them. Alamán arranged an interview with the vice-president but Rocafuerte could not attend because he arrived in the capital with a pulmonary disorder that confined him to bed. During his convalescence, Rocafuerte had many visitors including his old friend Congressman Carlos María Bustamante and various politicians.[4] They brought him up to date on Mexican politics.

When he recovered Rocafuerte met with Vice-President Busta-mante. The chief executive invited him to collaborate with the administration, but Rocafuerte, who wanted to retire from public affairs, requested the government's permission to return to Guaya-quil. Bustmante agreed and instructed the former chargé to apply for the necessary clearances. The following day Rocafuerte went to the treasury to initiate the complicated process. There Mangino asked his opinion of the new government. Rocafuerte replied that, although he respected the members of the present administration, Gómez Pedraza was the constitutionally elected president and, therefore, both Guerrero and Bustamante had come to office in violation of the constitution. In Rocafuerte's opinion, legitimacy, order, and stability should be restored by returning Gómez Pedra-za to the presidency. These declarations angered Mangino and the administration, which delayed issuing his passport clearance.[5]

Although Rocafuerte desired to avoid political conflict, his opinions and activities inevitably led to a confrontation with the government. In late April, James Thompson, the British and Foreign Bible Society's representative in Mexico and a friend of Rocafuerte's, sought his assistance. Eight boxes of Bibles had been impounded in January 1830, by the customs service at Veracruz. At first Thompson, who had encountered no official opposition since 1827, believed that a mistake had occurred and unsuccess-fully attempted to obtain the release of the boxes.[6] Then Thomp-son asked Rocafuerte to use his contacts with the government to obtain the release of the Bibles. On May 3, 1830, Rocafuerte wrote Minister of Interior Alamán informing him that, due to a mis-understanding on the part of local officials, the Veracruz customs had detained the scriptures. "It is one of those absurdities," he declared, "which ridicule the dignity of the Government and the enlightenment of the country and which reaffirm in the clergy pretensions which are incompatible with our [liberal Spanish American] institutions."[7] He asked Alamán, as a friend and liberal, to assure civil liberty and religious toleration by ordering the customs officials to release the Bibles. Rocafuerte's plea went unheeded since the minister of the interior had no intention of permitting religious freedom. The Bibles were released only after the Bustamante administration collapsed.[8]

2

Rocafuerte's interest in religious freedom was but part of his general concern for public welfare. He believed that the United States of Mexico, like other Spanish American nations, was divided into two groups: the wealthy and the poor. No country could prosper under those conditions. People could not be expected to understand the benefits of democracy or liberty if they lived in misery. Yet they would clearly understand the value of representative government if they could live more comfortably, dress better, enjoy adequate health care, in short, have a higher standard of living.[9] It was necessary, therefore, to introduce new industries to provide greater employment for the masses as well as prosperity for the nation. He advocated more than the expansion of opportunities for the proletariat; it was also necessary to assist the miniscule middle class. Rocafuerte's travels to Europe and the United States had convinced him that the growth of the middle sector was important for economic development as well as for political stability. He estimated that in Mexico City—the greatest metropolis of the New World—only ten percent of the population could be considered members of the middle class. This small and struggling group could not prosper because it was overburdened with the cost of living and because no institutions catered to its interests. Accordingly, he believed that both private enterprise and the state should cooperate to assist this sector.

The events of the previous decade, however, had disabused Rocafuerte of the notion that the state was the most efficient vehicle for modernization. Although he realized that governmental cooperation was necessary, he now believed that private initiative, unhampered by political considerations, would be more effective in resolving the problems of development. In particular, he believed that the major obstacles to modernization in the American nations were unemployment, urban discontent, outmoded transportation systems, antiquated social patterns, and governmental instability.

Since Mexico was the largest, wealthiest, and most advanced of the new countries, Rocafuerte decided to test his projects in the republic and, if they succeeded, extend them to other parts of Spanish America.

Although Rocafuerte believed Mexico was potentially very wealthy, inadequate communications made her and the other Spanish American nations "the poorest in the universe." He declared that outside the capital cities "one discovers [only] hunger, nakedness, and misery."[10] Improved transportation could change that, particularly in Spanish America where mountainous terrain and the absence of navigable rivers had increased costs to the point that the products of the interior could not compete with imports. In Rocafuerte's opinion only railroads could open up the interior, making agriculture and livestock-raising profitable.

Rocafuerte, who had witnessed the development of the first railroads in England, believed he could organize a company to construct a rail line. However, to arouse the interest of potential investors, he needed to create a demand for the new system. Accordingly, he published a series of articles in *El Sol* advocating the installation of gaslights in Mexico City. He maintained that the project would not only be useful, but it would also stimulate existing industries as well as create a demand for new products. Mines like Zimapán and Xantetelco in Puebla could supply iron for the numerous metal tubes required for the lighting project and a railroad would be necessary to transport iron from the mining districts to the capital. Later the line could be extended from Puebla to the port city of Veracruz, providing a direct connection between the principal port and the capital. Rocafuerte also believed that the project would stimulate development in other areas. For example, hydrocarbon was needed for the gas. Its acquisition and distribution would generate employment and increase expenditures, thereby creating new demand for manufactured and agricultural products. These and related industries would ultimately require the services of more and better railroads.[11] In short, Rocafuerte believed that his projects would generate great economic expansion.

Rocafuerte decided his development plans would gain acceptance if he could demonstrate the superiority of gaslighting in a city square. He had been planning the project for some time and had imported the necessary equipment and technical experts from England. When everything was ready, he began a publicity campaign. Rocafuerte also approached Minister of Interior Lucas Alamán seeking government backing for his demonstration. Although Alamán was attempting to establish the *Banco de Avío,* a development bank, he was primarily interested in assisting the textile industry and would not provide government funds for Rocafuerte's project. After many futile attempts to convince the federal government that his enterprise was important, the entrepreneur turned to the municipal administration.[12]

On October 7, 1830, Rocafuerte offered to sell the gaslighting equipment to the Federal District for seven thousand pesos. He proposed to install the lights in the portals of the Mercaderes and Agustinos squares and operate them for a period of three months. Thereafter, the municipal council would assume responsibility.[13]

The ayuntamiento accepted the proposal. However, since the Federal District lacked funds, the project could not be financed from current revenue. Instead the ayuntamiento allocated to the project seven thousand pesos that the federal government owed the city. When the governor of the Federal District requested payment from the national government, Minister of Interior Alamán informed the city that it would have to await a congressional appropriation. The municipal council decided not to sign a contract with Rocafuerte until the money was available.[14]

Rocafuerte considered Alamán's actions tantamount to killing the project. He knew that the minister of interior had a hundred thousand pesos at his disposal for special expenditures, some of which had already been employed to bring European theatrical productions to the capital. If he wished, Alamán could certainly have provided the meager sum the city required. Irate, Rocafuerte wrote to the newspapers explaining his project and criticizing the government for failing to support it.

Public response to Rocafuerte's article was favorable. *El Sol* received many letters deploring the government's unwillingness to aid the project. Some suggested that the installation of gaslights would have a beneficial psychological effect on Mexicans. It would demonstrate that complex enterprises were possible with domestic materials.[15] Others applauded linking the gaslight project with the construction of railroads. They pointed out that Mexico's high transportation costs hampered the growth of internal markets and restricted the development of agricultural exports.[16]

The interest generated by the discussion forced the federal government to explain its actions. Alamán stated that he did not oppose gaslighting. Indeed, the Bustamante regime declared that instead of merely financing a demonstration of new lights, the government wanted Rocafuerte to submit estimates for the cost of lighting the entire city. Although this announcement pleased the municipal council, Rocafuerte realized that he had been out-maneuvered. If it had been difficult to raise seven thousand pesos for the trial, it would be impossible to expect the government to allocate the four hundred thousand pesos that Rocafuerte estimated were needed to light the city. He decided to complete the project without governmental assistance. In December 1830 Rocafuerte published a long letter in *El Sol* explaining that despite governmental indifference to progress, he would introduce gaslights in Mexico. He proposed to establish a salon where the public might enjoy theater, dances, and *tertulias* in the comfort of gaslighting. Then he would turn the venture over to a joint stock company that could eventually provide lights for the entire city. Those interested in the project were invited to inspect the equipment and discuss the matter with the recently arrived English expert.[17]

Rocafuerte's announcement initiated a polemic in the official journal, *Registro oficial*, which gave the project added publicity. The *Registro* charged that Rocafuerte had misled the public; Alamán was not opposed to the project, as his recommendation to light the entire city demonstrated. The paper also declared that it was illegal to invest federal development funds in fields other than textiles. Rocafuerte countered that lights were as important as textiles and accused the minister of interior of using government funds to entertain the rich with frivolous comedies while the Lancasterian schools closed for lack of funds. Thereafter, the argument degenerated into personal insults.[18] The polemic prompted various experts to publish articles explaining the benefits of gaslighting and urging that the project be undertaken.[19]

Rocafuerte continued the preparation for a gaslighted salon. He remodeled a large building at 14 Zuleta Street where he installed the new lights. Subsequently, Rocafuerte convinced a group of entrepreneurs to purchase the enterprise. In March 1831 the new owners formally inaugurated the entertainment center, which sponsored dances and public functions; the center also had a modern restaurant and lounge. The success and popularity of the public hall made Rocafuerte a well-known and well-liked figure in Mexico City.[20]

Heartened by his initial success, Rocafuerte asked Congress on April 12, 1831, to grant him a concession to provide lighting for the city. He proposed to form two joint stock companies to undertake the project. One would install and operate gaslighting in Mexico City; the other would construct and operate a railroad needed to transport raw materials to the capital for the lights. If the companies proved successful, they could expand to other areas of Mexico. Certain that the Zuleta Street hall had aroused enough interest to attract investors, Rocafuerte looked confidently toward the future. Pro-administration congressmen, however, bottled up the proposal in committee.[21] As a result of such opposition, anti-Bustamante moderates, like Rocafuerte, were reluctantly coming to the conclusion that the government had become an obstacle to progress.

3

Rocafuerte's economic projects were not the only issues that brought him into conflict with the administration. His proposals for social and religious change also challenged the Bustamante regime. When he returned from England, friends with similar concerns urged him to participate in their efforts to improve social conditions in Mexico. In April 1830, his old colleague from the Cortes, the noted philanthropist Francisco Fagoaga, invited Rocafuerte to deliver an address at his home on the state of penal reform in the United States and Europe. The guests were influential moderates who had disliked popular democracy under Guerrero and now hoped that the Bustamante regime could pacify and unite Mexico. These wealthy businessmen, landowners, and politicians were abstaining from partisan politics and, instead, devoting their efforts to social welfare. Intrigued by Rocafuerte's talk, they asked him to write a pamphlet advocating prison reform. The speaker agreed and, late in 1830, he published an *Essay on the New System of Jails.*[22]

In the *Essay*, Rocafuerte argued that lack of education and employment had driven thousands of men and women to lives of crime. These unfortunates should be considered not merely lawbreakers but sick members of society. Crimes, he asserted, were usually committed for three reasons: hunger, ignorance, or passion. While the state had to correct criminals, jails should not be places of torture and punishment but of education and rehabilitation. He proposed a new penal system designed to transform inmates into useful productive citizens. Prisoners would be segregated so that hardened criminals could not influence new offenders. The institution would begin the process of rehabilitation by improving the diet, health, and personal hygiene of the prisoners. Then the jailers would develop the mind and character of their wards by teaching morality as well as reading and writing. Finally, and most important, prisoners would be taught a trade to make them productive members of society upon their release. To prove that such a system was beneficial, Rocafuerte cited the experience of prisons in the United States and Europe. In these countries the percentage of recidivism was greater among those who had served in antiquated jails than among inmates of the new prisons that followed policies similar to the ones he was advocating.

When public reaction to the *Essay on the New System of Jails* proved favorable, Rocafuerte's moderate friends decided to expand their campaign for social reform.[23] They encouraged him to write on behalf of the Lancasterian schools, which still lacked adequate support. However, Rocafuerte suggested a publication favoring religious liberty. Although some, like Carlos María Bustamante, feared that the country was not ready for public debate on the question, most agreed to support him.[24]

In March 1831, Rocafuerte published an *Essay on Religious Toleration*. In it, he argued that Mexico's liberal constitutional system of government should be modified to allow religious freedom. Although the charter of 1824 did not permit religious tolerance, the constitution could now be amended since the six-year prohibition on change had expired. Rocafuerte hoped that Mexico would not only accept religious heterodoxy but would also sever the ties between Church and state. Since the state dealt with man's material wants while the Church cared for his spiritual needs, the two were essentially different institutions and should be separate. He maintained that no church should have a monopoly because whenever any religion became dominant, it became oppressive.

Rocafuerte also associated religious freedom with material progress. As an example he cited Russia, which had been intolerant before Peter the Great and prospered after religious toleration had been introduced. In a few years she moved from the Middle Ages into modern times. Similarly countries, like Holland, Sweden, France, Germany, and Switzerland, prospered after introducing religious liberty. Among the new Spanish American nations, Argentina was also growing wealthy now that she permitted freedom of worship. In contrast, Spain, which had been affluent in the days when Christianity, Judaism, and Islam coexisted, sank into utter decay when the Jews and the Moslems were expelled.

Religious toleration induced prosperity because it instilled personal morality and habits of thrift and hard work. Rocafuerte argued that in countries were religious heterodoxy existed, the Sabbath was observed more faithfully than in Catholic nations were people tended to fulfill only the outward formalities while disregarding true religious feeling. A comparison of Spanish and Prussian experience demonstrated the value of toleration. Both nations had despotic governments and ten million inhabitants. Yet Prussia, which was poorer in natural resources, was more prosperous. Rocafuerte believed that the Germans worked harder than Spaniards because religious heterodoxy instilled better working habits among them. This, he explained, accounted for Prussia's wealth.

Mexico, Rocafuerte argued, had paid dearly for her intolerance. Many Englishmen had abandoned their plans to invest in the republic because they could not worship freely. If men would not invest in a country because it lacked religious liberty, they certainly would refuse to colonize it. Only by attracting immigrants could Mexico prevent underpopulated areas, like Texas, from falling to the expanding North Americans. Since few European Catholics were immigrating to Mexico, Rocafuerte maintained that European Protestants should be attracted. This could only be done if the constitution were changed. Thus, for the good of the nation, Rocafuerte urged the public to demand religious toleration.[25]

After the completion of the *Essay*, but before its publication, Rocafuerte requested his passport to Guayaquil. He had been unable to attract sufficient financial support for his proposed light and railroad companies. Although many were interested in economic development, the growing political unrest, which attended the government's increasing reliance on repressive tactics, frightened many investors. The wealthy moderates, who would otherwise have supported Rocafuerte's projects, now urged him to join a movement opposing the Bustamante regime. These moderates had come to believe that the price of stability had become excessive and they were returning to politics. Disillusioned with the apparent failure of Spanish American constitutional governments, Rocafuerte was unwilling to become involved in Mexico's internal struggles. Instead, he decided to return to his native land. The time was propitious. Gran Colombia had dissolved as a consequence of internecine divisions similar to the one now tormenting Mexico. If he returned home, Rocafuerte could participate in the formation of the recently organized Republic of Ecuador.

4

The Bustamante government, however, refused to allow him to leave. Minister of Treasury Mangino revived the old radical *yorkino* charge of Rocafuerte's criminal neglect in the Gran Colombia loan. Subsequently, the chamber of deputies undertook another investigation of the matter. The former chargé could not leave Mexico until he was either exonerated or charged with malfeasance in office.[26]

Thus Rocafuerte was in Mexico when the *Essay on Religious Toleration* appeared. Although Carlos María Bustamante warned him that at least another twenty years would have to pass before the matter could be discussed objectively in Mexico,[27] Rocafuerte ignored the warning because he believed he had handled an issue that vitally affected colonization, civil order, peace, and material progress with circumspection.[28] Many observers, including the

English and French envoys, agreed with him.[29] Others welcomed the pamphlet but felt that it dealt too openly with a highly controversial topic. James Thompson, who had returned to England, saw its publication as a great blow against Minister Alamán and the clerical party. Although he admired Rocafuerte's courage in publishing such a work in those reactionary times, Thompson feared for the writer's safety.[30]

Unfortunately for the author, the pamphlet appeared when clerical influence was at its zenith. Six new conservative bishops had been appointed since the Bustamente administration came to power. Minister of Interior Alamán favored the conservative clergy and Minister of Justice and Ecclesiastic Affairs José Ignacio Espinosa bowed to their pressure. The two ministers attempted to silence the liberal opposition by imposing crushing fines upon their newspapers. Consequently, pamphlets became the major vehicle for criticism and the government attempted to reduce their circulation through the Press Board.[31]

The Board to Protect the Freedom of the Press had originated under the Cortes. Established to safeguard the press from arbitrary government action, the Press Board investigated writings denounced as subversive. The Board's two attorneys evaluated the material; any publication deemed objectionable was submitted to a grand jury of nine men. If that body found cause for trial, the Board magistrate would select, by lot, another jury of twelve men to try the case. This threefold process was designed to protect freedom of expression, but the Bustamante administration used it to destroy that same liberty.[32]

When the *Essay on Religious Toleration* appeared, the minister of justice forced the Press Board to charge the author with sedition. Although the Press Board attorneys, Florentino Martínez Cornejo and José Cuevas, could find no fault with the *Essay*, the government insisted the pamphlet was seditious. On April 7, 1831, the Press Board declared that the pamphlet had violated various sections of the constitution, particularly article 3, which stated that the Roman Catholic faith was the religion of Mexico to the exclusion of all others.[33]

Ignoring the legally prescribed process, the government handpicked a grand jury composed entirely of clergymen. The hearing, which occurred on April 9, was a charade. The jurors not only refused to read the pamphlet, they would not listen to Rocafuerte's defense. After a brief deliberation, they declared that the author had indeed violated the law and should be detained, without bond, until his trial. Accordingly, Rocafuerte was taken into custody and incarcerated in a room in the municipal council building.[34]

When Carlos María Bustamante learned the outcome of the hearing he rushed to the Ayuntamiento to offer his services as defense attorney. Rocafuerte thanked him, explaining that he had already chosen another friend, Juan de Dios Cañedo, as his counsel. Carlos María Bustamante, who believed that a calm and serious defense was needed, was dismayed by the choice because Cañedo was one of the government's leading congressional opponents. Since both Cañedo and Rocafuerte were impetuous and given to caustic language, Carlos María Bustamente believed they would alienate the jury.[35] He also feared that disorders might occur during the proceedings if Rocafuerte's partisans filled the public galleries.

The trial, set for April 19, became a cause célèbre; people in Mexico City talked of nothing else. Rocafuerte was a popular figure, associated in the public's mind with the success of the gas-lighted hall on Zuleta Street. As a result of the extensive interest in the trial, the *Essay on Jails* was sold out and the unconfiscated copies of the *Essay on Religious Toleration* sold clandestinely at high prices.

The clergy, discounting the strength of public sympathy for the accused, believed that conservative principles had triumphed. A board of religious censorship, acting as if it were the old inquisition, began to study the pamphlet. Confident that the government would support its actions, the board acted with great impunity. It even had the temerity to dispatch a commission to review Rocafuerte's library and confiscate any books prohibited by the Church. The board's actions were so outrageous that they persuaded many moderates to oppose the clergy as well as the government. Indeed, moderate *yorkinos* and *escoceses* joined forces to ensure that Rocafuerte received a fair trial. Some even contemplated forming a new coalition to oppose the reactionary Bustamante administration.[36]

Although Tuesday, April 19, 1931, was an unusually hot day, thousands of people waited for hours in the square outside the courthouse to learn Rocafuerte's fate. The public galleries inside had been filled since early morning. As the day advanced, the crowds and the heat made the courtroom unbearable. Carlos María Bustamante expected a riot if the verdict did not please the belligerent multitude.

Before the trial began, Rocafuerte received a list of jurors. Since they were all clergymen, he rejected them, as was his privilege. Under the law, however, he would have to accept the next list. To everyone's surprise the second jury included only one priest; the other jurors were moderate *escoceses* and *yorkinos*. As soon as he could establish calm in the courtroom, the judge began by having the *Essay on Religious Toleration* read aloud. Throughout the hour long recitation, the crowd in the galleries applauded in behalf of the accused. After the reading, Rocafuerte was permitted to present a prepared defense.[37]

The essayist argued that he had not violated the law. True, article 3 of the constitution stipulated, "The religion of the United States of Mexico is, and will be permanently, Roman Catholic." But he had never advocated that Mexico adopt another faith. He had only suggested that other religions be tolerated. Was it possible, he asked that enslaved Italy could permit religious liberty while free Mexico would not even allow it to be discussed? Rocafuerte then read the second part of article 3, "The nation will protect it [the Catholic Church] with wise and just laws and prohibit the exercise of any other." Although the first part of article 3 stipulated that the Catholic religion was the national faith *permanently*, no similar injunction had been included in the part excluding other faiths. Therefore, Rocafuerte argued, it was not illegal to advocate the passage of a constitutional amendment permitting religious toleration. He concluded that the government had acted in an unjust and arbitrary fashion when it brought him to trial. Once again the public cheered and applauded.[38]

When calm had been restored, Juan de Dios Cañedo continued the case for the defense. Speaking for more than an hour and a half to the receptive crowd, Cañedo boldly attacked the government and the clergy. In Carlos María Bustamante's words, "Cañedo spoke horrible blasphemies and the spectators applauded him."[39] In contrast, the prosecution could only argue that Rocafuerte had attempted to subvert national morality and provoke political conflict. After a brief deliberation the jury voted to acquit

Rocafuerte. The "auditorium was insane" with joy; people shouted that justice had triumphed.[40] Rocafuerte left the court a hero. The crowd carried him home on its shoulders with a band leading the way.[41]

The Bustamante regime had miscalculated badly. As British Minister Pakenham reported to his government, "due pains were taken to obtain a conviction [yet] a sentence of acquittal was all but unanimously pronounced, one juror out of twelve having voted in the opposite sense."[42] The lone dissenter, Father Rocha, later apologized to Rocafuerte, explaining that he had no choice but to vote against him. The government had erred when it failed to consider Rocafuerte's popularity in the capital where the crowds lent support to his defense. Had the trial been held elsewhere, such influence would not have been forthcoming. Furthermore, the arrogance of the reactionary clergy drove many moderates into a new alliance that would ultimately attack the government. The trial, however, did not immediately lead to a more organized opposition. Instead, it was the Bustamante regime's overreaction to subsequent criticism that triggered a determined and organized opposition.[43]

Emboldened by the successful trial, some of Rocafuerte's friends convinced him to publish a second edition of the *Essay* with the defense as an appendix. Carlos María Bustamante, however, counseled caution, warning Rocafuerte that if he published Cañedo's caustic defense, there would be another trial which the essayist would lose. Although Carlos María Bustamante did not favor religious toleration, he, like many moderates, was opposed to clerical interference in politics. These moderates, who had assisted Rocafuerte during the trial, would not continue to support him if he pushed the religious issue too far. Accordingly, the author agreed not to publish Cañedo's arguments although he included a partial narrative of the trial as well as his own defense when he published the second edition of the *Essay on Religious Toleration*. The notoriety of the trial had created a great demand for the original pamphlet. Indeed, interested provincials ordered many copies of the *Essay* even before the second edition appeared. Consequently, the new edition was widely distributed in Mexico and Rocafuerte became known throughout the country.[44]

After Rocafuerte's acquittal, most moderates believed that the

Church censorship board would absolve the *Essay*. The clergy, however, responded by accusing Rocafuerte of heresy.[45] Although the Catholic hierarchy was understandably chagrined by Rocafuerte's suggestion that their religious monopoly be abolished, the board's accusation was unreasonable. Only by straining logic to its breaking point might one conclude that Rocafuerte's *Essay on Religious Toleration* attacked the Catholic religion. Such a charge was particularly difficult to prove because Rocafuerte was a practicing Catholic, who attended mass every Sunday, in a time when many conservatives honored their faith in the breach rather than in practice. Indeed, public reaction to the censorship board's action was so unfavorable that no bishop dared excommunicate Rocafuerte, although such a step would have been logical after the board's adverse report and the essayist's failure to repent. Instead, the Church hierarchy published the board's conclusions and distributed the booklet at a very low price to encourage its wide distribution.[46]

Led by Bishops Francisco Pablo Vázquez and Miguel Gordóa y Barrios, the Church hierarchy also organized a propaganda campaign against Rocafuerte and the concept of religious toleration. With the support and encouragement of Minister of Interior Alamán, conservative clergymen published countless articles and pamphlets vehemently denouncing the author of the *Essay on Religious Toleration*.[47] Fearing that the clerical attack might provoke a rash response from Rocafuerte, Carlos María Bustamante attempted to defend him while denouncing religious heterodoxy. On August 31, 1832, he wrote in his paper *Voz de la patria* that he was alarmed by news that Buenos Aires had permitted the erection of a Protestant church. He opposed religious freedom, he declared, as much as his good friend Rocafuerte favored it.[48] However, he assured his readers that Rocafuerte had written the *Essay* as a politician concerned with the needs of the nation and not as a theologian attacking the Holy Church. Finally, Carlos María Bustamante declared that he would vouch for the rectitude of the essayist's intentions "even with my head."[49]

Rocafuerte, who had remained silent up to that time, replied by publishing an open letter to Carlos María Bustamante. He reiterated the political considerations that had prompted him to write the *Essay*, reminding his friend that the nation's interests required religious heterodoxy. In an apparent attempt to appease the government and perhaps to receive his passport clearance, Rocafuerte also praised Minister of Treasury Mangino for his translation of one of Benjamin Franklin's religious works.[50] The compliment was wasted.

Although Rocafuerte once again requested his passport early in August, he had received no reply by October. Angered by the delay, he wrote a bitter letter to Alamán accusing the minister of not granting him the consideration he deserved. If the government would grant him a passport, Rocafuerte promised to be gone within fifteen days.[51] Alamán replied that his office could not issue a passport without a clearance from the ministry of finance.[52]

Once again, Rocafuerte offered to provide the treasury any information that would expedite his clearance and once again he was instructed to be patient; his case had yet to be resolved. The reply convinced Rocafuerte that the government was punishing him for his insolence; he would never receive a clearance as long as the Bustamante regime remained in power. Rocafuerte had hoped to avoid direct involvement in the internal politics of Mexico, believing that he could better serve the cause of Spanish Americanism by working in the international area and by introducing new methods, enterprises, and reforms to Spanish America. Reluctantly, he decided to join the opposition to Anastasio Bustamante.[53]

# XII

## ROCAFUERTE AND MEXICAN POLITICS

The success of republican, constitutional government was one of the goals of Spanish Americanists. The Spanish Cortes had provided many of them with experience in representative government. They hoped their own countries would adopt and perfect such liberal "institutions," which they believed were necessary for development and prosperity. Unfortunately, various groups both on the left and on the right turned to force as a means of resolving the social, economic, political, and religious conflicts that divided the nations of Spanish America. The Spanish Americanists' dream of peaceful, orderly government had begun to disintegrate in many areas of Spanish America by the 1830s.

1

When Rocafuerte joined the opposition to Anastasio Bustamante late in 1831, Mexico was undergoing a constitutional crisis similar to the ones ravaging other Spanish American countries. Vice-President Bustamante had overthrown the populist government of President Vicente Guerrero in December 1829. Many moderates and conservatives, who deplored insurrection in principle, willingly accepted Bustamante because they had been disturbed by what they considered to be Guerrero's abuse of popular democracy and because they hoped that the new government would restore order and tranquillity.

It soon became evident that the price of stability would be high. The new regime was not content merely to purge radical *yorkinos* and alleged malcontents from public life. In the months that followed it showed itself to be authoritarian, aristocratic, and pro-clerical. More important, however, it sought to destroy the federal system and replace it with authoritarian centralism. State insurrections occurred, but most were rapidly overwhelmed. By mid-1831, the opposition seemed defeated. In February, the government captured and executed ex-President Guerrero; the following month Juan Alvarez, the last remaining insurgent, laid down his arms and agreed to cooperate with the Bustamante administration.

Despite the end of insurgency, an armed truce continued to exist between the national government and the large states. Only a small group of congressmen openly opposed the regime. Led by Senators Antonio Pacheco Leál and Manuel Crescencio Rejón and deputies Andrés Quintana Roo and Juan de Dios Cañedo, the legislators braved threats and assaults to criticize the government. They instituted a press campaign to discredit the regime. In articles and pamphlets they attacked the administration insisting that only the return of Manuel Gómez Pedraza to the presidency would restore constitutional government in Mexico.[1]

Angered by these actions, the regime levied heavy fines on the opposition press, driving many anti-government sheets out of business. In an effort to curb pamphleteering, the administration declared Vicente Rocafuerte's *Essay on Religious Toleration* seditious and brought the author to trial. But, as has been shown, the tactic backfired and Rocafuerte was acquitted. Despite the setback, the Bustamante regime continued the campaign to silence its opponents. In the months that followed, the government imprisoned and exiled countless newspapermen and critics. Such tactics, however, were used only against the middle class. In the case of wealthy and powerful opponents, like Cañedo, it used other methods. The deputy was appointed minister to the nations of South America. Cañedo, who feared for his life, accepted the post, thereby ridding the government of a vocal leader of the opposition.[2]

As arrests and executions increased, more moderates began to protest. The price of stability was becoming too great. In August 1831, Carlos María Bustamante demanded in his *Voz de la patria* that no one be held without trial and that justice be prompt and impartial. He also accused Minister of War Facio of being responsible for the government's harsh policies. The minister did not reply, but one of his officers published veiled threats against the author in the government controlled *El Sol*.[3] The administration applied economic sanctions against the *Voz de la patria*, forcing the newspaper to cease publication on October 18, 1831. Congressman Carlos María Bustamante capped the final issue with a denunciation of the government's despotism.[4]

The demise of the *Voz de la patria* did not signify an end to press opposition. Senator Manuel Crescencio Rejón founded *El Tribuno del pueblo mexicano*, a paper devoted to "legal opposition." The paper aroused public opinion in the capital by reporting the military preparations of the federal government. *El Tribuno* recounted that a federal army of two thousand men had gathered in Orizaba, other soldiers were encamped in Veracruz, and the government planned further troop concentrations. Since no external enemy threatened the republic, Rejón demanded to know the reason for the movement of national armies. Was it, he asked, to attack the states? The administration let it be known unofficially that the troops were to be used in an invasion of Cuba. But, as Pakenham reported to his government, the news leak failed to dispel the fears of the opposition. They continued to believe the government was preparing to destroy the Federal system.[5]

Rejón's accusations angered many army officers. On October 29, soldiers ransacked the offices of *El Tribuno*. When this failed to prevent its publication, the military men used stronger action. On November 4, several officers set upon Rejón with drawn sabers but the senator escaped. An outraged Congress demanded to know why the military had violated legislative immunity. "Alamán appeared in Congress two days later to say that Rejón's senatorial immunity had not been violated, for the soldiers had accosted Rejón the writer, not Rejón the senator."[6] Later Minister of War Facio assured Congress the culprits would be apprehended. But the case was never solved. Fearing further attacks, Rejón ceased publication of *El Tribuno*. Infuriated by the regime's insolence toward the senator, Rocafuerte published a pamphlet deploring the government's policy of terrorizing journalists. He urged true patriots to defend the freedom of the press.[7]

The continuing excesses of the Bustamante regime and its treatment of Congress convinced a growing number of influential mod-

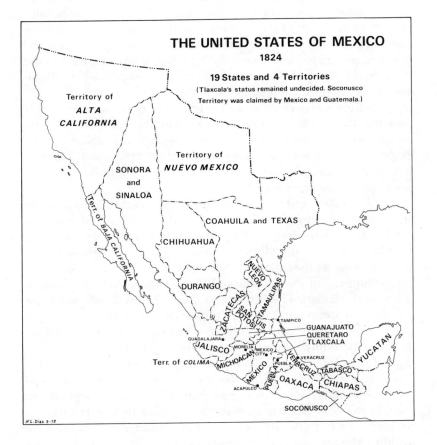

THE UNITED STATES OF MEXICO
1824

19 States and 4 Territories
(Tlaxcala's status remained undecided. Soconusco
Territory was claimed by Mexico and Guatemala.)

Territory of
ALTA
CALIFORNIA

Territory of
NUEVO MEXICO

SONORA
and
SINALOA

Terr. of BAJA CALIFORNIA

COAHUILA and TEXAS

CHIHUAHUA

DURANGO

NUEVO LEON

TAMAULIPAS

ZACATECAS

SAN LUIS POTOSI

TAMPICO

GUANAJUATO
QUERETARO
TLAXCALA

GUADALAJARA

JALISCO

MORELIA

MEXICO CITY

YUCATAN

Terr. of COLIMA

MICHOACAN

VERACRUZ

VERACRUZ

TABASCO

MEXICO

PUEBLA

PUEBLA

OAXACA

CHIAPAS

ACAPULCO

SOCONUSCO

N.L. Diaz 3-75

erates that they could no longer tolerate the progressive destruction of civil liberties. In mid-November, Quintana Roo, Rejón, Pacheco Leál, Mariano Riva Palacios (the son-in-law of the late Vicente Guerrero), and Juan Rodríguez Puebla formed a committee to unite former moderate *yorkinos, escoceses,* and other antigovernment forces. In the belief that the nation's constitutional process could not survive unless the laws were strictly enforced, the committee decided to demand the return of Gómez Pedraza to the presidency. They also agreed to coordinate congressional opposition with anti-government action in the states.

Once they had decided on a plan of action, the committee sought new members. Among those invited to join the group was Vicente Rocafuerte. The committee accepted his offer to establish a newspaper, the *Fénix de la libertad,* to represent the opposition. The new editor purchased the press of Las Escalerillas to publish the *Fénix* and opposition pamphlets.[8]

In November and December 1831, Rocafuerte challenged the government in three pamphlets entitled *General Considerations on the Goodness of Governments.*[9] Because, theoretically, the president had little power in the Mexican political system, criticism was often directed against the cabinet rather than against the chief executive. Accordingly, Rocafuerte attacked the ministers, concentrating on Facio and Alamán. The best governments, he declared, were those which used a minimum of force to govern. Rocafuerte argued that the present government of Mexico relied upon force and brutality because the ministers were cowards who had lacked the courage to fight for independence. To prove his point. Rocafuerte asserted that Facio had been a partisan of the detested Ferdinand VII and had not entered Mexico's service until 1823, after independence had been won. Rocafuerte's attack on Alamán was particularly virulent. He charged that, in spite of the minister's talent and education, Alamán was an avaricious reactionary, willing to sell his country to the clergy and to foreign princes. Rocafuerte reminded his readers that the minister of interior managed the properties of the Duke of Monteleone, the heir of Fernando Cortés. "Could the lackey of the Duke of Monteleone," asked Rocafuerte, also serve the interests of Mexico? Finally, he warned the public that the government was attempting to destroy federalism. And he exhorted the people to defend their liberty as Hidalgo and Morelos had done and to be prepared to die for their country "in the new struggle against tyranny."

The publications caused a sensation in Mexico. Some moderates, like Carlos María Bustamante, were pleased. "The ministers never expected to have this kind of enemy," he wrote in his diary. "They took the *Voz de la patria*, but now I have been avenged."[10] Others feared that Rocafuerte's intemperance had so antagonized the government that it would order his assassination. Yet the very virulence of his attack may have protected him by making Rocafuerte famous throughout the nation. So many state and local newspapers reprinted his diatribes against the government that the Bustamante regime dared not order his assassination lest it provoke riots.[11] Instead, an agent of the ministers, Colonel Antonio Gaona sued for libel on December 20, 1831. Gaona also demanded that the author retract his charges. Rocafuerte refused, promising to prove the veracity of his accusations in future publications. In view of the writer's intransigency, and aware of the growing hostility in the states, the government decided to avoid the scandal of a trial by withdrawing its charges. Ministers Facio and Alamán contented themselves with writing anonymous pamphlets attacking Rocafuerte.[12]

Outraged by Alamán's publication, *A New Year's Gift to Mr. Rocafuerte by Someone Who Knows Him*, Rocafuerte sued for libel. Although Alamán was merely replying in kind, Rocafuerte believed that he had written the truth about the minister, while Alamán had perverted the evidence to caricature him. The courts were initially reluctant to hear the case, but Rocafuerte refused to drop the charges. A grand jury was finally convened on January 5, 1832; it decided by a vote of eight to seven that there were insufficient grounds to try Alamán for libel. The ruling failed to placate Rocafuerte. Two days later he published an article in the *Fénix* criticizing the courts. He held that the jurors who had voted in favor of Alamán were biased and he asked the public to be impartial in judging the minister of interior. Rocafuerte reminded his readers that he had made serious accusations against Alamán. Any true gentlemen or man of honor would have defended his name. But what had the minister done? Had he taken Rocafuerte to court to

prove his allegations? No, replied the outraged journalist, Alamán
had merely hired a character assassin.[13]

2

While the government was preoccupied with Rocafuerte, other
members of the Mexico City Committee of Opposition were working to gain support in the states. This proved particularly difficult
because state politicians were loath to take the initiative and no
leader or cause had been found to weld their discontent into an
organized struggle against the national government. Finally, an
incident in Guadalajara, Jalisco, provided the committee with a
cause. On November 22, 1831, General Ignacio Inclán, the commander of the federal forces in Jalisco, ordered the arrest and execution of Juan Brambillas for printing pamphlets critical of the
Bustamante regime. Apparently, Inclán's actions were also designed to intimidate the state government, since Brambillas was the
printer of Jalisco state publications. Important dignitaries of
Guadalajara, among them the bishop, implored the federal commander to spare the printer. Although they obtained Brambillas'
pardon, Inclán's insolence and disregard for state authority convinced many moderates in the states to defend local government.
The state legislature fled to the city of Lagos and Governor Anastasio Cañedo asked other states to assist Jalisco. Fearful that
Inclán's act was the first step in an attempt to crush the federal
system, other states rallied to Jalisco's defense. The legislature of
Zacatecas invited Jalisco to move its government to Zacatecas until
General Inclán was removed and the federal government guaranteed states rights. Guanajuato and San Luis Potosí also pledged
their support to Jalisco. Although the minister of war relieved
General Inclán of his command, the Bustamante administration
refused to punish him as the states demanded.[14] Consequently, the
Brambillas incident became a symbol of the national government's
attempt to destroy the states.

The Mexico City Committee moved immediately to capitalize on
the discontent precipitated by General Inclán. Through contacts
such as Valentín Gómez Farías of Zacatecas and Sebastián Camacho
of Veracruz, the committee urged the states to raise forces to fight

the Bustamante regime. Although states like Zacatecas had powerful militias, it became evident that the dissidents would have to win
the support of some army commanders before they could overthrow the government. A few committee members were reluctant
to take such a step, fearing that once involved the military men
might demand the presidency. The 1829 coup against Guerrero
had already demonstrated that the army could force the federal
and state governments to accept an administration they disliked. In
spite of the danger, most committee members believed that Bustamante could not be removed without the assistance of the leading
army commanders. They decided to approach key military men in
the hope of winning them to their side. In an effort to control
military leaders who joined them, the committee insisted that
armed rebellion be linked to a demand for a return to constitutional government through the restoration of Gómez Pedraza to
the presidency.[15]

While the committee conspired secretly, Rocafuerte, undaunted
by government threats, began publishing *El Fénix de la libertad*. The
first issue, which appeared on December 7, 1831, declared that
press censorship was incompatible with a free government. In the
United States, England, France, and Holland, the press was the
proud guardian of the nation's civil liberties. But in countries like
Spain, Italy, Turkey, and now Mexico, where tyranny and corruption abounded, the press enjoyed no freedom. An unfettered
press, he declared, was the defense of a free people. Where that
liberty did not exist, as in Mexico, ordinary citizens could be
imprisoned, exiled, or executed at the whim of the government
while robbers, bandits, and assassins went unpunished. Accordingly, the *Fénix* pledged to restore and defend the freedoms Mexico
had lost.[16]

Rocafuerte's vitriolic journalism and the committee's secret activities convinced many observers that the government was in danger.
United States Minister Butler believed that the Bustamante regime
would fall within six months. Disturbed by growing rumors of a
conspiracy, Minister of Interior Alamán put the opposition leaders
under surveillance. Secret agents followed Rocafuerte, Rejón, and
Pacheco Leál, whom the administration considered its most dangerous opponents. Other spies haunted the markets, portals, and
cafés, hoping to unearth subversive activities.[17]

The administration, however, could not quell the growing discontent. Encouraged by the success of the *Fénix*, small clandestine opposition papers printed on portable presses began to appear. Their mobility make it extremely difficult for the government to destroy them. The most important of these small sheets was *El Duende* edited by Pablo Villavicencio who wrote under the pseudonym "El Payo del Rosario." Initially, the government attempted to silence the opposition papers with heavy fines. Since the *Fénix* was published openly from a fixed location, the Bustamante administration was determined to make it an example. On December 20, 1831, Rocafuerte was charged with violating press laws and the jury of first instance found cause for trial. Rocafuerte played into the government's hands by appealing; the judge ruled that the defendant had to post a bond of twenty thousand pesos until the appeal was heard. The sum was inordinately high since, even if the paper were found guilty, Rocafuerte could only be fined 1,500 reales or 187 pesos, 50 centavos. In order to continue publishing Rocafuerte posted bond. Then he published a long editorial castigating the government for having violated both the spirit and the letter of the law. Rocafuerte inquired whether the ministers' honor was so cheap that it could be appeased with twenty thousand pesos, five thousand per minister. Thereafter, the government fined the *Fénix* once a month in an attempt to drive it out of circulation. Finally, in March 1832, Press Board Attorney José Cuevas, who had previously followed the regime's instructions, refused to press charges against the paper. He was quickly replaced by someone who would carry out the government's wishes.

The *Fénix* was not the only newspaper subject to harassment, but the others were assessed lesser fines. Only Rocafuerte's wealth and the committee's resources permitted the *Fénix* to continue to exist. The relatively civilized tactic of large fines, however, was principally reserved for upper class critics of the government. Less influential journalists fared worse. On February 25, 1832, *El Duende* was charged with sedition; Villavicencio was imprisoned and later exiled fifty miles from the capital. When he continued to publish criticism of the regime and to distribute *El Duende* in Mexico City, the administration dispatched soldiers to destroy its presses. However, Villavicencio learned of the attack in time to flee with his press to Veracruz. By March 1832, the newspapers in the states had become highly critical of the government. In an effort to keep the population of the Federal District ignorant of the discontent in the states, the government banned the circulation of out-of-town newspapers in Mexico City.[18]

The regime's repressive actions only increased dissatisfaction. Even in the state of Mexico, the *Conservador de Toluca* echoed the Mexico City Committee when it criticized the minister of war and exhorted Congress to defend its prerogatives.[19] Despite the growing hostility toward the government, the committee had been unable to convince a military man to rebel against Bustamante. Fortunately for the conspirators, this time the government played into the hands of the opposition. Fearful that growing discontent in Veracruz might induce the senior commanders to betray the regime, the minister of war decided to change the state's military hierarchy. The Mexico City Committee used this information to convince Colonel Pedro Landero and other senior officers in Veracruz to oppose the government. The rebellious officers then invited General Santa Anna to assume the leadership of an insurrection.

Santa Anna agreed and after assuming titular command of the Veracruz insurrection, he tried to reach a compromise with the government. He informed Vice-President Bustamante that the army demanded changes. First, the orders modifying the Veracruz military structure were to be rescinded. Then, he insisted upon a change in cabinet, suggesting Sebastián Camacho for interior and foreign affairs, Melchor Múzquiz for war, Francisco García, the governor of Zacatecas, for treasury, and Valentín Gómez Farías for justice and ecclesiastic affairs. Although the vice-president's cabinet presented its resignation to give the chief executive freedom of action, the gesture proved meaningless. Despite the distinguished ministry proposed by General Santa Anna, the Mexico City Committe refused to accept any solution that would allow Bustamante to remain in office. Their intransigence convinced Santa Anna that no compromise was possible. Thus, in February 1832, a reluctant Santa Anna prepared to battle the Bustamante administration.[20]

The prospect of armed conflict, particularly one led by Santa Anna, alienated some moderates in Mexico City. Carlos María Bustamante argued that Santa Anna was an adventurer who would surely grasp for the presidency. When the other moderates proved willing to run that risk, Carlos María Bustamante broke with them, deciding to defend the existing government as the lesser of two evils. He founded a new paper, *La Marimba*, which criticized the Veracruz insurrection. The committee, on the other hand, increased its harassment of the regime in order to aid the rebellion.[21] Members waged an intensive press campaign, depicting the Veracruz officer as the champion of liberty. To their dismay, government forces defeated Santa Anna on March 3, 1832. Despite this setback, the *Fénix* and other opposition publications refused to mute their criticism. On March 7, Rocafuerte accused the government of responsibility for the civil war. When the editor learned that despite his defeat, Santa Anna had promised to continue the struggle, Rocafuerte published the general's proclamation in a special edition of the *Fénix*. Shortly thereafter, the committee learned that in Tamaulipas General Francisco Moctezuma, one of Guerrero's former ministers, had joined the struggle against the government. Hoping to spread the rebellion, Rocafuerte and the editors of other opposition papers escalated their criticism of the administration and openly encouraged armed resistance. The government reacted by increasing pressure on opposition papers and redoubling its surveillance of the leaders of the opposition. It arrested dozens of persons and executed "a criminal" nearly every day. The *Fénix* estimated that in March alone twenty "patriots" had perished.[22]

Realizing that its harsh tactics were alienating moderates and even conservatives, the government initiated a propaganda campaign of its own. In April, the *Registro oficial* reported that captured rebel documents indicated that, if he returned to office Gómez Pedraza would name Santa Anna minister of war, Gómez Farías minister of foreign and internal affairs, Rocafuerte minister of justice and ecclesiastic affairs, and García minister of treasury. The disclosure was designed to play upon the fears of moderates and conservatives who considered Santa Anna an adventurer and Rocafuerte an atheist, or, even worse, a Protestant. The suggestion that Gómez Farías and García of Zacatecas, who were noted for their staunch defense of the federal system, would also be cabinet members frightened those conservatives who believed federalism to be the first step toward anarchy.[23] The tactic temporarily halted the erosion of government support and converted a few former enemies into administration adherents.

On May 5, Rafael Dávila began publishing the pro-government *El*

*Toro.* During the following months the paper was largly devoted to attacking Rocafuerte, whom Dávila considered the leader of the opposition. The newspaper accused Rocafuerte of being a petulant malcontent. On various occasions, *El Toro* ridiculed the opposition by portraying Rocafuerte as the high priest of a heretical Protestant cult, who instructed his disciples, Pacheco Leál, Rejón, Quintana Roo, Villavicencio, and others, to destroy the nation. In other instances, *El Toro* asserted that the enemies of the government were swine and declared that their triumph would mean a government of pigs.[24]

Other pro-government publications agreed in blaming Rocafuerte for the upheaval and denounced as a traitor anyone who opposed the regime. In the guise of evaluating the source of the current political crisis, *El Sol* declared in an editorial that Rocafuerte had initiated the campaign against the government and that others, like Quintana Roo, Rejón, and Villavicencio, had followed his example.[25] The pro-government press centered its attacks on Rocafuerte because the Committee of Opposition worked covertly, while he had foolishly challenged the government openly. Moreover, by criticizing only a few men, the Bustamante administration attempted to convince the public that only a handful of malcontents opposed the government.

As late as May 1832, the Bustamante regime still hoped to defeat the rebels; despite widespread disaffection, most states had not openly taken the field against the vice-president. Only in the coastal states of Veracruz and Tamaulipas were rebels fighting the national government. However, the administration would not be safe until it reestablished control over these two states because the nation's two principal ports were in rebel hands. Custom revenues from Veracruz and Tampico were being diverted to finance the insurrection. Bustamante had dispatched two large armies to combat the insurgents. Initially, it appeared that the federal forces would crush Veracruz and Tamaulipas, as they had other rebellious states. However, government hopes for an easy triumph were shattered on May 13, when General Moctezuma won the first major anti-government victory by defeating a federal army at Tampico. Threatened by the debacle in the north, the other federal army abandoned its siege of Veracruz.

The events on the coast ended the government's illusions of victory. Bustamante sought to negotiate with the opposition, but no one would accommodate him. In an effort to permit him to form a more acceptable cabinet, the ministers resigned en masse. However, a mere change in cabinet was still not acceptable to the Committee of Opposition. The *Fénix* declared that they would continue to oppose Bustamante until he vacated the executive office and restored Gómez Pedraza to the presidency. Since the government would not accept these terms, the struggle continued. Santa Anna marched inland while Moctezuma advanced to San Luis Potosí.[26]

On May 27, to reemphasize the committee's position, Rocafuerte published a pamphlet entitled *To General Anastasio Bustamante*, in which he accused Bustamante of usurping power, destroying the nation's sovereignty, and presiding over an immoral, unjust, vengeful, and even cruel government. He warned that if Bustamante did not restore Gómez Pedraza to power, the constitutionality of any successor would be in doubt. Force, he concluded, was all that sustained the government and if Bustamante persisted in that folly, his regime would be overthrown by force.[27] Pro-government papers, like *La Marimba*, replied that the vice-president had assumed executive power legally and accused the opposition of lacking patriotism.[28] The ministry of justice denounced the pamphlet, but the courts did not find it subversive.

Indeed, juries were now refusing to convict newsmen for violating press laws. In May, the government lost eight out of nine cases brought to trial. As a consequence, a group of moderates founded a second opposition paper in the capital, *La Columna de la Constitución Federal de la República Mexicana*. Until then only the *Fénix* had been operating openly; all other opposition sheets had published clandestinely and without registering with the Press Board. In its first issue, *La Columna* declared that it would work to restore Gómez Pedraza, the lawful president of Mexico, to office.[29]

The open and growing opposition of moderates placed the Bustamante regime in a difficult situation. Although it used threats and force against common journalists, it could not use the same tactics against their upper class counterparts without alienating its conservative supporters. Earlier, the government had relied upon docile courts to control wealthy critics. Only the *Fénix* had continued to publish despite mounting fines. Once juries refused to convict journalists, the government either had to permit freedom of the press or use force against the upper class. In either case, it would lose support.

Realizing that the Bustamante regime was on the defensive, Rocafuerte redoubled his attacks. In June, one of the leaders of the movement in Veracruz, José Rincón, joined Rocafuerte in the capital. The new arrival informed him that preparations for the final campaigns were well underway and that Bustamante would soon fall. Heartened by the report, the journalist published another pamphlet on June 9, in which he predicted the government's demise. *El Toro* vehemently denied Rocafuerte's predictions, but the very intensity of Dávila's reaction seemed to indicate that the editor did not believe his own denials.[30]

The renewed vigor of the opposition caused the regime to increase its subsidies to pro-government newspapers. In June 1832, there were six pro-administration papers in the Federal District: the *Registro oficial, El Sol,* and *Los Amigos del pueblo,* which were directly under Alamán's control, and Francisco Ibar's *El Genio de la libertad,* Carlos María Bustamante's *La Marimba,* and Rafael Dávila's *El Toro* which, although not run by the government, were officially financed. These papers increased their attacks upon the "anarchists," as they labeled the opposition, insisting that to criticize the government was treason.[31]

As armed resistance spread throughout the country, Anastasio Bustamante again attempted to mollify the opposition by offering to change his cabinet. First, he removed Facio and Alamán, the most hated ministers. Then, he offered Sebastián Camacho, the governor of Veracruz and one of the important opposition leaders, the ministry of interior and foreign affairs, and General José María Calderón, the governor of Puebla, the ministry of war. José María Bocanegra, a former minister under Guerrero, was offered the ministry of justice and ecclesiastic affairs. Rafael Mangino, the least criticized member of the cabinet would remain. Despite Bustamante's entreaties, the three men refused the appointments when the committee insisted that Gómez Pedraza return to office as a precondition to holding elections.[32]

Unable to placate his opponents, Bustamante renewed pressure against the "anarchists" in the capital. It was rumored that the government would seek either to imprison or to murder the most vocal and visible leader of the opposition, Vicente Rocafuerte.

Although the administration believed that Rocafuerte's inflamma-
tory articles and pamphlets incited rebellion, it feared, under
present political conditions, that no jury would convict him. The
government needed proof that Rocafuerte had taken direct part in
organizing an armed revolt in order to imprison him and, perhaps,
later quietly assassinate him. The defeat of Colonel Pedro Pantoja
on June 8, 1832, seemed to provide the regime with an opportunity
to establish a case against its bitter antagonist.[33]

Colonel Pantoja had organized a group of guerrillas in Huepal-
co, a village near Cuautla (an area presently in the state of Morelos,
but then part of the state of Mexico). The insurgents encountered a
large federal force; during a brief struggle Pantoja was killed and
most of his followers imprisoned. The rebels were taken to a
federal prison in Chalco, near the capital. After a lengthy investigation, the government announced that it had proof that Rocafuerte
and Rejón had instigated and financed the insurrection. Accordingly, it ordered the immediate arrest of the two men.[34]

Soldiers and police searched for the two conspirators throughout
the city. Government supporters, like Carlos María Bustamante,
predicted that Rocafuerte would flee the country to elude justice.
They were wrong. Although Rejón went into hiding, Rocafuerte
openly continued his activities. He was apprehended in the atrium
of the cathedral on the evening of July 12. When an officer
detained him, Rocafuerte declared, "You can't arrest me: I've been
working for Mexican independence for fifteen years." Whereupon
the officer replied, "Well sir, I've been through the entire revolution and I have never seen your face. You, no doubt, have been
invisible."[35]

The prisoner was taken to the barracks of the national palace
where he was charged with inciting, sustaining, and directing
revolts against the government. The following day, Rocafuerte was
removed to Chalco where the other prisoners of the Pantoja rebellion were incarcerated.[36] The pro-government press was jubilant.[37]
But the opposition press led by the *Fénix*, now edited by Rodríguez
Puebla, warned the government that it was responsible for Rocafuerte's safety. On July 14, *La Columna* and the *Fénix* printed identi-
cal editorials declaring that Rocafuerte had been in good health
when apprehended, that he had not been armed, and that the
Bustamante regime could not claim the prisoner had either died of

ill health or been shot trying to escape. They threatened retaliation should Rocafuerte die.[38]

Despite the warnings of the press, Rocafuerte was handled roughly. He was placed in a dungeon for common criminals and held incommunicado for several days. The committee only learned of his whereabouts and condition on July 18. Relieved that Rocafuerte was alive, the *Fénix* thanked the jailers.[39] Moderates in the states also expressed concern for Rocafuerte's safety; many wrote editorials defending him. The municipal council of Guadalajara praised him and pledged to support his principles.[40] Thereafter, until he was released, the *Fénix* reminded its readers in every issue that Rocafuerte remained a prisoner, while the committee used its influence to arouse sympathy for him throughout the nation.[41]

Rocafuerte's arrest was only one facet of the renewed campaign to destroy the opposition in Mexico City. The government ordered the detention of hundreds of critics. Secret police and uniformed guards roamed through the city arresting suspected subversives. Despite their congressional immunity, Rejón and Quintana Roo went into hiding to avoid imprisonment. José Rincón, who had collaborated with Rocafuerte fled to Veracruz. On August 1, Santa Anna's sister was beaten by a group of soldiers as she stepped from a church where she had attended Sunday mass. She was later imprisoned and, although no charges were brought against her, held incommunicado. Government repression increased daily.

Then on August 6, to everyone's astonishment, the government relaxed its oppression and released Rocafuerte, ill but unharmed. The surprise move resulted from cabinet changes that took place early in August. The position of the Bustamante regime had deteriorated immensely in July. Jalisco, Veracruz, Zacatecas, and Durango were in open revolt; other states, like Puebla, were on the verge of joining them. When General Moctezuma occupied San Luis Potosí in August, Bustamante decided to take personal command of the federal armies, leaving Melchor Múzquiz as acting chief executive. In an attempt to end the civil war, Múzquiz invited leading conservative-moderates, Francisco Fagoaga, Juan Ignacio Godoy, Ignacio Alas, and Ignacio Iberri, to form a new cabinet. Before accepting the post of minister of foreign and internal affairs, Fagoaga had demanded that his friend Rocafuerte be released and that the government end all repression.[42]

The cabinet changes did not satisfy the Committee of Opposition, which privately pressured Fagoaga and the others to resign. On September 8, four days before the official announcement, the *Fénix* reported that Fagoaga was going to resign because he realized that, despite his best efforts, the government was not going to end its harsh policies. The other ministers also resigned shortly thereafter.[43]

Outraged by the intransigence of the opposition, the regime returned to the tactics of repression. *El Toro* insulted Rocafuerte, who, it claimed, had repaid the government's clemency by returning to the *Fénix* to attack Múzquiz and drive the new ministers from office. The administration issued orders for the arrest of countless "anarchists" and gave special instructions to the police and the army to apprehend immediately the principal leaders: Rocafuerte, Rejón, Quintana Roo, Pacheco Leál, and Villavicencio. Privately, the police were ordered to shoot them on sight. The search parties of soldiers and police who roamed through the city were unable to locate the "anarchist" leaders who had hidden in the houses of friends and sympathizers. Driven underground and ill, Rocafuerte officially relinquished the editorship of the *Fénix*. On October 1, a new editor began volume II. The paper, which had been the radical leader of the opposition, became a voice of moderation. The *Fénix* still insisted upon the return of Gómez Pedraza, but it no longer denounced the government with its former vehemence.[44]

Rocafuerte's sudden disappearance and the change in the editorial policy of the *Fénix* convinced many that he had fled the country. Others, like the editor of *El Sol*, maintained that he was on a secret mission to Veracruz to confer with the recently arrived Gómez Pedraza. None of these reports was true. Rocafuerte, who was quite ill, had been bedridden for two weeks beginning September 22 but as he recovered he began to venture cautiously into the streets to meet other leaders of the opposition. On the night of October 12, soldiers surprised Rocafuerte, Rejón, and Villavicencio "conspiring" in a small square in Mexico City. Although fired upon, they managed to escape. Thereafter parties of soldiers and secret police were constantly searching for the three men. In order to avoid detection, they moved about continuously for the next couple of months, sleeping in a different house every night. The seriousness of their plight became evident when the police discovered and killed Villavicencio. Rocafuerte, who suffered from a respiratory ailment all his life, found his health deteriorating under the stress of the struggle to remain hidden. On three occasions, Rocafuerte was so incapacitated that he could not flee when soldiers searched the houses in which he was hiding. However, secret spaces were available and he was spared Villavicencio's fate.[45]

Meanwhile, the insurgents in the states had won a series of victories. Santa Anna's forces were advancing on Mexico City from the east, Moctezuma from the northeast, García from the north, and Alvarez from the southwest. On October 5, 1832, the city of Puebla surrendered to Santa Anna. Unable to fight on all fronts, Bustamante concentrated his forces in the states of Puebla and Mexico. His tactic failed. On December 5, he was decisively defeated. Three days later he sued for peace. Bustamante and his leading officers met with Santa Anna, Gómez Pedraza, Ramos Arizpe, and Bernardo González Angulo at Zavaleta, a hacienda near Puebla City. They reached an agreement on December 23, whereby Bustamante and his officers were allowed to go into exile and Gómez Pedraza assumed the presidency to supervise state and national elections.[46]

The Treaty of Zavaleta resulted in an ambiguous victory for the constitutional moderates. Since it permitted the return of Gómez Pedraza, constitutionalists believed that legitimacy had been restored. But in reality, the commitment to legal succession had been broken when Gómez Pedraza was forced into exile in 1828 and it could not be restored merely by his return. Furthermore, the victory over Bustamante had been won by force of arms, with General Santa Anna erroneously receiving most of the credit. The Mexico City Committee had gambled that, with the return of constitutional government, they would be able to control the military. However, the fact that the principal leaders of the committee were not present at the signing of the peace diminished their power, influence, and prestige. Despite the presence of men like Gómez Pedraza and Ramos Arizpe at the negotiations, contemporaries, as well as later historians, generally assumed that Santa Anna had overthrown the Bustamante regime because the committee's propaganda campaign had depicted him as a hero. This, together with his earlier defeat of the invading Spaniards in 1829, made him the most popular man in Mexico. In 1833 he was elected president.

The failure of Mexican and other Spanish American constitutional moderates went beyond their inability to prevent the rise of military politicians.[47] They represented a liberal, sometimes radical, faction, committed to the constitutional process. As a result, they were theoretically forced to rely upon constitutional processes to restrain the left and the right. To do otherwise, they argued, would violate the very institutions they sought to develop. Unfortunately, neither the extreme right nor the extreme left felt bound by the same rules. This placed the constitutional moderates in a dilemma; they could not maintain the constitution if they did not follow the letter of the law, but they could not defend the constitutional process from extra-legal forces without violating the very principles they sought to protect. On the occasions when they resorted to force, as in opposition to Bustamante, they did so in the hope that they could restore the constitutional process. In this sense, the tragedy of Spanish Americanism and Spanish American liberalism was the inability of the constitutional moderates to convince other groups to operate within the limits of the constitution.

# XIII

## THE DEMISE OF SPANISH AMERICANISM

The persecuted "anarchists" emerged from their hiding places when Múzquiz lost control of Mexico City following Bustamante's defeat on December 5, 1832. Rocafuerte was finally able to consult doctors. The physicians advised him that the altitude and cold of the capital would never permit him to recover his health and prescribed a long convalescence in a warmer climate. Rocafuerte decided that his native Guayaquil would be an ideal place to recuperate. However, Gómez Pedraza wrote from Puebla inviting him to remain in the country, perhaps to participate in the new government or to act as a private citizen, fostering social reforms and introducing new enterprises in Mexico.[1]

As he lay in bed pondering the future, Rocafuerte recalled the two tumultuous decades that had passed since the promulgation of the Spanish Constitution in 1812. To reform-minded men like Rocafuerte, the new charter had seemed like the culmination of a century of change. Shortly after its adoption, filled with expectation, he had departed to take his place among the men who were creating a constitutional Spanish commonwealth. How elusive those hopes had been; political factionalism, Ferdinand VII, the Holy Alliance, and French troops had shattered that dream. Yet the constitutional years had formed a generation of Spanish Americanists who believed in the future of their continent and who wanted to continue the Spanish liberal tradition. These men, from all parts of Spanish America, were destined to cooperate in securing diplomatic recognition and promoting social and economic development in America.

Disappointed by the failure of Spanish constitutionalism, the Spanish Americanists turned to a new vision of American fraternity. Believing that the New World was better than the Old, they rejected monarchies and established republics. Since the United States was the first to recognize their independence, they turned for assistance to their elder sister republic. Although a few North Americans welcomed their brothers from the south, many others received them with suspicion. The interests of the United States and Spanish America did not coincide and the Spanish Americanists were unable to secure the support they needed in the North American nation. Eventually, the Spanish Americanists realized that they would have to forge their place in the family of nations alone.

Spanish Americanists were united by their common Spanish heritage, particularly liberalism, and the belief that Spanish America was destined to become great and powerful. The Spanish Americanists stressed the need for cooperation among the new republics so that they could take their rightful place among the nations of the world. They advanced their ideas officially as members of various governments and informally among themselves. Their efforts seemed destined to succeed when the governments of Spanish America began to forge ties by signing bilateral treaties among themselves. The same spirit of cooperation later prompted the convocation of international congresses, first in Panama and then in Tacubaya, to build Spanish American unity. However, official cooperation among the republics of Spanish America proved impractical.

The efforts by a group of Spanish Americanists who cooperated informally to gain European recognition for their governments were more fruitful. England, the first great power to proffer friendship, became the nerve center of Spanish American diplomacy in Europe. Her navy, financial resources, and commerce became invaluable allies in the struggle to create the new, modern nations the Spanish Americanists envisioned. However, aware that the influence of any one nation was dangerous, the Spanish Americanists tried to develop relations with all the countries of Europe. Their main weapon in this diplomatic offensive was commerce. Although European merchants were eager to trade with Spanish America, the aristocrats who governed Europe were more concerned with maintaining the principle of legitimacy. As a compromise, European politicians suggested that the new nations either accept European monarchs or pay large indemnities to gain Spanish recognition. The Spanish Americans rejected these humiliating solutions and turned once more to England as their best prospect for securing a place in the international community. Their efforts were rewarded in December 1824 when Great Britain became the first European nation to recognize the Spanish American republics.

Formal recognition gave additional impetus to the already rapidly growing commerce between England and Spanish America. This business activity finally convinced the smaller continental nations that they would have to recognize the new American states if they were to protect their trade with Spanish America. Merchants in the Hanseatic republics, Holland, and some German states, including Prussia, had been trading with Spanish America prior to independence. When the Spanish Americanists threatened to end that commerce unless recognition were forthcoming, the Northern European nations hesitantly entered into relations with Spanish America. Ultimately, they recognized the American nations because trade with Spanish America had grown enormously and they feared that failure to act would permit England to capture the entire Spanish American market.

In contrast, France, the nation which most Spanish Americans considered their natural friend and ally, refused to establish diplomatic relations with them in spite of the burgeoning trade between the two areas. France was not completely deaf to threats of economic sanctions and entered into commercial agreements with Spanish America, but French conservatives had sufficient strength to prevent their government from recognizing the new nations. Only after the Revolution of 1830 broke the power of the legitimists did France recognize the republics of Spanish America.

The papacy could not be intimidated by threats of economic reprisal. The Spanish Americanists wanted the Holy See to recognize their independence and confirm their right of *patronato*. The Vatican not only refused their requests but actively supported Ferdinand VII's claims to America, particularly his right to exercise the *patronato* in the New World. Rome did not recognize Spanish America until Spain had done so.

Spain finally recognized the independence of her former possessions after the death of Ferdinand VII, when the liberals returned to power. Some Spanish liberals had supported the cause of American independence for many years. These men cooperated with Spanish American diplomats by providing information about absolutist Spain and her attempts to reconquer the New World. The

Spanish Americanists in turn assisted the liberal Spanish émigrés. The kinship between Spanish and Spanish American liberals was strongest during the dark days of the "ominous decade" of Ferdinand's absolutism.

Until Spain recognized the new states, Spanish American governments were preoccupied with the threat of a Spanish invasion. As a result they negotiated large loans in Europe to purchase war material. Until the end of the decade Spanish American governments allocated the lion's share of their budgets for defense. Since the governments depended heavily on foreign loads, they were badly hurt by the European financial crisis of 1825–1826. The new republics lost millions of pounds when their London bankers became insolvent. The crisis also adversely affected Spanish America because foreign investors temporarily abandoned the New World.

The immense burden of defense and the destruction caused by the struggle for independence created intense political unrest in the American nations. Despite the attempts of Spanish Americanists and their liberal Spanish émigré friends to introduce mass education, social reforms, and technological innovations, the new countries entered a period of economic, social, and political dislocation in 1827. The dreams of Spanish American cooperation began to decline as internal stresses created divisions among the American nations. Unpaid debts between sister republics became a major point of contention when financial difficulties made it impossible for individual governments to meet their obligations. Economic decline and resulting unemployment and inflation exacerbated internal political divisions in the Spanish American nations. Political factionalism threatened their stability and regionalism threatened their very existence. These developments were inimical to Spanish Americanism.

By 1829, hope no longer existed even for a loose Spanish American confederation. In that year Gran Colombia and Peru went to war over boundary conflicts, the first of a series of struggles that were to mar Spanish American fraternity. The following year, regionalism, combined with political factionalism, destroyed Gran Colombia. It divided into three new nations: Venezuela, Ecuador, and New Granada (present-day Colombia). Later the Central

American union also failed, splitting into several countries. These events were among the most conspicuous of the regional crises that ravaged the disunited states of Spanish America in the first half-century of independence.

Even before the last of these crises erupted, Spanish Americanists began to turn inward. Some, like Arce and Vidaurre, became deeply embroiled in their country's politics and could find little time for international cooperation. Others, like Michelena and Olmedo, became disillusioned with the inability of the Spanish American governments to cooperate and returned to their homes. away from national as well as international politics. A few, like Cañedo and Rocafuerte, continued to encourage Spanish American cooperation. But, in general, most Spanish Americanists concentrated on national issues during the late 1820s and early 1830s.

Although in 1832 Rocafuerte could not foresee the total failure of Spanish Americanism, he realized that international cooperation was no longer practical. Since the intense political struggle that had gripped Mexico was being repeated throughout Spanish America, he abandoned the dream of being a citizen of America. Rather than remain in Mexico, he decided to return to his family in Guayaquil. When Rocafuerte asked for his passport, he received it without any difficulty.[2]

Rocafuerte left Mexico City for Acapulco in December 1832. The country was still unsettled and the trip was far from uneventful. First, he was captured by Lieutenant Colonel Luis Viera, the commander of Iguala, who recognized Rocafuerte as an antigovernment critic and had him chained to an open belltower where the captive could find no shelter from the elements. He was near death when Viera learned of Bustamante's surrender and released his prisoner. After convalescing, Rocafuerte continued his journey, only to fall into the hands of Francisco González, an illiterate guerrilla leader in Alvarez' army, who mistook him for a white conservative. Rocafuerte barely escaped execution. However, he managed to convince González that he was a hero of the anti-Bustamante struggle and so obtained his release.[3]

In January 1833, Rocafuerte finally reached Acapulco and boarded ship for Guayaquil. In Ecuador, he recovered his health and devoted himself to his long neglected estates. However, he was unable to curb his interest in government. Within a few months of his arrival, he entered politics, becoming the second president of Ecuador (1835–1839). Later he served as governor of the province of Guayas (1839–1842). He married late in life, not to his niece for whom he had requested papal dispensation in 1829, but to his cousin, Baltazara Calderón. Rocafuerte remained a staunch advocate of education, religious toleration, reform, and modernization. True to his beliefs, he continued his attempts to foster cooperation among the Spanish American countries. When war erupted between Chile and the Peru–Bolivian confederation during his presidency, Rocafuerte attempted to mediate. Although Ecuador and Peru had boundary questions pending, he refused a Chilean offer to settle them by entering the war against Peru. Later, in 1846, when General Juan José Flores attempted an invasion of Ecuador and Peru in the name of the Queen of Spain, Rocafuerte was among those who promoted a Spanish American conference to organize a common defense. He was in Lima attending that conference when he died in 1847.[4]

The attempts of men like Rocafuerte to rekindle the spirit of cooperation failed. Spanish Americanism was dead. The nations of America were too preoccupied with their own internal problems. Later, at the end of the century, a new form of international cooperation would develop: Pan Americanism. However, this movement, which was initiated by the United States, was not based on the same tenets as the earlier Spanish Americanism, for Pan Americanism rejected, indeed denied, Spanish liberalism, the basis of Spanish Americanism.

# NOTES

## Note to Introduction

1. R. A. Humphreys discusses the literature on independence in Charles C. Griffin (ed.), *Latin America: A Guide to the Historical Literature* (Austin, 1971), part V.

## I: The Spanish Heritage

1. Vicente Rocafuerte, *Bosquejo ligerísimo de la revolución de Mégico* [sic] *desde el grito de Iguala hasta la proclamación de Iturbide* (Philadelphia, 1822), 67; Francisco J. Ponte Domínguez, "José Antonio Miralla y Cuba," in Cuba: Archivo Nacional, *José Antonio Miralla* (Havana, 1960), 28–29.
2. Henry Kamen, *The War of Succession in Spain, 1700-1715* (Blooming-ton, 1969).
3. Henry Kamen, "El establecimiento de los intendentes en la adminis-tración española," *Hispania*, XXIV (1964), 374–378; Miguel Artola, "Campillo y las reformas de Carlos III," *Revista de Indias*, XII (1952), 687–690. On the eighteenth century, see also Jean Sarrailh, *La Espa-ña ilustrada de la segunda mitad del siglo XVIII* (Mexico, 1957); Richard Herr, *The Eighteenth Century Revolution in Spain* (Princeton, 1958); Marcelin Defourneaux, *Pablo de Olavide, el afrancesado* (Mexico, 1965); Ricardo Krebs Wilkens, *El pensamiento histórico, político y económico del Conde de Campomanes* (Santiago de Chile, 1960); Gonzalo Anes, *Econo-mía e Ilustración* (Barcelona, 1969).
4. David Brading, *Miners and Merchants in Bourbon Mexico, 1763-1810* (Cambridge, 1971), 33–92. Brading is a member of what could be called the "London School," a group of University of London stu-dents who argue that the Bourbon reformers "reconquered Spanish America," that is, that Spaniards took local control away from the creoles. The thesis has been brilliantly stated recently in John Lynch's *The Spanish American Revolutions, 1808-1826* (New York, 1973), 1–36. I question the notion of a "reconquest." All I wish to imply here is that

government was changed and expanded, and attempts were made to modernize it.

5. Artola, "Campillo y las reformas de Carlos III," 690–710.
6. William W. Pierson, "The Establishment and Early Functioning of the *Intendencia* in Cuba," in *The James Sprunt Historial Studies*, XIX (Chapel Hill, 1927), 74–123; John Lynch, *Spanish Colonial Administration, 1772-1810* (London, 1958); Lillian E. Fisher, *The Intendant System in Spanish America* (Berkeley, 1929).
7. Guillermo Céspedes del Castillo, *Lima y Buenos Aires* (Seville, 1949).
8. Nancy Farris, *Crown and Clergy in Colonial Mexico, 1759-1821* (London, 1968); Lyle McAlister, *The Fuero Militar in New Spain, 1764-1800* (Gainesville, 1957); Walter Howe, *The Mining Guild in New Spain and its Tribunal General, 1770-1821* (Cambridge, Mass. 1949).
9. Romeo Flores Caballero, "La consolidación de vales reales en la economía, la sociedad y la política novohispana," *Historia mexicana*, XVIII (1969), 334–378; Brian R. Hamnett, "The Appropriation of Mexican Church Wealth by the Spanish Bourbon Government," *Journal of Latin American Studies*, I (November 1969), 85–113; Michael P. Costeloe, *Church Wealth in Mexico* (Cambridge, 1967). Recently, Asunción Lavring has questioned the impact of this measure in Mexico; see "The Execution of the Law of *Consolidación* in New Spain: Economic Aims and Results," *Hispanic American Historical Review* (hereafter cited as *HAHR*) LIII (February 1973), 27–49.
10. Richard Herr *The Eighteenth Century Revolution*, 239–375.
11. Gabriel Lovett, *Napoleon and the Birth of Modern Spain*. 2 vols. (New York, 1965), I, 86–132; Miguel Artola, *Los orígenes de la España contemporanea*. 2 vols. (Madrid, 1959), I, 103–146.
12. Miguel Artola, *Los afrancesados* (Madrid, 1953).
13. Herr, *The Eighteenth Century Revolution*, 337–347; Federico Suárez, "La génesis del liberalismo político español," *Arbor*, VII, no. 21 (May-June 1947), 349–395.
14. Francisco Martínez Marina, *La teoría de las Cortes*. 2 vols. (Madrid, 1968. *Biblioteca de Autores Españoles*, vols. 219–220); Martínez Marina's critical introduction to the *Siete Partidas* has been reissued together with an excellent study of Martínez Marina as vol. 194 of *Biblioteca de Autores Españoles* (Madrid, 1966).
15. Jorge Castel, *La Junta Central Suprema y Gubernativa de España e Indias* (Madrid, 1950), 71–76.
16. Ibid.
17. Artola has published many replies of the "Consulta a la Nación" in *Los orígenes de la España*, II. The consultation also included the American Kingdoms; e.g., the Audiencia of Quito received the request on December 21, 1809, and the following month replies were sent from all

pertinent institutions in the kingdom. Archivo Nacional de Historia, Audiencia de Quito (hereafter cited as ANH, AQ), vol. 456, ff. 21–29.

18. The decree specified that in America a deputy should be elected "... por cada capital cabeza de partido de estas diferentes Provincias." ANH, AQ, vol. 460, ff. 40–51.

19. Artola, *Los orígenes de la España*, I, 282–284.

20. Lovett, *Napoleon and the Birth of Modern Spain*, I, 370–372.

21. ANH, AQ, vol. 460, ff. 122–125; Artola, *Los orígenes de la España*, I, 383–385.

22. A cursory review of books of cabildos from the years 1810-1814, will reveal how elections took place. The author has verified this for the cabildos of Quito and Guayaquil. On Peru see, John Preston Moore, *The Cabildo in Peru under the Bourbons* (Durham, N.C., 1966), 205–206. The best studies of the electoral process have been done for Mexico, see Charles R. Berry, "The Elections of the Mexican Deputies to the Spanish Cortes, 1810-1822," in Nettie Lee Benson, *Mexico and the Spanish Cortes, 1810-1822* (Austin, 1966), 10–42.

23. See Lovett, *Napoleon and the Birth of Modern Spain*, I, 371, fn. 33, for a review of the various estimates of the members of the Cortes.

24. Lovett, *Napoleon and the Birth of Modern Spain*, I, 373–374.

25. Benson, *Mexico and the Spanish Cortes*, 4.

26. ANH, AQ, vol. 465, fo. 95.

27. The only study of this important institution is, Nettie Lee Benson, *La diputación provincial y el federalismo mexicano* (Mexico, 1955).

28. The books of cabildos for this period contain important information on the new constitutional city council. For Quito in the 1820s see Gustavo Chiriboga, "El Ayuntamiento Constitutional de Quito," *Anuario histórico jurídico ecuatoriano*, II (1972), 433–463. However, the best study is Roger L. Cunniff, "Mexican Municipal Electoral Reform, 1810-1821," in Benson, *Mexico and the Spanish Cortes*, 59–86.

29. Agustín Argüelles, *Examen histórico de la reforma constitutional*. 2 vols. (London, 1835). For a comparison with later Spanish American constitutions see, Vicente Rocafuerte, "Examen analítico de las constituciones formadas en Hispano-américa," *Revista de historia de América*, no. 72 (July-December 1971), 419–484; Lovett, *Napoleon and the Birth of Modern Spain*, II, 415–490 and Artola, *Los orígenes de la España*, I, 257–490, discuss the framing of the constitution. Benson, *Mexico and the Spanish Cortes*, is a study of Mexican participation in that process.

30. For a good review of the literature on the Spanish liberals see the footnotes in Lovett, *Napoleon and the Birth of Modern Spain*, I, 370–378; II, 416–490.

31. Ibid., II, 438; Neptalí Zuñíga, *José Mejía, Mirabeau del Nuevo Mundo*

(Quito, 1949); Alfredo Flores, *Don José Mejía Llequerica en las Cortes de Cádiz de 1810 a 1813* (Barcelona, 1913).

32. Luis Alayza y Paz Soldán, *La constitutión de Cádiz: El egregio limeño Morales y Duarez* (Lima, 1946).

33. Enrique del Valle, *Los diputados de Buenos Aires en las Cortes de Cádiz y el nuevo sistema de gobierno económico de América* (Buenos Aires, 1912).

34. Benson, *Mexico and the Spanish Cortes.*

35. Benson, *La diputación provincial*, 11–41.

36. Ibid.; Lovett, *Napoleon and the Birth of Modern Spain*, II, 449.

37. Berry, "The Election of Mexican Deputies," 21–28.

38. María Cristina Diz-Lois, *El Manifiesto de 1814* (Pamplona, 1967), 28–39. She is a member of the conservative school of historians formed by Federico Suárez at the Estudio General de Navarra who, in the last twenty years, have engaged in a systematic criticism of the origins of Spanish liberalism.

39. *El Español Constitucional*, III, 21–25.

40. Berry, "The Election of Mexican Deputies," table 4, p. 26–27.

41. Lovett, *Napoleon and the Birth of Modern Spain*, II, 809–810; Artola, *Los orígenes de la España*, I, 618–620.

42. Raymond Carr, *Spain, 1808-1939* (Oxford, 1966), 97, 119.

43. Benson, *Mexico and the Spanish Cortes*, 4.

44. Lovett, *Napoleon and the Birth of Modern Spain*, II, 813.

45. Diz-Lois, *El Manifiesto*, 79–192; the manifesto is reproduced on pages 193–277.

46. Federico Suárez argues that the Persians were not reactionaries. They were, to use his terminology, *renovators* rather than *innovators*, see his *La crisis política del antiguo régimen en España, 1800-1840* (Madrid, 1958), 88–100.

47. José Luis Comellas, *Los primeros pronunciamientos en España* (Madrid, 1958), 45–49.

48. Lovett, *Napoleon and the Birth of Modern Spain*, II, 752–808.

49. Ibid., II, 828–29.

50. Comellas, *Los primeros pronunciamientos*, 58–105.

51. Vicente Llorens, *Liberales y románticos, una emigración española en Inglaterra* (2d ed. Madrid, 1968), 10.

52. Comellas, *Los primeros pronunciamientos*, 48–49.

53. Charles W. Fehrenbach, "Moderados and Exaltados: The Liberal Opposition to Ferdinand VII, 1814-1823," *HAHR*, L (February 1970), 52–59.

54. Romeo Flores Caballero, *La contrarevolución en la independencia* (Mexico, 1969), 78.

55. Carlos Martínez Silva, *Biografía de don José Fernández Madrid* (Bogotá, 1935), 11–15. José Fernández de Madrid was a relative of the then

conservative minister of the Indies, Miguel Lardizabal y Uribe. In this case blood proved to be thicker than ideology.

56. Captain General Gabino Gaínza, a conservative, was Vicente Rocafuerte's brother-in-law.

57. ANH, Libro de Cédulas, XVI, ff. 239–240.

58. Comellas, *Los primeros pronunciamientos*, 6–7. For an attempt to rehabilitate Ferdinand see María del Carmen Pintos Vieites, *La política de Fernando VII entre 1814-1820* (Pamplona, 1958).

59. This point was generally acknowledged by participants. Evaristo San Miguel declared that "masonic lodges became liberal and conspiratorial juntas [and the terms] constitutionalist and mason became synonymous." Evaristo San Miguel, *Vida de D. Agustín Argüelles*. 4 vols. (Madrid, 1851-52), II, 62–63.

60. Herr, *The Eighteenth Century Revolution*, 154–200; Robert J. Shafer, *The Economic Societies in the Spanish World, 1763-1821*. (Syracuse, 1958).

61. Bolívar, San Martín and Miranda's careers are well known. For the others mentioned see Vicente Rocafuerte, *A la nación* (Quito, 1908), 235–244; Bradford Hadley, "The Enigmatic Padre Mier" (Ph.D. dissertation, University of Texas, Austin, 1955); Harold Bierck, "Pedro Gual and the Patriot effort to Capture a Mexican Port, 1816," *HAHR*, XXVII (August 1947), 456–466; Ponte Domínguez, "Miralla y Cuba," 1–94; Carlos María Bustamante, "Diario de lo especialmente ocurrido en México," V (June 25, 1825), manuscript, Zacatecas.

62. Dolores F. Rovirosa, "Antonio José Valdez: Maestro, periodista, historiador y hombre de América," (unpublished manuscript, Latin American Collection, Austin, 1970).

63. Wilbert H. Timmons, "Tadio Ortíz, Mexican Emissary Extraordinary," *HAHR*, LI (August 1971), 463–477.

64. Jaime E. Rodríguez O., "An Analysis of the First Spanish American Constitutions," *Revista de Historia de América*, no. 72 (July-December 1971), 413–419. In studying the Americans' criticism of Spain one must distinguish between their hatred of Ferdinand and his supporters and their dislike of things Spanish. When this distinction is made, much of what appear to be anti-Spanish attitudes on the part of the liberals turn out to be, merely, anti-Ferdinand and anti-absolutist views.

65. Harris G. Warren, "The Origin of General Mina's Invasion of Mexico," *Southwestern Historical Quarterly*, XLII (July 1938), 1–20.

66. Comellas, *Los primeros pronunciamientos*, 165–186.

67. Harris G. Warren, "Xavier Mina's Invasion of Mexico," *HAHR*, XXIII (February 1943), 52–76.

68. Comellas, *Los primeros pronunciamientos*, 187–302.

69. Carr, *Spain*, 127. José Fontana Lazaro's *La quiebra de la monarquía*

*absoluta, 1814-1820* (Barcelona, 1971) provides the first truly scholarly economic and political study of the period. Unfortunately, it came to my attention too late to be incorporated into this work.

70. Antonio Alcalá Galiano, *Recuerdos de un anciano* (Madrid, 1955. *Biblioteca de Autores Españoles*, vol. 83), 91–131; Charles W. Fehrenbach, "A Study of Spanish Liberalism: The Revolution of 1820," (Ph.D. dissertation, University of Texas, Austin, 1961), 73–85.
71. Carr, *Spain*, 128–129.
72. Ramon Mesonero Romanos, *Memorias de un setentón* (Madrid, 1967. *Biblioteca de Autores Españoles*, vol. 203), 97–99; Fehrenbach, "A Study of Spanish Liberalism," 80–85.
73. Cunniff, "Mexican Municipal Reform," 82.

## II: The Spanish Constitution Restored

1. Rodríguez, "An Analysis," 414–416.
2. José Fernández de Madrid, *A la restauración de la Constitución española* (Havana, 1820).
3. *El Argos*, June 3, 1820, 16.
4. *El Argos*, October 5, 1820, 8.
5. Genaro García collected some of these pamphlets. Thirty-five of them, all published in 1820, are to be found in *Miscelanea para la historia de México*, IV, Latin American Collection, University of Texas, Austin. See also Carlos María Bustamante's recently reprinted *La Constitución de Cádiz, o motivos de mi afecto a la Constitución* (Mexico, 1971).
6. Ponte Domínguez, "Miralla y Cuba," 28–29.
7. Manuel Lorenzo de Vidaurre, *Votos de los americanos a la nación española y a nuestro amado monarca el señor don Fernando VII; verdadero concordato entre españoles, europeos y americanos* (Mexico, 1820).
8. Tomás Romay, "Purga Urbem," *Diario del Gobierno Constitucional de la Habana*, May 20, 1820, 1–3. As the secretary of the provincial deputation of Havana, Romay seems to have felt compelled to give lip service to the constitution.
9. Jaime E. Rodríguez O., "Vicente Rocafuerte and Mexico, 1820-1832" (Ph.D. dissertation, University of Texas, Austin, 1970), 3–9; Manuel L. de Vidaurre, *Plan del Perú* (Philadelphia, 1823), 126; Bolívar to José Joaquín Olmedo, San Carlos, June 13, 1821, in Vicente Lecuna, *Cartas del Libertador*, 12 vols. (Caracas, 1929–1959), XII, 235–237.
10. Vicente Rocafuerte, *Rasgo imparcial* (Havana, 1820), 1–7.
11. Diego Tanco, *Lo más y lo menos* (Havana, 1820).

12. *El Argos*, June 13, 1820, p. 10; José Antonio Miralla, *Análisis del papel titulado lo más y lo menos* (Havana, 1820).

13. Félix Varela, *Observaciones sobre la Constitución Política de la Monarquía Española* (Havana, 1821); Enrique Gay Calbo, "Varela y El Habanero," in *Biblioteca de Autores Cubanos*, IX (Havana, 1945), ix–xxxix.

14. See José Antonio Miralla, "Soberanía del pueblo y elecciones populares, conforme a la Constitución Política de la Monarquía Española," *El Argos*, August 14, 1820, 1–10; José Fernández de Madrid, "Nuestras diferencias: sus peligros: sus remedios," *El Argos*, December 16, 1820, 2–6. In general most of the political articles published in *El Argos* during 1820–1821 are favorable to reform within the Spanish Constitution.

15. José Manuel Restrepo, *Historia de la Revolución de la República de Colombia*. 4 vols. (Bencazon, 1858), III, 33; Simón Bolívar to Francisco de Paula Santander, Rosario de Cucutá, May 7, 1820, Lecuna, *Cartas*, II, 194–197; José Revenga to Santander, Angostura, August 2, 1820, in Colombia: Academia de Historia, *Archivo Santander*. 24 vols. (Bogotá, 1914-1932), V, 75–76.

16. Miralla, *Análisis del papel*, 14; Rocafuerte, *A la nación*, 262; Bolívar to Vicente Rocafuerte, Bogotá, January 10, 1821, Lecuna, *Cartas*, II, 297.

17. Miralla, *Análisis del papel*, 16–18; Roque E. Garrigó, *Historia documentada de la conspiración de los Soles y Rayos de Bolívar*. 2 vols. (Havana, 1929), II, 153.

18. San Miguel, *Argüelles*, II, 101; Alcalá Galiano, *Recuerdos de un anciano*, 149–152; Mesonero Romanos, *Memorias de un setentón*, 101–102; José L. Comellas, *El trienio constitucional* (Madrid, 1963), 105–117.

19. Mesonero Romanos, *Memorias de un setentón*, 109–110; Comellas, *El trienio constitucional*, 37–38.

20. Carr, *Spain*, 130; San Miguel, *Argüelles*, II, 94–101.

21. Spain: Cortes, *Diario de las sesiones de Cortes: legislatura de 1820*. 3 vols. (Madrid, 1871), I, 16–18.

22. Fehrenbach, "A Study of Spanish Liberalism," 113–128; Miguel Artola, *La España de Fernando VII* (Madrid, 1968), 733–767.

23. Rocafuerte, *A la nación*, 244; Joaquín L. Villanueva, *Vida literaria*. 2 vols. (London, 1825), II, 384.

24. *El Constitucional*, no. 507 (September 27, 1820), 3–4.

25. Fehrenbach, "A Study of Spanish Liberalism," 157–169; Artola, *La España de Fernando*, 677–695; Comellas, *El trienio constitucional*,

26. *El Constitucional*, no. 583 (December 12, 1820), 4; no. 513 (October 3, 1820), 4; William S. Robertson, *France and Latin American Independence* (New York, 1967) 226–343; Guillaume de Bertier de Sauvigny, *The Bourbon Restoration* (Philadelphia, 1966), 176. Even after France intervened in Spain in 1823, most liberals still believed that she had been

the unwilling ally of the conservative powers. Later, Spanish Americans seeking recognition felt that France would be their friend if she could be torn away from the Holy Alliance.

27. Rocafuerte, *A la nación*, 263.
28. Pedro Gual to Santander, Bogotá, July 12, 1821, *Archivo Santander*, VI, 315.
29. Jaime Delgado, *España y México en el siglo XIX*. 3 vols. (Madrid, 1950), I, 42–45.
30. O'Donojú's instructions are reproduced in *ibid.*, I, 46–54.
31. Flores, *La contrarevolución*, 81–82; William S. Robertson, *Iturbide of Mexico* (Durham, N.C., 1952), 76–83. The Plan of Iguala also appealed to some Mexican liberals because it proclaimed the Spanish Constitution the fundamental law of the nation. Thus it attracted constitutionalists who were disenchanted by the bureaucracy's unwillingness to abide by the charter. As a result, constitutional monarchists, like José María Fagoaga, joined the movement to ensure that their principles were honored. See Doris M. Ladd, "The Mexican Nobility at Independence, 1780–1826" (Ph.D. dissertation, Stanford University, 1972), 228–243. The initial joy of independence and the subsequent disappointment in Iturbide's government are masterfully discussed in Javier Ocampo's *Las ideas de un dia* (Mexico, 1969).
32. Delgado, *España y México*, I, 25–79; Timothy E. Anna, "Francisco Novella and the Last Stand of the Royal Army in New Spain," *HAHR*, LI (February 1971), 92–111; Margaret L. Woodward, "The Spanish Army and the Loss of America, 1810-1824," *HAHR*, XLVIII (November 1968), 602–603.
33. Fehrenbach, "A Study of Spanish Liberalism," 202–225; Artola, *La España de Fernando*, 695–705; Comellas, *El trienio constitucional*, 208–295.
34. José Revenga to William White, Madrid, June 15, 1821, *Archivo Santander*, VII, 138; W. Woodrow Anderson, "Reform as a Means to Quell Revolution," in Benson, *Mexico and the Spanish Cortes*, 197–203.
35. As Pedro Gual commented, "the Spaniards have caused more of an uproar in two years than the French did in twenty years of revolution." Gual to Bolívar, Bogotá, February 15, 1822, Simón O'Leary, *Memorias del General O'Leary*. 29 vols. (Caracas, 1880). VIII, 427–428.
36. Gual to Santander, Pamplona, September 24, 1821, *Archivo Santander*, VII, 147–148.
37. Gual to Bolívar, Bogotá, February 15, 1822, O'Leary, *Memorias*, VIII, 427–428; Anderson, "Reform," 203–206.
38. Fehrenbach, "A Study of Spanish Liberalism," 225–266; Artola, *La España de Fernando*, 767–830; Comellas, *El trienio constitucional*, 336–443.

39. Richard Herr, *Spain* (Englewood Cliffs, 1971), 86.
40. Woodward, "The Spanish Army and America," 602–603; Charles W. Arnade, *The Emergence of the Republic of Bolivia* (Gainesville, 1957), 106, 102–107.
41. Arnade, *The Emergence of Bolivia*, 109–149; Enrique Gandía, "Las guerras de los absolutistas y liberales en América," *Revista de Indias*, XIV (July-December 1954), 427–430, 407–408; Vicente Lecuna, *La liberación del Perú* (Caracas, 1941), 6–11.
42. Arnade, *The Emergence of Bolivia*, 108.
43. Gandía, "Las guerras de los absolutistas y liberales," 413.

## III: Politics and Progress

1. Ponte Domínguez, "Miralla y Cuba," 61–63.
2. Carlos María Bustamante, "Diario de lo especialmente ocurrido en México," V (June 25, 1825); Rocafuerte, *A la nación*, 264–266; *El Argos*, August 14, 1821, 2.
3. Rocafuerte to Gual, New York, June 1, 1823 Colombia: Archivo Nacional, La República (hereafter cited as CANR), Guerra y Marina, 1464.
4. Disappointed by the failure of Spanish constitutionalism, many Spanish Americanists turned briefly to what has been called the Western Hemisphere Idea: the belief in the purity and goodness of America and the contrasting evil and corruption of Europe. See for example, Rocafuerte to Mier, New York, July 31, 1821, Mier Correspondence. This belief was attractive then because Spanish Americanists hoped that the United States would assist their countries. While they believed in the Western Hemisphere Idea for a time, they ultimately based their hopes on Spanish America rather than on the entire continent. Furthermore, the Spanish Americanists did not reject Spanish liberalism. Their apparent dislike of Spain and things Spanish was merely a reaction to Ferdinand VII's absolutism and his insistence upon reconquering America. This is clearly demonstrated by the ties of friendship Spanish Americansts retained with liberal Spanish exiles. In fact, they invited the émigrés to work for liberalism in Spanish America. See, Delgado, *España y México*, I, 337, and passim.
5. *The North American and United States Gazette*, LXV, no. 16,700 (July 26, 1847), 2; Rocafuerte to José Servando Teresa de Mier, New York, July 31, 1821, Mier Correspondence, Latin American Collection, Uni-

versity of Texas, Austin; Charles H. Bowman, "The Activities of Manuel Torres as Purchasing Agent, 1820-1821," *HAHR*, XLIII (May, 1968), 234–246; Arthur P. Whitaker, *The United States and the Independence of Latin America, 1800-1830* (New York, 1964), 58, 69, 158–160; Thomas P. Govan, *Nicholas Biddle, Nationalist and Public Banker, 1786-1844* (Chicago, 1959), 54, 74. Nicholas Biddle to Rocafuerte, Philadelphia, November 6, 1824; Jonathan [Roberts] to Biddle, Washington, April 13, 1820; Richard Forrest to Biddle, Baltimore, March 29, 1822; Nicholas Biddle Papers, Library of Congress, Washington, D.C. Rocafuerte to Thompson D. Shaw, Guayaquil, May 15, 1841, Simon Gratz Collection, Pennsylvania Historical Society, Philadelphia. Rocafuerte to Elie A. F. Lavallete, Quito, August 2, 1837, Elie A. F. Lavallete Collection, Duke University, Durham, N.C.

6. Rocafuerte to Mier, New York, July 31, 1821, Mier Correspondence.

7. Vicente Rocafuerte, *Ideas necesarias a todo pueblo americano independiente que quiera ser libre* (Philadelphia, 1821), 5–17, 19–137; Thomas Longworth, *New York Directory* (New York, 1821), 137; Benson, *La diputación provincial*, 86. Rocafuerte's tract induced Father Mier to hasten publication of a pamphlet that also exhorted the leaders of Mexico to establish a republic. [José Servando Teresa de Mier], *Memoria política-instructiva enviada desde Filadelphia en Agosto de 1821 a los gefes* [sic] *independientes de Anahuac llamado por los españoles Nueva España* (Philadelphia, 1821); Mier to Gual, Philadelphia, September 12, 1821, Mier Correspondence.

8. Manuel Torres to Mier, Philadelphia, September 24, 1821, Mier Correspondence; Torres to Rocafuerte, Philadelphia, September 29, 1821, locker no. 5, 4th shelf from the top, box no. 6, American Catholic Historical Society, Philadelphia; Rocafuerte to Macedonio Chavez, Havana, November 18, 1821, Mier Correspondence.

9. D.U.L.A., *Idea general sobre la conducta política de D. Miguel Ramos Arizpe, natural de la provincia de Coahuila, como diputado que ha sido por esta provincia en las Cortes generales y extraordinarias de la monarchía* [sic] *española desde el año 1810 hasta el de 1821* (Mexico, 1822), 20; Benson, *La diputación provincial*, 90–91; Rocafuerte explains his attitude at this time in, Rocafuerte to Bolívar, London, September 27, 1826, O'Leary, *Memorias*, IV, 398–401.

10. Torres to Mier, Philadelphia, December 16, 1821, Mier Correspondence; Rocafuerte, *A la nación*, 266; Flores Caballero, *La contrarevolución*, 98; Rocafuerte, *Bosquejo ligerísimo*, 87–92.

11. José Manuel de Herrera to José Gorantes, Mexico, February 13, 1822, Archivo General de la Secretaría de Relaciones Exteriores, Mexico (hereafter cited as AGSREM), H/310.11 (72:73) "822"/1. 5-15-8485.

12. Mariano Herrero to Captain General of Cuba, Guanabacoa, July 13,

1822, in Cuba: Archivo Nacional, *Documentos para la historia de Mexico* (Havana, 1961), 252–253.

13. Carlos María Bustamante, *Continuación del cuadro histórico de la revolución de México*. 4 vols. (Mexico, 1953-1963), I, 42–44; *Gazeta imperial de México*, II, no. 17–28, from April 6, 1822, to April 25, 1822; Rocafuerte, *Bosquejo ligerísimo*, 90–91, 103–110. Iturbide's proclamation is reproduced on 104–106.

14. Rocafuerte, *A la nación*, 266–267; Rocafuerte, *Bosquejo ligerísimo*, 100–111; Bustamante, *Continuación del cuadro*, I, 44–45.

15. Robertson, *Iturbide*, 170–172; Rocafuerte, *Bosquejo ligerísimo*, 113–136.

16. Miguel de Santamaría to Santander, Veracruz, March 26, 1822, *Archivo Santander*, VIII, 153–154; Herrera to Santamaría, Mexico, May 11, 1822 in Mexico: Secretaría de Relaciones Exteriores, *La diplomacia mexicana*. 3 vols. (Mexico, 1910-1913), I, 24; Rocafuerte, *A la nación*, 167–168.

17. Rocafuerte, *A la nación*, 268; Indice de los individuos que estan en arresto [Mexico, September, 1822], Iturbide Papers, Library of Congress, Washington, D.C.; Lucas Alamán, *Historia de Méjico*. 5 vols. (Mexico, 1942), V, 490–492; Horace V. Harrison, "The Republican Conspiracy Against Agustín de Iturbide," in Thomas Cotner and Carlos Castañeda (eds.), *Essays in Mexican History* (Austin, 1958), 143–144.

18. Rocafuerte, *A la nación*, 266–269; Carlos María Bustamante, *Diario histórico de México* (Zacatecas, 1896), 25.

19. Vicente Rocafuerte, "Report of the Mexican Minister, at the Twenty-first Annual Meeting of the British and Foreign School Society," in British and Foreign School Society,*Twenty-first Report* (London, 1826), 109; *El Sol*, January 26, 30, 1822; March 20, 1822. There is no agreement on the date the first Lancasterian school was inaugurated. I am using the date given by Rocafuerte. For a discussion of the problems in establishing an accurate date see, Evelyn Blair, "Educational Movements in Mexico, 1821-1836" (Ph.D. dissertation, University of Texas, Austin, 1941); and Eleanor J. Marshall, "History of the Lancasterian Educational Movements in Mexico" (M.A. thesis, University of Texas, Austin, 1951).

20. Henry Clay to Agustín Iturbide, Washington, March 23, 1822, in Mexico: *La diplomacia mexicana*, I, 67; John Quincy Adams to Herrera, Washington, April 23, 1822, AGSREM, H/310,11 (72:73) "822"/1. 5-15-8485; Joel R. Poinsett to James Monroe, Charleston, July 20, 1822, Monroe Papers, series I, Library of Congress, Washington, D.C.; *Aurora*, no. 10,342 (June 29, 1822), 2.

21. Santamaría to Santander, Mexico, August 2, 1822, *Archivo Santander*,

VIII, 339–340; Santamaría to Poinsett, Veracruz, November 25, 1822, in the Poinsett Papers, II, fo. 67, Pennsylvania Historical Society, Philadelphia; Rocafuerte to Santander, Philadelphia, February 15, 1823, *Archivo Santander*, IX, 252–253.

22. Herrera to Santamaría, Mexico, August 7, 1822; Santamaría to Herrera, Mexico, August 9, 1822; Herrera to Santamaría, Mexico, August 14, 1822; Herrera to Gual, Mexico, September 28, 1822: Mexico, *La diplomacia mexicana*, I, 25–29, 33–35. Santamaría to Poinsett, Veracruz, November 25, 1822, Poinsett Papers, II, 67, Philadelphia; Harrison, "The Republican Conspiracy," 144–160.

23. Rocafuerte to Santander, Philadelphia, February 15, 1823, *Archivo Santander*, IX, 252–253; Rocafuerte, *A la nación*, 270; Rocafuerte's *Bosquejo ligerísimo* was supposed to have been published by the Philadelphia press of *Teracrouef y Naroajeb*, which is nothing more than a rearrangement of the author's name *Rocafuerte y Bejarano*. Rocafuerte states that he wrote the work in the United States and had it published in Cuba, see *A la nación*, 270. However various Cuban scholars maintain that the book was written as well as published in Havana. See Ponte Domínguez, "Miralla y Cuba," 65–67; and Antonio Fernández de Castro, *Vicente Rocafuerte, un americano libre* (Mexico, 1947), 75. In light of the three-month interval between the time Rocafuerte left Mexico and the time he arrived in Philadelphia, that point of view seems reasonable.

24. Rocafuerte, *A la nación*, 271–272; Rocafuerte to Santander, Philadelphia, February 15, 1823, *Archivo Santander*, IX, 252–253; Rocafuerte to Gual, Philadelphia, February 15, 1823, CANR, Guerra y Marina, MCDLXIV, ff. 133–136; Rocafuerte to Josiah S. Johnston, Philadelphia, March 1, 1823, Johnston Papers, Pennsylvania Historical Society, Philadelphia; John Quincy Adams, *Memoirs*. 12 vols. (Philadelphia, 1874-1877), VI, 77.

25. Francisco de Arillaga to José Ignacio Pavón, Mexico, May 15, 1823, AGSREM, H/121.32 "823-24"/1. 40-11-22; Rocafuerte to Gual, Philadelphia, February 15, 1823, CANR, Guerra y Marina, MCDLXIV, ff. 133–136; *Aurora*, December 16, 1822, 2; December 18, 1822, 2.

26. José Manuel Zozaya to Herrera, Puebla, October 1, 1822, AGSREM, H/310.11 (72:73) "822"/1. 5-15-8484; Santamaría to Poinsett, Veracruz, November 25, 1822, Poinsett Papers, II, fo. 67, Herrera to Eugenio Cortés, Mexico, October 31, 1822; Zozaya to Herrera, Washington, December 7, 1822, AGSREM, H/310.11 (72:73) "822"/1. 5-15-8485.

27. Zozaya to Herrera, Washington, December 13, 1822, December 20, 1822, December 26, 1822, AGSREM, H/310.11 (72:73) "822"/1. 5-15-8485.

28. Zozaya to Herrera, Washington, December 26, 1822, AGSREM, H/310.11 (72:73) "822"/1. 5-15-8485; Rocafuerte to Gual, Philadelphia, February 15, 1823, CANR, Guerra y Marina, MCDLXIV, ff. 133–136.

29. Rocafuerte, *A la nación*, 269–270; Zozaya to Herrera, Washington, January 11, 1823; February 3, 1823, AGSREM, H/310.11 (72.73) "822"/1. 5-15-8485; Rocafuerte to Johnston, Philadelphia, March 1, 1823, Johnston Papers.

30. Rocafuerte to Gual, Philadelphia, February 15, 1823, CANR, Guerra y Marina, MCDLXIV, ff. 133—136; Zozaya to Herrera, Washington, January 11, 1823; February 3, 1823, AGSREM, H/310.11 (72:73) "822"/1. 5-15-8485; Adams, *Memoirs*, VI, 72–74.

31. Zozaya to Herrera, Washington, February 3, 1823, Mexico, *La diplomacia mexicana*, I, 107; Zozaya to Herrera, Washington, January 11, 1823, AGSREM, H/210 (73:72) /5. LE 2220 (XII); Rocafuerte to Gual, Philadelphia, February 15, 1823, CANR, Guerra y Marina, MCDLXIV, ff. 133–136; "Decreto de gracias al Honorable Henrique Clay," in Aurelio Noboa (ed.), *Recopilaciones de Leyes del Ecuador*. 5 vols. (Guayaquil, 1900), II, 6–7.

32. Benson, *La diputación provincial*, 90–92; Nettie Lee Benson, "The Plan of Casa Mata," *HAHR*, XXV (February 1945), 46–48; Zozaya to Herrera, Washington, February 28, 1823, Mexico, *La diplomacia mexicana*, I, 108.

33. Rocafuerte to Gual, February 15, 1823; New York, June 1, 1823, CANR, Guerra y Marina, MCDLXIV, ff. 133–136; Rocafuerte to Gual, Maracaibo, November 21, 1823, in Colombia, *Revista del Archivo Nacional*, IV, no. 39 (May 1942), 241–243.

34. "Minutes of the Managers of the Pennsylvania Hospital," VII, fo. 381 (April 28, 1823), Archives of the Pennsylvania Hospital, American Philosophical Society, Philadelphia; Rocafuerte, *A la nación*, 270; Vicente Rocafuerte, *Ensayo sobre el nuevo sistema de cárceles* (Mexico, 1830), passim; Rocafuerte to Gual, New York, June 1, 1823, CANR, Guerra y Marina, MCDLXIV.

35. Vicente Rocafuerte, *Lecciones para las escuelas de primeras letras, sacadas de las Sagradas Escrituras, siguiendo el texto literal de la traducción del Padre Scio, sin notas ni comentarios* (New York, 1823).

36. *New York Daily Advertiser*, May 7, 1823, 2; May 9, 1823, 2. Rocafuerte's speech is reproduced in *Paulson's American Daily Advertiser*, no. 14,493 (May 12, 1823), 3.

37. British and Foreign School Society, *Eighteenth Annual Report* (London, 1823), 114; Rocafuerte, "Report of the Mexican Minister," 110.

38. Rocafuerte to Gual, Philadelphia, February 15, 1823, CANR, Guerra y Marina, MCDLXIV, ff. 133–136; Vicente Rocafuerte, *Ensayo político*,

*el sistema colombiano, popular, electivo, y representativo, es el que más conviene a la América independiente* (New York, 1823).

39. Rocafuerte, *Ensayo político*, 11–216.
40. Rocafuerte described the pamphlet as an "Italian salad." Rocafuerte to Gual, Maracaibo, November 21, 1823, Colombia, *Revista del Archivo Nacional*, IV, no. 39 (May 1942), 241–243.

## IV: The Great Cuban Conspiracy

1. Garrigó, *Soles y rayos de Bolívar*, I, 154–155, 162.
2. José del Castillo to Poinsett, Havana, April 6, 1823, Monroe Papers, series I, Washington, D.C.; Ponte Domínguez, "Miralla y Cuba," 67.
3. Ponte Domínguez, "Miralla y Cuba," 67–68. For an extensive discussion of Cuban attempts to join the U.S. during these years see Herminio Portell-Vilá, *Historia de Cuba en sus relaciones con los Estados Unidos y España*. 4 vols. (Havana, 1938), I, 200–243.
4. Castillo to Poinsett, Havana, April 16, 1823, Monroe Papers, series I; Washington, D.C.; John Sibly to Johnston, New Orleans, March 11, 1822, Johnston Papers.
5. Adams, *Memoirs*, VI, 69–74; Poinsett to James Monroe, Charleston, May 7, 1823, Monroe Papers, series I; Washington, D.C. For a general account of U.S. views on the annexation of Cuba see John A. Logan, *No Transfer, An American Security Principle* (New Haven, 1961), 149–160.
6. Garrigó, *Soles y rayos de Bolívar*, I, 190–191; Manuel Lorenzo de Vidaurre to Bolívar, Guayaquil, December 20, 1823, O'Leary, *Memorias*, X, 371–372.
7. Gaspar Betancourt Cisneros wrote a series of biographical letters, fragments of which are found in Vidal Morales y Morales, *Iniciadores y primeros mártires de la revolución cubana* (Havana, 1901), 36–37.
8. José Aniceto Iznaga, "Peregrinación patriotica a Colombia" in Morales y Morales, *Iniciadores y primeros mártires*, 38.
9. Zozaya to Herrera, Washington, January 11, 1823, AGSREM, H/310.11 (72:73) "822"/1. 5-15-8485; Poinsett to John C. Calhoun, Charleston, n.d. [1823], Poinsett Papers, I, 72; Philadelphia; H. U. Addington to George Canning, Washington, December 1, 1823, in Charles Webster, *Britain and the Independence of Latin America, 1812-1830*. 2 vols. (London, 1938), 498–499.
10. *Paulson's American Daily Advertiser*, no. 14,437 (March 7, 1823); Hilario de Rivas to Francisco Dionicio Vives, Philadelphia, August 1, 1823, in Cuba, *Boletín del Archivo*, XXVII (1928), 152–153.

11. Castillo to Poinsett, April 16, 1823; Poinsett to Monroe, Charleston, April 16, 1823, and May 7, 1823, Monroe Papers, Series I, Washington, D.C.

12. Thomas Jefferson to Monroe, Monticello, June 23, 1823, Jefferson Papers, vol. 224, Library of Congress, Washington, D.C.; Ponte Domínguez, "Miralla y Cuba," 68–69; Adams to Hugh Nelson, Washington, April 28, 1823, Diplomatic Instructions to All Countries, IX, National Archives, Washington, D.C.

13. José A. Torrens to Minister of Foreign Affairs (Mexico), Philadelphia, May 31, 1823, Mexico, *La diplomacia mexicana*, II, 9–11; Manuel José de Arce to    , Philadelphia, July 26, 1823, in Miguel A. García, *General Don Manuel José de Arce*. 3 vols. (San Salvador, 1944), I, 275.

14. The article was reprinted in *El Sol*, no. 113 (October 5, 1823), 450–452.

15. Manuel José de Arce and Juan M. Rodríguez to John Quincy Adams, Washington, September 9, 1823; September 11, 1823; September 13, 1823: Notes from the Central American Legation, I, ff. 1, 5–7, 29, National Archives, Washington, D.C. Daniel Brent to Monroe, Washington, September 11, 1823, Monroe Papers, New York.

16. Rocafuerte to Adams, New York, October 16, 1823, Notes from the Central American Legation, I, fo. 33; Torrens to Lucas Alamán, Philadelphia, August 21, 1823, Mexico, *La diplomacia mexicana*, II, 20–24.

17. José María Salazar to Santander, New York, May 27, 1823; Leandro Palacios to Santander, New York, June, 1823, *Archivo Santander*, X, 170–172, 255–256.

18. Joaquín Anduaga to Spanish Secretary of State, New York, January 1, 1823; January 15, 1823, Estado, leg. 5649, Archivo Histórico Nacional, Madrid (hereafter cited as AHN).

19. Rivas to Vives, Philadelphia, August 1, 1823; August 8, 1823: Cuba, *Boletín del Archivo*, XXVII (1928), 152–153.

20. Vives to Overseas Ministry, Havana, August 14, 1823, Cuba, *Boletín del Archivo*, II, no. 6 (January-February 1903), 17–21; José María Heredia to Francisco Hernández, Matanzas, November 6, 1823, in Garrigó, *Soles y rayos de Bolívar*, II, 180–182. Garrigó's work is a detailed study of the internal aspects of the revolt.

21. Vives to Rivas, Havana, May 18, 1823; Vives to Tomás Gener, Havana, September 6, 1823; September 30, 1823: Cuba, *Boletín del Archivo*, XXVII, no. 1–6 (1928), 173–174; XV, no. 1 (January-February 1916), 27–28.

22. Rocafuerte to Gual, Maracaibo, November 21, 1823, Colombia, *Revista del Archivo Nacional*, IV, no. 39 (May 1942), 241–243; Rocafuerte, *A la nación*, 273–275; José A. Torrens to Alamán, Philadelphia, October 23, 1823, Mexico, *La diplomacia mexicana*, II, 40–43.

23. Mariano Manrique to Santander, Maracaibo, June 18, 1823; José Padilla to Santander, Maracaibo Bay, June 20, 1823; Manrique to Santander, Carigua, July 10, 1823; Avila y Compañía to Francisco Carabaño, Maracaibo, August 20, 1823; Manrique to Santander, San Carlos Castle, August 20, 1823: *Archivo Santander*, X, 243–246, 246–247, 300–301; XI, 18–19, 29–30.

24. Rocafuerte to Gual, Maracaibo, November 21, 1823, Colombia, *Revista del Archivo Nacional*, IV, no. 39 (May 1942), 242–243; Leandro Palacios to Santander, Washington, December 4, 1823, *Archivo Santander*, XI, 146–149; Iznaga, "Peregrinación patriotica," 38–39.

25. Iznaga, "Peregrinación patriotica," 39; Vidaurre to Bolívar, Guayaquil, December 30, 1823, O'Leary, *Memorias*, X, 371–372; Rivas to Vives, Philadelphia, February 23, 1824, Cuba, *Boletín del Archivo*, XXVII (1928), 171–172.

26. Rocafuerte, *A la nación*, 273–275; Rocafuerte to Gual, Maracaibo, November 21, 1823, Colombia, *Revista del Archivo Nacional*, IV, no. 39 (May 1942), 241–243; Bustamante, *Diario histórico*, 25.

27. Addington to Canning, Washington, December 1, 1823, Webster, *Britain and Latin America*, II, 498–499; Rivas to Vives, Philadelphia, September 12, 1823, Cuba, Archivo Nacional, *Documentos para la historia de Venezuela* (Havana, 1960). Rivas to Vives, Philadelphia, December 5, 1823; February 23, 1824; April 20, 1824; Vives to Rivas, Havana, May 18, 1824: Cuba, *Boletín del Archivo*, XXVII (1928), 164–165, 171–172, 172–173, 174; Rivas to Spanish Secretary of State, Philadelphia, April 25, 1824; May 27, 1824, AHN, Estado, leg. 5650.

28. Rocafuerte, *A la nación*, 275–276; Santander to Bolívar, Bogotá, November 6, 1823, and January 6, 1824, *Archivo Santander*, XI, 133–135, 233–235.

29. Rocafuerte, *A la nación*, 275–276; Santander to Bolívar, n. 1, December 16, 1823, *Archivo Santander*, XI, 188–190; Rocafuerte to Gual, Maracaibo, November 21, 1823, Colombia, *Revista del Archivo Nacional*, IV, no. 39 (May 1942), 242–243.

30. Iznaga, "Peregrinación patriotica," 39–42; Santander to José A. Paéz, Bogotá, February 22, 1824, *Archivo Santander*, XI, 314–316, Bolívar to Santander, Lima, December 20, 1824, Lecuna, *Cartas del Libertador*, IV, 225–230; Ponte, Domínguez, "Miralla y Cuba," 79–94.

31. Quoted in Hugh Thomas, *Cuba, the Pursuit of Freedom* (New York, 1971), 104.

32. José Fernández de Madrid to Bolívar, Bogotá, October 29, 1825, O'Leary, *Memorias*, XI, 267–268; Bustamante, "Diario," XVII (August 12, 1830), ff. 109–110; Eduardo Labougle, "José Antonio Miralla," in Cuba, Archivo Nacional, *Miralla*, 150–152.

## V: The Politics of Recognition

1. Rocafuerte, *A la nación*, 276–277.
2. Rodríguez, "An Analysis," 414–416; on Father Mier's federalism see, Nettie Lee Benson, "Servando Teresa de Mier, Federalist," *HAHR*, XXVIII (November 1948), 514–525.
3. Bustamante, "Diario," IV (January 13, 1824), 11; IV (January 20, 1824), 17. *Aguila mexicana*, no. 282 (January 21, 1824), 2.
4. José María Bocanegra, *Memorias para la historia de México independiente.* 2 vols. (Mexico, 1892), I, 339–343, 338–339. Other documents concerning the revolt are published in *El Iris de Jalisco*, no. 28 (February 2, 1824), 1–3; no. 31 (February 9, 1824), 2–4; no. 32 (February 11, 1824), 2; Bustamante, "Diario," IV (January 23, 1824), 19–23; IV (January 24, 1824), 23–25; Rocafuerte, *A la nación*, 277–278.
5. Most of the relevant correspondence on this question may be found in Mexico, *La diplomacia mexicana*, II, 99 passim, and in Webster, *Britain and Latin America*, I, 431–436; Arthur Wavell to Ignacio García Illueca, London, May 7, 1823, AGSREM, H/311.1 (42:72) "828"/1. 1-1-44; Alamán to Francisco de Borja Migoni, Mexico, August 6, 1823, AGSREM, H/121.32 "823–24"/1. 40-1121.
6. Lionel Hervey to George Canning, Mexico, January 18, 1824, in Webster, *Britain and Latin America*, I, 446–450.
7. Juan Antonio Mateos, *Historia parlamentaria de los congresos mexicanos de 1821-1857*. 25 vols. (Mexico 1877-1912), II, 683–703. Alamán to Pablo de la Llave, Mexico, February 18, 1824; De la Llave to Alamán, Córdoba, February 29, 1824; March 18, 1824: Mexico, *La diplomacia mexicana*, II, 261–262, 268, 278–279, 282–283, Bustamante, "Diario," IV (February 14, 1824), 58–60; IV (March 15, 1824), 92.
8. Rocafuerte, *A la nación*, 177–178; Rocafuerte to Juan de Díos Cañedo, London, May 3, 1828, AGSREM, H/131 "825"/6. LE 1616 (2). For a discussion of how little the Monroe Doctrine influenced the political realities of Spanish American independence, see Dexter Perkins, *The Monroe Doctrine, 1823-1826* (Cambridge, Mass., 1927), 149, and passim.
9. Minuta del nombramiento de D. Vicente Rocafuerte para Secretario de La Legación de Londres, Mexico, February 26, 1824, Mexico, *La diplomacia mexicana*, II, 263–264; Rocafuerte to Alexander von Humbolt, London, December 17, 1824, Ecuador: Academia Nacional de

Historia, *Boletín*, XXIV (July-December 1954), 285; Mateos, *Historia parlamentaria*, II, 715, 717, 719, 720, 724; *El Iris de Jalisco*, no. 53 (March 31, 1824), 1; Bustamante, *Continuación al cuadro*, II, 206; Bustamante, "Diario," IV (March 11, 1824), 89–90. It is possible that Rocafuerte may have had to purchase property to meet such a requirement since he left Juan Nepomuceno de Pareda to care for his interests in Mexico.

Rocafuerte's appointment was not unusual. In the years following independence, various Spanish American countries named men born elsewhere to represent them abroad. This was possible because many men considered themselves citizens of America, meaning, of course, Spanish America. Indeed, Spanish Americanists were proud of this fact and they discussed it openly during the Panama conference in 1826. See the extract from the *Archivo diplomático del Perú* quoted in Luis Quintanilla, *A Latin American Speaks* (New York, 1943), 94–96.

10. Instrucciones para el Ministro de México en Londres, Mexico, *La diplomacia mexicana*, II, 272–275.

11. Instrucciones reservadas para el Ministro de México en Londres, Mexico, *La diplomacia mexicana*, III, 10.

12. Instrucciones, Mexico, *La diplomacia mexicana*, III, 10.

13. José Mariano Michelena to Alamán, Tampico, April 16, 1824, Hernández y Dávalos Papers, Latin American Collection, University of Texas, Austin (hereafter cited as HD), 17-3.4022; Michelena to Alamán, London, June 26, 1824, AGSREM, H/311.1 (42:72) "824"/1. 1-1-44. The mission included the following persons: Michelena, minister; Rocafuerte, secretary; Tomás Murphy, Sr., first officer and agent in Paris; Juan Gambóa, second officer; Angel Guerra, third officer; Pedro Fernández del Castillo and Juan N. Almonte, military attaches; Maximo Garro and Juan Mancebo, scribes. Manuel Eduardo Gorostiza was later named confidential agent to the Low Countries.

14. Robertson, *France and Latin America*, 296–350; Harold Temperley, *The Foreign Policy of Canning, 1822-27* (London, 1927), 103–142; Webster, *Britain and Latin America*, 18–26; Manfred Kossok, *Im Schatten der Heiligen Allianz Deutschland und Lateinamerika 1815-1830. Zur Politik der deutschen Staaten gegenüber der Unabhängigkeitsbewegung Mittel- und Südamerikas* (Berlin, 1964).

15. Michelena to Alamán, London, June 26, 1824, AGSREM, H/311.1 (42:72) "824"/1. 1-1-44. Throughout this and other chapters dealing with diplomacy, the names of Michelena and Rocafuerte will be linked closely. There are several reasons for this. Michelena spoke neither English nor French, while Rocafuerte was fluent in both. They were together most of the time if for no other reason than

Michelena's need for a translator. The two men, however, were close friends and had known each other for a long time. They shared common experiences and outlooks. See the correspondence in the Hernández y Dávalos Papers, especially, Rocafuerte to Michelena, London, July 7, 1825, HD 18-6.4450.

16. Michelena to Canning, London, June 25, 1824; Canning to Michelena, London, June 26, 1824; Foreign Office Papers, London (hereafter cited as FO), FO 97/270, ff. 1, 5.

17. Michelena to Alamán, London, June 26, 1824; July 17, 1824; AGSREM, H/311.1 (42:72) "824"/1. 1-1-44.

18. Michelena to Alamán, London, July 3, 1824 (letters 16, 17), AGSREM, H/311.1 (42:72) "824"/1. 1-1-44.

19. Michelena to Alamán, London, October 27, 1824, HD 17-5.4165; Michelena to Alamán, London, July 12, 1824; Canning to Michelena, and Canning to Rocafuerte, July 7, 1824; Segunda conferencia con el señor Canning, London, July 9, 1824; AGSREM, H/311.1 (42:72)/1. 1-1-44.

20. Michelena to Alamán, London, July 24, 1824; Borja Migoni to Juan Guzmán, London, July 13, 1824; Borja Migoni to Supreme Executive Power, London, August 10, 1824; Mexico, *La diplomacia mexicana*, III, 218–221; II, 200–205.

21. Michelena to Borja Migoni, London, July 18, 1824, HD 17-4.4086.

22. Michelena to Borja Migoni, London, July 18, 1824; July 24, 1824; August 2, 1824; Borja Migoni to Michelena, London, July 20, 1824; Michelena to Alamán, London, July 25, 1824; HD 17-4.4086, 4087, 4088, 4092, 4089. Michelena to Alamán, London, July 25, 1824, Mexico, *La diplomacia mexicana*, III, 218–221. Alamán's extensive correspondence with Borja Migoni was carried on privately. Therefore, it is not in the Foreign Ministry Archive, but in the papers of the Hospital de Jesús now housed in the Archivo General de la Nación in Mexico.

23. The Mexican government named Borja Migoni consul general even though Canning requested that someone else be appointed. Canning to Ward, London, January 3, 1825, Webster, *Britain and Latin America*, I, 459–462; Rocafuerte to Cañedo, London, June 18, 1828, AGSREM, H/131 "828"/14. LE 1621 (6); Joseph Blackmore to Rocafuerte, London, November 20, 1828, FO 50/51, fo. 34. Michelena tried to influence Alamán through private correspondence. He told him, "I repeat that the matter of [Borja] Migoni is not my personal affair; it involves the nation. I have acted as a public man [in the matter]." Michelena to Alamán, London, May 18, 1825, Alamán Papers, folder II, no. 122, Latin American Collection, University of Texas,

Austin. The fact that nothing changed until Borja Migoni died in 1832 indicates the strength and influence that the mining interests had in the government.

24. The correspondence on the difficulties with Borja Migoni is extensive. Some of it was published in Mexico, *La diplomacia mexicana*, III, 215−245. But the bulk of the correspondence, including Murphy and Gorostiza's reports, is in the Hernández y Dávalos Papers, HD 17-4.4043 through 18-1.4319.

25. Michelena to Alamán, London, July 17, 1824; July 25, 1824; Joseph Planta to Michelena, London, July 13, 1824; Planta to Michelena and Rocafuerte, London, n.d.: AGSREM, H/311.1 (42:72) "824"/1. 1-1-44.

26. Felisberto Caldeira Brant and Manuel Rodríguez Gameiro Pessoa to Luis José de Carvalho e Melo, London, July 14, 1824 in Mexico, Secretaría de Relaciones Exteriores, *Relaciones diplomáticas entre México y Brasil* (Mexico, 1964), 34. Michelena to Brant and Gamiero, London, August 7, 1824; Brant and Gameiro to Michelena, London, August 10, 1824; Michelena to Alamán (secret), London, August 31, 1824: HD 17-4.4032, 4036, 4062. Harold Bierck, *La vida pública de Don Pedro Gual* (Caracas, 1947), 334−338.

27. Manuel E. Gorostiza to Michelena, Brussels, August 9, 1824; Tomás Murphy to Michelena, St. Sauverne, August 17, 1824: HD 17-4.4035, 4046.

28. Michelena to Alamán, London, August 21, 1824, AGSREM, H/311.1 (42:72) "824"/1. 1-1-44. Michelena to Alamán, London, August 31, 1824 (nota cifrada no. 1); Murphy to Ramos Arizpe, n.p., August 31, 1824: HD 17-4.4061, 4063.

29. Murphy to Michelena, San Salvador, September 2, 1824; September 5, 1824; Gorostiza to Michelena, Antwerp, September 1, 1824; Michelena to Murphy, London, September 15, 1824: HD 17-4.4070, 4074, 4067, 4083.

30. Gorostiza to Michelena, Amsterdam, September 13, 1824, HD 17-4.4078.

31. Michelena to Murphy, London, September 10, 1824; September 14, 1824; September 16, 1824: HD 17-4076, 4080, 17-7.7083.

32. Memorándum de la conferencia tenida entre el Sr. Planta y el ciudadano General José Mariano Michelena, London, September 22, 1824; Michelena to Alamán, London, September 23: HD 17-4.4107, 4102.

33. Murphy to Michelena, Paris, September 27, 1824, HD 17-4.4112; Gorostiza to Michelena, The Hague, September 29, 1824 (letters 1, 2, 3, 4—confidential): HD 17-4.4107, 4109, 4115, 4119.

34. There is an extensive correspondence on France and Spain for the

months of October, November, and December in the Hernández y Dávalos Papers, HD 17-5.4121 through 17-7.713.

This initial failure did not end conspiratorial activities between Spanish exiles and Spanish Americanists. In 1825 and 1826 various Spanish liberal groups received financial assistance from Spanish Americanists. Even in exile, however, the Spanish liberals maintained their political divisions. The moderates rallied around General Francisco Espoz y Mina while the *exaltados* and *comuneros* supported General José María Torrijos. The two factions became even more divided in 1827 when Torrijos invited all exiled Spaniards to join a junta to liberate Spain. The moderates refused to participate. But the radical Spaniards formed the Supreme Junta of the Free and Independent Spanish Nation. Many of the members of the Supreme Junta had intimate contacts with Spanish Americanists and particularly with the members of the Mexican legation who had encouraged and supported several attempts to free Spain from the "tyrant" Ferdinand VII.

In 1827 and 1828, the Spaniards entered into conversations with Vicente Rocafuerte and Gran Colombian Minister José Fernández de Madrid. All parties agreed that only if Spanish and Spanish American liberals cooperated could absolutism be destroyed. Otherwise, Spain would remain enslaved and America would continue to be threatened. After extensive discussions, Rocafuerte entered into an agreement with the Spaniards. On March 25, 1828, the representatives of the United States of Mexico and the Supreme Junta signed a treaty whereby Mexico recognized the Supreme Junta as the only legal government of Spain and the Supreme Junta recognized the independence of Mexico. Rocafuerte insisted that the treaty also include a recognition of the independence of the other nations of Spanish America, as well as a promise that the Supreme Junta would negotiate similar treaties with those nations as soon as possible. Finally, the Mexicans agreed to subsidize the liberal invasion of Spain until such time as the Supreme Junta could negotiate a five-million-peso loan. Thereafter, a Mexican-Spanish claims commission would settle the debts outstanding between the two nations.

The treaty was never ratified. Although Rocafuerte forwarded the accord to Mexico, his government found it expedient not to submit the treaty to Congress. At that time Mexico was bitterly divided over laws expelling Spaniards from the republic. It seemed unlikely that the nationalist Mexican radicals would approve aid to Spaniards, even if they were liberal and were willing to recognize Mexico. Indeed, *El Sol*'s suggestions that Spain might recognize the independence of Mexico were met with great skepticism.

The setback in Mexico did not alienate Torrijos and his supporters. They continued to aid the new nations in any way they could. For example, they provided the Mexican legation with detailed information of Ferdinand's invasion of Mexico the following year. Unfortunately, Mexico's political unrest, particularly the radicals' ouster of Manuel Gómez Pedraza prevented further cooperation between Rocafuerte and the Supreme Junta. Torrijos continued, however, to seek Mexican support. After Rocafuerte departed, he renewed negotiations with the new Mexican minister and former *exaltado*, Manuel Eduardo Gorostiza. Llorens, *Liberales y románticos*, 103–105; Rocafuerte, *A la nación*, 294; "Tratado celebrado en Londres, entre la **República de los Estados Unidos Mexicanos y la Junta Suprema de la** Nación Española libre e independiente," in Iris M. Zavala, *Masones, comuneros y carbonarios* (Madrid, 1971), 295–296; Flores Caballero, *La contrarevolución*, 136–138; Delgado, *España y México*, 346–350.

35. Memorandum de la conferencia entre el agente Michelena y el ministro Canning, London, October 13, 1824, HD 17-5.4179.

36. Michelena to Alamán, London, October 30, 1824; Murphy to Ramos Arizpe, Paris, October 17, 1824: HD 17-5.4178, 4144. Michelena to Alamán, London, November 4, 1824, Alamán Papers, folder II, no. 116.

37. Michelena to Alamán, London, November 6, 1824, HD 17-6.4196; Temperley, *The Foreign Policy of Canning*, 160–161, 240–242.

38. Michelena to Gorostiza, London, October 6, 1824; Gorostiza to Michelena, The Hague, October 15, 18, and 28, 1824; Gorostiza to Murphy, Brussels, November 9, 1824; Michelena to Gorostiza, London, October 26, 1824; Memorándum de la conferencia con el Sr. Falk, London, October 28, 1824; Gorostiza to Michelena, Brussels, November 19 and 26, 1824: HD 17-5.4129 4243, 4148, 4161; 17-6.4201; 17-5.4162, 4181; 17-6.4209, 4216.

39. Michelena to Gorostiza, London, November 17, 1824; Gorostiza to Michelena, Brussels, November 30, 1824; Michelena to Gorostiza, December 7, 1824: HD 17-6.4208, 4218, 17-7.701.

40. Gorostiza to Michelena, Brussels, December 10, 1824; December 14, 1824; n.d. [December, 1824]; December 28, 1824: HD 17-7.703, 708, 709, 735.

41. Conferencia del 30 de noviembre de 1824; Michelena to Alamán, London, December 7, 1824: HD 17-7.700, 699.

42. Rocafuerte to Planta, London, December 4, 1824, HD 17-7.696.

43. Planta to Michelena, London, December 6, 1824; Michelena to Alamán, London, December 20, 1824: HD 17-7.715, 714. Rocafuerte to Planta, December 10, 1824, FO 97/270, ff. 137–140.

44. Michelena to Alamán, London, December 21, 1824; January 4, 1824

(Letters 83, 84): HD 17-7.723, 18-1.4264, 4265. Temperley, *The Foreign Policy of Canning*, 142–156; Rocafuerte, *A la nación*, 297.
45. *Times*, January 4, 1825, 3.

## VI: The Politics of Credit

1. Mexico, *Legislación mexicana*, IV, 617; Alamán to Borja Migoni, Mexico, April 24, 1823; March 4, 1823: AGSREM, H/121.32 "823-24/1. 40-11-21 Mexico, *La diplomacia mexicana*, II, 144–145.
2. *El Sol*, no. 71 (August 24, 1823), 283; Borja Migoni to Alamán, London, March 2, 1824, AGSREM, H/121.32 "823-24"/1. 40-11-21. The difficulties encountered in ratifying the Barclay contract are discussed later in this chapter.
3. Francisco de Borja Migoni, "Esposición del Consul General de México en Londres, sobre el empréstito que fue encargado," *El Amigo del Pueblo*, September 12, 1827, 3–7. The official correspondence Borja Migoni exchanged with the government on this matter is found in, Mexico, *La diplomacia mexicana*, II, 137–206; Michelena to Alamán, London, July 24, 1824, Mexico, *La diplomacia mexicana*, III, 218–221; Rocafuerte to Juan de Dios Cañedo, London, January 28, 1828, and November 19, 1828, AGSREM, H/300 (72:861) "823-30"/1. LE 1700 and H/131 "823"/14. LE 1621 (6).
4. Borja Migoni, "Esposición sobre el empréstito," 9–18. Michelena later denounced Borja Migoni's activities. After reading the legation papers, he referred to Borja Migoni's official correspondence as "lies and contradictions," which he and his associates entertained the government with while they made their preparations. Michelena to Alamán, London, July 24, 1824, Mexico, *La diplomacia mexicana*, III, 218–221.
5. Borja Migoni, "Esposición sobre el empréstito," 10, 20.
6. *Times*, no. 12,088 (January 20, 1824), 2; no. 12,094 (January 27, 1824), 2; no. 12,097 (February 11, 1824), 2. Borja Migoni, "Esposisión sobre el empréstito," 18–20.
7. Borja Migoni to José Ignacio Esteva, London, February 9, 1824, Mexico, *La diplomacia mexicana*, II, 185–194. The Goldschmidt contract is reproduced in José María Luis Mora, *Obras sueltas*. 2d ed. (Mexico, 1963), 437–444.
8. For criticisms of the loan see Michelena to Alamán, London, June 26, 1824 and July 24, 1824, AGSREM, H/311.1 (42:72) "824"/1. and Mexico, *La diplomacia mexicana*, III, 218–221; Rocafuerte to Cañedo,

London, January 22, 1828, and November 19, 1828, AGSREM, H/300 (72:861) "823-30"/1. LE 1700 and H/131 "823"/14. LE 1621 (6); Murphy to Michelena, Paris, October 1, 1824, HD 17-5.4122. Borja Migoni profited from the loan twice. The first time he nad his associates bought Mexican bonds at 58 percent and resold them at 84 percent. Then, after Michelena arrived, the value of Mexican bonds declined temporarily to 48 percent in October because it was feared that Iturbide would overthrow the government. Michelena tried to use six million pesos in the hands of Goldschmidt to buy the bonds at that low price, planning to resell them when the scare was over and the bonds returned to a high price, which would have earned a large sum for the nation. Borja Migoni refused. Instead, he and his friends bought the bonds as individuals and resold them later at a profit. Michelena to Carlos de Alvear, London, November 10, 1824, HD 17-4.4203.

9. Manuel de Mier y Teran to Michelena, Mexico, April 4, 1824; B. A. Goldschmidt to Barclay, Herring, Richardson, & Co., London, January 12, 1824; David Barclay and Charles Herring to Borja Migoni, London, March 26, 1824 and March 31, 1824; Borja Migoni to Barclay and Herring, London, March 30, 1824 and April 3, 1824; Borja Migoni to Alamán, London, March 30, 1824: AGSREM, H/121.32 "823-24"/1. 40-11-21.

10. Barclay, Herring, Richardson, & Co., to Esteva, London, April 1, 1824 and May 7, 1824, AGSREM, H/131.32 "823-24"/1. 40-11-21.

11. Manuel de Mier y Terán to Michelena, Mexico, April 4, 1824; September 5, 1825: AGSREM, H/121 "823-24"/1. 40-11-21. Mier y Teran to Michelena, Mexico, September 4, 1824, HD 17-4.4073.

12. Michelena to Alamán, London, August 21, 1824, AGSREM, H/131.1 (42:72) "824"/1. When Michelena told Borja Migoni that the Barclay Company expected to be paid for its efforts, Borja Migoni replied sarcastically: "I have deduced that the government expected the generous patriotism of those gentlemen to provide an advance to cover the cost of military purchases. . . . The extraordinary outpouring of gratitude which the government and the Minister bestow upon them, does not permit me to believe that these gentlemen expect money to make the purchase. If I am in error, I do not have the power to correct that error." Borja Migoni to Michelena, London, July 31, 1824; Michelena to Alamán, London, August 1, 1824: HD 17-4.4090, 4093.

13. Murphy to Michelena, St. Sauveur, August 7, 1824; September 5, 1824: HD 17-4.4034, 4073.

14. Manuel E. Gorostiza to Michelena, Antwerp, August 15, 1824; August 31, 1824; Gorostiza to Michelena, Amsterdam, September 16, 1824: HD 17-4.4045, 4065, 4085.

15. Michelena to Alamán, London, August 21, 1824, AGSREM H/311.1
    (42:72) /1. 1-1-44. Michelena to Alamán, London, August 31, 1824;
    September 1, 1824; Instrucciones que observará el primer ayudante
    del Estado Mayor D. Juan Nepomuceno Almonte para la conducción
    de las armas, September 2, 1824 (in code): HD 17-4.4061, 4066, 4068,
    4069.
16. Barclay, Herring, Richardson, & Co. to Michelena, London, Septem-
    ber 8, 1824, HD 17-4.4075.
17. Michelena to Alamán, London, September 23, 1824 (letters 1, 2),
    HD 17-4.4108. Michelena to Alamán, London, November 4, 1824;
    November 23, 1824: Alamán Papers, folder II, no. 116, 117.
18. The correspondence among all parties in the acquisition of the *Arvens
    Prindsen* is located in the Hernández y Dávalos Papers, HD 17-5.4142
    through 18-2.4367.
19. [Decreto autorizando el contrato de Barclay y Cía. para vender los
    bonos de México en Londres]. Mexico, August 25, 1824, AGSREM,
    H/121.32 "823-24"/1. 40-11-21; Esteva to Michelena, Mexico, Octo-
    ber 27, 1824, HD 17-5.4170. The Mexican agents in Europe were
    shocked at the government's actions. After reading the latest Mexi-
    can papers, Murphy wrote: "Is it possible that no one in Mexico has
    found fault with that [Goldschmidt] loan and that the newspapers
    should lose all sense of proportion in praising that contract?" Murphy
    to Michelena, Paris, October 1, 1824, HD 17-5.4122. The only one who
    was critical of the loan in Mexico appears to have been Pablo Villa-
    vicencio, but even he did not realize the magnitude of the loss involved.
    [El Payo del Rosario], *De coyote a perro inglés voy al coyote ocho a tres*
    (Mexico, 1825).
20. The contract for the Barclay loan is reproduced in Mora, *Obras sueltas,*
    445–449. Michelena to Esteva, London, December 25, 1824; Michelena
    to Alamán, London, January 4, 1825: HD 17-7.731, 18-1.4266.
21. *Times*, February 8, 1825, 2; February 11, 1825, 4. It is often asserted
    that Bolívar's victories in Peru were instrumental in contributing to the
    high price of American bonds in London. This is not the case. Accounts
    of Gran Colombian victories did not appear in the London press until
    March, a month after the loan was made. *Times*, March 3, 1825, 2.
22. Contrato de armamento y vestuario para el servicio de la República,
    October 27, 1824, HD 17-5.4164. Carlos María Bustamante main-
    tained that the arms that arrived from England were of inferior
    quality. He commented they were quite different from those which
    had been sent as samples. Bustamante, "Diario," IV (January 25,
    1825).
23. Mexico: Senate, "Dictamen de la comisión de la Cámara de Senadores
    sobre el paradero del bergantín *Guerrero*," *Correo de la federación mexi-*

*cana*, I, no. 22 (November 22, 1826), 1–3; no. 2 (November 2, 1826), 2; no. 5 (November 5, 1826), 4; no. 24 (November 24, 1826), 1–2; Rocafuerte to Juan José Espinosa de los Monteros, Mexico, February 23, 1827, *Aguila mexicana*, no. 68 (March 9, 1827), 2–3.

24. Michelena to Alamán, London, February 6, 1825; Murphy to Michelena, Paris, March 1, 1825: HD 18-1.4299, 18-2.4321.

25. Autorización de Vicente Rocafuerte para promover relaciones de amistad y comercio con las potencias europeas, Mexico, March 20, 1825, AGSREM, H/510 "825"/2-2-2024.

26. Rocafuerte, *A la nación*, 279–289; Rates of pay grades to the officers and individuals of the British Navy admitted in the Mexican Navy, HD 18-6.4476. The correspondence relating to the ships and men with which Michelena returned to Mexico is found in HD 18-6.4470 to 4478; Rocafuerte to Alamán, London, August 6, 1825, HD 18-6.4488.

27. Alamán to Rocafuerte, Mexico, June 8, 1825; Rocafuerte to Gómez Pedraza, London, October 2, 1825; October 19, 1825; October 31, 1825: AGSREM, H/310 (72:00) "825"/1. 14-2-36; H/510 (85-0) "825" 2-2-2024; 1-13-1527.

28. John Clapham, *The Bank of England*. 2 vols. (Cambridge, 1958), II, 89–100.

29. Vicente Rocafuerte, *Esposición de las razones que determinaron a Vicente Rocafuerte a prestar a la República de Colombia la suma de £63,000* (London, 1829), 4–9; Gómez Pedraza to Rocafuerte, Mexico, October 31, 1825, AGSREM, H/310 (72:00) "825"/1. 4-2-36; *El Sol*, no. 69 (August 22, 1823), 276. Rocafuerte to Espinosa de los Monteros, London, n.d.; Rocafuerte to Cañedo, London, March 19, 1828: AGSREM, H/300 (72:861) "823-24"/1. LE 1700.

30. Rocafuerte, *Esposición de las razones*, 6–9, 18–19. The correspondence between Rocafuerte and Barclay is published on pages 9–17. Esteva to Michelena, Mexico, May 16, 1825, HD 18-4.4409. Rocafuerte to Camacho, London, May 4, 1826; Alamán to Rocafuerte, Mexico, August 19, 1825: AGSREM, III/352 (72:42)/2. 7-16-61; H/122.32 (72:42) "825"/1.

31. Rocafuerte to Camacho, London, February 15, 1826, partially reproduced in Joaquín D. Casasús, *La deuda contraída en Londres* (Mexico, 1885), 103. The number of bankruptcies grew to immense proportions at the turn of the year. The *Index to the Times Newspaper* shows this clearly. The January-March, 1825, *Index* has ten pages of bankruptcies; the one for April-June has eight pages and, thereafter, the number declines drastically. *Palmer's Index to the Times Newspaper* (London, 1898), January-March, 5–14; April-June, 4–11. On the economic situation of England see, *Times*, May 2, 1826, 4; May 4, 1826, 2. The Peruvian envoys reported to their government, "The great and extra-

ordinary shock which the English economy has suffered appears to have no equal in its history. More than 500 bankruptcies have occurred and some of them were great and wealthy [commercial] houses." José G. Paredes and José Joaquín Olmedo to Peruvian minister of foreign relations, London, February 3, 1826, in José Joaquín Olmedo, *Espistolario* (Puebla, 1960), 522–523.

32. Rocafuerte to Camacho, London, March 2, 1826, Joaquín Ramírez Cabañas (ed.), *El empréstito de México a Colombia* (Mexico, 1930), 5–7.

33. Rocafuerte to Cañedo, London, March 19, 1828, AGSREM H/300 (72:861) "823-30"/1. LE 1700.

34. Although Gran Colombia made attempts to repay the loan, she was unable to do so for many years. This caused contemporary and later writers to criticize Rocafuerte unduly. The details of the loan are treated at greater length in Jaime E. Rodríguez O., "Rocafuerte y el empréstito a Colombia," *Historia mexicana*, XVIII (April-June, 1969), 485–515.

35. José María del Castillo to Goldschmidt & Co., Bogotá, April 8, 1826, *El Sol*, no. 1176 (September 2, 1826), 1780; Olmedo to José de La Mar, London, June 10, 1826, Olmedo, *Espistolario*, 535–543.

36. Rocafuerte to Camacho, London, May 4, 1826, AGSREM, III/352 (72:42) 2. 7-16-61. Olmedo described the situation in the following terms: "The principal cause of our worry is that April 15 has passed, the day on which the dividends should have been paid and Mr. Kinder has not paid them. . . . The government which does not pay, be it because of its own bad will or that of its agents, be it because of poverty, or because its funds have been accidentally delayed, always, always loses its credit. . . . The creditors do not let us live in peace one instant; they come to see us in droves; they complain; they lament; they ask us for explanations; they ask us for hope; in short they don't leave us alone. Because as I have said, not to be paid is bad in any circumstances, in the present it is horrible and deadly since many families live from these interests. Everything is paralyzed today; more than 600 bank-ruptcies have occurred. Money does not circulate and no one has the means to live." Olmedo to Bolívar, London, April 22, 1826 in Olmedo, *Espitolario*, 532–533.

37. Rocafuerte to Camacho, London, May 4, 1826, AGSREM, III/352 (72:42) 2. 7-16-61.

38. Olmedo to La Mar, London, June 10, 1826, Olmedo, *Epistolario*, 535–543; *Times*, June 21, 1826, 3.

39. Rocafuerte to Camacho, London, June 9, 1826, AGSREM, H/300 (72:861) "823-30"/1. LE 1700; *Times*, June 18, 1826, 2.

40. Rocafuerte to Espinosa de los Monteros, London, [July] 1, 1826, AGSREM, H/300 (72:861) "823-30"/1. LE 1700.

41. *Times*, August 10, 1826, 2.
42. On August 30 the *Times* could find no grounds for believing that Mexico could pay its dividends. *Times*, August 30, 1826, 2. Barclay & Co. to Rocafuerte, London, September 10, 1826; Rocafuerte to Alexander Baring, London, September 11, 1826; Baring to Rocafuerte, London, September 13, 1826: AGSREM, 2-5-25-4. Esteva to Directores de las Aduanas Maritimas, Mexico, December 28, 1825; Agreement by which D. Vicente Rocafuerte Chargé d'affaires of Mexico transfers to Baring Brothers the Agency of Mexico which Barclay, Herring, Richardson and Company held previously, London, September 20, 1826. AGSREM, H/121.32 "823-24"/1. 40-11-21.
43. *Times*, September 13, 1826, 2; September 14, 1826, 2; September 15, 1826, 2; September 16, 1826, 2. Rocafuerte to Holders of Mexicans Bonds, London, September 15, 1826, *Times*, September 15, 1826, 2.
44. Rocafuerte to Espinosa de los Monteros, London, November 9, 1826, AGSREM, III/352 (72:42)/2. 7-16-61; *El Sol*, no. 1276 (December 14, 1826), 2190; no. 1280 (December 17, 1826), 1206 [sic] (in error for 2206); no. 1275 (December 12, 1826), 2186.
45. Elmer W. Flaccus has attempted to explain Victoria's weak leadership by suggesting that he suffered from hypoglycemia, "a disturbance of the brain functions resulting in weakness and visual changes, coma and epileptic type gyrations." See his "Guadalupe Victoria: His Personality as a Cause of his Failure," *The Americas*, XXIII (January 1967), 297–311. However, Flaccus has failed to notice the nature of the Mexican political system during Victoria's administration and later. No president until Juárez was able to exercise power effectively. Even Juárez was unable to resolve the government's inherent contradiction between a presidential system and ministerial responsibility. See Frank A. Knapp, *The Life of Sebastián Lerdo de Tejada, 1823-1889* (Austin, 1951), 122–127.
46. José Ignacio Pavón to Espinosa de los Monteros, Mexico, January 7, 1828, AGSREM, H/122.32 (72:42) "827" 79; Rocafuerte to Cañedo, London, November 19, 1828, AGSREM, H/632 "828"/1.
47. Fernández de Madrid to Bolívar, London, September 21, 1827, O'Leary, *Memorias*, IX, 299–300.
48. Joel Warrington, an English bondholder, was among the many who demanded their dividends. He voiced a commonly held opinion when he said: "Now your nation is *without honor, without credit*, derided and despised by every honest man in Europe." Joel Warrington to Rocafuerte, London, February 16, 1828; Rocafuerte to Camacho, London, February 20, 1828: AGSREM, H/122.32 (72:42) "827"/79.
49. Rocafuerte to Cañedo, London, November 19, 1828 (letters 1, 2), and December 18, 1828, AGSREM, H/632 "828"/1.

50. Rocafuerte to Cañedo, London, April 20, 1828; Esteva to Cañedo, Mexico, April 22, 1828; AGSREM, H/122.32 (72:42) "827"/79. Rocafuerte to Dudley, London, April 19, 1828, FO 50/51, ff. 9–13.
51. *El Amigo del Pueblo*, IV (April 2, 1828), 2, 4–5.
52. Fernández de Madrid to Rocafuerte, London, March 9, 1828, AGSREM, III/242 (72:861)/1. LE 1044 (2); Rocafuerte to José María Bocanegra, London, April 18, 1828, AGSREM, H/300 (72:861) "823-30"/1. LE 1700. The *oficial mayor* of the Mexican foreign ministry assured the minister of treasury that the ships were worth three times the amount owed by Gran Colombia. José María Ortíz de Monasterio to Pavón, Mexico, January 19, 1829, AGSREM, III/242 (72:861)/1. LE 1044 (2). Mexico could have used the vessels for, as the British minister reported to London, "This country does not at this moment possess a single ship fit to be sent to sea for a warlike purpose." Richard Pakenham to Lord Aberdeen, Mexico, October 5, 1830, FO 50/61, fo. 184. As a result of their disagreement, Rocafuerte and the ministry of treasury published documented accounts of their positions. Rocafuerte wrote *Espocisión de las razones* and the treasury published *Cuaderno que contiene el prestamo hecho a Colombia por D. Vicente Rocafuerte* (Mexico, 1829).
53. Alexander Baring to Rocafuerte, London, December 25, 1828; Rocafuerte to Cañedo, London, January 22, 1829; Pavón to Baring Brothers, March 30, 1829: AGSREM, H/300 (72:861) "823-30"/1. LE 1700.

## VII: The English Treaty

1. *Times*, January 5, 1824, 3; Michelena to Canning, London, October 11, 1824, Webster, *Britain and Latin America*, I, 458–459; Memorándum de Michelena a Planta, London, March 4, 1825, HD 18-2.4329.
2. Canning to Ward, London, January 3, 1825, Webster, *Britain and Latin America*, I, 459–462.
3. Canning to Mornier and Ward, London, January 3, 5, 8, 1825, FO, 50/9, ff. 1–7, 9–11, 13–16, 17–18.
4. Memorándum de la conferencia entre el Honorable Sr. George Canning, el Sr. Planta y el General Michelena y el Sr. Rocafuerte, London, May 21, 1825, HD 18-4.4418.
5. Planta to Michelena, London, June 24, 1825; Memorandum of the British Board of Trade, London, n.d.: HD 18-5.4439, 4440.
6. Michelena to Planta, June 24, 1825, HD 18-5.4438; Rocafuerte to

Michelena, London, July 7, 1825, HD 18-6.4450. Rocafuerte to Esteva, London, July 9, 1825; Rocafuerte to Alamán, London, July 9, 1825 (letters 1, 2): AGSREM, H/510 (85-0) "825" / 2-2-2024.

7. Tratado de amistad, comercio y navegación entre Inglaterra y México, Mexico, April 6, 1825, HD 18-3.4379; Mornier and Ward to Canning, Mexico, April 10, 1825, Webster, *Britain and Latin America*, I, 468–470.

8. Alamán to Rocafuerte, Mexico, May 21, 1825, AGSREM, H/310 (72:00) "825"/1. 14-2-36; Ward to Canning, Mexico, May 21, 1825: FO 50/13, ff. 3–5.

9. Rocafuerte to Alamán, London, August 2, 1825; August 6, 1825 (letters 85, 111): AGSREM, H/352 (72:42) "825"/38. 1–138.

10. Rocafuerte to Gómez Pedraza, London, October 19, 1825, AGSREM, H/510 (85-0) "825" 2-2-2024; *Times*, September 10, 1825, 3.

11. Memorándum de la conferencia entre el Sr. Planta y el Sr. Rocafuerte, London, November 16, 1825; Rocafuerte to Gómez Pedraza, London, November 17, 1825: AGSREM, H/510 (85-0) "825" 2-2-2024. Rocafuerte to Alamán, London, July 14, 1825, AGSREM, H/300 (72:861) "823-30"/1. LE 1700.

12. Ward to Camacho, Mexico, December 13, 1825; December 17, 1825; Decreto presidencial, Mexico, January 2, 1826; Camacho to Congress, Mexico, January 18, 1826; Mornier and Ward to Camacho and Esteva, Mexico, January 29, 1826: AGSREM III/352 (72:42)/2. 7-17-61. Mornier and Ward to Canning, Mexico, January 15, 1826; January 30, 1826: FO 97/271, ff. 1–17, 11–20.

13. Decreto de Guadalupe Victoria, nombrando Sebastián Camacho Plenipotenciario ante la corte de S. M. B. Mexico, n.d., AGSREM, III/352 (72:42)/2. 7-16-61; Mornier and Ward to Canning, Mexico, March 17, 1826, FO 97/271, ff. 108–116.

14. Camacho to Canning, Portsmouth, October 13, 1826; Canning to Camacho, Paris, October 20, 1826: FO 50/29, ff. 35–38, 41–42. Rocafuerte was to play the same role with Camacho that he had with Michelena. The United States Minister to Britain reported to his government, "As Mr. Camacho unfortunately speaks neither English nor French, our communications have been carried out principally through Mr. Rocafuerte." Gallatin to Clay, London, December 16, 1826, Manning, *Diplomatic Correspondence*, III, 1583–1585.

15. Rocafuerte to Planta, London, October 19, 1826; Memorandum of the Conference of November 29, 1826: FO 50/29, ff, 55–60. Tratado de Amistad, Comercio y Navegación entre Gran Bretaña y Los Estados Unidos Mexicanos, London, December 26, 1826, AGSREM, H/(352: 42) 826/. 7-17-7. Camacho made a gift of £1,000 to the British Chancellery, as was customary when negotiating a treaty. [Receipt of a gift of £1,000], London, December 26, 1826; Camacho to Espinosa de los

Monteros, London, December 26, 1826: AGSREM, III/352 (72:42) 2. 7-16-61.

16. *Correo de la federación mexicana*, I, no. 117 (February 24, 1827), 4; *Aguila mexicana*, no. 56 (February 24, 1827), 4; Poinsett to Clay, Mexico, February 21, 1827, Dispatches from Mexico, II, National Archives, Washington, D.C.; Pakenham to Canning, Mexico, May 7, 1827: FO 50/34, ff. 40–41.

17. Flores Caballero, *La contrarevolución*, 115–118; Ward to Canning, Mexico, April 18, 1827, FO, 50/32, ff. 54–69.

18. Mexico: Senate, "Dictamen de la comisión de la Cámara de Senadores sobre el paradero del bergantín *Guerrero*," *Correo de la federación mexicana*, I, no. 22 (November 22, 1826), 1–3; Ward to Canning, Mexico, March 15, 1827, FO 50/31B, ff. 159–162.

19. Rocafuerte to Gómez Pedraza, Mexico, February 23, 1827; February 27, 1827; *Aguila Mexicana*, no. 68 (March 9, 1827), 2–3. Rocafuerte to Michelena, London, December 20, 1827, HD 19-2.4577.

20. *Correo de la federación mexicana*, I, no. 5 (November 5, 1826), 4.

21. Manuel Rincón to Espinosa de los Monteros, Mexico, February 22, 1827; Rocafuerte to Espinosa de los Monteros, Mexico, February 24, 1827, AGSREM, H/583 (8-5) "827"/2-1-1841.

22. José Morán to Michelena, Mexico, April 25, 1827, HD 19-2.4544.

23. Gómez Pedraza to Michelena, Mexico, July 7, 1827, HD 19-2.4551. There is an extensive correspondence on this question in HD 18-5.4441 through 19-2.4554.

24. *Aguila mexicana*, no. 79 (March 20, 1827), 2–3; no. 102 (April 10, 1827), 2–3. Espinosa de los Monteros to Senate, *Aguila mexicana*, no. 69 (March 10, 1827), 2. On Rocafuerte's reasons for making the loan see Rodríguez, "Rocafuerte y el empréstito a Colombia," 496–508, 512–515.

25. Mexico: Senate, "Dictamen de la comisión inspectora sobre el préstamo hecho a Colombia por D. Vicente Rocafuerte en Londres," *Correo de la federación mexicana*, II, no. 152 (April 1, 1827), 1–3; *Aguila mexicana*, no. 147 (May 27, 1827), 1; *Correo de la federación mexicana*, II, no. 175 (April 21, 1827), 1–2; II, No. 176 (April 25, 1827), 4.

26. Rocafuerte to Editors, Mexico, April 2, 1827, *Aguila mexicana*, no. 92 (April 2, 1827), 4.

27. Ward to Canning, Mexico, March 15, 1827, FO, 50/31B, ff. 159–162; Pakenham to Canning, Mexico, May 7, 1827, FO 50/34, ff. 40–41.

28. Ward to Canning, Mexico, March 2, 1827; March 15, 1827: FO 50/31B, ff. 98–102, 159–162. Espinosa de los Monteros to Camacho, Mexico, March 2, 1827, AGSREM, III/353 (72:42)/2. 7-16-61.

29. [Dictamen de la comisión de la Cámara de Senadores sobre el tratado celebrado entre Su Magestad Británica y los Estados Unidos Mexi-

canos], Mexico, March 27, 1827; [Ratificación del tratado], Mexico, April 3, 1827; Espinosa de los Monteros to Rocafuerte, April 2, 1827: AGSREM, III/352 (72:42)/2. 7-16-61. Ward to Canning, Mexico, March 31, 1827, FO 50/31B, fo. 217; Guadalupe Victoria to Canning, Mexico, April 3, 1827, FO 50/39, fo. 247.

30. Rocafuerte to Espinosa de los Monteros, Veracruz, May 8, 1827, AGSREM, III/352 (72:42)/2. 7-16-61; *Correo de la federación mexicana*, II, no. 199 (May 19, 1827), 4; no. 232 (June 21, 1827), 4. *Aguila mexicana*, no. 161 (June 9, 1827), 4; no. 181 (June 29, 1827), 4.

31. *Correo de la federación mexicana*, III, no. 286 (August 14, 1827), 2. Rocafuerte may have been accused of harboring "a Spanish accomplice" because he had a Spanish servant whom he took to London. The man never arrived, however, because he became ill aboard ship and died en route. Henry G. Ward, *Mexico*, 2d ed., 2 vols. (London, 1829), II, 392–395. Juan N. Pereda, who handled Rocafuerte's affairs in Mexico, gathered the information to exonerate him. Pereda was a Mexican patriot who was expelled by the Law of December 20, 1827, because he had been born in Spain. He went to Bordeaux where he wrote a pamphlet defending Mexico's independence. Later he returned to Mexico and was given a diplomatic mission. See *Voz de la Patria*, I, no. 15 (April 13, 1829), 4–7; Jorge Flores (ed.), *Juan Nepomuceno de Pereda y su misión secreta en Europa* (Mexico, 1964).

32. Rocafuerte to Espinosa de los Monteros, New York, June 20, 1827; Espinosa de los Monteros to Camacho, Mexico, April 30, 1827: AGSREM, III/352 (72:42)/2. 7-16-61. Rocafuerte to Espinosa de los Monteros, London, July 20, 1827, AGSREM, H/300 (72:861) "823-30"/1. LE 1700; Temperley, *The Foreign Policy of Canning*, 441–446.

33. Rocafuerte, *A la nación*, 290.

34. Temperley, *The Foreign Policy of Canning*, 446.

## VIII: Northern Europe

1. This work concentrates on Mexican activities because the author was unable to carry out detailed archival research in the other Spanish American countries. This deficiency is partially offset by the existence of a work which discusses, although from a different point of view, the relations between the German states and Spanish America. See Kossok, *Im Schatten der Heiligen Allianz*.

2. Gorostiza to Rocafuerte, The Hague, n.d.; Michelena to Gorostiza,

London, January 3, 1825; Gorostiza to Michelena, Brussels, January 7, 1825: HD 17-8.4259a, 4263, 4273, *Times*, January 4, 1825, 3.

3. Gorostiza to Michelena, Elberfelt, January 24, 1825, HD 18-1.4292.

4. Gorostiza to Michelena, Berlin, February 2, 1825; Gorostiza to Michelena, Hamburg, February 18, 1825: HD 18-1.4295, 4307.

5. Gorostiza to Michelena, Hamburg, February 22, 1825; March 8, 1825, Gorostiza to Murphy, Hamburg, March 1, 1825: HD 18-1.4311, 4335, 4322.

6. Sieveking to Gorostiza, Hamburg, May 18, 1825; Gorostiza to Michelena, Brussels, May 24, 1825: HD 18-4.4425, 4419.

7. Memorandum d'une conference entre M. de Colquhoum chargé d'affaires et Consul general des Villes Anseatiques et le citoyen General José Mariano Michelena Ministre Plenipotentiare des Estas Unis du Mexique, London, June 10, 1825, HD 18-6.4453.

8. J. J. Colquhoum to Rocafuerte, London, July 9, 1825; Rocafuerte to Colquhoum, London, July 9, 1825; Colquhoum to Rocafuerte, July 12, 1825; Rocafuerte to Colquhoum, July 12, 1825; Rocafuerte to Michelena, London, July 18, 1825: HD 18-6.4455, 4457, 4460, 4461, 4464.

9. Kossok, *Im Schatten der Heiligen Allianz*, 142–154. Rocafuerte to Camacho, London, June 5, 1825; Rocafuerte to Bocanegra, London, June 20, 1829; AGSREM, H/311.2 "828"/3. 1-4-858.

10. Gorostiza to Michelena, Brussels, April 5, 1825; Gorostiza to Michelena, The Hague, April 29, 1825: HD 18-3.4378, 18-4.4391.

11. A. R. Falk to Michelena, London, May 5, 1825; Gorostiza to Michelena, Brussels, June 18, 1825; Instrucciones para D. Manuel E. Gorostiza, Agente y Consul General, London, June 30, 1825: HD 18-4.4402, 4435, 18-5.4444.

12. Rocafuerte to Gómez Pedraza, London, October 19, 1825, AGSREM, H/510 (85-0) "825" 2-2-2024. Rocafuerte to Gorostiza, London, August 3, 1826; Gorostiza to Rocafuerte, Brussels, September 9, 1826; Gorostiza to Cañedo, The Hague, May 14, 1824: AGSREM, H/131/1377. 3-10-14, Tratado de Amistad, Navegación y Comercio entre los Estados Unidos Mexicanos y Su Magestad el Rey de los Países Bajos, London, June 15, 1827, in Manuel Mestre Ghigliazza (ed.), *Las Relaciones diplomáticas entre México y Holanda* (Mexico, 1931), 47–55.

13. Rocafuerte to Alamán, London, August 9, 1825, AGSREM, H/510 (85-0) "825"/. 2-2-2024.

14. Gorostiza to Rocafuerte, Brussels, August 30, 1825; Rocafuerte to Gorostiza, London, August [sic] (in error for September) 2, 1825: AGSREM, H/131/1377. 3-10-14.

15. Kossok, *Im Schatten der Heiligen Allianz*, 163–167.

16. Ibid., 167–169, Canning to Viscount Strangford, London, March 17, 1826; Strangford to Canning, St. Petersburg, April 4, 1826: Webster, *Britain and Latin America II*, 304–306.

17. Rocafuerte to Gómez Pedraza, London, October 31, 1826, AGSREM, 1-13-1527; Gallatin to Clay, London, December 16, 1826, Manning, *Diplomatic Correspondence*, III, 1583–1585.

18. Kossok, *Im Schatten der Heiligen Allianz*, 170–172; Rocafuerte to Michelena, London, November 14, 1827, HD 19-2.4570. Prussia's interest in Mexico grew so rapidly that the Rhine West India Company dispatched its director, Carl Becher, to investigate, see Carl Becher, *Mexico in den errignisvollen Jahren 1832 und 1833* (Hamburg, 1834); Primeras declaraciones cambiadas entre México y Prusia sobre comercio y navegación. Aquisgram, June 18, 1827, in Mexico, *Tratados y convenios celebrados y no ratificados por la República Mexicana.* 2 vols. (Mexico, 1878), II, 47–49.

19. Flores Caballero, *La contrarevolución*, 104–155.

20. Barón von Bulow to Rocafuerte, London, February 25, 1828; Rocafuerte to Von Bulow, London, February 25, 1828; Von Bulow to Rocafuerte, London, November 13, 1828: AGSREM, H/352 (72:43) "831". 14-3-120. Rocafuerte to Bocanegra, London, June 20, 1829, AGSREM, H/311.2 "828"/3. 1-4-858; Mexico, *Tratados y convenios*, II, 34–43.

21. Rocafuerte to Camacho, London, April 12, 1826; [Decreto del Rey de Württemberg], Stuttgart, February 22, 1826; Count von Beroldingen to Camacho, Stuttgart, April 29, 1826: AGSREM, III/353 (72:43)/1. 7-19-17.

22. Rocafuerte to Camacho, London, June 5, 1826; Camacho to Von Beroldingen, Mexico, August 19, 1826; Camacho to Rocafuerte, Mexico, August 20, 1826: AGSREM, III/353 (72:43)/1. 7-19-17.

23. Rocafuerte to Mandestohl, London, October 31, 1826; Gorostiza to Von Beroldingen, Brussels, November 10, 1826; Von Beroldingen to Gorostiza, Stuttgart, January 29, 1827; Tratado de Amistad y Comercio entre los Estados Unidos Mexicanos y Su Magestad el Rey de Württemberg, London, January 18, 1832: AGSREM, III/353 (72:43)/1. 7-19-17.

24. [Decreto de Su Magestad, Ludwig, Rey de Bavaria], Munich, May 7, 1827; Barón von Cetto to Rocafuerte, London, May 27, 1826; Rocafuerte to Von Cetto, London, June 2, 1826; Rocafuerte to Camacho, London, June 5, 1826; Von Cetto to Rocafuerte, London, November 1, 1826; Rocafuerte to Espinosa de los Monteros, London, November 26, 1826: AGSREM, III/352 (72:43)/2. 7-12-6.

25. Murphy to Espinosa de los Monteros, London, February 20, 1827, AGSREM, III/352 (72:43)/2. 7-12-6.

26. Memorándum del Barón von Cetto a D. Vicente Rocafuerte, London, December 4, 1827; Rocafuerte to Espinosa de los Monteros, London, January 15, 1828: AGSREM, III/352 (72:43)/2. 7-12-6.
27. Rocafuerte to Barón von Cetto, London, February 4, 1828; Rocafuerte to Espinosa de los Monteros, London, February 19, 1828: AGSREM, III/352 (72:43)/2. 7-12-6.
28. Tratado de Amistad y Comercio entre los Estados Unidos Mexicanos y Su Magestad el Rey de Bavaria, London, May 14, 1832, AGSREM, III/352 (72:43)2. 7-12-6.
29. Gorostiza to Camacho, Brussels, December 7, 1826; Gorostiza to Espinosa de los Monteros, Brussels, April 12, 1827; August 10, 1827: AGSREM, H/131/1377 (i). "Tratado de Amistad y Comercio entre los Estados Unidos Mexicanos y la Unión Helvética," London, December 31, 1832, Mexico, *Tratados y convenios*, II, 345–348.
30. Camacho to Espinosa de los Monteros, London, March 12, 1827, AGSREM, H/353 (72:485)/1. 1-11-1146.
31. Rocafuerte to Cañedo, London, November 19, 1828, AGSREM, H/353 (72:485)/1. 1-11-1146.
32. Rocafuerte to Cañedo, London, December 18, 1828; Bocanegra to Rocafuerte, Mexico, February 28, 1829; Gorostiza to Alamán, London, January 20, 1830: AGSREM, H/353 (72:485)/1. 1-11-1146.

## IX: France and Rome

1. Murphy to Michelena, Paris, January 11, 1825; February 1, 1825; London, April 6, 1825: HD 18-1.4276, 4294; 18-3.4382. Robertson, *France and Latin America*, 354–362.
2. Alamán to Michelena, Mexico, February 23, 1825; José Moreno Guerra to Rocafuerte, Paris, March 25, 1825: HD 18-1.4313; 18-4.4416.
3. Memorándum de la conferencia entre el Honorable Sr. George Canning, el Sr. Planta, y el General Michelena y el Sr. Rocafuerte, London, May 21, 1825, HD 18-4.4418.
4. Estracto de un despacho del Señor Vizconde de Granville el Exmo. Sr. George Canning, Paris, June 14, 1825, AGSREM, 1-13-1527; Rocafuerte to Alamán, London, August 9, 1825, AGSREM, H/510 (85-0) "825"/2. 2-2024.
5. Murphy to Michelena, Paris, September 15, 1825, HD 18-7.4485.
6. Murphy to Alamán, Bordeaux, June 26, 1825, Luis Weckman (ed.), *Las relaciones franco-mexicanas*. 2 vols. (Mexico, 1961-62), I, 22; Roca-

fuerte to Michelena, London, July 8, 1825, HD 18-6.4451; Rocafuerte to Alamán, London, July 9, 1825, AGSREM, H/510 (85-0) "825"/2-2-2024.

7. Rocafuerte to Gómez Pedraza, London, October 19 and 31, 1825, AGSREM, 1-13-1527.

8. Rocafuerte to Murphy, London, August 23, 1825; Murphy to Rocafuerte, Paris, September 24, 1825, Weckman, *Relaciones franco-mexicanas*, I, 45−46; Rocafuerte to Alamán, London, August 9, 1825; Rocafuerte to Gómez Pedraza, London, October 19 and 31, 1825: AGSREM, H/510 (85-0) "825"/2-2-2024.

9. Murphy to Rocafuerte, Paris, December 20, 1825; Rocafuerte to Murphy, London, December 24, 1825; Murphy to Rocafuerte, Paris, December 25, 1825; Camacho to Guy Duperré, Mexico, May 11, 1826: Weckman, *Relaciones franco-mexicanas*, I, 23, 50, 51.

10. Murphy to Rocafuerte, Paris, December 25, 1825, Weckman, *Relaciones franco-mexicanas*, I, 23−24. For the correspondence on French trade see Weckman, *Relaciones franco-mexicanas*, I, 63−80.

11. Rocafuerte, *A la nación*, 281; Murphy to Rocafuerte, Paris, February 13, 1826. Rocafuerte to Murphy, London, February 25, 1826; Murphy to Rocafuerte, Paris, April 26, 1826: Weckman, *Relaciones franco-mexicanas*, I, 56−57, 24.

12. Martínez Silva, *Fernández Madrid*, 200−203; Robertson, *France and Latin America*, 383−386.

13. José Gabriel Pérez to Pedro Gual and Pedro Briceño Méndez, Lima, August 11, 1826, Vicente Lecuna and Harold A. Bierck, *Selected Writings of Bolívar*. 2 vols. (New York, 1951), II, 631−632.

14. Ibid.

15. Murphy to Rocafuerte, Paris, May 22, 1826; June 6, 1826; June 9, 1826; Rocafuerte to Murphy, London, June 16, 1826; Murphy to Rocafuerte, Paris, June 26, 1826; Camacho to Murphy, London, November 29, 1826; Murphy to Camacho, Paris, December 14, 1826: Weckman, *Relaciones franco-mexicanas*, I, 25, 29−30.

16. For the correspondence on Camacho's mission to France, see Weckman, *Relaciones franco-mexicanas*, I, 130−135; Murphy to Cañedo, Paris, September 27, 1828, Weckman, *Relaciones franco-mexicanas*, I, 51.

17. Rocafuerte, *A la nación*, 294−295; Rocafuerte to Bocanegra, London, August 2, 1829, AGSREM, H/131 "825"/6. LE 1616 (2); Marie Paul Marquis de La Fayette, *Memoires, correspondence et manuscripts*. 6 vols. (Paris, 1838), VI, 311−312. The treaty was not ratified in Mexico. Several decades passed before the two nations ratified treaties of friendship and commerce.

18. Herr, *The Eighteenth Century Revolution*, 11−36; Nancy Farris, *Crown*

*and Clergy in Colonial Mexico*; Anne Staples, "Ecclesiastical Affairs in the First Mexican Federal Republic," Master's thesis, University of Texas (Austin, 1967), 32–65.

19. James M. Breedlove, "Effects of the Cortes, 1810-1822, on Church Reform in Spain and Mexico," in Benson, *Mexico and the Spanish Cortes*, 113–133; Staples, "Ecclesiastical Affairs," 9–66; Farris, *Crown Clergy*, 237–253.

20. Juan Guzmán to Giulio Della Somaglia, Cardinal Secretary of State, Mexico, July 21, 1824; Michelena to Alamán, London, February 25, 1825: HD 17-5.4176, 4177.

21. The encyclical is reproduced in Pedro Leturia, *Relaciones entre la Santa Sede e Hispano-América*. 3 vols. (Caracas, 1959), II, 264–283.

22. Ibid.; Michelena to Alamán, February 25, 1825, **HD, 17-5.4177.**

23. Guadalupe Victoria to Pope Leo XII, Mexico, October 27, 1824, HD 17-5.4174.

24. Michelena to Della Somaglia, London, [March, 1825]; Michelena to Alamán, London, March 24: HD 18-2.4362, 4361.

25. Alamán to Rocafuerte, Mexico, June 7, 1825, AGSREM, H/310 (72:45.631) "825"/1. 14-2-37.

26. José Joaquín de Moral to Rocafuerte, Paris, August 3, 1825, **AGSREM, H/311.2 (72:45.631) "824"/14-3-30; Rocafuerte to Alamán, London, September 10, 1825, AGSREM, H/131 "825"/7. LE 1616** (3); Miguel Ramos Arizpe to Rocafuerte, Mexico, October 15, 1825, Archivo General de la Nación (Mexico, D.F.), Justicia Eclesiastica (hereafter cited as AGN, JE), vol. 45, fo. 9.

27. Rocafuerte to Bocanegra, London, May 6, 1829, AGN, JE, Vol. 94, ff. 323, 324.

28. Rocafuerte to Bolívar, London, January 8, 1824 [*sic*] (in error for 1825), O'Leary, *Memorias*, IV, 385–386. On Jesuit activity in France see Bertier de Sauvigny, *The Bourbon Restoration*, 365–390.

29. Rocafuerte to Gómez Pedraza, London, October 3, 1825; October 8, 1825: Joaquín Ramírez Cabañas (ed.), *Las relaciones entre México y el Vaticano* (Mexico, 1928), 12–14. Vázquez to Gómez Pedraza, London, October 7, 1825, AGN, JE. vol. 46, ff. 5–6.

30. Vázquez to Della Somaglia, Brussels, January 29, 1826; Vázquez to Ramos Arizpe, Brussels, January 2, 1826: Ramirez Cabañas, *México y el Vaticano*, 14–20. In order to compare the difference in the way Vázquez and a liberal lay diplomat dealt with the Vatican, see Camacho to Ramos Arizpe, Paris, April 24, 1827, AGN, JE, vol. 82-1, ff. 160–161.

31. Leturia, *La Santa Sede e Hispanoamerica*, II, 281; Alfonso Alcalá Alvarado, *Una pugna diplomática ante la Sante Sede: El restablecimiento del Episcopado en México, 1825-1831* (Mexico, 1967), 19–36.

32. Rocafuerte to Camacho, London, May 15, 1826, AGSREM, H/131 "825"/LE 1616 (3).
33. Rocafuerte to Alamán, London, January 7, 1826, AGSREM, H/131 "825"/7. LE 1616 (3).
34. Rocafuerte to Camacho, London, April 11, 1826, AGN, JE, vol. 45, ff. 236–238.
35. Della Somaglia to Vázquez, Rome, May 10, 1826, AGN, JE, vol. 45, fo. 232; Vázquez to Ramos Arizpe, London, June 7, 1826, AGSREM, H/131 "825"/7. LE 1616 (3).
36. Rocafuerte to Camacho, London, June 7, 1826, AGSREM, H/131 "825"/7. LE 1616 (3).
37. Alcalá Alvarado, *Una pugna diplomatica*, 45–54.
38. José Canga Argüelles, *Ensayo sobre las libertades de la inglesia española en ambos mundos* (London, 1826); Pablo Mendíbil, *Revue Encyclopédique*, XXX (1826), 410–411; Joaquín L. Villanueva, *Juicio de la obra del señor arzobispo De Pradt intitulada "Concordato de México"* (London, 1827).
39. Moral to Camacho, Paris, October 25, 1826; Camacho to Ramos Arizpe, London, November 15, 1826; Ramos Arizpe to Camacho, Mexico, January 16, 1827: AGN, JE, vol. 45, ff. 221–229; vol. 84-1, ff. 94–97.
40. Ward to Canning, Mexico, March 6, 1827, FO 50/31B, ff. 144–158.
41. Extracto del resumen de la conferencia entre Damas, Camacho y el Nuncio apostolico, Paris, April 18, 1827," in Luis Medina Ascensio, *La Santa Sede y la emancipación mexicana*, (Mexico, 1965), 240–242; Camacho to Ramos Arizpe, Paris, April 24, 1827, AGN, JE, vol. 8-21, ff. 160–161.
42. Tejada to Rocafuerte, Rome, August 17, 1827; Tejada to Vázquez, Rome, August 17: 1827, AGSREM, H/131 "825"/7. LE 1616 (3).
43. Rocafuerte to Espinosa de los Monteros, London, September 18, 1827 (letters 3, 4, 5), AGSREM, H/131 "825"/7. LE 1616 (3).
44. Vázquez to Espinosa de los Monteros, Paris, July 28, 1828; September 25, 1828: AGN, JE, vol. 84-1, ff. 159–160, 173–175. Murphy to Vázquez, London, January 27, 1828, AGSREM, H/131 "825"/1. LE 1615 (17); Baring Brothers to Vázquez, London, June 2, 1829, AGN, JE, vol. 94, fo. 222; José Ignacio Espinosa to Vázquez, Mexico, June 9, 1830, AGN, Gobernación, vol. 69.
45. Rocafuerte to Cañedo, London, October 15, 1828, AGSREM, H/131 "825"/7. LE 1616 (3); Tejada to Rocafuerte, Rome, April 11, 1828; Rocafuerte to Bocanegra, London, April 28, 1829; May 6, 1829: AGN, JE, vol. 94, ff. 321–322, 319–320, 323–324.
46. Alcalá Alvarado, *Una pugna diplomatica*, 119-236; Medina Ascensio, *La Santa Sede*, 193-218. Vázquez returned to Mexico where he became

bishop of Puebla, distinguishing himself for his conservative views. Years later, during the war with the United States, he had another opportunity to choose between the interests of his Church and that of his country. True to his beliefs, he opposed the liberal government, which he feared might despoil the Church of some of its privileges, and opened the gates of Puebla—the strategic fortified city on the road to Mexico City—to the invading North Americans.

## X: The Spanish Liberals, Rocafuerte, and America

1. Rocafuerte, *A la nación*, 287–288. On the liberal emigration see Llorens Castillo, *Liberales y románticos*, 9-54.
2. Rocafuerte to José Canga Argüelles, London, July 30, 1824; Canga Argüelles, to Rocafuerte, London, July 31, 1824, in José Canga Argüelles, *Elementos de la ciencia de hacienda* (London, 1825), 1.
3. Bustamante, "Diario," VI (July 19, 1825), ff. 21–22; Canga Argüelles to Alamán, London, November 20, 1825, AGSREM, H/120 (5-2) "825" 2-1-1869.
4. José Canga Argüelles, *Diccionario de hacienda con aplicación a España*. 5 vols. (London, 1826-1827).
5. Rocafuerte, *A la nación*, 290–291; Llorens Castillo, *Liberales y romanticos*, 170–177; William J. Burke, *Rudolph Ackerman* (New York, 1935), 22–23. Very few of these publications reached Spain during the reign of Ferdinand VII. After his death, other interests kept the liberal exiles from introducing these works at home. As a result, their efforts benefited America rather than Spain.
6. José Joaquín Mora, *Cuadro de la historia de los árabes desde Mahoma hasta la conquista de Granada*. 2 vols. (London, 1826); Francisco S. Clavigero, *Historia antigua de México*, translated by José Joaquín Mora, 2 vols. (London, 1826).
7. Evaristo San Miguel, *Elementos del arte de la guerra*. 2 vols. (London, 1826-1827); Rocafuerte, *A la nación*, 291.
8. Rocafuerte, *A la nación*, 291; Villanueva, *Vida literaria*; William Paley, *Teología natural, o demonstración de la existencia y de los atributos de la divinidad fundada en los elementos de la naturaleza*, translated by Joaquín L. Villanueva (London, 1825). In order to win support in Mexico, Rocafuerte persuaded Villanueva to dedicate the translation to their mutual friend from the Cortes, Father Miguel Ramos Arizpe, then Mexico's minister of justice and ecclesiastic affairs;

Domestic and Foreign Missionary Society, *Quarterly Papers*, II (June, 1828), 13.

9 .Rocafuerte to Bolívar, London, May 26, 1825, O'Leary, *Memorias*, IV, 397–398; Rocafuerte to Alamán, London, November 16, 1825, AGSREM, H/555.1 (016) "825"/1; Domestic and Foreign Missionary Society, *Quarterly Papers*, II (June, 1828), 13–14.

10. British and Foreign School Society, *Eighteenth Annual Report* (London, 1823), 114; *Nineteenth Annual Report* (London, 1824), 102. See other yearly reports until 1829.

11. Rocafuerte, "Report of the Mexican Minister," 108–111.

12. [Vicente Rocafuerte and James Thompson], *Representación de la Sociedad Britanica y estrangera de escuelas mutuas dirigida al congreso de Tacubaya* (London, 1827).

13. British and Foreign School Society, *Twenty-Fourth Annual Report* (London, 1828), lxxxvii; James Thompson to British and Foreign School Society, Jalapa, April 23, 1828 in *Twenty-Fifth Annual Report* (London, 1829), 102–104.

14. British and Foreign School Society, *Twenty-Second Annual Report* (London, 1827), xv.

15. Lloyd Sanders, *The Holland House Circle* (London, 1908).

16. Rocafuerte, *Ensayo sobre cárceles*, 16–17, 31–34; Llewellyn Woodward, *The Age of Reform, 1815-1870*. 2d ed. (Oxford, 1962), 371, 467–468, 621.

17. [Vicente Rocafuerte], "Arreglo de las prisiones," *Ocios de los españoles emigrados*, Segunda época (April, 1827), 161–175.

18. Llorens Castillo, *Liberales y románticos*, 255–263.

19. When Rocafuerte returned to Mexico in February, 1827, he was accused of using government funds to support the *Ocios*. However, the administration denied that this was the case. See *Correo de la federación mexicana*, I, no. 52 (December 22, 1826), 4; Espinosa de los Monteros to the Senate, Mexico, December 23, 1826, *Correo de la federación mexicana*, II, no. 128 (March 28, 1827), 2.

20. Simon Collier, *Ideas and Politics of Chilean Independence, 1808-1833* (Cambridge, 1967), 260–322.

21. Rocafuerte, *A la nación*, 292.

22. [Vicente Rocafuerte and José Canga Argüelles], *Cartas de un americano sobre las ventajas de los gobiernos repúblicanos federativos* (London, 1826); Llorens Castillo, *Liberales y románticos*, 165–166.

23. Mariano Egaña to Juan Egaña, London, November 20, 1826 and [December, 1826], Mariano Egaña, *Cartas de don Mariano Egaña a Su Padre* (Santiago, 1948), 174–185, 212–215.

24. Rocafuerte to Bolívar, London, September 27, 1826, O'Learly, *Memorias*, IV, 398–401.

25. Ibid.

26. Gallatin to Clay, London, December 16, 1826, Manning, *Diplomatic Correspondence*, III, 1,583–1,585.

27. Rocafuerte to Gual, Quito, March 28, 1843 in Rocafuerte, *A la nación*, 413.

28. Rocafuerte to Bolívar, New York, June 20, 1827, O'Leary, *Memorias*, IV, 401.

29. Bolívar to Fernández de Madrid, Bogotá, February 7, 1828; Bolívar to Daniel F. O'Leary, Guayaquil, September 13, 1829: Lecuna, *Cartas del Libertador*, VII, 143–144; IX, 120–127.

30. Rocafuerte to Michelena, London, December 20, 1827, HD 19-2.4577; Rocafuerte to Cañedo, London, September 18, 1828, AGSREM, H/210 (861:72) "828"/1. LE 1700 (3).

31. Rocafuerte to Bolívar, London, June 6, 1829, O'Leary, *Memorias*, IV, 401–402; O'Leary later maintained that Rocafuerte quarreled with Bolívar over the question of relations with the Vatican. Their correspondence, however, indicates that their disagreement over federalism was greater, and the cause of the rupture. O'Leary to Carlos Soublette, Rome, October 15, 1838, Nicolás Navarro (ed.), *Actividades diplomáticas del General Daniel Florencio O'Leary en Europa* (Caracas, 1938), 142–150.

32. Rodríguez, "An Analysis," 418–484.

33. Rocafuerte, *A la nación*, 292; Pablo Mendíbil, *Resumen histórico de la revolución de los Estados Unidos Mejicanos sacado del "Cuadro histórico" que en forma de cartas escribió el Lic. D. Carlos María Bustamante* (London, 1828), viii; Bustamante, *Continuación del Cuadro*, I, 3.

34. Rocafuerte to Michelena, London, December 20, 1827, HD 19-2.4577; Pakenham to Dudley, Mexico, January 5, 1828, FO 50/42, ff. 1–10.

35. Rocafuerte to Blackmore, London, November 25, 1828, FO 50/51, ff. 36–37; Pakenham to Charles R. Vaugham, Mexico, January 13, 1829, FO 50/53, ff. 56—69.

36. Rocafuerte to Cañedo, London, February 23, 1829, AGSREM, H/623 "828"/1.

37. Rocafuerte to Bocanegra, London, April 28, 1829, AGN, JE, vol. 94, ff. 319–320; Manuel Gómez Pedraza, *Manifiesto que Manuel Gómez Pedraza ciudadano de la República de Méjico dedica a sus compatriotas; o sea una reseña de su vida pública*. 2d ed. (Guadalajara, 1831).

38. Rocafuerte to Aberdeen, London, June 18, 1829, FO 50/58, ff. 68–69. Rocafuerte to Bocanegra, London, June 18, 1829; June 20, 1829; Aberdeen to Bocanegra, London, June 24, 1829: AGSREM, H/311.2 "828"/3. 1-4.858. *Times*, June 18, 1829, 2.

39. Rocafuerte to Bocanegra, London, March 24, 1829; July 16, 1829: AGSREM, H/210 (42:72) 4.1-12-1308; H/311.2 ("828")/3. 1–4–858.

40. Rocafuerte to Alamán, London, July 14, 1825; Rocafuerte to Victoria,

London, [February, 1826]; Camacho to Rocafuerte, Mexico, April 21, 1826; Rocafuerte to Espinosa de los Monteros, London, August 3, 1826: AGSREM, H/131 "825"/6. LE 1616 (2).

41. Rocafuerte to Cañedo, London, May 3, 1828, AGSREM, H/131 "825"/6. LE 1616 (2); Fernández de Madrid to his wife, London, October 18, 1827, Martínez Silva, *Fernández Madrid*, 343.

42. *El Amigo del pueblo*, May 21, 1828, 242–246.

43. Pakenham to Dudley, Mexico, May 28, 1828, FO 50/43, ff. 252–253. Pakenham believed that Rocafuerte was being relieved because he was an *escoces*. However, Rocafuerte had no political connection with that group, although he was on friendly terms with many *escoceses*. Dudley to Pakenham, London, August 21, 1828, FO 50/43, ff. 57–58; *Voz de la patria*, II, no. 19 (March 29, 1830).

44. The extensive correspondence on the question is found in AGSREM, H/131 "828"/14. LE 1621 (6). Rocafuerte to Blackmore, London, November 18, 1828; Blackmore to Rocafuerte, London, November 20, 1828: FO 50/51, ff. 33–34.

45. Rocafuerte to Bocanegra, London, March 18, 1828, AGSREM, H/131 "825"/6. LE 1616 (2); Borja Migoni to Bocanegra, London, March 19, 1828, AGSREM, H/131 "823"/4. LE 1612 (9). Borja Migoni's case is strange. The government continued to consider him its consul general after he refused to accept the appointment of chargé d'affaires. When he died in May, 1832, Gorostiza attempted to take care of his estate in order to save some of Mexico's funds which Borja Migoni had deposited in the bank along with his own money. However, English courts intervened because, to Gorostiza's surprise, Borja Migoni had long since become a citizen of England. See Bustamante, "Diario," XX (June 30, 1832), fo. 377; *Times*, May 25, 1832, 3.

46. Bocanegra to Pakenham, Mexico, January 31, 1829, FO 50/53, ff. 180–181; Bocanegra to Rocafuerte, Mexico, June 4, 1829, AGSREM, H/131 "825"/6. LE 1616 (2).

47. Gorostiza to Bocanegra, London, December 16, 1829, AGSREM, H/131 "825"/6. LE 1616 (2); Alamán to Santamaría, New York, July 17, 1829, Lucas Alamán, *Obras*. 10 vols. (Mexico, 1942), IX, 514–518.

48. Rocafuerte to Alamán, Veracruz, March 13, 1830, Alamán Papers, folder III, no. 149; Rocafuerte to His Holiness, London, December 24, 1829, CANR, Negocios Eclesiasticos, II, ff. 34–35.

## XI: Rocafuerte and Mexican Reforms

1. Rocafuerte to Alamán, Veracruz, March 13, 1830, Alamán Papers, folder III, no. 149.
2. Both Mangino and Facio had been attached to the Mexican legation in London. See list of persons attached to the Mission of the United States of Mexico in London, June 27, 1828, FO 50/51, fo. 21.
3. Rocafuerte wrote Alamán two letters, an official one informing him of his arrival and a personal one expressing his pleasure at Alamán's being minister. Rocafuerte to Alamán, March 13, 1830, AGSREM, H/300 (72:861) "823-30"/1. LE 1700; Rocafuerte to Alamán, Veracruz, March 13, 1830, Alamán Papers, folder III, no. 149.
4. Alamán to Rocafuerte, Mexico, March 20, 1830, AGSREM, H/131 "825"/6. LE 1616 (2); Bustamante, "Diario," (April 12, 1830), ff. 162–164.
5. Rocafuerte, *A la nación*, 296–297.
6. James Thompson to Pakenham, Mexico, February 18, 1830; Pakenham to Alamán, Mexico, February 20, 1830; Alamán to Pakenham, Mexico, March 31, 1830: FO 50/51, ff. 319–320.
7. Rocafuerte to Alamán, Mexico, May 3, 1830, Alamán Papers, folder III, no. 154.
8. Thompson to José María Luis Mora, London, February 31, 1831, Mora Papers, Latin American Collection, University of Texas, Austin. Rocafuerte was not the only one who was confused by Alamán's ideology. Nearly a year later Thompson wrote: "I am very sorry that Alamán has lent himself to the highest degree in favor of the pretention of the clergy. He is a man whom, in truth, I do not understand and it appears that he has failed others' faith in him as he has mine." Thompson to Mora, London, July 18, 1831, Mora Papers. Part of the reason for such confusion lies in the fact that ideology tended to move rapidly to the left because of changing circumstances. Thus, without changing his position, a man who was a liberal in 1821 might be considered a moderate in 1825 and a conservative in 1830. Furthermore, few men had consistent ideologies; in some instances liberals and conservatives were in agreement while in others they were bitterly divided. Historians are still attempting to comprehend Mexican liberalism and conservatism. Recently Charles Hale has concluded in *Mexican Liberalism in the Age of Mora, 1821-1852* (New Haven, 1968) that liberals and conservatives had much in common; Michael Costeloe argues, in a book soon to be published

by the Fondo de Cultura Económica, that Mexicans had no ideology whatsoever. See also Moisés González Navarro, *El pensamiento político de Lucas Alamán* (Mexico, 1952).

9. Rocafuerte to Editors, Mexico, December 20, 1830, *El Sol*, II, no. 542 (December 21, 1830), 2,166—1,267. Minister of Interior Alamán was also concerned with the development of industry. During his administration the Banco de Avío, a development bank, was founded; see Robert A. Potash, *El Banco de Avío de México* (Mexico, 1959).

10. Rocafuerte is quoted in Lorenzo de Vidaurre, *Plan del Perú* (Philadelphia, 1823), 172; Rocafuerte to Editors, Mexico, September 27, 1830, *El Sol*, II, no. 508 (November 16, 1830), 2,054. Most contemporary observers agreed that Mexico was indeed quite wealthy, although the transportation bottleneck prevented all but silver from being exported. It also prevented the rapid development of the agricultural interior. On this point consult David R. Ringrose, *Transportation and Economic Stagnation in Spain, 1750-1850* (Durham, N. C., 1970), which considers similar questions in the mother country.

11. Bustamante, "Diario," XXVII (August 12, 1830), fo. 110. Rocafuerte to Editors, Mexico, September 27, 1830; December 17, 1830, *El Sol*, II, no. 508 (November 20, 1830), 2,029; III, no. 558 (January 10, 1831), 2,230-2,232.

12. Rocafuerte to Editors, Mexico, December 27, 1830, *El Sol*, III, no. 558 (January 11, 1831), 2,230-2,232; *Registro oficial*, IV, no. 11 (January 11, 1831), 43–44; Pakenham to Lord Palmerston, Mexico, May 31, 1831, FO 50/56, fo. 215; [Lucas Alamán], *Un regalo de año nuevo para el señor Rocafuerte, o consideraciones sobre sus consideraciones* (Mexico, 1832), 4–5.

13. Rocafuerte to Ayuntamiento, Mexico, October 7, 1830; Rocafuerte to Editors, Mexico, September 27, 1830, *El Sol*, II, no. 508 (November 20, 1830), 2,029-2,030.

14. Comisión de Hacienda to Ayuntamiento, Mexico, October 8, 1830; Gobernador del Distrito Federal to Alamán, Mexico, October 12, 1830; Alamán to Gobernador del Distrito Federal, Mexico, October 30, 1830; Comisión de Hacienda to Ayuntamiento, Mexico, November 11, 1830: *El Sol*, II, no. 508 (November 20, 1830), 2,030.

15. D. P. to Editors, Mexico, n.d., *El Sol*, II, no. 514 (November 26, 1830), 2,054.

16. *El Anahuacence* to Editors, Mexico, n.d., *El Sol*, II, no. 514 (November 26, 1830), 2,054-2,055.

17. Rocafuerte to Editors, Mexico, December 20, 1830, *El Sol*, II, no. 542 (December 21, 1830), 2,166–2,167.

18. *Registro oficial*, III, no. 103 (December 26, 1830), 412; IV, no. 11 (January 11, 1831), 43–44. Rocafuerte to Editors, Mexico, Decem-

ber 27, 1830, *El Sol*, III, no. 558 (January 10, 1831), 2,230—2,232; II, no. 516 (December 28, 1830), 2,181—2,184. Alamán later maintained that Rocafuerte turned against the government in 1831 because it did not support his projects. The minister believed he had given Rocafuerte privileged treatment when he allowed him and the supporters of gas lights and railroads to make free use of the government controlled *El Sol* at a time when the press was muzzled by censorship. Alamán, *Un regalo de año nuevo*, 4—5.

19. *El Sol*, II, no. 516 (December 28, 1830), 2,181—2,184.

20. Ibid., III, no. 625 (March 17, 1831), 2,500.

21. Ibid., III, no. 670 (May 1, 1831), 2,677.

22. Rocafuerte to Editors, Mexico, December 27, 1830, *El Sol*, III, no. 558 (January 10, 1831), 2,230—2,232; Rocafuerte, *A la nación*, 307; Vicente Rocafuerte, *Ensayo sobre el nuevo sistema de cárceles* (Mexico, 1830).

23. Public reaction to the *Essay on Jails* was so favorable that the government felt obliged to praise the work in a series of articles, presumably written by Alamán, which appeared in the *Registro oficial*, IV, no. 86 (March 27, 1831); IV, no. 104 (April 11, 1831).

24. Rocafuerte, *A la nación*, 301. The French chargé to Mexico believed that the work had been inspired by the English minister. But Rocafuerte was not Pakenham's friend, as he had been Ward's, and the former's correspondence does not indicate any connection between the two men. Ernesto de la Torre Villar (ed.), *Correspondencia diplomática franco-mexicana, 1808-1839* (Mexico, 1957), 259; Pakenham to Palmerston, Mexico, May 3, 1831, FO 50/56, fo. 215.

25. Vicente Rocafuerte, *Ensayo sobre tolerancia religiosa*. 2d ed. (Mexico, 1831).

26. Rocafuerte, *A la nación*, 297; *El Sol*, III, no. 626 (March 18, 1831), 2,501; Mateos, *Historia parlamentaria*, VII, 219.

27. Bustamante, "Diario," XVIII (April 17, 1831), fo. 198.

28. Rocafuerte, *A la nación*, 301.

29. Pakenham to Palmerston, Mexico, May 3, 1831, FO 50/56, fo. 215. De la Torre Villar, *Correspondencia franco-mexicana*, 259. Un Español, *Dos años en México, o memorias críticas sobre los principales sucesos de la República de los Estados Unidos Mexicanos* (Valencia, 1838), 86—87.

30. Thompson to Mora, London, July 18, 1831, Mora Correspondence. Carlos María Bustamante described Rocafuerte's *Essay* in the following manner: "He has discussed it [religious toleration] as a politician, and he does not merit the reproaches and insults that certain men have heaped prodigiously upon him. They have not understood the rectitude of his intentions which I would assure even with my head." *Voz de la patria*, V, no. 22 (August 31, 1831), 7. Years later

when he had become more conservative Bustamante changed his views. See Bustamante, *Continuación del Cuadro*, IV, 18–19.

31. *El Sol*, II, no. 185 (January 1, 1830), 740.

32. Clarise Neal, "Freedom of the Press in New Spain," in Benson, *Mexico and the Spanish Cortes*, 87–112, 111.

33. Rocafuerte, *Tolerancia religiosa*, 85; Rocafuerte, *A la nación*, 301–302; Pakenham to Palmerston, Mexico, May 3, 1831, FO 50/56, fo. 215; *El Sol*, III, no. 652 (April 13, 1831), 2,608; Bustamante, "Diario," XVIII (April 17, 1831), fo. 198.

34. Rocafuerte, *A la nación*, 301-302; Bustamante, "Diario," XVIII (April 17, 1831), fo. 198; *El Sol*, III, no. 652 (April 13, 1831), 2,608; Rocafuerte, *Tolerancia religiosa*, 86–93.

35. Bustamante, "Diario," XVIII (April 16, 1831), fo. 198.

36. Ibid., XVIII (April 19, 1831), fo. 203; Rocafuerte, *A la nación*, 302; De la Torre Villar, *Correspondencia franco-mexicana*, 259. *El Sol*, III, no. 625 (March 17, 1831), 2,500; III, no. 652 (April 13, 1831), 2,608.

37. Bustamante, "Diario," XVIII (April 17, 1831), fo. 198; (April 19, 1831), fo. 203. Rocafuerte, *A la nación*, 302–303.

38. Rocafuerte, *Tolerancia religiosa*, 93–94. His defense in reproduced on pages 95–108.

39. Bustamante, "Diario," XVIII (April 19, 1831), fo. 203.

40. Rocafuerte, *A la nación*, 302–303.

41. Un Español, *Dos años en México*, 86–87.

42. Pakenham to Palmerston, Mexico, May 3, 1831, FO 50/56, fo. 215.

43. Bustamante, *Continuación al Cuadro*, IV, 18–19. Some apologists for José María Luis Mora claim that he convinced Minister of War Facio to oppose Alamán and the clerical party in the trial. See Robert Florstedt, "Mora contra Bustamante," *Historia mexicana*, XII (July–September 1962), 27. The only proof for this assertion is Mora's statement that the clerical party was unable to convict Rocafuerte "among other reasons because of the united efforts of Mora and Facio and because of Rocafuerte's civic courage. . . ." Mora, *Obras sueltas*, 32–33. The other evidence adduced by Florstedt to prove that Mora defended Rocafuerte is James Thompson's letter to Mora praising Rocafuerte's courage and rejoicing in the outcome of the trial. Thompson wrote Mora because the latter was an agent of the English Bible Society. The communication merely proves that Thompson knew both Mora and Rocafuerte; nothing in the letter indicates that Mora had anything to do with the trial. Furthermore, it is unlikely that Facio helped Rocafuerte because he and his friends, particularly Cañedo, opposed the minister of war.

44. Bustamante, "Diario," XVIII (April 19, 1831), fo. 203; Rocafuerte,

*Tolerancia religiosa,* 85–118; Pakenham to Palmerston, Mexico, May 3, 1831, FO 50/56, fo. 215; *El Sol,* III, no. 660 (April 21, 1831), 2,640.

45. Bustamante, "Diario," XVIII (April 19, 1831), fo. 203; Pakenham to Palmerston, Mexico, May 3, 1831, FO 50/56, fo. 215; De la Torre Villar, *Correspondencia franco-mexicana,* 259; José María Guerrero, *Dictamen teológico que el presbitero licenciado José María Guerrero consultor de la Junta de Censura Religiosa de México presentó a la misma respetable Junta y fué aprobado con unanimidad en sesión del 20 corriente mayo contra el "Ensayo sobre tolerancia religiosa"* (Mexico, 1831), 5, and passim.

46. *Registro oficial,* V (June 12, 1831), 172.

47. Bishop José Miguel [Gordoa y Barrios] to Alamán, Zapopán, January 8, 1832, Alamán Papers, folder III, no. 194. The following are some of the many pamphlets that denounced Rocafuerte: Un Imparcial, *Refutación del ensayo político sobre tolerantismo* (Mexico, 1831); Anonymous, *Impugnación a la nueva secta, sublimes cristianos, contenida en el ensayo sobre tolerancia religiosa por el ciudadano Vicente Rocafuerte (Mexico, 1832);* J.B.M., *Disertación contra tolerancia religiosa* (Mexico, 1833); Un Eclesiastico de Durango, *Disertación sobre la tolerancia de cultos* (Chihuahua, 1834). The clergy also reacted against foreigners, particularly the English who were all considered Protestants, by banning masked balls under pain of major excommunication. According to "ecclesiastic authorities" these festivities were unusually licentious. *El Sol,* III, no. 641 (April 2, 1831), 2,563.

48. *Voz de la patria,* I, no. 22 (August 31, 1831), 7.

49. Ibid.

50. Vicente Rocafuerte, *Carta al ciudadano Carlos María Bustamante* (Mexico, 1831), 3–12.

51. Rocafuerte to Alamán, Mexico, October 8, 1831, Alamán Papers, folder III, no. 185.

52. Alamán to Rocafuerte, Mexico, October 10, 1831, Alamán Papers, folder III, no. 186.

53. Rocafuerte, *A la nación,* 297.

## XII: Rocafuerte and Mexican Politics

1. Jaime E. Rodríguez O., "Oposición a Bustamante," *Historia mexicana,* XX (October–December 1970), 199–208.

2. Alamán to Cañedo, Mexico, June 3, 1831, in Francisco Cuevas Cansino, *El Pacto de familia* (Mexico, 1962), 160–161; Robert I.

Ward, "Juan de Dios Cañedo: Político y diplomático," Licenciatura thesis, Universidad Ibero-Americana (Mexico, 1968), 171–172.

3. *Voz de la patria*, V. No. 22 (August 31, 1831), 7–8; Felipe Collados to Editors, *El Sol*, III, no. 799 (September 7, 1831), 3,196.

4. *Voz de la patria*, V, Supplemento no. 14 (October 18, 1831), 1–8.

5. Rocafuerte, *Observaciones sobre la carta*, 8; Pakenham to Palmerston, Mexico, October 6, 1831, FO 50/56, ff. 224–226.

6. Stanley Green, "Lucas Alamán," (Ph.D. dissertation, Texas Christian University, Fort Worth, 1971), 145–146; Bustamante, "Diario," XIX (November 4, 1831), fo. 230; Bustamante, *Continuación del cuadro*, IV, 24–27; Rocafuerte, *Observaciones sobre la carta*, 8; *Fénix de la libertad*, I, no. 3 (December 14, 1831), 13–14.

7. Rocafuerte, *Observaciones sobre la carta*, 3–20.

8. Bustamante, "Diario," XIX (November 30, 1831), ff. 245–246; Butler to Livingston, Mexico, November 23, 1831, National Archives, Washington, D.C., Dispatches from the United States' Ministers to Mexico (hereafter cited as NA, DUSMM); *El Sol*, IV, no. 1,113 (August 27, 1832), 4,436; Rocafuerte, *A la nación*, 304–306; Un Español, *Dos años en Mexico*, 110; José María Tornel, *Breve reseña histórica de los acontecimientos más notables de la Nación Mexicana desde el año de 1821 hasta nuestros dias* (Mexico, 1852), 295; *Fénix de la libertad*, I, no. 1 (December 7, 1831), 1.

9. Vicente Rocafuerte, *Consideraciones generales sobre la bondad de un gobierno aplicadas a las actuales circunstancias de la República de México* [in three parts with continuous pagination] (Mexico, 1831).

10. Bustamante, "Diario," XIX (December 16, 1831), ff. 299–308. The *Voz de la patria*, the "Voice of the Fatherland," was Bustamante's paper. Thus, he is referring both to the freedom of the press and to his defunct newspaper.

11. *El Censor*, VIII, no. 1,302 (March 7, 1832), 2–3; VIII, no. 1,301 (March 8, 1832), 1–2. Bustamante, "Diario," XIX (December 16, 1831), ff. 299–308; (December 24, 1831), fo. 331.

12. *El Fénix de la libertad*, I, no. 6 (December 24, 1831), 28; [José Antonio Facio], *Contestación, o sea banderilla a Don Vicente Rocafuerte, acerca del primer número de los impresos en que se propuso aplicar las bondades de un gobierno a las actuales circunstancias de la República Mexicana* (Mexico, 1831); [Lucas Alamán], *Un regalo de año nuevo*, 3–29.

13. *El Fénix de la libertad*, I, no. 9 (January 4, 1832), 40; I, no. 10 (January 7, 1832), 43–44.

14. *El Fénix de la libertad*, I, no. 2 (December 10, 1831), 5–7; I, no. 5 (December 21, 1831), 17–18; I, no. 14 (January 18, 1832), 56. Green, "Lucas Alamán," 253–254.

15. Butler to Livingston, Mexico, December 6, 1831, NA, DUSMM; Andrés Quintana Roo to [Valentín Gómez Farías], Mexico, June 13, 1832, Gómez Farías Papers, Latin American Collection, University of Texas, Austin, GF 67 F 44A.

16. *El Fénix de la libertad*, I, no. 1 (December 7, 1831), 1–2, 4.

17. Butler to Livingston, Mexico, December 6, 1831, NA, DUSMM; Bustamante, "Diario," XIX (December 16, 1831), ff. 299–308; Rocafuerte, *A la nación*, 297–298; Mexico, Cámara de diputados, *Proceso de los ex-ministros*, 44.

18. *El Fénix de la libertad*, I, no. 7 (December 28, 1831), 29–32; no. 11 (January 11, 1832), 49–50; no. 20 (February 11, 1832), 89; no. 24 (February 25, 1832), 104; no. 33 (March 28, 1832), 141; no. 34 (March 31, 1832), 145; no. 36 (April 7, 1832), 153; no. 46 (May 12, 1832), 194.

19. *El Conservador de Toluca* (December 3, 1831). Reprinted in *El Fénix de la libertad*, I, no. 3 (December 14, 1831), 9.

20. Antonio López de Santa Anna to [Anastasio Bustamante], Veracruz, January 4, 1832 (letters 1, 2); [Bustamante] to Santa Anna, Mexico, January 12, 1832; Santa Anna to [Bustamante], Veracruz, January 25, 1832: Mariano Riva Palacio Papers, Latin American Collection, University of Texas, Austin. Mateos, *Historia parlamentaria*, VIII, 13–16; *El Fénix de la libertad*, I, no. 19 (February 8, 1832), 82–84.

21. *La Marimba*, I, no. 1 (January 28, 1832), 1–11; Andrés Quintana Roo, *Ampliación que el C. Andrés Quintana Roo hace a la acusación que formalizó ante la Cámara de Diputados contra el Ministro de Guerra D. José Antonio Facio por haber atropellado la inviolabilidad de la representación nacional* (Mexico, 1832).

22. *El Fénix de la libertad*, I, no. 27 (March 7, 1832), 117; Alcance al no. 28 (n.d.); I, no. 33 (March 28, 1832), 139–140. *El Duende*, I, no. 16 (March 17, 1832), 64; Bustamante, "Diario," XX (March 11, 1832), fo. 100.

23. *El Duende*, I, no. 31 (April 27, 1832), 124.

24. *El Toro*, May 5, 1832, 1–8; May 9, 1832, 9—16; May 12, 1832, 17–24; May 16, 1832, 25–32; May 19, 1832, 33–40. *La Marimba*, I, no. 19 (May 11, 1832), 153.

25. *El Sol*, IV, no. 1,113 (August 27, 1832), 4,463.

26. *Fénix de la libertad*, I, no. 49 (May 23, 1832), 205–207; Bustamante, "Diario," XX (May 25, 1832), fo. 223.

27. [Vicente Rocafuerte], *Al Excmo. Sr. General de división D. Anastasio Bustamante* (Mexico, 1832), 2–20.

28. *La Marimba*, I, no. 21 (May 29, 1832), 205–216; I, no. 22 (June 2, 1832), 223–231.

29. *Fénix de la libertad*, I, no. 55 (June 13, 1832), 231. *La Columna de*

*la Constitución Federal de la República Mexicana*, I, no. 1 (June 1, 1832), 1–3; I, no. 4 (June 11, 1832), 15.

30. José Joaquín Rincón to Gómez Farías, Huatusco, September 7, 1847, Gómez Farías Papers, GF 1737, F 50; [Vicente Rocafuerte], *La tumba prócsima del gobierno usurpador* (Mexico, 1832). *El Toro* (June 13, 1832), 101–102; (June 16, 1832), 109–120.

31. *La Columna* provides an interesting analysis of these papers in vol. I, no. 8 (June 20, 1832), 20.

32. *Fénix de la libertad*, I, 57 (June 20, 1832), 239; Quintana Roo to [Gómez Farías], [Mexico], June 13, 1832, Gómez Farías Papers, GF 44 A.

33. *La Columna*, I, no. 25 (July 31, 1832), 100; *Fénix de la libertad*, I, no. 63 (July 11, 1832), 260—263.

34. Gabriel Durán to Minister of War, Hacienda Atlapango, June 8, 1832, *El Sol*, III, no. 1,036 (June 9, 1832), 4,148. Bustamante, "Diario," XX (June 9, 1832), 324–325; XX (June 25, 1832), fo. 368.

35. Bustamante, "Diario," XXI (July 12, 1832), fo. 10.

36. Ibid., XXI (July 13, 1832), fo. 10. Instancia del Comandante General de México, para que se designe interprete que reconosca la documentación recogida a Vicente Rocafuerte, [July 12, 1832], Secretaría de la Defensa Nacional, Archivo Histórico, XI/481.3/947 (1832).

37. *La Marimba*, I, no. 28 (July 13, 1832), 296. *El Sol*, III, no. 1,071 (July 15, 1832), 4,292; III, no. 1,099 (August 31, 1832), 4,406. *El Toro* (July 18, 1832), 218; (July 28, 1832), 258.

38. *La Columna*, I, no. 18 (July 14, 1832), 72; *El Fénix de la libertad*, I, no. 64 (July 14, 1832), 266–267.

39. *Fénix de la libertad*, I, no. 66 (July 18, 1832), 275.

40. *El Fénix de la libertad*, I, no. 96 (July 25, 1832), 284–285.

41. Ibid., I, no. 65 (July 16, 1832), 217 *[sic]* (in error for 271); I, no. 67 (July 21, 1832), 287; I, no. 69 (July 25, 1832), 287; I, no. 71 (July 30, 1832), 295; I, no. 72 (August 1, 1832), 299. *La Columna*, I, no. 30 (August 11, 1832), 120.

42. Rincón to Gómez Farías, Huatusco, September 7, 1847, Gómez Farías Papers, GF 1737, F 50. *La Columna*, I, no. 25 (July 31, 1832), 100; no. 26 (August 1, 1832), 104. *El Fénix de la libertad*, I, no. 70 (July 28, 1832), 289–290; no. 74 (August 6, 1832), 307; no. 76 (August 11, 1832), 315. *El Sol*, IV no. 1,090 (August 3, 1832), 4,372; no. 1,106 (August 20, 1832), 4,436; no. 1,112 (August 26, 1832), 4,459–4,460. *El Toro*, (August 1, 1832), 273–284.

43. *Fénix de la libertad*, I, no. 88 (September 8, 1832), 362–363; no. 90 (September 12, 1832), 373.

44. *El Sol*, IV, no. 1,108 (August 22, 1832), 4,444; no. 1,118 (September 1, 1832), 4,483–4,484; no. 1,120 (September 3, 1832), 4,491.

*El Toro* (September 12, 1832), 478—479; *El Fénix de la libertad*, II, no. 1 (October 1, 1832).

45. Bustamante, "Diario," XXI (September 25, 1832), fo. 205; (October 12, 1832), ff. 300—301. *El Sol*, IV, no. 1,444 (September 27, 1832), 4,600; no. 1,666 (October 18, 1832), 4,688; no. 1,820 (November 1, 1832), 4,879—4,880. *El Fénix de la libertad*, II, no. 16 (January 13, 1833), 4.

46. Manuel Gómez Pedraza to Gómez Farías, Puebla, December 14, 1832, Gómez Farías Papers, GF 85, F 44 A; Bocanegra, *Memorias*, II, 322—330.

47. Historians of Spanish America have often attributed political initiative to strongmen called *caudillos*, literally leaders. Santa Anna, for example, is often given credit for overturning governments at will. Wilfred H. Calcott even entitled the general's biography, *Santa Anna: The Story of an Enigma Who Once Was Mexico* (Norman, 1936). Such views fail to consider the complex nature of interest groups, which have always participated in politics. It is no more than the discredited great-man theory in disguise. Military politicians were indeed important in Spanish America but, as Richard Herr remarks about the same phenomenon in Spain, "This did not mean that Spain had become the plaything of the army or that parliamentary government had ceased to exist. It meant that generals made better political leaders than most men. They could capture the popular imagination. . . . But the issues were between political parties based on different social groups, not between army and society. The army was not monolithic. Almost every shade of opinion found a general to turn to who could rally some troops to his side." Herr, *Spain*, 88. For a different interpretation of Santa Anna see Fernando Díaz Díaz, *Caudillos y Caciques, Antonio de López de Santa Anna y Juan Alvarez.* (Mexico, 1972).

## XIII: The Demise of Spanish Americanism

1. *Fénix de la libertad*, II, no. 16 (January 13, 1833), 4; Rocafuerte, *A la nación*, 306—307.

2. *Fénix de la libertad*, II, 16 (January 13, 1833), 4.

3. Rocafuerte, *A la nación*, 306—312; Vicente Rocafuerte, "Narración de los actos de despotismo y arbitrariedad que ha ejercido en la persona de Vicente Rocafuerte D. Luis Gonzaga Viera, teniente

coronel retirado y actual comandante principal de la demarcación de Iguala." *Fénix de la libertad*, II, no. 16 (January 13, 1833), 2–3.

4. On Rocafuerte's activities in Ecuador see Isaac J. Barrera, *Rocafuerte* (Quito, 1911), and Luis Robalino Dávila, *Rocafuerte* (Quito, 1964). The best source for Rocafuerte's activities after 1831 is his own correspondence, which I am publishing in Guayaquil as part II of *Estudios sobre Vicente Rocafuerte*. On nineteenth-century diplomacy in South America see Robert N. Burr, *By Reason or Force: Chile and the Balancing Power in South America, 1830–1905* (Berkeley, 1967).

# BIBLIOGRAPHY

I. *Primary Sources*

A. Manuscripts

*Colombia*

Archivo Nacional: La República (Bogotá)
Negocios Eclesiasticos
Secretaría de Guerra y Marina

*Ecuador*
Archivo Nacional de Historia (Quito)
Audiencia de Quito
Libros de Cédulas

*Great Britain*
Public Record Office (London)
Foreign Office Papers: FO 50, FO 97, FO 270

*Mexico*
Archivo General de la Nación (Mexico, D. F.)
Gobernación: 69
Justicia Eclesiastica: 45, 46, 82-1, 82-2, 83-1, 83-2, 84-1, 85, 86, 93, 94
Pasaportes, 32
Archivo General de la Secretaría de Relaciones
Exteriores (Mexico, D. F.)
The numbers of the legajos consulted in this archive are not listed because the numbering is so complex. They appear in the footnotes.
Archivo Histórico de la Secretaría de la Defensa Nacional (Mexico, D. F.)
Expediente, XI/481.3/942 (1832)
Biblioteca del Estado de Zacatecas (Zacatecas)
Bustamante, Carlos María, "Diario de lo especialmente ocurrido en México." 44 vols.

287

*Spain*
  Archivo Histórico Nacional (Madrid)
    Estado: 5649, 5650

*United States*
  American Catholic Historical Society Archives (Philadelphia)
  American Philosophical Society (Philadelphia)
    Archives of the Pennsylvania Hospital
  Duke University Library (Durham)
    Elie A. F. La Vallete Papers
  Library of Congress (Washington, D. C.)
    Nicholas Biddle Papers
    Agustín Iturbide Papers
    Thomas Jefferson Papers
    James Monroe Papers
  National Archives (Washington, D. C.)
    Department of State, RG 59
      Diplomatic Instructions to all Countries: 9
      Dispatches from the United States' Ministers to Mexico: 1–5
      Notes from the Central American Legation: 1
  New York Public Library (New York)
    James Monroe Papers
    Joel R. Poinsett Papers
  Pennsylvania Historical Society (Philadelphia)
    Simon Gratz Collection
    Josiah Stoddart Johnston Papers
    Joel R. Poinsett Papers
  University of Texas (Austin)
    The Latin American Collection
      Lucas Alamán Papers
      Valentín Gómez Farías Papers
      Juan E. Hernández y Dávalos Papers
      José Servando Teresa de Mier Papers
      José María Luis Mora Papers
      Mariano Riva Palacio Papers


B. Printed Documents


Colombia: Academia de Historia, *Archivo Santader*. 24 vols. Bogotá:
  Editorial Aguila Negra, 1914-1932.
Cuba: Archivo Nacional, *Documentos para la historia de Venezuela*. Havana:
  Archivo Nacional, 1960.

————, *José Antonio Miralla*. Havana: Archivo Nacional, 1960.

————, *Documentos para la historia de México*. Havana: Archivo Nacional, 1961.

————, *José Fernández de Madrid y su obra en Cuba*. Havana: Archivo Nacional, 1962.

Cuevas Cancino, Francisco (ed.), *El Pacto de Familia*. Mexico: Secretaría de Relaciones Exteriores, 1964.

De la Torre Villar, Ernesto (ed.), *Correspondencia diplomática franco-mexicana, 1808-1839*. Mexico: El Colegio de México, 1957.

Dublán, Manuel and Lozano, José María (eds.), *Legislación mexicana, o colección completa de las disposiciones legislativas expedidas desde la independencia de la República*. 34 vols. Mexico: Dublán y Lozano Hijos, 1876-1904.

Egaña, Mariano, *Cartas de don Mariano Egaña a su padre*. Santiago de Chile: Editorial Nascimiento, 1948.

Flores, Jorge (ed.), *Juan Nepomuceno de Pereda y su misión secreta en Europa*. Mexico: Secretaría de Relaciones Exteriores, 1964.

Garrigó, Roque E., *Historia documentada de la conspiración de los Soles y Rayos de Bolívar*. 2 vols. Havana: Imprenta El Siglo XX, 1929.

Lecuna, Vicente (ed.), *Cartas del Libertador*. 12 vols. Caracas: Imprenta El Comercio & others, 1929-1959.

Lecuna, Vicente and Bierck, Harold (eds.), *Selected Writings of Bolívar*. 2 vols. New York: Colonial Press, 1951.

Manning, William R. (ed.), *Diplomatic Correspondence of the United States Concerning the Independence of the Latin American Nations*. 3 vols. New York: Oxford University Press, 1925.

Mateos, Juan Antonio (ed.), *Historia parlamentaria de los congresos mexicanos de 1821-1857*. 25 vols. Mexico: V. S. Reyes, 1877-1912.

Mestre Ghigliazza, Manuel (ed.), *Las relaciones diplomáticas entre México y Holanda*. Mexico: Secretaría de Relaciones Exteriores, 1931.

Mexico: Chamber of Deputies, *Proceso instructivo formado por la sección del Gran Jurado de la Cámara de Diputados del Congreso General en averiguación de los ex-ministros D. Lucas Alamán, D. Rafael Mangino, D. José Antonio Facio, y D. José Ignacio Espinosa*. Mexico: Imprenta de Ignacio Cumplido, 1833.

Mexico: Congress, *Colección de las leyes y decretos expedidos por el Congreso General de los Estados Unidos de México en los años de 1829-1830*. Mexico: Imprenta de Galván, 1831.

Mexico: Ministry of Foreign Affairs, *La diplomacia mexicana*. 3 vols. Mexico: Tipografía Artistica & others, 1910-1913.

————, *Relaciones diplomáticas entre México y Brasil*. Mexico: Secretaría de Relaciones Exteriores, 1964.

Mexico: Ministry of Treasury, *Cuaderno que contiene el Préstamo hecho a Colombia por D. Vicente Rocafuerte*. Mexico: Imprenta del Aguila, 1829.

Mexico: Senate, "Dictamen de la comisión de la Cámara de Senadores sobre el paradero del bergantín *Guerrero,* leido en la sesión del 17 de noviembre de 1826," *Correo de la federación mexicana,* I, no. 22 (November 22, 1826), 1–3.

Mexico, *Tratados y convenios celebrados y no ratificados por la República Mexicana.* 2 vols. Mexico: Imprenta de Esteva, 1878.

Navarro, Nicolás (ed.), *Actividades diplomáticas del General Daniel Florencio O'Leary en Europa.* Caracas: Tipografía Americana, 1938.

Noboa, Aurelio (ed.), *Recopilaciones de Leyes del Ecuador.* 5 vols. Guayaquil: Imprenta de El Telégrafo, 1900.

O'Leary, Simón, *Memorias del General O'Leary.* 29 vols. Caracas: Imprenta de la Gazeta Oficial, 1880.

Olmedo, José Joaquín, *Epistolario.* Puebla: Editorial Cajica, 1960.

Ramírez Cabañas, Joaquín (ed.), *Las relaciones entre México y el Vaticano.* Mexico: Secretaría de Relaciones Exteriores, 1928.

————, *El empréstito de México a Colombia.* Mexico: Secretaría de Relaciones Exteriores, 1930.

Spain: Cortes, *Diario de las sesiones de Cortes: legislatura de 1820.* 3 vols. Madrid: Imprenta de García, 1871.

Webster, Charles (ed.), *Britain and the Independence of Latin America, 1812-1830.* 2 vols. London: Oxford University Press, 1938.

Weckman, Luis (ed.), *Las relaciones franco-mexicanas.* 2 vols. Mexico: Secretaría de Relaciones Exteriores, 1961-62.

## C. Contemporary Accounts

Adams, John Q., *Memoirs.* 12 vols. Philadelphia: J. B. Lippincott & Co., 1874-1877.

[Alamán, Lucas], *Un regalo de año nuevo para el señor Rocafuerte, o consideraciones sobre sus consideraciones.* Mexico: Imprenta de Valdéz, 1832.

————, *Historia de Méjico.* 5 vols. Mexico: Editorial Jus, 1942.

————, *Obras.* 10 vols. Mexico: Editorial Jus, 1942.

Alcalá Galiano, Antonio, *Recuerdos de un anciano* (vol. 83, *Biblioteca de Autores Españoles*). Madrid: Ediciones Atlas, 1955.

Anonymous, *Impugnación a la nueva secta sublimes cristianos, contenida en el ensayo sobre tolerancia religiosa, por el ciudadano Vicente Rocafuerte* Mexico: Imprenta de Rivera, 1832.

Argüelles, Agustín, *Examen histórico de la reforma constitucional.* 2 vols. London: C. Wood & Sons, 1835.

Becher, Carl C., *Mexico in den ereignisvollen Jahren 1832 und 1833.* Hamburg: Perthes & Besser, 1834.

Bocanegra, José María, *Memorias para la historia de México independiente.* 2 vols. Mexico: Imprenta del Gobierno Federal, 1892.

Borja Migoni, Francisco de, "Esposición del C. Francisco de Borja Migoni consul-general de México en Londres, sobre el empréstito que fue encargado," London, February 11, 1826 in *El Amigo del Pueblo*, September 12, 1827, 1–34.

Bustamante, Carlos María, *Diario histórico de México.* Zacatecas: Tipografía de la Escuela de Artes y Oficios de la Penitenciaría, 1896.

———, *Continuación del cuadro histórico de la Revolución de México.* 4 vols. Mexico: Biblioteca Nacional and Instituto de Antropología e Historia, 1953-1963.

———, *La Constitución de Cádiz, o motivos de mi afecto a la Constitución.* Mexico: Federación Editorial Mexicana, 1971.

Cañedo, Juan de Dios, *Defensa de la acusación hecha en la Cámara de Diputados contra el ministro de guerra.* Mexico: Imprenta de Agustín Guiol, 1831.

Canga Argüelles, José, *Elementos de la ciencia de hacienda.* London: Macintosh, 1825.

———, *Ensayo sobre las libertades de la iglesia española en ambos mundos.* London: Imprenta de Salvá, 1826.

———, *Diccionario de hacienda con aplicación a España.* 5 vols. London: Imprenta de Calero, 1826—1827.

Clavigero, Francisco S. *Historia antigua de México.* 2 vols. Translated by José Joaquín de Mora. London: Ackerman, 1826.

Dávila, Rafael, *Testamento del General Guerrero.* Mexico: Imprenta de Rivera, 1831.

D.U.L.A., *Idea general sobre la conducta política de D. Miguel Ramos Arizpe, natural de la provincia de Coahuila, como diputado que ha sido por esta provincia en las Cortes generales y extraordinarias de la monarchía [sic] española desde el año de 1810 hasta el de 1821.* Mexico: Imprenta de Herculana de Villa, 1822.

Un Eclesiastico de Durango, *Disertación sobre la tolerancia de cultos.* Chihuahua: Imprenta del Estado, 1834.

Un **Español**, *Dos años en México, o memorias críticas sobre los principales sucesos de la República de los Estados Unidos Mexicanos, desde la invasión de Barradas, hasta la declaración del Puerto de Tampico, contra el gobierno del gral. Bustamante.* Valencia: Imprenta de Cabrerizo, 1838.

[Facio, José Antonio], *Contestación, o sea banderilla a don Vicente Rocafuerte, acerca del primer número de los impresos en que se propuso explicar las bondades de un gobierno a las actuales circunstancias de la República Mexicana.* Mexico: Imprenta de T. Guiol, 1831.

Fernández de Madrid, José, *A la restauración de la Constitución española.* Havana: Imprenta de Palmer, 1820.

———, "Nuestras diferencias; sus peligros; sus remedios," *El Argos*, December 16, 1820, 2–6.

Gómez Pedraza, Manuel, *Manifiesto que Manuel Gómez Pedraza, ciudadano de la República de Méjico dedica a sus compatriotas; o sea una reseña de su vida pública*. 2d ed. Guadalajara: Imprenta de Brambillas, 1831.

Guerrero, José María, *Dictamen teológico que el presbitero licenciado José María Guerrero consultor de la Junta de Censura Religiosa de México presentó a la misma respetable Junta y fué aprobado con unanimidad en sesión del 20 corriente mayo contra el "Ensayo sobre tolerancia religiosa" publicado en México por el ciudadano Vicente Rocafuerte*. Mexico: Imprenta de Valdés, 1831.

Un Imparcial, *Refutación del ensayo político sobre tolerantismo y defensa de los diezmos*. Mexico: Imprenta de las Escalerillas, 1831.

Iznaga, José Aniceto, "Peregrinación patriotica a Colombia," in Vidal Morales y Morales, *Iniciadores y primeros mártires*. Havana: Imprenta Avisador Comercial, 1901, 38–52.

J.B.M., *Disertación contra tolerancia religiosa*. Mexico: Imprenta de Galván, 1833.

La Fayette, Marie Paul Marquis de, *Memoires, correspondence et manuscripts*. 6 vols. Paris: H. Fournier Aine, 1838.

Longworth, Thomas, *New York Directory*. New York: Longworth, 1821.

Martínez Marina, Francisco, *La teoría de las Cortes* (vols. 219–220, *Biblioteca de Autores Españoles*). Madrid: Ediciones Atlas, 1968-1969.

Mendíbil, Pablo, *Resumen histórico de la Revolución de los Estados Unidos Mejicanos sacado del "Cuadro histórico" que en forma de cartas escribió el Lic. D. Carlos María Bustamante*. London: Ackerman, 1828.

Mesonero Romanos, Ramón, *Memorias de un setentón* (vol. 203, *Biblioteca de Autores Españoles*). Madrid: Ediciones Atlas, 1967.

[Mier, José Servando Teresa de], *Memoria política-instructiva enviada desde Filadelfia en Agosto de 1821 a los gefes independientes de Anahuac llamado por los españoles Nueva España*. Philadelphia: F. Hurtel, 1821.

Miralla, José Antonio, *Análisis del papel titulado lo más y lo menos*. Havana: Imprenta de Palmer, 1820.

———, "Soberanía del pueblo y elecciones populares, conforme a la Constitución Política de la Monarquía Española," *Argos*, August 14, 1820, 1–10.

Mora, José Joaquín, *Cuadro de la historia de los árabes desde Mahoma hasta la conquista de Granada*. 2 vols. London: Ackerman, 1826.

Mora, José María Luis, *Obras sueltas*. 2d ed. Mexico: Editorial Porrua, 1963.

Paley, William, *Teología natural, o demonstración de la existencia y de los atributos de la divinidad fundada en los fenómenos de la naturaleza*. Translated by Joaquín L. Villanueva. London: Macintosh, 1825.

[El Payo del Rosario], *De coyote a perro inglés voy al coyote ocho a tres.* Mexico: Juan Cabrera, 1825.

Quintana Roo, Andrés, *Acusación presentada en la Cámara de Diputados el 2 de diciembre contra el ministro de guerra.* Mexico: Imprenta de Rivera, 1830.

———, *Cuarta representación a la Cámara de Diputados sobre la acusación pendiente contra el ministro de guerra.* Mexico: Imprenta de las Escalerillas, 1831.

———, *Ampliación que el C. Andrés Quintana Roo hace a la acusación que formalizó ante la Cámara de Diputados contra el Ministro de Guerra D. José Antonio Facio por haber atropellado la inviolabilidad de la representación nacional.* Mexico: Imprenta de las Escalerillas, 1832.

Rocafuerte, Vicente, *Rasgo imparcial, breves observaciones al papel que ha publicado el Dr. D. Tomás Romay en el Diario del Gobierno.* Havana: Imprenta de Palmer, 1820.

———, *Ideas necesarias a todo pueblo americano independiente que quiera ser libre.* Philadelphia: D. Huntington, 1821.

———, *Bosquejo ligerísimo de la revolución de Mégico* [sic] *desde el grito de Iguala hasta la proclamación de Iturbide.* Philadelphia: Imprenta de Teracrouef y Naroajeb [sic] (in error for Havana: Imprenta de Palmer), 1822.

———, *Lecciones para las escuelas de primeras letras, sacadas de las Sagradas Escrituras, siguiendo el texto literal de la traducción del Padre Scío, sin notas ni comentarios.* New York: A. Paul, 1823.

———, *Ensayo Político, el sistema colombiano popular, electivo, y representativo, es el que más conviene a la América independiente.* New York: A. Paul, 1823.

———, "Report of Mr. Vicente Rocafuerte, the Mexican Minister, at the Twenty-first Annual Meeting of the British and Foreign School Society," in British and Foreign School Society, *Twenty-first Annual Report.* London: J. B. G. Vogel, 1826, 108–111.

[Rocafuerte, Vicente and Canga Argüelles, José,] *Cartas de un americano sobre las ventajas de los gobiernos repúblicanos federativos.* London: Imprenta de Calero, 1826.

[Rocafuerte, Vicente and Thompson, James,] *Representación de la Sociedad Britanica de escuelas mutuas dirigida al congreso de Tacubaya.* London: n.p., 1827.

Rocafuerte, Vicente, "Examen analítico de las constituciones formadas en Hispano-américa," *Revista de historia de América*, no. 72 (July–December 1971), 419–484.

———, *Esposición de las razones que determinaron a D. Vicente Rocafuerte a prestar a la República de Colombia la suma de £63,000.* London: Macintosh, 1829.

————, *Ensayo sobre el nuevo sistema de cárceles*. Mexico: Imprenta de Galván, 1830.

————, *Ensayo sobre tolerancia religiosa*. 2d ed. Mexico: Imprenta de Rivera, 1831.

————, *Carta de Vicente Rocafuerte al ciudadano Carlos María Bustamante*. Mexico: Imprenta de Rivera, 1831.

————, *Observaciones sobre la carta inserta en el Registro oficial del 4 de octubre, del célebre Obispo Flechier sobre la ilicitud de los matrimonios entre los católicos y los protestantes*. Mexico: Imprenta de Rivera, 1831.

————, *Consideraciones generales sobre la bondad de un gobierno aplicadas a las actuales circunstancias de la República de México* (in three parts with continuous pagination). Mexico: Imprenta de las Escalerillas, 1831.

————, *Al Excmo. Sr. General de división D. Anastasio Bustamante*. Mexico: Imprenta de las Escalerillas, 1832.

————, *La tumba prócsima del gobierno usurpador*. Mexico: Imprenta de las Escalerillas, 1832.

————, *A la nación*. Quito: Tipografía de la Escuela de Artes y Oficios, 1908.

————, *Colección Rocafuerte*. 16 vols. Quito: Talleres Gráficos Nacionales, 1947.

Romay, Tomás, "Purga urbem," *Diario del Gobierno Constitucional de La Habana*, no. 141 (May 20, 1820), 1-3.

San Miguel, Evaristo, *Elementos del arte de la guerra*. 2 vols. London: E. S. Miguel, 1826-1827.

————, *Vida de D. Agustín Argüelles*. 4 vols. Madrid: Imprenta del Colegio de Sordo-Mudos, 1851-1852.

Tanco, Diego, *Lo más y lo menos del discurso del Dr. D. Tomás Romay y del Rasgo Imparcial del ex-diputado Rocafuerte*. Havana, n.p., 1820.

Tornel Y Mendívil, José María, *Breve reseña histórica de los acontecimientos más notables de la Nación Mexicana desde el año de 1821 hasta nuestros dias*. Mexico: Imprenta de Cumplido, 1852.

Varela, Félix, *Observaciones sobre la Constitución Política de la Monarquía Española*. Havana: Imprenta de Palmer e hijos, 1821.

Vidaurre, Manuel Lorenzo de, *Votos de los americanos a la nación española y a nuestro amado monarca el señor don Fernando VII; verdadero concordato entre españoles, europeos y americanos*. Mexico: Arispe, 1820.

————, *Plan del Perú, defectos del gobierno español antiguo, necesarias reformas*. Philadelphia: J.F. Hurtel, 1823.

Villanueva, Joaquín Lorenzo, *Vida literaria de Joaquín Lorenzo Villanueva, o memorias de sus escritos y de sus opiniones eclesiásticas y políticas de algunos sucesos notables de su tiempo*. 2 vols. London: Macintosh, 1825.

———, *Juicio de la obra del señor arzobispo de Pradt intitulada "Concordato de México."* London: Macintosh, 1827.
Ward, Henry G. *Mexico.* 2d ed. 2 vols. London: Henry Colburn, 1829.
Zavala, Lorenzo de, *Venganza de la colonia.* Mexico: Empresas Editoriales, 1950.

## D. Contemporary Newspapers

*El Aguila mexicana* (Mexico), 1823-1829.
*El Amigo de la patria* (Mexico), 1824.
*El Amigo del Pueblo* (Mexico), 1827-1828.
*El Argos: periodico político, científico y literario* (Havana), 1820-1821.
*El Atleta* (Mexico), 1827-1828.
*The Aurora* (Philadelphia), 1821-1822.
*El Censor* (Veracruz), 1832.
*La Columna de la Constitución Federal de la República Mexicana* (Mexico), 1832-1833.
*El Constitucional: o sea, crónica científica, literaria y política* (Madrid), 1820-1821.
*Correo de la federación mexicana* (Mexico), 1826-1828.
*Diario del gobierno constitucional de Cuba* (Havana), 1820.
*El Duende* (Mexico), 1832.
*El Español Constitucional* (London), 1820.
*El Fénix de la libertad* (Mexico), 1831-1833.
*Gazeta imperial de México* (Mexico), 1822.
*El Iris de Jalisco* (Guadalajara), 1824.
*La Marimba* (Mexico), 1832.
*The New York Daily Advertiser* (New York), 1823.
*The North American and United States Gazette* (Philadelphia), 1847.
*El Observador de la República Mexicana* (Mexico), 1830.
*Ocios de los españoles emigrados* (London), 1824-1827.
*Paulson's American Daily Advertiser* (Philadelphia), 1823.
*Registro oficial del gobierno de los Estados Unidos Mexicanos* (Mexico), 1830 1833.
*El Sol* (Mexico), 1821-1829; 1830-1833.
*The Times* (London), 1824-1832.
*El Toro* (Mexico), 1832.
*Voz de la patria* (Mexico), 1828-1831.

## II. *Secondary Sources*

Alayza y Paz Soldán, Luis, *La constitución de Cádiz: El egregio limeño Morales y Duarez*. Lima: Talleres Gráficos Lumen, 1946.

Alcalá Alvarado, Alfonso, *Una pugna diplomática ante la Santa Sede: El restablecimiento del Episcopado en México, 1825-1831*. Mexico: Editorial Porrua, 1967.

Anderson, W. Woodrow, "Reform as a Means to Quell Revolution" in Benson, *Mexico and the Spanish Cortes*, 185−207.

Anes, Gonzalo, *Economía e Ilustración en la España del siglo XVIII*. Barcelona: Ediciones Ariel, 1969.

Anna, Timothy E., "Francisco Novella and the Last Stand of the Royal Army in New Spain," *HAHR*, LI (February 1971), 92−111.

Arnade, Charles, *The Emergence of the Republic of Bolivia*. Gainesville: University of Florida Press, 1957.

Artola, Miguel, "Campillo y las reformas de Carlos III," *Revista de Indias*, XII, (October−December 1952), 685−714.

———, *Los afrancesados*. Madrid: Instituto de Estudios Políticos, 1953.

———. *Los orígenes de la España contemporanea*. 2 vols. Madrid: Instituto de Estudios Políticos, 1959.

———, *La España de Fernando VII*. Madrid: Espasa Calpe, 1968.

Barrera, Isaac, *Rocafuerte: Estudio histórico-biografico*. Quito: Imprenta Nactional, 1911.

Benson, Nettie Lee, "The Plan of Casa Mata," *HAHR*, XXV (February 1945), 45−56.

———, "Servando Teresa de Mier, Federalist," *HAHR*, (November, 1948), 514−525.

———, *La diputación provincial y el federalismo mexicano*. Mexico: El Colegio de México, 1955.

———, (ed.), *Mexico and the Spanish Cortes, 1810-1822*. Austin: University of Texas Press, 1966.

Berry, Charles R., "The Election of Mexican Deputies to the Spanish Cortes, 1810-1822," in Benson, *Mexico and the Spanish Cortes*, 10−42.

Bertier de Sauvigny, Guillaume de, *The Bourbon Restoration*. Philadelphia: University of Pennsylvania Press, 1966.

Bierck, Harold, *La Vida pública de Don Pedro Gual*. Caracas: Ministerio de Educación, 1947.

———, "Pedro Gual and the Patriot Effort to Capture a Mexican Port, 1816," *HAHR*, XXVII (August 1947), 456−466.

Bowman, Charles H., "The Activities of Manuel Torres as Purchasing Agent, 1820-1821," *HAHR*, XLIII (May 1968), 234-246.

Blair, Evelyn, "Educational Movements in Mexico, 1821-1836," Ph.D. dissertation, University of Texas, Austin, 1941.

Brading, David, *Miners and Merchants in Bourbon Mexico, 1763-1810.* Cambridge: University of Cambridge Press, 1971.

Breedlove, James M., "Effects of the Cortes, 1810-1822, on Church Reform in Spain and Mexico," in Benson, *Mexico and the Spanish Cortes*, 113-133.

Burke, William J., *Rudolph Ackerman, Promoter of the Arts and Sciences.* New York: New York Public Library, 1935.

Burr, Robert N., *By Reason or Force: Chile and the Balancing of Power in South America, 1830-1905.* Berkeley and Los Angeles: University of California Press, 1967.

Calcott, Wilfred H., *Santa Anna, the Story of an Enigma Who Once Was Mexico.* Norman: University of Oklahoma Press, 1936.

Carr, Raymond, *Spain, 1801-1939.* Oxford: Oxford University Press, 1966.

Casasús, Joaquín D., *La deuda contraída en Londres.* Mexico: Imprenta del Gobierno, 1885.

Castel, Jorge, *La Junta Central Suprema y Gubernativa de España e Indias.* Madrid: Imprenta Marte, 1950.

Céspedes del Castillo, Guillermo, *Lima y Buenos Aires.* Seville: Escuela de Estudios Hispano-Americanos, 1949.

Chiriboga, Gustavo, "El Ayuntamiento Constitucional de Quito," *Anuario histórico jurídico ecuatoriano*, II (1972), 433–463.

Clapham, John, *The Bank of England.* 2 vols. Cambridge: Cambridge University Press, 1958.

Collier, Simon, *Ideas and Politics of Chilean Independence, 1808-1833.* Cambridge: Cambridge University Press, 1967.

Comellas, José L., *Los primeros pronunciamientos en España.* Madrid: Consejo Superior de Investigaciones Científicas, 1958.

———, *El trienio constitucional.* Madrid: Ediciones Rialp, 1963.

Costeloe, Michael P., *Church Wealth in Mexico.* Cambridge: Cambridge University Press, 1967.

Cunniff, Roger L., "Mexican Municipal Electoral Reform, 1810-1821," in Benson, *Mexico and the Spanish Cortes*, 59–86.

Defourneaux, Marcelín, *Pablo de Olavide, el afrancesado.* Mexico: Editorial Renacimiento, 1965.

Delgado, Jaime, *España y México en el siglo XIX.* 3 vols. Madrid: Consejo Superior de Investigaciones Cientficas, 1950.

Del Valle, Enrique, *Los diputados de Buenos Aires en las Cortes de Cádiz y el nuevo sistema de gobierno económico de América.* Buenos Aires: M. Garcia, 1912.

Díaz Díaz, Fernando, *Caudillos y Caciques, Antonio López de Santa Anna y Juan Alvarez.* Mexico: El Colegio de México, 1972.

Diz-Lois, María Cristina, *El Manifiesto de 1814.* Pamplona: Estudio General de Navarra, 1967.

Farris, Nancy, *Crown and Clergy in Colonial Mexico, 1759-1821.* London: The Athlone Press, 1968.

Fehrenbach, Charles W., "A Study of Spanish Liberalism, The Revolution of 1820" Ph.D. dissertation, University of Texas, Austin, 1961.

————, "Moderados and Exaltados: The Liberal Opposition to Ferdinand VII, 1814-1823," *HAHR*, L (February 1970), 52−69.

Fernández de Castro, Antonio, *Vicente Rocafuerte, un americano libre.* Mexico: Secretaría de Educación Pública, 1947.

Fisher, John R., *Government and Society in Colonial Peru.* London: The Athlone Press, 1970.

Fisher, Lillian E., *The Intendant System in Spanish America.* Berkeley: University of California Press, 1929.

Flores, Alfredo, *Don José Mejía Llequerica en las Cortes de Cádiz de 1810 a 1813.* Barcelona: Casa Editorial Macci, 1913.

Flores Caballero, Romeo, "La consolidación de vales reales en la economía, la sociedad y la política novohispana," *Historia mexicana*, XVIII (January−March 1969), 334−378.

————, *La contrarevolución en la independencia.* Mexico: El Colegio de México, 1969.

Florestedt, Robert, "Mora contra Bustamante," *Historia mexicana*, XII (July−September 1962), 26−52.

Fontana Lazaro, José, *La quiebra de la monarquía absoluta, 1814-1820.* Barcelona: Ediciones Ariel, 1971.

Gandía, Enrique, "Las guerras de los absolutistas y liberales en América," *Revista de Indias*, XIV (July−December 1954), 407−430.

García, Miguel A., *General Don Manuel José de Arce.* 3 vols. San Salvador: Imprenta Nacional, 1944.

González Navarro, Moisés, *El pensamiento político de Lucas Alamán.* Mexico: El Colegio de México, 1952.

Govan, Thomas P., *Nicholas Biddle, Nationalist and Public Banker, 1786-1844.* Chicago: University of Chicago Press, 1959.

Green, Stanley, "Lucas Alamán: Domestic Activities, 1823-1835" Ph.D. dissertation, Texas Christian University, Fort Worth, 1971.

Hadley, Bradford, "The Enigmatic Padre Mier" Ph.D. dissertation, University of Texas, Austin, 1955.

Hale, Charles, *Mexican Liberalism in the Age of Mora.* New Haven: Yale University Press, 1968.

Hamnett, Brian R., "The Appropriation of Mexican Church Wealth by the Spanish Bourbon Government," *Journal of Latin American Studies*, I (November 1969), 85–113.

Harrison, Horace V., "The Republican Conspiracy Against Agustín de Iturbide," in Thomas Cotner and Carlos Castañeda (eds.), *Essays in Mexican History*. Austin: University of Texas Press, 1958, 142–165.

Herr, Richard, *The Eighteenth Century Revolution in Spain*. Princeton: Princeton University Press, 1958.

———, *Spain*. Englewood Cliffs: Prentice Hall, 1971.

Howe, Walter, *The Mining Guild in New Spain and its Tribunal General, 1770-1821*. Cambridge, Mass.: Harvard University Press, 1949.

Humphreys, R. A., "Independence," in Charles C. Griffin (ed.), *Latin America: A Guide to the Historical Literature*. Austin: University of Texas Press, 1971.

Kamen, Henry, "El establecimiento de los intendentes en la administración española," *Hispania*, XXIV (July–September 1964), 368–395.

———, *The War of Succession in Spain, 1700-1715*. Bloomington: University of Indiana Press, 1969.

Knapp, Frank A., *The Life of Sebastián Lerdo de Tejada, 1823-1889*. Austin: University of Texas Press, 1951.

Kossok, Manfred, *Im Schatten der Heiligen Allianz, Deutschland und Lateinamerika 1815-1830. Zur Politik der deutschen Staaten gegenüber der Unabhängigkeitsbewegung Mittel- und Südamerikas*. Berlin: Akademie-Verlag, 1964

Krebs Wilkens, Ricardo, *El pensamiento histórico, político y económico del Conde de Campomanes*. Santiago, Chile: Universidad de Chile, 1960.

Ladd, Doris, "The Mexican Nobility at Independence, 1780-1826." Ph.D. dissertation, Stanford University, 1972.

Lecuna, Vicente, *La liberación del Perú*. Caracas: Litografía del Comercio, 1941.

Leturia, Pedro, *Relaciones entre la Santa Sede e Hispano-América*. 3 vols. Caracas: Sociedad Bolivariana de Venezuela, 1959.

Llorens, Vicente, *Liberales y románticos, una emigración española en Inglaterra*. 2d ed. Madrid: Editorial Castellana, 1968.

Logan, John A., *No Transfer: An American Security Principle*. New Haven: Yale University Press, 1961.

Lovett, Gabriel, *Napoleon and the Birth of Modern Spain*. 2 vols. New York: New York University Press, 1965.

Lynch, John, *Spanish Colonial Administration, 1772-1810*. London: The Athlone Press, 1958.

———, *The Spanish-American Revolutions, 1808-1826*. New York: W. W. Norton & Company, 1973.

McAlister, Lyle, *The Fuero Militar in New Spain, 1764-1800*. Gainesville: University of Florida Press, 1957.

Marshall, Eleanor J., "History of the Lancasterian Educational Movements in Mexico." M.A. thesis, University of Texas, Austin, 1951.

Martínez Silva, Carlos, *Biografía de don José Fernández Madrid*. Bogotá: Imprenta: Nacional, 1935.

Medina Ascencio, Luis, *La Santa Sede y la emancipación mexicana*. Mexico: Editorial Jus, 1965.

Moore, John P., *The Cabildo in Peru under the Bourbons*. Durham, N.C.: Duke University Press, 1966.

Morales y Morales, Vidal, *Iniciadores y primeros mártires de la revolución cubana*. Havana: Imprenta Avisador Comercial, 1901.

Neal, Clarise, "Freedom of the Press in New Spain," in Benson, *Mexico and the Spanish Cortes*, 87–112.

Ocampo, Javier, *Las Ideas de un día, el Pueblo Mexicano ante la consumación de su independencia*. Mexico: El Colegio de México, 1969.

Perkins, Dexter, *The Monroe Doctrine, 1823-1826*. Cambridge, Mass.: Harvard University Press, 1927.

Pierson, William W., "The Establishment and Early Functioning of the *Intendencia* in Cuba," *The James Sprunt Historical Studies*, XIX. Chapel Hill: University of North Carolina Press, 1927, 74–133.

Pintos Vieites, María del Carmen, *La política de Fernando VII entre 1814-1820*. Pamplona: Estudio General de Navarra, 1958.

Ponte Domínguez, Francisco, "José Antonio Miralla y Cuba," in Cuba: Archivo Nacional, *José Antonio Miralla*, 1–94.

Portell Vilá, Herminio, *Historia de Cuba en sus relaciones con los Estados Unidos y España*. 4 vols. Havana: Jesus Montero, 1938.

Potash, Robert A., *El Banco de Avío de México, el fomento de la industria, 1821-1846*. Mexico: Fondo de Cultura Economica, 1959.

Quintanilla, Luis, *A Latin American Speaks*. New York: Macmillan Company, 1943.

Restrepo, Jose Manuel. *Historia de la Revolución de la República de Colombia*. 4 vols. Bencazon: Imprenta de José Joaquín, 1858.

Ringrose, David R., *Transportation and Economic Stagnation in Spain, 1750-1850*. Durham, N.C.: Duke University Press, 1970.

Robalino Dávila, Luis, *Rocafuerte*. Quito: Talleres Gráficos Nacionales, 1964.

Robertson, William S., *Iturbide of Mexico*. Durham, N.C.: Duke University Press, 1952.

———, *France and Latin American Independence*. New York: Octagon Books, 1967.

Rodríguez O., Jaime E., "Rocafuerte y el empréstito a Colombia," *Historia mexicana*, XVIII (April–June 1969), 485–515.

────────, "Vicente Rocafuerte and Mexico, 1820-1832." Ph.D. dissertation, University of Texas, Austin, 1970.

────, "Oposición a Bustamante," *Historia mexicana*, XX (October-December 1970), 199–234.

────────, "An Analysis of the First Spanish American Constitutions," *Revista de Historia de América*, no. 72 (July–December 1971), 412–484.

Rovirosa, Dolores F., "Antonio José Valdez: Maestro, periodista, historiador y hombre de América." Austin: (unpublished manuscript) Latin American Collection, 1970.

Sanders, Lloyd, *The Holland House Circle*. London: Methuen & Company, 1908.

Sarrailh, Jean, *La España ilustrada en la segunda mitad del siglo XVIIII*. Mexico: Fondo de Cultura Economica, 1957.

Shafer, Robert J., *The Economic Societies in the Spanish World, 1763-1821*. Syracuse: Syracuse University Press, 1958.

Staples, Anne, "Ecclesiastical Affairs in the First Mexican Federal Republic." M.A. thesis, University of Texas, Austin, 1967.

Suárez, Federico, "La génesis del liberalismo político español," *Arbor*, VII, no. 21 (May–June 1947), 349–395.

────────, *La crisis política del antiguo régimen en España, 1800-1840*. Madrid: Ediciones Rialp, 1958.

Temperley, Harold, *The Foreign Policy of Canning, 1822-1827*. London: Bell & Sons, 1927.

Thomas, Hugh, *Cuba: the Pursuit of Freedom*. New York: Harper & Row, 1971.

Timmons, Wilbert H., "Tadeo Ortíz, Mexican Emissary Extraordinary," *HAHR*, LI (August 1971), 463–477.

Ward, Robert J., "Juan de Dios Cañedo: Político y diplomático." Licenciatura thesis, Universidad Ibero-Americana, Mexico, 1968.

Warren, Harris G., "The Origin of General Mina's Invasion of Mexico," *Southwestern Historical Quarterly*, XLII (July 1938), 1-20.

────────, "Xavier Mina's Invasion of Mexico," *HAHR*, XXIII (February 1943), 52–76.

Whitaker, Arthur P., *The United States and the Independence of Latin America, 1800-1830*. New York: Norton, 1964.

Woodward, Llewellyn, *The Age of Reform, 1815-1870*. 2d ed. Oxford: Oxford University Press, 1962.

Woodward, Margaret L., "The Spanish Army and the Loss of America, 1810-1824," *HAHR*, XLVIII (November 1968), 586–607.

Zavala, Iris M., *Masones, comuneros y carbonarios*. Madrid: Siglo XXI de España, 1971.

Zuñíga, Neptalí, *José Mejía, Mirabeau del Nuevo Mundo*. Quito: Talleres Gráficos Nacionales, 1949.

# INDEX

Aberdeen, Lord, 189-190
Ackerman, Rudolf, 180
Adams, John Quincy: opposes annexation of Cuba, 70-71, 73, 76; as secretary of state, 58, 62; skeptical about Spanish America, 49
Alamán, Lucas: critical of Vatican, 169-170; criticism of, 198-199, 214, 215-216; ideology of, 194, 277n; as minister of foreign affairs, 100, 125, 131, 161; as minister of interior, 194-195, 212, 217, 223; opposes gaslights, 198-199; opposes religious toleration, 133, 195-196; opposition to, 135; and Rocafuerte, 192, 194, 195, 209, 215; supports Borja Migoni, 96; supports Church, 204
Alas, Ignacio, 225
Alcalá Galiano, Antonio, 12, 23, 32
Alpuche, José María, 136, 139, 189
Alvarez, Juan, 211, 227, 233
Alvear, Carlos de, 101
Amati, Bernardino, 41
American Bible Society, 51, 65-66
Anduaga, Joaquín, 76
Anguolême, Duke, 162
Aranda, Count of, 5
Arango, José Agustín, 71, 81
Arce, José Manuel de: and Cuban invasion, 79-81, 82, 83; and mission to United States, 74-76; and Spanish Americanism, 84, 233
Arenas, Joaquín, 135
Argüelles, Augustín, 12, 16, 33, 35, 40
Army: and constitution, 44-45; and Cortes, 16, 39; and freemasonry, 20-21, 22-23, 69; and *fueros*, 4; in politics, 217, 227-228, 285n; relations with Ferdinand VII, 16-17; relations with Iturbide, 56, 63-64; threatens Congress, 212

Articles of Confederation (USA), 85
Astorga, Marquess of, 96
Austria: and Spanish America, 144, 154, 156
Ayacucho, battle of, 45

Barbour, Philip, 60, 71
Barclay, David, 112, 182
Barclay, Herring, Richardson and Company, 94, 108, 109, 137; bankruptcy of, 123; financial soundness of, 120-121; loan to Mexico, 116-118, 124; purchases arms for Mexico, 113-114, 115, 116; restricted by Goldschmidt clause, 112-114
Baring, Alexander, 124, 127
Baring Brothers, 109, 124, 127, 177
Bavaria: and Mexico, 155-156
Becher, Carl, 149, 268n
Bedford, Duke of, 182
Bernadotte (Sweden), 187
Bernstorff, Count, 144, 150
Betancourt, José Ramón, 71, 80
Betancourt Cisneros, Gaspar, 71, 81
Biddle, Nicholas, 50, 59
Biddle, Thomas, 50
Blackmore, Joseph, 191
Bocanegra, José María, 176, 223
Bolívar, Simón, 17, 19, 20, 22, 31, 67, 259n; attitude toward Cuba, 81, 84; criticism of, 186-188; death of, 188; liberates Peru, 44-45, 82, 83; and Rocafuerte, 28, 185-188, 275n; and Spain, 99, 164
Bonaparte, Joseph, 6, 7, 29
Bonaparte, Napoleon, 6, 8, 16
Borja Migoni, Francisco de, 88, 93, 94, 119, 258n; and Barclay, 112-114; as consul general, 120, 127, 276n; criticism of, 191; negotiates loan, 108-